ANTIBLACKNESS

ANTIBLACKNESS

EDITED BY

MOON-KIE JUNG AND

JOÃO H. COSTA VARGAS

DUKE UNIVERSITY PRESS DURHAM AND LONDON 2021

Library of Congress Cataloging-in-Publication Data
Names: Jung, Moon-Kie, editor. | Vargas, João Helion Costa, editor.
Title: Antiblackness / [edited by] Moon-Kie Jung, João H. Costa Vargas.
Description: Durham : Duke University Press, 2021. | Includes
bibliographical references and index.
Identifiers: LCCN 2020025015 (print) | LCCN 2020025016 (ebook)
ISBN 9781478010692 (hardcover)
ISBN 9781478011811 (paperback)
ISBN 9781478013167 (ebook)
Subjects: LCSH: Anti-racism. | Racism. | Race relations.
| Blacks—Race identity.
Classification: LCC HT1523 .A585 2021 (print) | LCC HT1523 (ebook) |
DDC 305.8—dc23
LC record available at https://lccn.loc.gov/2020025015
LC ebook record available at https://lccn.loc.gov/2020025016

Cover art: Radcliffe Bailey, *Door of No Return*, 2019. Mixed media
including paint on tarp, black glitter, and a photograph on canvas.
102 × 120 inches. © Radcliffe Bailey. Courtesy of the artist and
Jack Shainman Gallery, New York.

In solidarity with Black freedom struggles

for the abolishment of this world

and

with deep gratitude to all whose efforts—

political, theoretical,

practical, artistic, editorial, personal—

made this book possible

CONTENTS

ANTIBLACKNESS OF THE SOCIAL

AND THE HUMAN

JOÃO H. COSTA VARGAS / MOON-KIE JUNG

"The brutality with which Negroes are treated in this country simply cannot be overstated. . . . For the horrors of the American Negro's life there has been almost no language." Of the approaching centenary of the Emancipation Proclamation, James Baldwin noted, "You know, and I know, that the country is celebrating one hundred years of freedom one hundred years too soon" (1962, 22, 94–95). In the past decade, the U.S. public was made aware of certain spectacular brutalities presently borne by Black people, owing largely to numerous video-recorded police and vigilante killings and the Movement for Black Lives. Reaching a tipping point in 2020, a series of such murders—of Ahmaud Arbery (February 23), Breonna Taylor (March 13), and, above all, George Floyd (May 25)—set off an unprecedented wave of protests; the violent deaths of Black trans people—Nina Pop (May 3), Tony McDade (May 27), Brayla Stone (June 25), Merci Mack (June 30), Shaki Peters (July 1), and Bree Black (July 3)—generated far less outrage.[1] This ongoing moment has been important, but, as is too often missed in academic as well as non-academic discussions, these cruelties, the latest additions to a vast and uncatalogued archive, were not exceptional but of a piece with a long history of global scale. Even those who sought to take full measure of the horrors continually understated them: some things, maybe many things, needed fixing, but surely, it was no longer 1963, much less 1863. There was still almost no language.

This book grew out of our dissatisfaction with not only liberal but also most leftist analyses that failed to contend, unflinchingly, with *antiblackness*—its enduring depth, breadth, and violence. Wishing to address this failure collectively and interdisciplinarily, we reached out to scholars whose work we hold in utmost respect and asked them to engage with antiblackness without compromise—to summon the necessary language. As the following chapters suggest, such an endeavor entails a thoroughgoing critique and a fundamental overhaul of the social sciences and the humanities. For our part, in this introduction, we posit and think through the constitutive antiblackness underpinning the foundational categories of the modern world, the Social and the Human.[2] As a corollary, we then draw a conceptual distinction between antiblackness and racism, the latter proving to be inapt and inadequate in capturing the former.

* * *

To conclude *Logics of History: Social Theory and Social Transformation*, historian William Sewell Jr. returns to a most basic question: "So, then: What *is* 'the social' in social science?" (emphasis in original). Distilling a lifetime of interdisciplinary work across the social sciences, he answers, "The social is the complex and inescapable ontological ground of our common life as humans." In the modern "disenchanted world," the Social is the foundation of collective human existence and the "foundational term" for the scientific study of it (Sewell 2005, 325, 329, 369). Yet the social sciences fail to grasp what W. E. B. Du Bois (1935, 727) refers to as "the most magnificent drama in the last thousand years of human history": the transoceanic, transcontinental enslavement of Africans. For example, the broadest of the social sciences that likewise claims the entirety of the Social, the modern social world, as its domain, sociology, despite thriving subfields on race and historical sociology, almost completely ignores racial slavery (Jung 2019). Even when the social sciences do acknowledge it and document it empirically, their theories of the Social—that is, social theories—inexorably misrecognize and euphemize it, most typically as a variety of coerced labor. In short, the social sciences—disciplines born of modernity that theorize, empirically investigate, and, indeed, do their part in constructing modernity—either do not or cannot comprehend arguably the most decisive and defining development in modern history.

How do we make sense of this wholly unnoticed yet fundamental paradox? A profoundly *antisocial* condition, slavery breaches the bounds of the Social, the social sciences' self-defined limits. The Social is not common ground for all. That slavery presents such an "extreme antisocial situation" (Steinmetz 2016, 101–2) is prefigured by the work of Orlando Patterson, ironically a sociologist, whose *Slavery and Social Death*, though influential outside his discipline, has had little theoretical impact within it. In the book, he carries out a comprehensive historical survey of slavery and identifies its "constituent elements": "slavery is the permanent, violent domination of natally alienated and generally dishonored persons." The enslaved is "a socially dead person" or, alternatively, "a social nonperson" (Patterson 1982, 1, 5, 7, 13). In other words, to be enslaved is to have no recognized social existence: in and against the social world but not of it.

Articulated to transoceanic trade, empire building, and capitalism, the modern enslavement of Black people, racialized through enslavement as Black, assumes global scale and significance, distinguishing it from premodern cases of slavery. In an earlier publication, Charles Mills (2013, 35), one of this book's contributors, reflects on the singular position of Black people in the modern world:

> The peculiar experience of Africans under Western modernity, which originally turned them into "negroes" (lowercase), creating a race where previously none had existed, impressed a forced diaspora on them that took them to Europe and the Americas . . . , made the extraction of their labor central to the making of the modern world, . . . while still leaving them globally identifiable as the people who were appropriately designated a "slave race" in modernity, the very period when slavery was [otherwise] dead or dying in the West.

Taking the Social for granted as the universally shared ontological ground, social theories cannot but fail to see enslavement for what it is. A social nonperson is not a type of dominated social person among others, and social death is not a form of social injury among others. The "life" of the enslaved is radically, incommensurably insecure. They have no legitimate standing in the social world. They have no legitimate claims to power or resources, including their very "own" selves. For example, in the antebellum United States, the enslaved were subject to sale, and the ever-present threat of sale, and the internal slave trade forced the relocation of over two million, half of them "involv[ing] the break up of a family" (Johnson 1999, 5–7; 2013, 14). As Hortense Spillers alerts us, *kinship* or *family*, as well as all other categories that constitute and make sense of so-cial life, "loses meaning" in social death *since it can be invaded at any given and arbitrary moment by the property relations*" (2003, 218, emphasis in orig-inal). The point is not that the enslaved always, continuously suffer such invasions. Constant terror does not require constant violation. Rather, "the fact of its possibility [is] experienced as an ever-present sense of impend-ing doom that shadow[s] everything, every thought, every moment of [the enslaved's] existence." Basic needs of humans as social beings—such as senses of belonging, trust, and efficacy—are under relentless, "prolonged assault," and "all ties [are] precarious" (Patterson 2018, ix). What we are suggesting is that relative to such extreme antisocial conditions, we must continually doubt the adequacy of and rethink all social categories of prac-tice and analysis, including, as we discuss below, racism.

This state of abjection does not end with formal emancipation. Against the predominant narrative of progress and freedom across the humanities and the social sciences, Saidiya Hartman (2002, 757) argues that the "time of slavery" has yet to pass, that the present is still in its grip. Chattel slav-ery may be, for the most part, no more (Patterson and Zhuo 2018), but what follows in the wake of the "nonevent of emancipation" is the "afterlife of slavery": "Slavery had established a measure of man and a ranking of life and worth that has yet to be undone. . . . Black lives are still imperiled and devalued by a racial calculus and a political arithmetic that were en-trenched centuries ago" (Hartman 1997, 116; 2007, 6). Antiblackness, part and parcel of racial slavery and its afterlife, remains the extreme antisocial condition of possibility of the modern social world. To those who would dismiss out of hand a homologous continuity between racial slavery and the present, the stranglehold of the former on the latter, and insist upon a cat-egorical break, we pose the questions: When did Black life start mattering? When were Black people freed from the ever-present sense of impending doom?

Since the dawn of modernity, Black people have been progressively, singularly positioned—materially and symbolically—as the "slave race" around the globe. By the end of the seventeenth century, for instance, slavery in the Spanish Empire, from the Americas to Asia, was abolished for all—in law, if not fully in practice—with the sole exception of Black people, which mirrored the contemporaneous hardening of Black enslave-ment in the English colonies (Seijas 2014; van Deusen 2015). Further, the ever-expanding antiblackness underwrote white as well as other nonblack claims to Humanity and freedom the world over (Buck-Morss 2000), including in contexts without Black people, such as precolonial Korea (see chapter 7). Of the various color lines that have crisscrossed the planet, the one closing off Blackness, we contend, has been the most decisive and definitive, marking the outer boundary of the Human.

At the conclusion of the nineteenth century, in *The Philadelphia Negro*, Du Bois ([1899] 1996, 386–87) made a profound, underappreciated observation:

> And still this widening of the idea of common Humanity is of slow growth and today but dimly realized. We grant full citizenship in the World-Commonwealth to the "Anglo-Saxon" (whatever that may mean), the Teuton and the Latin; then with just a shade of reluctance we extend it to the Celt and Slav. We half deny it to the yellow races of Asia, admit the brown Indians to an ante-room only on the strength of an undeniable past; but with the Negroes of Africa we come to a full stop, and in its heart the civilized world with one accord denies that these come within the pale of nineteenth century Humanity.

⟩ What Du Bois claimed about the nineteenth century, we affirm and extend to the twentieth and the twenty-first, and it is still precisely this "core concept of 'the human' that anchors so many humanities disciplines— history, literature, art history, philosophy, religion, anthropology, political theory, and others" (Lowe and Manjapra 2019, 23). The Human is to the humanities what the Social is to the social sciences: their foundational concept, the declared and assumed universality of which is ultimately belied and bounded by its "full stop" antiblackness. The Human, the modern human, defines itself in opposition to the Black (alleged) nonbeing: "The distaste must be for her. . . . Her blackness is static and dread," as Toni Morrison writes of Pecola in *The Bluest Eye* ([1970] 2007, 49). Frantz Fanon (1967a) places this fear and hatred of Black people at the core of what he describes as the modern collective unconscious. The hatred of Black people is the hatred of the nonbeing, of the placeless, of the alleged nonhuman. As Rinaldo Walcott (2014, 93) notes,

> What it means to be Human is continually defined against Black people and Blackness. The very basic terms of social Human engagement are shaped by anti-Black logics so deeply embedded in various normativities that they resist intelligibility as modes of thought and yet we must attempt to think them. . . . This global anti-black condition produced in the post-Columbus era, still and again manifests itself in numerous ways that have significantly

limited how Black people might lay claim to human-ness and therefore how Black people might impact on what it means to be Human in a post-Columbus world.

* * *

Following Baldwin, Spillers, Hartman, and others, we call attention to the perpetual, if unnoticed and ignored, theoretical incoherence generated by the deep-seated antiblackness of modernity. Applied to the plight of Black people, concepts and theories meant to index *social* domination and *human* suffering invariably falter and fall short. Under racial slavery, for instance, "the captive female body . . . could be converted into cash, speculated and traded as commodity, worked to death, taken, tortured, seeded, and propagated like any other crop, or murdered," Hartman reminds us. "The work of sex and procreation was the chief motor for reproducing the material, social, and symbolic relations of slavery [that] . . . inaugurated a regime of racialized sexuality that continues to place black bodies at risk" (Hartman 2016, 168–69). In apperceiving such antisocial, antihuman conditions, even the most radical theories of the Social and the Human, much less their mainstream counterparts, cannot but misrepresent. What conceptual vocabulary is up to the task? Exploitation or primitive accumulation? Patriarchy or misogyny? Hegemony or subalternity? Relative to antiblackness, such categories "are all thrown in crisis" (Spillers 2003, 221). Misrecognition and euphemism are inevitable.

There are at least two possible readings of the passage from *The Philadelphia Negro* quoted above. Humanity can be imagined as a continuum, with the full inclusion of the "Anglo-Saxon" on one end and the full exclusion of the "Negroes of Africa" on the other. One could then read hope into the phrase "widening of the idea of common Humanity" and envisage the ultimate inclusion of Black people. Explicitly and implicitly, this reading is manifest in more than a century of social-scientific research since the publication of what is now increasingly considered a foundational text of social science: Black people's continued position on the wrong end of countless social measures, yoked to an enduring hope, or at least possibility, of eventual equality and freedom. Even if unuttered, the hope is ingrained in the analytical assumption that the same social theories, concepts, models, and variables must obtain from one end to the other of any posited continuum.

A second, alternative reading, which this book puts forth, is to take seriously the nature of the difference that the "full stop" denotes and, as the ensuing chapters demonstrate, the character of the "one accord" that "denies" Blackness from the pale of Humanity. Even when viewed through radical social theories, all the world is a continuum, and Black people are not excepted. For instance, their enslavement is most frequently conceptualized as one, if the most extreme, regime of modern labor exploitation among others. Adopting and adapting Marxism, Du Bois himself would later, in *Black Reconstruction in America*, conceive of the Black enslaved as the "Black worker," and in between the enslaved Black worker and the "white worker" is arrayed a range of racialized and coerced workers—the other members of the "dark proletariat" (1935, 15–17). Unsurprisingly, the "worker" here is "as a category absent gender and sexual differentiation" (Hartman 2016, 166).[3] Still, even on its own terms, Du Bois's Marxism, and its central figure of the worker, could not but come up against its intrinsic limitations as it sought to make the Black (male) enslaved legible to the world: "No matter how degraded the factory hand, he is not real estate. . . . In this vital respect, the slave laborer differed from all others of his day. . . . It was a sharp accentuation of control over men beyond the modern labor reserve or the contract coolie system" (Du Bois 1935, 10–11).[4] Not an anomalous appurtenance to sameness or similarity, this vital difference is *the* difference that makes all the difference in and for the world. For Blackness and Black people, to be rendered recognizable to the Social and the Human is to be misrecognized beyond recognition. Like Du Bois's pale of Humanity, analytical categories of the Social and the Human do not extend to the antisocial, antihuman condition of antiblackness without being overstretched, and analogies and appeals to antiblackness, such as *wage slavery*, to represent nonblack suffering and domination register as overwrought.

The incongruity, the conceptual crisis, bespeaks the incommensurability of antiblackness and the need to distinguish antiblackness from racism.[5] The analytical and political imperative of establishing a break from the social concept of racism emanates from the recognition of antiblackness as an ontological condition of possibility of modern world sociality, whereas racism is an aspect of that sociality. A world without racism requires deep transformations in social practices and structures. A world without antiblackness necessitates an entirely new conception of the social, which is to say a radically different world altogether.

A framework of antiblackness stresses the uniqueness of Black positionality and experiences relative to those of nonblack social groups. It proposes that the defining antagonism of modernity is Black-nonblack (Wilderson 2010). Deriving from theoretical efforts and historical and sociological analyses, such a perspective suggests that Black people (a) are not only exceptionally and systematically excluded socially—from housing markets, quality education, effective health care, safety, and life—but (b) are the nonbeing that underpins and engenders modern nonblack subjectivities. These propositions assume a logic of social and ontological abjection, rather than domination or subjection, of Black people. Such logic is antiblackness.

Whereas from the perspective of racism, racial and other related and intersecting forms of oppression can be eliminated, or at least ameliorated, from the perspective of antiblackness such an assumption, or hope, is suspended relative to Black people.[6] Antiblackness suggests that rather than with a set of social and institutional practices, the problem lies with the very notions of the Social and the Human underlying these practices and their constitutive rejection of Blackness and Black people. What would be the effect of reforming social and institutional practices if the basic assumptions authorizing such practices are left untouched? Or, to put the problem more directly, how would we go about proposing an entirely new type of sociality or humanity? How would we go about rejecting Humanity without rejecting the modern world, the Social?

Fanon emphasizes the singular positionality of the Black, who "has no ontological resistance in the eyes of the white man" (1967a, 110). In an antiblack world, the Black nonsubject is constitutive of an asymmetrical social space of positionalities from which she is excluded. The Black nonsubject provides the fixed point against which all other positionalities attain social freight and legibility, yet her presence is negated, erased, ignored. Put differently, per our reading of the passage from *The Philadelphia Negro*, while Black people fall outside the continuum of Humanity, they generate and define the continuum precisely because they are its constitutive, asymptotic other—the alleged nonbeings who delimit the social world but are not of it. By contrast, though subject to various types of combined oppressions, nonblack subjects of varied racial categories, genders, sexual orientations, social classes, and nationalities nonetheless occupy legible positions on the continuum of Humanity. Having any, even minimal, ontological resistance in the eyes of the white cisheteronormative propertied man is an all-important difference from having none—"the total absence of human recognition" (Morrison [1970] 2007, 48)—a difference in kind that is continually misrecognized as a difference in degree.

Antiblackness is an antisocial logic that not only dehumanizes Black people but also renders abject all that is associated with Blackness.[7] This generalized abjection helps us grasp the ways in which, historically and contemporarily, Black people's embattled bodies, spaces, knowledge, culture, citizenship, and humanity have served as the counterpoints to safety, rationality, belonging, and life. Unlike racism, which tends to focus on analogous experiences of oppression, antiblackness stresses the singularity of Black people's dehumanization, antihumanization.

To fully engage with this perspective's implications and consequences, it is important that we avoid a common and understandable tendency: the identification of counterexamples that affirm Black people's humanity. Of course, we know of countless examples, historical and contemporary, of a radical Black humanity—a vital humanity that exceeds the present social world, one that operates according to ethical and aesthetic principles not reducible to normative parameters, one that categorically rejects dehumanization. It is the humanity of "the commodity who speaks," of those who inhabit the space of the fantastic and "refuse victimization."[8]

Black humanity is never in question. The point of stressing antiblackness is not to negate Black people's humanity or accept Black a-humanity. Rather, it is to locate in the globally shared notion of the Human the source of Black people's dehumanization, suffering, and death. It is not to negate or dismiss Black people's agency, but rather to reframe Black agency as necessarily and always engaging the fundamentally antiblack world as it is and projecting radically alternative conceptions of what it is to be human and live in society.

* * *

"Slavery is with us still. We are haunted by slavery. We are animated by slavery," Anthony Paul Farley, one of this volume's contributors, argues in an earlier publication. Antiblackness "is slavery *and* segregation *and* neosegregation *and* every situation in which the distribution of material or spiritual goods follows the colorline" (Farley 2005, 221; emphases in original). The persistence, multiplicity, and interconnectedness of diasporic antiblack forces that trace to racial slavery are impossible to negate, given the greatly disproportionate presence of Black people in spaces of dispossession and death, physical and social. Singular in their extensiveness and intensiveness, such antiblack dynamics include the targeted criminalization and industrial warehousing of people in jails, prisons, immigration detention centers, juvenile facilities, and foster care institutions; intensifying protocols of punishment and confinement of ostensibly uncoercive institutions, such as schools, universities, hospitals, and welfare; intractable levels of unemployment and subemployment; absurd deficit in wealth accumulation; hypersegregation in housing and schools, as well as looming gentrification; blocked access to quality education; exposure to environmental toxins leading to birth defects, chronic illnesses, and death; premature death by preventable causes, including treatable cardiovascular, stress, and birth-related conditions; the AIDS/HIV pandemic; and ever-outlying rates of homicide, domestic violence, and other forms of state and nonstate coercion. This litany is but a sample of the afterlife of slavery that characterizes the Black diaspora.[9]

The essays assembled in this book examine antiblackness across expansive coordinates of time, across the modern era. Antiblackness, they find, fundamentally structures the past and the present, from nineteenth-century slavery to the 2020 U.S. Census, from precolonial to colonial to postcolonial formations of state, empire, nation, and civil society. The chapters collectively disrupt the deeply taken-for-granted assumption of an inexorable, if halting, march through history toward recognition and rights for all, including Black people. Rather than a relic, anomaly, or contradiction being gradually overcome, antiblackness is conceptualized as foundational to modernity.

The essays likewise span vast coordinates of space, from Great Britain, France, and the United States to Haiti, India, Korea, Palestine, and South Africa, from the White House to plantations, convict lease camps, prisons, and schools. Across such disparate geographies, we find a coherent pattern of antiblackness, as modern subjects—not only Europeans or whites but also various nonblack subalterns—define themselves and construct a world, the modern social world, in opposition to the Black nonsubject. The challenge, which the contributors confront head-on rather than sidestepping, is to grapple with the common fact of antiblackness while attending to the specific inflections of particular historical moments and contexts.

The present book is unique in bringing together scholars in and beyond Black studies. Black studies scholars provide robust retheorization of antiblackness and novel empirical investigations. Deployed to trouble seemingly critical or liberatory categories such as democracy, mass incarceration, feminism, and citizenship, antiblackness gains conceptual complexity as it reveals essential but previously hidden dimensions of theoretical discourses, everyday interactions, and institutional processes, historical and contemporary.

Placing antiblackness at the center, contributors whose primary specialization is not Black studies scrutinize anew apparently unconnected histories and peoples. Antiblackness shapes and haunts plantation agriculture in colonial India in the nineteenth century, Koreans' Declaration of Independence in 1919, Indigeneity and settler colonialism in the contemporary United States and Palestine, and politics over the racial categorization of Latinx. What the authors glean are not merely overlooked stories and data to be assimilated into existing literatures but fundamental reorientations. In heterogeneous contexts far and wide, antiblackness structures and bounds the Social and the Human.

What holds this book together is not theoretical consensus. Not every contributor would wholly agree with this introduction or all of the other chapters. Rather, the gathered authors each consider antiblackness from their particular vantage points but with the common goal of pushing past accepted understandings. Working in a humanities discipline that is starkly devoid of and hostile to Black people and Black thought (Botts et al. 2014; Curry and Curry 2018), philosopher **CHARLES W. MILLS** contends that Black philosophy, born of "racial subordination in modernity," is singularly positioned to illuminate the workings of race and modernity as "the position of Blacks is unique among all the groups racialized as nonwhite by the modern West": "For no other nonwhite group has race been so enduringly constitutive of their identity, so foundational for racial capitalism, and so lastingly central to white racial consciousness and global racial consciousness in general." Interweaving theory and autobiography, **FRANK B. WILDERSON III** provides a precis of Afropessimism and illustrates it with personal experiences that, in part, inspired it. Recalling white comrades in the African National Congress and a Palestinian friend in Minneapolis, he lays bare the "ruse of analogy" at play in even revolutionary politics and social theories as they relate to Blackness and Black people. In critical dialogue with Afropessimism, **IYKO DAY** takes up the question that, according to Patrice Douglass (2018, 116), is being insistently asked of it—"does Afro-pessimism adequately deal with the question of black gender?"—and ultimately answers in the negative through a heterodox Marxist critique of racial capitalism. Juxtaposing Marx, Freud, the Gospels, Goethe, Wittgenstein, C. L. R. James, and others, legal scholar **ANTHONY PAUL FARLEY** outlines a general theory of antiblackness that, among other things, posits "the rule of law [as] nothing other than the endless unfolding of the primal scene of accumulation" of the Middle Passage.

The next set of chapters ground their analyses in histories of the nineteenth and early twentieth centuries. Focusing on the production and circulation of Carolina rice, **ZACH SELL** narrates a global history of racial capitalism and colonial empires, linking settler slavery of antebellum Georgia and South Carolina to the mills and markets of England to colonial plantations of British India. At bottom, antiblackness was the "foundation stone" (Du Bois 1935, 5) not only in the form of enslaved labor but also in the form of "negative recognition," of the enslaved's indispensable but overlooked knowledge of rice cultivation without which colonial efforts to introduce Carolina rice production in India were predestined to fail.[10] Hartman's generative concepts of the nonevent of emancipation (1997, 116) and the afterlife of slavery (2007, 6) are vividly borne out in **SARAH HALEY**'s account of Black women ensnared in the Jim Crow carceral regime. Under ever-present conditions of physical and sexual terror, they were compelled to materially and symbolically "reproduce white life at the detriment of their own" and forced to engage in "a form of perverse social reproduction": the reproductive labor of their own incarceration— "activity that maintains the barest life . . . for the maintenance and naturalization of the category of Black prisoner and the maintenance of a system of captivity that extracted industrial and agricultural labor to the point of human expiration." Studying a context halfway around the globe from the U.S. South, **JAE KYUN KIM** and **MOON-KIE JUNG** make sense of Black people's persistent presence in the public discourse of, despite their physical absence in, precolonial Korea at the turn of the twentieth century. Buffeted by closing imperial forces, Koreans managed their intense colonial vulnerability and imagined their place in the modern world through the figure of its absolute other, the enslaved African, to lasting colonial and postcolonial consequences.

Exploring dimensions of captivity as political subjugation, the four subsequent chapters provide analytical insights into the carceral logics of antiblackness. **DYLAN RODRÍGUEZ** examines the ways in which the term "mass incarceration" has been politically domesticated to conform to a reformist agenda. Such an approach ultimately fails to address incarceration as a fundamentally antiblack logic and methodology of social management. Focusing on the experiences of a Black woman in Britain who for decades fought against police abuse in London, and providing a genealogy of the repression against African Caribbean women contesting state violence in postcolonial Britain, **MOHAN AMBIKAIPAKER** shows how gendered antiblackness is at the core of Western liberal juridical rule. **CONNIE WUN** presents an analysis of the narratives of six Black girls disciplined in their high school and argues that antiblackness includes everyday forms of surveillance and punishment enacted in accordance with institutional protocols. As part of a larger structure of carcerality, schools draw from and reproduce antiblack logics according to which captivity is policy. Framing Sally Hemings, Michelle Obama, and Deborah Danner as *captive maternals*, **JOY JAMES** argues that their experiences, including survival strategies, suggest the limits of democracy. Their experiences as feminized bodies link antiblackness, violence, and presidential powers. Despite the different historical periods they inhabit, the three women share vulnerabilities traceable to global racial slavery.

The final part of the book is composed of studies of contemporary dynamics that unsettle received narratives, assumptions, and theories to reveal the breadth and depth of antiblackness. **CRYSTAL M. FLEMING** asserts that in France, antiblackness is both quotidian and structurally embedded—it is part of what it means to be French. Yet, in the French context, antiblack racism is seldom related to chattel slavery. Such denial, or what Charles Mills (1997) calls "epistemology of ignorance," makes it difficult to grasp historical and structural aspects of antiblack racism, including the ways in which European whites continue to benefit from it. Analyzing U.S. as well as Latin American census information, **TANYA KATERÍ HERNÁNDEZ** argues that antiblack racism and its corresponding aversion to Blackness explain Latinxs' strong preference for the white racial category, regardless of one's physical characteristics. Thus, the proposal to collapse "Hispanic" ethnicity into a single racial category—replacing the current two-part question about "Hispanic" ethnicity and racial identity—would make it even more difficult to collect data on Black Latinxs and effectively render them invisible. Drawing from Joy James's (2016; this volume) theorizations of the womb and the captive maternal, **SARAH IHMOUD** contends that Zionist settler violence against Palestinians in occupied territory is energized by an antiblack logic that seeks to preserve the Jewish body from the imagined threat of contamination. Grappling with seemingly irreconcilable critiques of settler colonialism and antiblackness, **JODI A. BYRD** reflects on "how Indigeneity situates itself in and benefits from antiblackness" and proposes that "choosing a return to what remains will allow us to turn away from nationhood, sovereignty, and jurisdiction and toward governance, relationality, kinship, and land."

Notes

1   This book went into production in early 2020, before the protests.

2   We capitalize the Social and the Human to specify their modernity.

3   Hartman goes on to demonstrate how "gender" and "sexual differentia-
    tion" as social concepts lose coherence when applied to "the captive female
    body": "Depending on the angle of vision or critical lexicon, the harnessing
    of the body as an instrument for social and physical reproduction unmakes
    the slave as gendered subject or reveals the primacy of gender and sexual
    differentiation in the making of the slave" (2016, 168).

4   For a more detailed analysis of the enslaved and the worker in relation
    to Du Bois's *Black Reconstruction in America*, see Jung (2019). In rela-
    tion to Gramsci, see Wilderson (2003).

5   In our view, the dominant way of thinking about antiblackness has been to
    conceptualize it, whether explicitly or implicitly, as a synonym for antiblack
    racism. Our own previous work, including earlier versions of this chapter,
    has not been clear on this point.

6   Derrick Bell's writings, of course, are an exception to the assumption that
    racism can be eliminated (see, e.g., Bell 1995).

7   Here we reference Fred Moten's longer discussion of Black abjection. It is
    important to note that in Moten's work, Black people object to their abjec-
    tion in multiple ways, including aesthetic practice (see Moten 2003).

8   "The commodity who speaks" is, of course, Fred Moten's (2003, 8) formu-
    lation. The space of the fantastic is Cedric Robinson's rendition of Black
    spaces, expressed at an event at the Southern California Library in 2012
    (see Vargas 2018). Joy James (this volume) has written on the refusal to be
    victimized. See also Jared Sexton's (2011) "The Social Life of Social Death."

9   Especially in officially postracial contexts, we could speak of saturation
    points beyond which antiblack processes spill onto and affect even non-
    blacks (Vargas 2018).

10 With regard to the cotton industry of the same period, Du Bois (1935, 5)
    wrote, "Black labor became the foundation stone not only of the South-
    ern social structure, but of Northern manufacture and commerce, of the
    English factory system, of European commerce, of buying and selling on a
    world-wide scale."

PART I

OPENINGS

THE ILLUMINATION OF BLACKNESS

CHARLES W. MILLS

No discipline in Western thought is more centrally linked to the general ideal of enlightenment, as well as to modernity's specific historical Enlightenments, than philosophy, the oldest discipline of them all. The metaphor of bringing light into darkness, of illuminating blackness, is most famously expressed, after all, in Plato's celebrated Allegory of the Cave, from the book generally seen as one of the foundational texts of the Western tradition, the *Republic* (Plato 2012, bk. 7). Analogized to the sun, the Form of the Good (uppercase because for Plato it's a transcendental entity) has the capacity to illuminate the cave dwellers' world of shadows with both factual and moral insight, knowledge of what actually is the case and of what, accordingly, should be done. Moreover, light is, of course, paradigmatically associated with whiteness, and—in the standard array of synonyms and antonyms to be found in any dictionary or thesaurus—opposed to blackness. In terms of actual electromagnetic radiation, any physicist will be happy to inform us that white light already includes all the colors of the visible spectrum, whereas blackness turns out to be not really a color at all, but the absence of all light and color. Given the racialization that accompanies modernity, it is then unsurprising that metaphor, color symbolism, and Euro-identity all fuse: whiteness becomes the identity of both enlightenment and of the human bearers of enlightenment. Whiteness is light; whiteness is all-encompassing; whiteness is the universal; whiteness is Euro-illumination. So how could enlightenment possibly be Black, considering that this is the very color, or noncolor, of the darkness we want illuminated and eliminated? Don't any metaphors drawn from this realm automatically foredoom the enterprise?

And the obvious answer is . . . it all depends on how you choose your metaphors (Lakoff and Johnson 2003).

Consider another way of looking at things, another set of linked metaphors—though still within the realm of the visual—drawn from a very different text, one classic in its own way as a representation of the racialized optics of modernity: Ralph Ellison's *Invisible Man* ([1952] 1995, 5). Here we are given a very different perspective on whiteness and enlightenment: whiteness as glare, whiteness as dazzle, whiteness as blinding, whiteness as "Monopolated Light & Power." In the prologue to Ellison's novel, his nameless Black narrator—surrounded in his secret basement by 1,369 lightbulbs—tells us, "I've illuminated the blackness of my invisibility— and vice versa" ([1952] 1995, 13). But the illumination he has attained over the novel's quest (as he looks back in a prologue that is really a postscript) has been achieved despite, not with the help of, the Jim-Crowed white power source represented by Monopolated, and its attempted totalitarian control of his vision. Whiteness here is constructed not by inclusion of the other colors but by their official exclusion, an "Optic White" for "Keeping America Pure," even if an unacknowledged Black base lies at the heart of its "purity" (Ellison [1952] 1995, 196, 212–18). Figuring whiteness in this way demystifies its chromatic pretensions and the related illusions of the Eurocentric worldview that has biased objective inquiry into the work- ings of the world. Through this alternative prism, whiteness is a willed darkness; whiteness is segregated investigation; whiteness is the partic- ular masquerading as the universal (Alcoff 2015). So, from this reversed perspective, it is not Blackness that needs illumination but Blackness that does the illuminating. The meaning of my title—assuming you, the reader, took it the conventional way—has been shockingly inverted.

Periodizing "Black" Philosophy

In this opening chapter, I want to explore the concept of a Black Enlighten- ment, in philosophy and more generally, that has historically been aimed at illuminating the darkness of whiteness. By now it is a familiar criticism that the definite article in "the Enlightenment" is misleading (Outram 2005). There are multiple Enlightenments, demarcated, for example, by geography, chronology, and political orientation. Thus, we have the standard lineup, both within and outside continental Europe (though not outside the European world order), of, for instance, the Scottish, Dutch, German, French, and Ibero-American enlightenments, each with their respective timings. External to that world (at least in conventional cartographies) we have the less familiar Islamic Enlightenment, whether of eighteenth-century modernity onward (de Bellaigue 2017), or—challenging standard periodizations as well as standard mapmaking—in the Arab influence on the putatively self-created, springing from its own brow, earlier European Renaissance (al-Khalili 2012). Then there are political categorizations, as in Jonathan Israel's (2001) contrast between conservative/moderate and radical enlightenments. So the potential plurality of reference of the concept must be borne firmly in mind: the space, time, and politics of enlightenment are all variable.

Here I am urging us to formally recognize a variety not only not usually included in these accepted taxonomies, but indeed—as just indicated above—likely to appear oxymoronic in its very conception: the Black Enlightenment, linked with Black philosophy. But obviously I need to clarify how I understand the latter term, and since this is a contested issue, my discussion will be not just a reporting of different usages, but will be in part stipulative, making a case for what I think is the most appropriate one.

First, a quick reminder. Since humanity as a whole comes out of Africa, the philosophy produced by Afro-descendant populations really includes all philosophy. So—as an ironic twist on the opening section—far from whiteness being in a position to exclude Blackness, whiteness (including all the European Enlightenments) would have been subsumed into Blackness from the start. But that would just be a glib debating point. Obviously, the reference is to the populations of the sub-Saharan continent conventionally characterized as Black today, not those who left it thousands of years earlier, whose Afro ancestry is from a different epoch.

However, at least in my recommended usage, Black philosophy does not include all the philosophizing of the former group either. Blackness for me denotes not just a particular range of skin colors and phenotypical features, a designation that can be applied by us to populations in past epochs independently of how these populations actually thought of themselves, but to populations racialized as Black, and (generally) identifying themselves as such. As I am suggesting we use the term, then, Blackness is a racial category, not just a physical description, and as such it cannot exist before racial Blackness exists, and thus not before race exists. Given the stigmatization of Afro-descendant populations as intellectual inferiors, certainly in modernity but possibly in premodernity also, one can completely understand why some scholars would want to insist on a tradition of Black philosophy that goes all the way back to antiquity, including ancient Egypt. See, for example, *I Am Because We Are: Readings in Black Philosophy* (Hord and Lee 1995). The rationale is obvious. People categorized as white today take pride in the achievements of classical Greek and Roman civilization, identifying the luminaries of the period as their white ancestors regardless of whether they thought of themselves that way or not. So the idea is to establish a comparable genealogy of age and prestige of Black thought. For our purposes, though, the crucially defining features of Blackness and the Black Enlightenment do not have this transhistorical character but arise specifically in opposition to racial subordination.

Thus at least three necessary conditions have to be met: the existence of race as a social category, the existence of Blackness as one of the extant racial categories, and the subordination of Africans and Afro-descendant populations under that designation. Suppose, to begin with, that race (race-thinking, racism) is a product of the modern period, as many historians of race have contended, such as Ivan Hannaford (1995), Nell Irvin Painter (2011), and George Fredrickson (2015). They recognize, of course, that the premodern world, like our own, was filled with prejudices and bigotries of all kinds—tribal, ethnic, national, religious—but deny that any of them, singularly or in synthesis, mutated into a racial form. It is really only with modernity, and the simultaneous developments of the European taxonomizing of the world and the European voyages of discovery of the world (or, less euphemistically, conquest), that racialized categorization and racialized stigmatization begin. So Black philosophy (as shaped by racial Blackness) cannot exist because race does not exist. Thinkers in the Africa of, say, 1000 CE would not have been Black, and so would not have been doing Black philosophy when they philosophized. Rather, they would have been philosophizing as Yoruba, Akan, Kikuyu, and so forth.

However, this short periodization of race has come under increasing challenge in recent decades. A new body of work in medieval studies— for example, that of Debra Higgs Strickland (2003) and Geraldine Heng (2018)—is arguing that Christian iconography in the Middle Ages involved representations of enemy populations that at least approached, and possibly became, racialization, albeit not in modern terms. For Strickland (2003), as indicated by her title (*Saracens, Demons, and Jews*), the inclusion of actual human beings (Jews, "Saracens" [Muslims], "Ethiopians" [Africans], and

Mongols) among the "monstrous races" inherited from Pliny the Elder's *Natural History* had the effect of creating a human teratology of the bestial alongside the one-legged, one-eyed, and dog-headed demonic creatures of myth and nightmare. Heng (2018) adds Gypsies and "Skraelings" (North American Indians) to the list of stigmatized groups. So, the point would be that long before what we now think of as the birth of modern scientific Enlightenment racism, Christian culture had demarcated, among the ranks of humanity, those whose humanity was at best questionable, at worst untenable. And as noted, "Ethiopians" (the designation for Africans in general) were part of this derogated group of subhumans.

Strickland points out "the interchangeability of demons and Ethiopians" in these texts, with Ethiopians often "number[ing] among Christ's tormentors in Passion imagery," "based primarily on one physical characteristic: blackness" (2003, 81–83). As she summarizes things:

> The central idea in these writings is the symbolic equation of black with spiritual darkness, implying the concomitant equivalence of white with spiritual enlightenment, as expressed in the Gospel verse . . ."God is light and in him there is no darkness.". . . . In effect, the blackness of the Ethiopians obliterated their humanity, paving the way for the abstract understanding necessary for ethnic stereotyping. That is, Ethiopians were transformed from living humans into symbols [of the demonic]. (2003, 84, 86)

Similarly, Heng writes:

> *Within* Christianity the color black accrued a slate of negative significations that yoked the "abstraction" of blackness . . . to sin, ignorance, shame, error, and the state of unredemption preceding forgiveness and salvation, as well as—more perniciously and unforgivingly—to the devil, the demonic, the infernal, and the damned. . . . A more troubling development was the visualization of *black skin in tandem with a sub-Saharan phenotype*, in the portrayals of torturers and executioners, especially the killers and tormentors of revered people such as John the Baptist and Christ. (2018, 186–87)

Unquestionably, then, we have here a religiously based, antiblack ethnocentrism of a premodern kind. But do we yet have racialization and racism? Strickland (2003) does not take that step—indeed, the term "race" does not even appear in her index. But in the later work by Heng (2018), any theoretical ambivalence and ambiguity are removed, as boldly announced in her title, *The Invention of Race in the European Middle Ages*. We need, in Heng's opinion, to recognize the protean character of race and not tie ourselves to the biologistic concept associated with modernity. Thus, for her the established short periodization is mistaken and needs to be extended to the medieval period.

But an even more radical challenge comes from a cohort of classical scholars. Agreeing that dominant conceptions of race and racism in the literature are tendentious, they reject both the short and what could be designated the medium periodization for a long one. Here the crucial text is Benjamin Isaac's (2004) *The Invention of Racism in Classical Antiquity*, that—in another unequivocal title—backdates the origins of race and racism long beyond Heng's medieval periodization, indeed beyond the birth of Christianity, all the way to the classical world. In fact, Isaac (2004, 172–81) argues that the pioneering racist theorist of the Western tradition is none other than Aristotle. Though Aristotle concedes that no visible markers identify the "natural slaves" he discusses in the *Politics*, the fact that he links them with non-Greeks, particularly Persians, is, for Isaac, sufficient for this to count as racialization (Aristotle 2013, bk. 1). Indeed, part of the point of Isaac's book is to contest what he sees as the question-begging conception of races presupposed by race-as-modern theorists (color-coded populations—white, Black, brown [sometimes "yellow" also], red—originating from different continents or subcontinents). For Isaac, such a conceptualization turns the question of the periodization of race into a stipulative verbal exercise rather than an open-ended empirical historical investigation, since terms are being so defined that only modern race will be recognized as race. Instead, we should work with a nontendentious definition that focuses on the essentials (unalterable group hierarchy, in his view) rather than accidental traits like skin color.

A later conference volume coedited with other like-minded scholars, *The Origins of Racism in the West*, further explores the implications of such a revisionist view for various human groups (Eliav-Feldon, Isaac, and Ziegler 2013). And once again it turns out—see the chapter by Goldenberg—that negative "racial" representations of Blacks (as, once more, "Ethiopians") can be found in the period, in Greco-Roman antiquity, before even the Christian epoch (CE), and inherited by the Church Fathers, such as Origen (Goldenberg 2013). Moreover, as Goldenberg documents in his own earlier book, *The Curse of Ham*, the biblical story in Genesis (9: 18–25) of Noah's curse on Ham, supposedly dooming his son Canaan's descendants to perpetual slavery, would come to be interpreted in both the Arab and Christian worlds as referring to Africans, thereby becoming "the single greatest justification for Black slavery for more than a thousand years" (Goldenberg 2003, 1).

In sum, if the argument in these works of revisionist racial scholarship is vindicated, it would mean that antiblack racialization at the ideological level does indeed long predate modernity, fundamentally shaping the iconography and eschatology of Christianity. So two of my suggested three necessary conditions would have been met. But still, they alone would not suffice for the emergence of Black philosophy as I am proposing we conceptualize it. What is also required is that such stigmatizing representations be part of material structures of racial domination, racializing Africans ontologically, and thereby shaping an oppositional Black consciousness, in which this imputed demeaning identity is resisted and Blackness revalorized.

In other words, people from the classical pagan Greco-Roman world and the later medieval Christian world could have had such negative views about "Ethiopians" without in general also having the power to inflict them in the form of group-subordinating institutions. Africans could have been completely out of reach, in African nations beyond Greco-Roman or medieval Christian European power, completely oblivious to the fact that they were being so racialized and stigmatized. Or it could be that even as minority African inhabitants of these polities, they were subject only to individual discriminatory acts, not systemic race-based oppression. Ancient and medieval slavery in the West, for example, is generally seen as raceless, both because of the aforementioned conventional judgment that this was a preracial epoch, and because people from all ethnic groups and communities were enslaved. So even if—in the light of this new body of revisionist scholarship—we do now need to entertain the possibility of premodern racialized slavery, it does not, on the evidence, seem to have targeted Blacks as such.

(Slavery in the medieval Islamic world is another story, and some scholars have contended that differential treatment of Black slaves can indeed be found here [Lewis 1992; Segal 2002]. The fact that the Arabic word for Blacks, *abīd*, is the same as the word for slaves is certainly linguistic testimony to such a connection [Hardy 2002]. So this would be a possible example of premodern Black racial subordination in the non-Western world, which might have generated oppositional texts that meet our definition. But our focus in this chapter is on what has come to be characterized as the Western world.)

My claim, then, is that even if the existence of premodern Western racism, including antiblack racism, can be established, it is only with Western modernity that we begin to get the systematized racial subordination of

Africans as Blacks, and the corresponding experience of such subordination, that lays the grounds for Black philosophy in my recommended sense, and the possibility of a Black Enlightenment. So modernity remains crucial in my preferred periodization; Black philosophy would constitute one component of what has recently come to be termed "Afro-modern political thought" (Gooding-Williams 2009; Hanchard 1999). As against negative but socially impotent characterizations in the distant Euro-world, or isolated discriminatory transactions within the Euro-world, it is the advent of the Atlantic slave trade at a time when European enslavement of its own population was dying out, and the later colonial conquest of Africa, that racializes Blacks as a group, that indeed creates Blacks as a category. Only then can we talk about material and ideological circumstances pervasive and enduring enough to act as the ground for the development of Black philosophy.

But possibility must be distinguished from actuality. Even after the emergence of Blackness as a racial social category and institutionalized reality in particular geographical locations, it seems dubious to me to categorize all the philosophizing of Blacks in these locations as Black philosophy. If the mere identity of the practitioners constituted a sufficient condition, then work by Blacks in mainstream metaphysics, epistemology, logic, philosophy of language, value theory, history of philosophy, and so on that is in no way informed by Blackness or race or the African American experience would count as Black philosophy even if it were indistinguishable from work in these areas produced by mainstream European and Euro-American philosophers. Clearly such a conclusion is quite counterintuitive. So we need to differentiate the identity of the philosophers from the identity of the philosophy and separate the question of who they are from the question of what it is. Think of the analogy of women philosophers, some of whom take gender as their primary theme, others of whom do not. Blackness, as I am suggesting we understand it, is to race as feminism is to gender (though there will be non-Black critical racial philosophies also). Black philosophy will, of course (at least at the present), be done predominantly by Black philosophers—this is not a contingent correlation. But it cannot be turned into a definitional truth. And by the same token, just as men can be feminists and do feminist philosophy, so other people of color, and indeed whites, can do Black philosophy. The crucial criteria are not identity based but content based: philosophical engagement with a particular set of problems, a certain body of literature, a historical tradition, a distinctive outlook on the world.

Black Philosophy and Black Enlightenment

So what is that tradition and outlook? In my opinion, the best way to conceptualize the defining features of Black philosophy is as the philosophy that develops out of the distinctive experience of racial subordination in modernity—a philosophy that, in its effort to understand and end that subordination, has the potential for illuminating modernity more thoroughly and relentlessly, more free from illusions, than its (typically) white antagonist. (I emphasize "potential" because, although my own sympathies are with the radical strain in Black philosophy, the term cannot be so narrowly defined as to exclude Black conservative thinkers also grappling, from their opposed political perspective, with the problem of race.)

Here, of course, I am presupposing a familiarity with the claims of standpoint theory—the general thesis, arguably first articulated in Marxism, and then subsequently developed by feminism—that in a system of subordination, or interlocking and overlapping subordinations, the perspective of those at the bottom is more likely to be the foundation of an objective assessment of its workings than the perspective of those more favorably located. In other words, material advantage comes at an epistemic cost: the likelihood that, because of one's unrepresentative group experience and vested interests in the established order, one will find it more difficult to see that order as it really is. One will be more prone to illusions, more susceptible to rationalizations and denials of its injustice. Those at the bottom are certainly not thereby guaranteed a veridical view of the social structure. But the mere fact of having no group interest in its perpetuation is a great cognitive advantage, while the everyday experience of oppression will make them less likely to accept dominant accounts that deny or gloss over the ugly realities on which it is based. If social subordination affords one distinctive insights, this means that Blacks have been peculiarly well placed to theorize, from the underside (think of Ellison's narrator in his basement), the actual material and normative topography of this racialized world. So Blackness really indicates not a particular band of wavelengths but a particular societal position, and not just any subordinated nonwhite position but a peculiar location within the nexus of multiple oppressions created by white supremacy. In comparison to the Euro-Enlightenments discussed at the start, the geography in this case is not limited to a particular national or even continental region, but is literally global. For it is shaped first by the forced diaspora of modern Atlantic slavery that transported captured Africans to the Americas (Canada and the United States, the Caribbean, Latin America) and Europe—what Paul Gilroy (1993) famously designated the "black Atlantic"—and then by the resulting transnational stigmatization of this population across the planet, even in countries without such a history—producing what Lewis Gordon (1995) has termed "an anti-black world."

From this perspective, we can appreciate how a philosophy coming out of Blackness could actually be better situated to carry out the Enlightenment project than its designated legitimate representatives, whose supposedly illuminating vision was (and is) darkened in various ways by their commitment to the existing racial order. Pronouncements about general human equality all too often stopped at the global color line. Being more centrally shaped by social oppression than any of the earlier listed Euro-Enlightenments, the Black Enlightenment is—unsurprisingly—more potentially radical than any of them. (Israel's [2001] examples of the "radical Enlightenment," whether his controversial main candidate, Spinoza, or even in the anti-imperialism he finds in such French *encyclopédistes* as Diderot, are all European thinkers, with the limitations one would correspondingly expect in the depth of their challenges to the global order.) The Haitian Revolution was more genuinely universalist, more consistently a realization of (ostensible) enlightenment values, than either the American or French Revolutions, and precisely for that reason it has generally been written out of the European Enlightenment narrative (Nesbitt 2008; Trouillot 2015). The diasporic experience of Black racial subordination, enduring into the postemancipation period, indeed enduring until today, generates a distinctive perspective on modernity that, though overlapping in part with the general experience of people of color under Euro-domination, is marked by peculiar features unique to it. Hence the idea of a Black Enlightenment, a "black light" analogous to a penetrating X-ray vision into the workings of Euro-created polities and related patterns of Euro-cognition, both factual and moral. Think of it as W. E. B. Du Bois's ([1903] 1997, ch. 1) "second sight" extrapolated from its specific U.S. context to the diaspora in general. Metapositioned with respect to the European white Enlightenment, drawing on the higher (Black?) frequencies beyond the visible spectrum, it tracks the chiaroscuro of light and darkness of white normative exclusions, moral and conceptual and juridico-political, and their consequences across multiple different geographical borders and white political ideologies. The very invisibility of Blacks as human equals has helped to make visible for them ongoing structures of inequality taken for granted by the whites privileged by them, even when the pretensions of their political philosophies have been radical. And given the historic gender hierarchies within Blackness, we would likewise expect that Black women—at the bottom of the bottom—would be differentially and more favorably positioned to recognize intraracial inequities unperceived by Black males (Guy-Sheftall 1995; Taylor 2017).

Consider the big three of structural social oppression: gender, class, and race. Of these, both gender and class clearly predate the modern period, in patriarchal systems of various kinds stretching back to the early formation of the species, and in class societies evolving in separate continents out of hunter-gatherer communities. But race is different. As just argued, even if race as ideology, discourse, and iconography is older than the conventional postwar narrative claimed, race as a planetary system is unambiguously modern. It is European expansionism in the modern period that internationalizes race, creating—through colonialism, imperialism, white settlement, and racial slavery—a white supremacy that becomes global by the early twentieth century (Du Bois [1903] 1997; Lake and Reynolds 2008; Mills 1997; Winant 2001). So at the very same time that liberalism as the putatively most important political ideology of modernity is supposedly eliminating premodern social hierarchies, it is establishing new modern hierarchies of race. As George Fredrickson points out in his short history of racism:

> What makes Western racism so autonomous and conspicuous in world history has been that it developed in a context that presumed human equality of some kind. . . . If equality is the norm in the spiritual or temporal realms (or in both at the same time), and there are groups of people within the society who are so despised or disparaged that the upholders of the norms feel compelled to make them exceptions to the promise or realization of equality, they can be denied the prospect of equal status only if they allegedly possess some extraordinary deficiency that makes them less than fully human. (2015, 11–12)

So race is ontologized in a way that it is not in premodernity because inherited discourses of racial stigmatization, whether secular or Christian, now have coercive power behind them in the form of the racial state (Goldberg 2002; Mills 2020). (Note: If the defenders of the existence of premodern racial ideologies can also make a case for their institutionalization, then premodern racial states could exist also, and in fact Heng [2019] later argues that the first Western racial state is actually a premodern one, twelfth–thirteenth-century England oppressing its Jewish population.

However, such racialization would still be local rather than global, and not in sharp contrast to declared universal equality, as with the modern racial state.) Race becomes ontological—and thus an appropriate subject for philosophical inquiry—because race becomes the signifier of full or diminished humanity, a signifier that is enforced by material practices in a modern racialized world. In affirming their racial identity, whites are in effect affirming their humanity and distancing themselves from the less-than-human. Insofar as philosophy is supposed to investigate, at the most foundational level, the human condition, race then needs to be taken up philosophically, since it will henceforth shape social reality, the (differentiated) experience of social reality, conceptions of the ethically right and the aesthetically beautiful, and the norms of belief: in short, ontology, phenomenology, value theory, and epistemology.

But the critical distancing on race necessary to denaturalize it, and to develop such a philosophy, will be very difficult to attain for the Europeans privileged by this new system. Their new whiteness will act as a cognitive barrier. The mainstream (class-privileged white male) Enlightenment's complicity with colonialism, imperialism, white settlement, and racial slavery is, after several decades of decolonial exposé, a completely familiar story by now. But the point is that even white radical theory, such as class theory and feminism, will also be affected. For though class and gender are, of course, also part of this matrix of interlocking oppressions generated by empire, race is the element that is new and whose synthesizing and catalytic effects shape the transmutation of these premodern categories into their distinctively modern forms. To the extent that white supremacy gradually spreads, in material structures and overarching norms, across the planet, it henceforth ceases to be possible to speak simply of class and gender, for these identities will now be racialized.

And this means, as the disproportionately Black and female pioneering theorists of intersectionality have taught us, that insofar as white racial identity tends to trump gender and class—with the white woman and the white worker generally making common cause with the white male bourgeois directors of the colonial project rather than with their sisters and brothers of color in resistance to it—both white class theory and white feminism will be cognitively handicapped (Collins 2019; Crenshaw 2020; Guy-Sheftall 1995). The white working class is, of course, still oppressed and exploited by capitalism. But it is central to the Marxist narrative that—unlike the subordinated classes of premodernity—the (white) wage worker attains equal normative status within the liberal polity and

　　　　　　　　　　　　CHARLES W. MILLS

the capitalist system. That is why, in *Capital*, volume 1, Marx (1976) sees himself as facing, and successfully meeting, the challenge of explaining where the capitalist's profits come from, considering that in the wage relationship equivalents are being exchanged with each other. And though white women are certainly subordinated by white patriarchy, they attain at least a virtual personhood through their relation to white males (fathers, husbands, brothers, coracials in general) that is denied to people of color.

So in general the white working class and white women will find it harder to recognize, condemn, and theorize racial oppression, from which they benefit psychically (as the official full humans) and materially, whether through the land and resources from Indigenous expropriation in white settler states, the racial exploitation of African slavery and the subsequent post-Emancipation social denial of equal opportunities to freed Blacks, or the privileged European citizenship of the imperial powers dominating the planet. This is not to deny the existence of that historic handful of white progressives, male and female, who have overcome their socialization to demand an end to all forms of subordination. But the reality is that white racial privilege has generally distorted the clarity of vision one would have hoped for from those experiencing intrawhite gender and class oppression. It is not in general the case that white workers and white women as a group have joined forces with those people of color trying to abolish white supremacy. So while white Marxism and white feminism have produced distinctive and invaluable insights as oppositional bodies of thought within the Western tradition, they have usually failed even to see white supremacy as an oppressive system in itself, let alone sought to theorize and overturn it. (Recognizing racism as individual belief, behavior, and transaction is not the same as recognizing the existence of a structure of racial domination that can continue to function even in the absence of most whites having racist sentiments and beliefs.) It is people of color who become the unqualified subpersons, those "less than fully human," of modernity, precisely at the time, as Fredrickson (2015) emphasizes, when equality becomes the general epochal norm, as trumpeted in the slogans of the American and French Revolutions, and the new egalitarian philosophy of liberalism. As George Mosse (1997) argued decades ago, the most important and influential political ideology of modernity actually turns out to be not liberalism but racism.

Black philosophy, then, particularly in its intersectionalist rather than its dominant Black male form, emerges as the philosophy of those at the bottom of this interlocking set of oppressions. And I would suggest that the distinctive racialization of Blacks offers insights into the workings of white supremacy not always as readily available from other nonwhite cognitive locations in this system. For if the umbrella category—nonwhite, people of color—is useful in many contexts, it also conceals deep differences and divisions, and in other contexts these are differences that make a difference.

Consider the other major varieties of white Western racism of the modern period: anti–Native American racism; anti–Australian Aborigine racism; anti-Asian racism; anti-Arab racism; anti-Latinx racism.

Anti–Native American racism was, obviously, central to the founding of the United States, and the white settler states of the Americas more generally. But the creation of the reservation system means that today they are a marginal presence in the daily life of the white American polity. Moreover, both in the U.S. and the Latin American nations where they make up a larger proportion of the population, their relation to race is ambivalent. Though their racial categorization—Indians—was, of course, crucial to white settler ideology, it is not generally one that they have embraced themselves, except for contingent reasons of political solidarity against the white man, since they retain their preconquest civilizational identities. So their philosophical opposition to the conquest really involves the reclaiming of these distinct and disparate ethnic identities and their linked philosophical outlooks: it is not a philosophy of race as such. The same could be said about Australian Aborigines, who have sometimes self-identified as Blacks—both as a reclamation and a positive inversion of the derogatory white settler term used for them ("blackfellows") and in partial emulation of the Black American struggle—but have their diverse ethnic belongings to fall back on.

Asians as a racial, as against continental, category attempts to subsume into one group people from very different nations with different languages and cultural traditions, and in some cases histories of extensive conflict and war with one another (for example, India and Pakistan; Japan, China, and Korea). And again, their national ethnocultural identities, even in immigrant communities in the U.S., often trump their imputed/constructed racial identity, since overall they suffered less damage from Western colonialism's attempted eradication of their national cultures through violence and the lure of assimilation. In addition, some—though admittedly not all—Asian American groups have been assigned model minority status, a prerequisite of which is a social and political distancing from African Americans and the African American civil rights struggle, as can be witnessed in recent Asian-Black tensions over preferential admissions policies for Blacks. The current—as I revise this chapter in July 2020—national and global protests over the police murder of George Floyd have both exposed these rifts and generated hopeful signs of a possible greater degree of political solidarity in the future. See, for example, the following news stories and opinion pieces: Dewan (2020); Ebrahimji and Lee (2020); Lang (2020); Roy and Constante (2020); Yoon (2020).

Islamophobia has been judged by some theorists to be a form of medieval cultural anti-Arab racism, and thus long embedded in the Western Christian tradition (Strickland 2003; Heng 2018), even before its renascence in recent decades as a result of Middle Eastern politics and the growth of anti-Western terrorist movements. But this history did not stimulate any systemic critical Arab theorization of race. Rather, nationalism and religion were the banners under which the Arab anticolonial struggle was classically fought. Moreover, as noted earlier, in part because of the legacy of the medieval Arab slave trade, Blacks have themselves often been seen in racist terms by Arabs. Human rights activists have characterized the kafala system of migrant labor in the Arab states as a form of modern-day slavery, reducing African workers to a second-class status permitting widespread routine exploitation and mistreatment, and reinforcing long-standing antiblack prejudices. Even President Obama was often referred to as *al-abīd*, the slave. The heightened global consciousness about racism has forced open a discussion about these dark matters in the Arab World also (Dadouch 2020; Nusairat 2020).

Finally, Latinxs are not only, like Asians, citizens of families originating from many different nations, but they do not even have the racial commonalities that would justify a clear-cut racial category. Hence the ongoing debate as to whether they should really be seen as a race in the first place or as an ethnic group composed of many races—Euro-Latinxs, Afro-Latinxs, Indo-Latinxs, mulattoes, and mestizos—with whiteness a preferred choice for many of them, and a tradition in their own countries, dating back to the Iberian conquests and African slavery, of the oppression and derogation of Indigenous peoples and Afro-Latinxs (Gracia 2007). Though Euro-Latinx immigrants may be seen as people of color in the United States, their positioning at home, quite contrary to the myths of racial democracy promulgated in many of these nations, is one of the subordination of racial others through a system of pigmentocracy subtler in its dynamics of exclusion than the unabashed white supremacy of the United States, but no less a hierarchical ethnoracial order (Andrews 2004; Hernández 2013; Telles 2014). Afro-Latinx theorists like Eduardo Bonilla-Silva (2008) have argued that the U.S. is moving toward the Latin model of race, in which white-ness will be expanded to include Hispanic whites rather than becoming a minoritarian identity—clearly not any kind of material basis for a criti-cal indictment of, and subversive interest in, the overturning of the racial system as such. And Richard Alba (2018) is similarly skeptical of the much-ballyhooed supposed impending demographic shift to a nonwhite majority.

Consider now the contrasting situation of Blacks, and of antiblack racism, in the global order.

To begin with, as emphasized from the start, the forced migration of At-lantic slavery spreads the population of captured Africans to the Americas and Europe, globalizing in the West distinctively antiblack structures of subordination (racial chattel slavery) as well as an awareness on the part of both the slaves and the free of this fundamental division in the population. Indigenous peoples in the Americas and Australia, by contrast, generally stayed at home, and so did not have the same presence in the global imagi-nary. Moreover, this presence was, of course, an unambiguously degraded one. The pivotal role of African slavery in the new modern world system meant that for hundreds of years, "negro" was virtually synonymous with "slave," and this would become part of planetary consciousness. Whether through the Curse of Ham (theological racism), or pre-Darwinian scientific racism, Blacks were judged to be natural slaves, indeed a slave race, the manifestation of Aristotle's (2013) category from classical antiquity. Being a natural slave is different from being a savage warrior (like, say, Native Americans) or the member of a barbaric civilization (like, say, Asian Indi-ans); there is conceptual room in these latter cases for some kind of white admiration, even of a condescending kind, that there is not for chattel. Thus, it is standardly the case that in the racist hierarchies of the period, for example in Gobineau's (1999) work, Blacks are located at the bottom of the pyramid, from a continent itself characterized as "Dark."

Second, the distinctiveness of the Black body, both literal and metaphorical—recall the religious color symbolism inherited from medi-eval Christendom—means that Blacks stand out in a way that no other people do. More distant in their skin color, hair texture, and facial features from the European somatic norm than, say, Native American, Asian, and Arab ethnic groups, Blacks constitute the antipode to whiteness (as race, as virtue, as cleanliness, as light . . .). To use Hegelian language, the icono-graphy of Blackness becomes "world-historical," though of course not in a positive but in a negative sense, a degraded status immediately recogniz-able even in countries with no history of African slavery. So even after the

CHARLES W. MILLS

different nineteenth-century emancipations in the Americas, North and South, the stigmata of the Black body remain as the marker of inferiority: Blacks as the descendants of (natural) slaves. With racial chattel slavery, the n***** is born as a distinctive creature of the modern age (Jordan 2012; Pieterse 1995; Robinson 2000).

Relatedly, and in only apparent contradiction, the n***** category is sometimes expanded to include the other nonwhite races, becoming a generic racial term if special circumstances—the need to bring them down—call for the underlining of their inferiority. After the Sepoy Uprising against the British (the Indian Mutiny), for example, British soldiers resumed the routine use of the epithet for the Indian troops under their command. As recently as the contemporary wars in the Middle East, one could find the phrase "sand-n*****s" sometimes being employed by Americans about the Arab population. In 1968, the Quebec nationalist Pierre Vallières published *Nègres Blancs d'Amérique* about the English Canadian subordination of his fellow French Canadians, which was translated into English as *White Niggers of America* (Vallières 1972). Ex-Beatle John Lennon and his wife Yoko Ono cowrote the song "Woman Is the Nigger of the World" in 1972 as a statement of feminist solidarity. So the term would become a floating signifier not merely racial but transracial, yet achieving its impact always through comparison to the population universally recognizable as the uncontroversially debased.

Third, though not with the same success in all diasporic destinations, the peculiar subordination of chattel slavery was meant to erase the languages and cultures Africans had brought with them to the New World, given their possible role as a source of resistance. So unlike colonized populations in Asia and the Arab World, or Indigenous communities in the Americas and Australia, they did not generally have a precolonial tradition that, though suppressed, was still readily accessible. African survivals, while still existing, became syncretized across various ethnic groups in the forging of a new ethnic identity: what we now think of, in the United States, for example, as African Americans, Black Americans, or Afro-Latinx in Latin America. And race became central to this process precisely because this ethnicity was constructed in opposition to an oppression for which racist ideology and racial domination was constitutive. The negro, the Black, the n*****, had to rethink and reinvent and re-assert himself or herself as a person of equal moral standing, not through the attempt to escape the taint of Blackness, the racial sign of the natural slave (since it was inescapable, despite attempted cultural assimilation, though exogamous marriage and the progressive whitening of one's descendants did provide one kind of eventual exit), but through its revalorization and resignification. Race could not be avoided, so race had to be confronted and then suitably transformed. With other colonial peoples, by contrast, precolonial ethnicity and national origins were more available as anticolonial resources. For these populations, race was not really their identity but a Euro-imposed one.

Fourth, and finally, the very centrality of African slavery to the making of the modern world means that the global achievement of Black racial equality would be tectonic in both its repercussions and its costs. Recent work by mainstream historians like Sven Beckert on the crucial contribution of African slavery to the development of capitalism, vindicating such pioneering Black radical theorists as Du Bois, C. L. R. James, and Eric Williams (radical at the time), makes clear what a dramatic overturning of the modern world order would be required to provide rectificatory justice for today's descendants of African slaves (Beckert 2014; Du Bois 1935; James 1989; Williams [1944] 1994). As Cedric Robinson writes in his classic *Black Marxism*, in the transition from medievalism to modernity,

> Satanic [depictions] gave way to the representation of Africans as a different sort of beast: dumb, animal labor, the benighted recipients of the benefits of slavery. Thus the "Negro" was conceived. . . . The creation of the Negro was obviously at the cost of immense expenditures of psychic and intellectual energies in the West. The exercise was obligatory. It was an effort commensurate with the importance Black labor power possessed for the world economy sculpted and dominated by the ruling and mercantile classes of Western Europe. (2000, 4)

So the stakes involved are immense, not just material but also psychic, thereby giving whites (and others aspiring to whiteness) an overwhelming vested interest in not raising these questions, in learning to avoid this past history and its implications for the structures of disadvantage of the present. Hence the phenomenon of white ignorance, linked, of course, to other processes of racial domination also, and affecting white cognition not merely at the layperson level but within the academy as well (Mills 2007, 2015). Since this is not a philosophy text, readers might be particularly interested in my own experience in the discipline of philosophy. For the past fifty years, since its revival by John Rawls's (1999) *A Theory of Justice* in 1971, white political philosophy as a subfield in the discipline has been thriving, with a vast literature dedicated to the question of what a just society would look like. But across the political spectrum, from left to right, virtually none of this work raises any questions about racial justice. It is not, of course, that racial justice is too minor an issue to get theoretical attention, but rather the converse. It is too major, in the sense that the whole system was founded on racial injustice and so for that very reason it has to be ignored as a subject, disciplinarily tabooed. Not just the material costs of reparations in the financial economy, national and international, but the costs to the Western psychic economy of admitting the magnitude of the wrong done to the human beings represented as n*****s for hundreds of years in Western consciousness, might just be too great for whites to bear. No wonder, then, that the very centrality of race to the architecture of the modern world precludes its acknowledgment by its beneficiaries; no wonder that the various white Enlightenments, no matter what their national and political variations, cannot face the central darkness on which they were founded. The position of Blacks is unique among all the groups racialized as nonwhite by the modern West. For no other nonwhite group has race been so enduringly constitutive of their identity, so foundational for racial capitalism, and so lastingly central to white racial consciousness and global racial consciousness in general.

My claim is, then, that Black philosophy is better positioned to be systematically devoted to the project of developing a consistently antiracist understanding of race and modernity than the racial philosophies (to the extent that they exist) of the other nonwhite racialized groups. No other group has had the distinctive combination of experience, group interest, motivation, brutal racial exploitation, lack of alternative identitarian resources, and intimate and quotidian familiarity with the ideologies and practices of the West to be better located to understand race from the inside. So it is no accident that what has recently been christened "critical philosophy of race" has been pioneered by Blacks, for no other race has felt so imperatively the need to make sense of a world that has been more thoroughly and unforgivingly structured by race for them than for any other group, with no way out except to turn race to emancipatory purposes.

And that brings us back, in conclusion, to philosophy's promise of the universal. As the phrase implies, "standpoint theory" is a theory about epistemic locations, not individuals. The claim is not that Blackness confers any kind of automatic veridical insight upon you: Blacks are as capable of being racist and sexist as everybody else. After all, Black womanism arose in significant measure precisely because of the need to combat Black male sexism. What standpoint theory presumes is that taking up a perspective shaped by social subordination, especially when it is open to admitting multiple varieties of subordination, orients one epistemically in a way more likely to be illuminating of the true nature of the social system than viewpoints taking class, race, and gender privileges and their accompanying phenomenology for granted. Onora O'Neill (1993) has famously argued that the problem with mainstream ethics and political philosophy is that it typically employs idealizing abstractions, not in the innocuous sense of selecting certain features of reality to take to the higher level of the model (since any theoretical abstraction necessarily does this), but in the problematic sense of abstracting away from social oppression and its fundamental shaping effect on people and society in carrying out such modeling. The flawed abstractions typical of white social and political philosophy are of this form; they whitewash, they white-out, crucial aspects of social reality, above all the fact of white racial domination and its holistic impact over the past few hundred years. In the phrase of Joe Feagin's (2013) book, they provide a distortional "white racial frame" through which to apprehend the world. So what are being represented as abstract universals are really whitewashed particulars that have been polished up and Platonized.

In theorizing the intersection of gender, class, and race, Black philosophy thus holds the potential for a correction of the deficiencies that white racial privilege introduces into other bodies of oppositional theory, such as white feminism and white class theory, and the deficiencies of flawed Black male theorizations as well. It is in this respect that Black philosophy is potentially better positioned to realize the genuine (as against bogus) universal, overcoming Europe's "Monopolated" white cognitive power and its darkening of a universalist emancipatory beacon. From the famous judgment of the Combahee River Collective—"We . . . find it difficult to separate race from class from sex oppression because in our lives they are most often experienced simultaneously. . . . We are not just trying to fight oppression on one front or even two, but instead to address a whole range of oppressions" (cited in Taylor 2017, 19, 22)—to the Black Lives Matter movement (Ransby 2018) originally founded by three queer Black women (Alicia Garza, Patrisse Khan-Cullors, Opal Tometti) that is currently resonating around the world—the hope is that through such a rethinking, the consistently radical enlightenment viewpoint of a transformative Black philosophy can be developed that will be a rainbowed vision, potentially containing all colors, for all of us.

AFROPESSIMISM AND THE RUSE OF ANALOGY: VIOLENCE, FREEDOM STRUGGLES, AND THE DEATH OF BLACK DESIRE

FRANK B. WILDERSON III

A psychotic episode is no picnic, especially when you realize you've been having it your whole life; it cannot be called madness because madness assumes a change in the weather. A season of sanity is required.

I was moaning. Sobbing. The crisp disposable sheet that lined the gurney rasped as I shifted. I sat up when they came into the room. No one was going to strap me down. But I didn't climb down for fear of giving them cause. In the glare of fluorescence they, the doctor and the nurse, were white as dust. The gurney rattled as I shook and cried. They didn't approach. They didn't call for help, not for themselves or for me, a monstrous aphasic too Black for care. That's how I saw them see me. And my urge to save them from me eclipsed my desire to be cured. But I couldn't speak. Not even to tell them this.

Cluster bombs spiked in my heart. I clutched my chest and cried out. Did they take a step back? Is it your heart, the doctor asked. I wanted to laugh. The funny thing about a mouth is that it needs to close as well as open if a word is to be made. Mine wouldn't close; if it closed it wouldn't open. The hinges of my jaws made moans or howls but not words. I thought, *how funny is that?* I answered him in the words of a bird as its throat is slit. They left the room.

When they returned I was able to speak. But this, I knew, would only make it worse. They asked what had brought this on. I told them it was the stress of graduate school. The best way to deal with an interrogation is to weave a bit of truth into your lie. I couldn't tell them I had suddenly realized what it meant to be an Afropessimist; that my breakdown was brought on by a breakthrough; one in which I finally understood why I was too Black for care.

Lens Crafting

Afropessimism is a lens of interpretation, a way of analyzing and understanding social phenomena, much like Marxism, feminism, or postcolonial studies. It shares certain affinities with Marxism, radical feminism, postcolonial studies, and radical LGBT theory in that the desire foundational to its inquiry is decidedly revolutionary and not reformist. A social theory animated by reformist desire would ask how an otherwise ethical world discriminates against certain types of people (workers, women, gender-nonconforming individuals, and/or people living under foreign occupation) and posit what could be done to improve living conditions of those subjects in need of redress without completely undoing the basic arrangements of power; meaning without destroying the world. A revolutionary theory is grounded in the assumptive logic that the world itself is unethical and that no amount of reform will improve life for the subject of redress (that subject being the woman for radical feminism, the gender-nonconforming subject for LGBT studies, the worker for Marxism, and the native for postcolonial studies). For revolutionary feminists, the world is out of joint, not because women cannot get equal pay or are abused in the home and workplace but because the entire psychic and economic life of institutional relations is overdetermined by the need to posit the female as the Other. Such a theory is invested in examining and, ultimately, undoing the ontology of gender, which will undo the world.

Ontology is the philosophical study of the nature of being, becoming, existence, or reality, as well as the basic categories of being and their relations. Ontology often deals with questions concerning what entities exist or may be said to exist and how such entities may be grouped, related

FRANK B. WILDERSON III

within a hierarchy, and subdivided according to similarities and differences. Ontology is the examination of what is meant by the word "thing." In this respect, feminism based on a revolutionary, rather than reformist, desire would ask, What is the ontological status of the word "woman" and the word "man" and how does that ontological status (or lack thereof in the case of "woman") structure the institutional capacity of every institution from the family to the church to the stock market to the state? In other words, how does the structural antagonism between man and woman lay the foundation for what we call "world"? Furthermore, it asks how violence is necessary to initiate and sustain the ontological capacity of constructed categories that reformists would, by contrast, take at face value; as though man and woman were not social constructs but forces of nature.

The difference between Afropessimism and the major revolutionary theories of modernity are as glaring as the similarities. True Afropessimism is not animated by reformist desire to end discriminatory practices in the world; it is animated by an understanding that world itself is unethical and needs be undone. Also, it is a theory, like Marxism, radical feminism, postcolonial studies, and radical LGBT theory, which argues that violence is necessary to form an unethical paradigm (to create world) and, ultimately, violence is necessary to undo an unethical paradigm (to bring about the end of the world). Again, Afropessimism parts company with these theories, however, in that it does not offer an alternative worldview. The reasons for this refusal of the prescriptive gesture are complex, but, to state it simply, Afropessimists argue that whereas the paradigmatic antagonism that the aforementioned theories posit as being central to the formation of world are all subject positions of one kind or another, in other words, all various categories within the same species, that species being the Human (woman/man, worker/boss, native/settler, queer/straight are, in various paradigms, antagonists, to be sure, but they are also all Human beings), the Black or Slave is not a category of Human. We have here a critique that is far more comprehensive and whose implications are more far reaching than the implications of its theoretical counterparts. The antagonist of the woman is the man; the antagonist of the worker is the boss; the antagonist of the queer is the straight—but the antagonist of the Black is the Human. If revolutionary feminism is an immanent critique of the family or the paradigm of kinship, if Marxism is an immanent critique of capitalism or the paradigm of political economy as a structure, then Afropessimism is an immanent critique of the Human or the paradigm of Humanity.[1] This is why Afropessimists are loath to offer what in revolutionary circles are called "alternative visions." Whereas it is possible to imagine an alternative filial world (a kinship void of patriarchy) and it is possible to imagine an alternative economic world (an economy void of capitalism), it is epistemologically impossible to imagine an alternative Human world (a world void of relationality). Heretofore, revolutionary theory has concerned itself with unethical modes of relation: gender and economic, for example. These theories have performed immanent critiques in order to show how and why the way relations are organized and empowered (or disempowered) within a (filial or economic) paradigm are unethical. By contrast, Afropessimists argue that these immanent critiques do not go far enough; that if one were to deploy Blackness (or Slaveness) as one's lens of interpretation, one would be able to critique not just the way relations are organized and empowered and find those modes of organization and empowerment to be unethical; but one would be armed with a theoretical apparatus that would allow one to perform an immanent critique of relationality itself. Looked at through the lens of Blackness, one would be able to see how relationality itself (all relations of any kind) is unethical because relationality, the capacity to be, is predicated on antiblackness. To be is to be other than Black. "Simple enough one has only not to be a nigger" (Fanon 1967a, 115). What Fanon alerts us to is another key Afropessimist tenet: that there is no analogy between the suffering of Black people and those others who find themselves subjugated by unethical paradigms (such as patriarchy and capitalism). Analogy is a ruse, in part because, once the subjects of unethical paradigms are liberated from their chains, they will still stand in contradistinction to the Slave. They will still be Human. Ergo, they will still be the Black's antagonists.

Afropessimism connects the work of scholars such as Saidiya Hartman, Jared Sexton, Hortense Spillers, David Marriott, Frank B. Wilderson III, and others, and builds on its own unique reading of the seminal works of Frantz Fanon, Orlando Patterson, and Sylvia Wynter. The vital and decisive move made by these writers is one that takes the Black out of the Human; or, more accurately, Afropessimism demonstrates how a Human is always already not a Black. Blackness, Afropessimists argue, is what makes the Human conceptually coherent because, if the positive attributes of what it means to be Human are ever in doubt, the meaning can be secured by a reflection upon what it is not: to be Human, one has simply not to be Black (just as capitalist stands in ontological contradistinction to worker and as man stands in ontological distinction to woman). In other words, Afropessimism argues that we cannot take the word "Human" at face value. Like any other word or concept, "Human" does not come with its meaning neatly tied in a bow. The Human is a construct. To know the Human is to know, first and foremost, what it is not. Humans are sentient beings who are not Black. Blacks are sentient beings who are not Human. There is a structural (which is to say, necessary) antagonism between Blacks and Humans; and this antagonism hinges on violence. The paradigm of violence that positions and oppresses degraded forms of Humanity, such as colored immigrants, women (who are not Black), LGBT people, Indigenous people, and working-class folks (who are not Black), cannot be analogized with the paradigm of violence that positions and oppresses Blackness. Any analogy between the grammar of suffering of degraded Humans and the grammar of suffering of Blacks is hobbled by the ruse of analogy. Degraded forms of Humans are positioned and oppressed by a grammar of suffering known as exploitation and alienation. But Black people are positioned and oppressed by a grammar of suffering known as "fungibility and accumulation" (Hartman 1997). Blacks are objects and implements to be possessed (accumulated) and exchanged (made fungible) in the material and psychic life of Human subjects. Black people are the things that belong to Humans. In this way, all Humans are Masters in their relation to Blacks; and all Blacks are Slaves in their relation to Humans—and this paradigmatic arrangement holds true, Afropessimists argue, whether we are speaking about exalted Human formations, such as heterosexual White males, or degraded Human formations, such as the LGBT community or Brown immigrants or the working class.

Afropessimists interrogate the historic development of the Human, and what that development has meant for the creation of the Black as non-Human. Blackness is an ontological position; that is, as a grammar of suffering, the Slave is not a laborer but an anti-Human, a positionality against which Humanity establishes, maintains, and renews its coherence, its corporeal integrity. In this way, the socially dead or fungible Slave is a necessary foil for the construction of the socially alive Human.

This relationship is both fundamentally destructive and necessary for the construction of liberated Human subjects. For example, the circulation of Blackness as metaphor and image within progressive multiracial (meaning, decidedly nonblack) movements produces dreams of liberation which are, as we will see, parasitic on the suffering of Blacks without, in any essential way, contributing to the liberation of Black suffering. As Black people, we often mistake this as being the highest form of empathy and recognition. In point of fact, to paraphrase Hartman, it's just an extension of the master's prerogative. We facilitate the imagination of people and worlds in which we play no part. Afropessimism is not a politics, but it does point to the need for a new kind of politics that resonates with Fanon's call for the "end of the world": a complete revolution of what currently exists. And this undoing is aimed at exalted Humanity (White men), as well as degraded Humanity (oppressed people of color).

Afropessimism is not a politics, in part, because the politics that arise from modernity's treatises of Human liberation (e.g., Marxism, feminism, postcolonialism, Indigenism) are all constructed by two scaffolds—one of which is conspicuously absent from Afropessimism. Those two scaffolds are description and prescription. Marx, for example, describes the world as being out of joint, as being unethical in its essential arrangements because of the distribution of capacities in political economy: capitalists are the only ones with the capacity to accumulate surplus value. This mode of accumulation is parasitic on the labor power of the working class. Therein lies the descriptive scaffold, and it is thoroughly explicated in over three thousand pages in Marx's (1976) *Das Kapital*. To put it simply, the world is unethical and out of joint due to a structural antagonism between the haves and the have-nots. The prescriptive scaffold is Marx's answer to the question, What is to be done? Here Marxism is unwavering in its answer: destroy capitalist capacity, bring about the end of the capitalist political economy, and usher in a communist political economy, by any means necessary. The prescriptive scaffold can be summed up in a word—communism; or in a phrase—the dictatorship of the proletariat. His prescription offers not just the promise of redress and renewal in some abstract, ideal, or spiritual sense, but a concrete proposal as to how the working class will be liberated and what liberation will look like on the other side of capitalism. No such concept or proposal is offered by Afropessimism, for who can say what liberation looks like on the other side of Humanity?

Instead of interrogating the capitalist and the capacity of her or his position, Afropessimism interrogates the Human and its capacity as being parasitic on the absence of the Slave's, or Black's, capacity (the absence of agency). Therein lies the descriptive scaffold of Afropessimism, and it is explicated by the scholars cited above, as well as in countless articles and an archive of monographs that are being written and published. The Human has three constituent elements: natality, honor, and contingent violence. These constituent elements of Human subjectivity are not embodied by the Slave or Black, and their conceptual coherence is vouchsafed in contradistinction to the Slave's or Black's lack of them. (Just as the capitalist has the capacity to accumulate surplus value, and this capacity is necessarily lacking in the worker; but the absence of this capacity in the worker is required to give its presence coherence in the capitalist.) The social death of the Slave, or Black, has three constituent elements: natal alienation, general dishonor, and naked or gratuitous violence (Patterson 1982). Gratuitous violence secures natal alienation and general dishonor. The Black body, or Black "flesh," as Spillers (2003) would say, is a sentient being for which no form of violence is psychically beyond the limit. In other words, there is nothing one can do to this body, in the collective unconscious or the libidinal economy, that would be deemed "violence beyond the limit" (Eltis 1993).

The Political Is Personal

Why is antiblack violence not a form of racist hatred but the genome of Human renewal? Why must the world reproduce this violence, this social death, so that social life can regenerate Humans and prevent them from suffering the catastrophe of psychic incoherence?

This question complicates not just coalition politics, but interracial "love" (and we should be mindful of the scare quotes, as Spillers would say) and "friendship" between Blacks and Humans. If the necessary and ritualistically violent exclusion of Blacks secures subjective capacity for relations between Humans, what does this imply for Black and Human friendships and love? It returns us to James Baldwin's dilemma in "The Black Boy Looks at the White Boy": "There is a difference between Norman [Mailer] and myself in that I think he still imagines that he has something to save, whereas I have never had anything to lose" (1993, 217). How do friendships and love manifest between one species with something to salvage and another species with nothing to lose?

My relationship with my White former underground commander, Heinrich, and my White wife, Anita, are my conduits for thinking about this. That's because I never speak honestly to White people—it's too dangerous; it's too debilitating. White people are the most violent and naive people on the planet; especially progressives and radicals, the ones who think they're for social justice and revolution. Get too close, or remain around them for too long, and what you find is that they are really no better than loyal opposition. This is true whether you're dealing with Bernie Sanders Democrats, or even socialists, in the U.S., or you're dealing with British radicals and

African National Congress (ANC) antiapartheid veterans in South Africa. So one must perform a Blackness with responsible rage; because in your irresponsible rage they will see only a threat to their own persons or to their way of life. They won't see their very existence, their capacity to be as Humans, their life, as the place from which the threat originated. So one performs Black rage responsibly, in an attempt to make them feel safe, even at the expense of one's own safety.

Heinrich and Anita are two White people to whom I have spoken openly, honestly, and over a long period of time; they earned their roles as auditors, and it's not a two-way street. Nor should it be, for there's no reciprocity in the Master-Slave dynamic. As an urban guerilla and my commander in the armed wing of the ANC, Umkhonto we Sizwe (MK), Heinrich had earned that role long before I met him. That does not mean that all, or even most of the Whites in MK were like that. I can recall some really disturbing conversations that I had with Derek Andre Hanekom and something I saw at a meeting with Ronnie Kasrils.[2]

When I first arrived in South Africa in 1989, I was a Marxist. Toward the end of 1996, two and a half years after Nelson Mandela came to power, I left not knowing what I was. This is not to say that I, like so many repentant Marxists, had come around to what policy wonks and highly placed notables within the ANC National Executive Committee (NEC) called for then, a so-called mixed economy—a phrase that explained less than nothing but was catchy and saturated with common sense, thus making it unassailable. No, I had not been converted to the ethics of the free market, but I was convinced the rubric of exploitation and alienation (or a grammar of suffering predicated on the intensification of work and the extraction of surplus value) was not up to the task of (a) describing the structure of the antagonism, (b) delineating a proper revolutionary subject, or (c) elaborating a trajectory of institutional iconoclasm comprehensive enough to start "the only thing in the world that's worth the effort of starting: the end of the world, by God!" (Aime Cesaire, as quoted in Fanon 1967a, 96).

In June 1992, not long after the massacre at Biopatong, Ronnie Kasrils cochaired a Tripartite Alliance Rolling Mass Action meeting with a CO-SATU (Congress of South African Trade Unions) central committee member and an ANC NEC member. They sat together at a long table on the stage in the basement auditorium of the Allied Bank Building in Johannesburg. One hundred delegates of the Tripartite Alliance had been sent there to plan a series of civil actions designed to paralyze the urban nerve centers of South African cities (the Leipzig Option, as some called it). I was one

FRANK B. WILDERSON III

of the delegates. Out of one hundred people, it seemed as though no more than five to ten were White or Indian. There were a few Coloureds. One Black American—me; and eighty to ninety Black South Africans.

We began with songs that lasted so long and were so loud and so pointed in their message (Chris Hani is our shield! Socialism is our shield! Kill the Farmer, Kill the Boer!), that by the time the meeting finally got underway one sensed a quiet tension in the faces of Kasrils and his cochairs. An expression I'd seen time and again since 1991 on the faces of Charterist notables; faces contorted by smiling teeth and knitted brow, solidarity and anxiety; faces pulled by opposing needs—the need to bring the state to heel and the need to manage the Blacks, and it was this need that was looking unmanageable.

Planning for a mass excursion was on the table: an armada of buses filled with demonstrators was to ride to the border of the homeland of the Ciskei, which was ruled by the notorious General Joshua Oupa Gqozo. We would disembark, hold a rally, then a march, then, at one moment in the march, we would crash through the fence, thus liberating the people of the homeland by the sheer volume of our presence. Kasrils and his cochairs looked one to the other. Yes, things were indeed getting out of hand. As a round of singing and chanting ensued, they leaned their heads together and whispered.

Comrade Kasrils rises. He exits, stage right. He returns with a small piece of paper. An important intelligence report, comrades, news that should give us pause. Reading from the slip of paper, he says he has just received word that, were we to actually pass the motion on the floor to cross the Ciskei border en masse, to flood the homeland with our belligerent mass, General Joshua Oupa Gqozo would open fire on us with live ammunition. To Comrade Kasrils's horror, the room erupts in cheers and applause. This, I am thinking, as I join the cheering and the singing, is not the response his intelligence was meant to elicit.

Had Comrade Kasrils been hoisted by his own petard, or was there dissonance between the assumptive logic through which he and the Tripartite Alliance posed the question, What does it mean to suffer? and the way that question was posed by—or imposed upon—the mass of Black delegates? The divergence of our joy and what appeared to be his anxiety was expressed as divergent structures of feeling, which I believe to be symptomatic of a contrast in conceptions of suffering and to be symptomatic of irreconcilable differences in how and where Blacks are positioned, ontologically, in relation to nonblacks. In the last days of apartheid, we failed to imagine the fundamental difference between the worker and the Black. How we understand suffering and whether we locate its essence in economic exploitation or in antiblackness has a direct impact on how we imagine freedom; and on how we foment revolution.[3]

Perhaps the bullets that were promised us did not manifest within our psyches as lethal deterrents because they manifested as gifts, rare gifts of recognition; gifts unbequeathed to Blackness; acknowledgment that we did form an ensemble of Human capacity instead of a collection of kaffirs, or a bunch of niggers. We experienced a transcendent impossibility: a moment of Blackness-as-Presence in a world overdetermined by Blackness-as-Absence.

I am not saying that we welcomed the prophecy of our collective death. I am arguing that the threat of our collective death, a threat in response to the gesture of our collective—our living—will, made us feel as though we were alive, as though we possessed what in fact we could not possess, Human life, as opposed to Black life (which is always already "substitutively dead," "a fatal way of being alive"); we could die because we lived (Marriott 2000, 15, 19). It was as though we had penetrated three layers of Absence in the libidinal economy, an economy that organized the structure of reality in ways that were too often eschewed by South African Marxists, and Charterists more broadly, in favor of the verifiable data of political economy; an economy which in many respects was at the center of Steven Biko's meditations and the foundation of Black Consciousness. Like Steven Biko before him, Lewis Gordon (1995, 103), also a close reader of Frantz Fanon, reminds us of the serious pitfalls and "limitations [in] excluding the evasive aspects of affect from interpretation of reality." Building on Lewis Gordon's ontological schema of Absence and Presence, which is a reconstruction and elaboration of Fanon's ontological arguments in *Black Skin, White Masks*, I designate three layers of Black Absence, subjective, cartographic, and political, through which we might read the cheering that erupted as affective (rather than discursive) symptoms of an ontological discovery.

ABSENCE OF SUBJECTIVE PRESENCE

The world cannot accommodate a Black(ened) relation at the level of bodies, subjectivity. Thus, Black "presence is a form of absence," for to see *a* Black is to see *the* Black, an ontological frieze that waits for a gaze, rather than a living ontology moving with agency in the field of vision. The

Black's moment of recognition by the Other is always already Blackness, upon which supplements are lavished, American, Caribbean, Xhosa, Zulu, and so on. But the supplements are superfluous rather than substantive; they don't unblacken. As Gordon points out, "there is 'something' absent whenever blacks are present. The more *present* a black is, the more absent is this 'something.' And the more absent a black is, the more *present* is this something." Blackness, then, is the destruction of presence, for Blacks "seem to suck presence into themselves as a black hole, pretty much like the astrophysical phenomenon that bears that name" (Gordon 1995, 99).

The inverse is even more devastating to contemplate vis-à-vis the dim prospects for Blacks in the world. For not only are Whites "prosthetic Gods," the embodiment of "full presence," that is, "when a white is absent *something* is absent," there is "a lacuna in being," as one would assume given the status of Blackness, but Whiteness is also "the standpoint from which others are seen," (Gordon 1995, 100) which is to say Whiteness is both full Presence and absolute perspectivity. "To look at a black body is to look at a mere being-among-beings . . . [but] the white body, being human (Presence), doesn't live as a mere-being-among-beings. It lives with the potential to be a being that stands out from mere beings. Its being-in-itself ironically enables it to be a being-for-itself" (Gordon 1995, 100–101).

Human value is an effect of recognition that is inextricably bound with vision. Human value is an effect of perspectivity. What does it mean, then, if perspectivity, as the strategy for value extraction and expression, is most visionary when it is White and most blind when it is Black? It means that "to be valued [is to] *receive* value outside of blackness" (Gordon 1995, 100). Blacks, then, void of Presence, cannot embody value, and void of perspectivity, cannot bestow value. Blacks cannot be. Their mode of being becomes the being of the NO.

ABSENCE OF CARTOGRAPHIC PRESENCE

In a passage richly suggestive of maps, Gordon writes, "The worlds of the black and the white become worlds separated by Absence leading to 'fate' on the one hand and Presence leading to 'freedom' on the other. Put differently, the former lives in a world of WHEN and the latter lives in a world of WHETHER" (1995, 101). Here the Absence of cartographic Presence resonates in the libidinal economy in the way Black homeland (in this case, the Ciskei) replicates the constituent deficiencies of Black body or subject. The Black homeland is a fated place where fated Black bodies are domiciled. It is the nowhere of no one. But it is more—or less—for homeland cartography suffers from a double inscription. The homeland is an Absence of national Presence drawn on the Absence of continental Presence; a Black nation on a Black continent; nowhere to the power of two. Lamenting Africa's status as *terra nullius* in the Human psyche, Sartre wrote, "A great many countries have been present in their time at the heart of our concerns, but Africa . . . is only an absence, and this great hole in the map of the world lets us keep our conscience clean" (as quoted in Gordon 1995, 100). Just as the Black body is a corpus (or corpse) of fated WHEN (when will I be arrested, when will I be shunned, when will I be a threat), the Black homeland, and the Black continent on which it sits, is a map of fated WHEN, "battered down by tom-toms, cannibalism, intellectual deficiency, fetishism, racial defects, slaveships, and above all else, above all 'Sho good eatin'" (Fanon 1967a, 112). From the terrestrial scale of cartography to the corporeal scale of the body, Blackness suffers through homologies of Absence.

ABSENCE OF POLITICAL PRESENCE

The third manifestation of Black Absence that our ecstasy assailed, or perhaps simply recognized, that afternoon, was Black Absence from the political hegemony of the Charterist grammar of suffering—a grammar of suffering that ran from the tepid ANC/UDF formulation in which the political subject is imagined to be dispossessed of citizenship and access to civil society, to the lukewarm, the South African Communist Party's formulation in which the political subject is imagined to be dispossessed of labor power. Neither formulation rises to the temperature of the Black's grammar of suffering. How, inside the Charterist movement, would it have been possible to articulate a political line that was essential, as opposed to supplemental, to the suffering of Blacks; a grammar of suffering in which the subject is not simply dispossessed of labor power but a sentient being dispossessed of being? The second question implied here is whether or not Steven Biko's presence on that stage, instead of Ronnie Kasrils and the Charterist generals', would have been sufficient to transpose our felt recognition of a Black grammar of suffering (Absence in a world of Presence) into discourse, and from there into a new political hegemony. Were the seeds of this articulation and transposition in Black Consciousness? If not, why not? And if so, why did they not take root? Such questions have great bearing upon our thinking about the political past, present, and future of

FRANK B. WILDERSON III

South Africa, if for no other reason than the fact that the presence of Ronnie Kasrils (as the prototypical White, Charterist, radical) on stage that afternoon had been vouchsafed by the absence of Steven Biko from that stage and others like it.[4]

As we roared, toyi toyied, and sang, we had the feeling that we'd rent the three layers of Absence. It was exhilarating; a shattering of the WHEN of Black Absence; a breaking through to the WHETHER of Human Presence—recognition of ourselves as beings void of the inertia of objects; endowed at last with the force of subjects.

It was, I suspect, that burst of desire for recognition, and the shocking realization of what Blackness as Presence would really entail—the violence necessary to enact one moment of Black recognition—that gave comrade Kasrils pause. It would have given us pause as well had we thought it instead of felt it—had it been transposed from affect into discourse. For turning Absence into Presence is not the same as turning waged workers into free workers. The latter reorganizes the world; the former brings it to an end.

Unlike the delegates, Comrade Kasrils's answer to the question, What does it mean to suffer? was predicated on economic exploitation and not on antiblackness. As a Marxist, Ronnie Kasrils could not imagine a fundamental difference between the worker and the Black. Kasrils could think historically, politically, and economically, but not ontologically. Or maybe he did know the difference, as we knew it, intuitively, and was compelled all the more to manage it.

It may seem sacrilegious to accuse White antiapartheid Charterists of antiblackness. People like Ronnie Kasrils, Derrick Hanekom, and Albie Sachs risked their lives and ostracization from their families and communities—they gave blood and spilled blood. To imbue them, or the structure of feeling through which they conducted their political life, with the same antiblackness that they fought against appears, at first blush, to impose upon them an injudicious form of double jeopardy. The record, however, indicates that antiblackness cannot be disentangled from the story of their political ascent.

You turn your head sideways and listen to people like Ronnie Kasrils, and you would hardly know that they were high-ranking guerillas. So I think what I'm saying is that Anita (as a one-time White progressive who threw her labors into the project of Black liberation) and Heinrich (as an MK operative and later as an aboveground politico) sought ways and means through which they could be authorized by Black revolutionary ensembles of questions. What do I mean by that? Well, I know what I don't mean. For a long time, Heinrich, like most of us in the ANC in general and MK in particular, were fixated on the idea that if you destroy capitalism you destroy civil society. And Anita thought that the essential antagonism was between men and women. Neither one of them had raced their paradigmatic views, much less Blackened those views.[5] But both of them, by becoming predisposed to be authorized by the most abject subject (or nonsubject) in the room, evolved to where they are today.

I want to say that it's great, what has happened between me and Anita, and me and Heinrich; but I also want to say I don't offer that as any kind of vision of the future. Because I love Anita and Heinrich and they love me doesn't mean that anything essential has changed in the calculus of life; it doesn't mean that the antagonism that structures our relationship has been conquered or lessened by love. In fact, I think that both those encounters bring up more problems than possibilities. One's sentiments run the risk of blinding one. Though perhaps no Afropessimist, Baldwin at least understands the antagonism when he writes, "Norman [Mailer] still imagines that he has something to save, whereas I have never had anything to lose." If you remove economic dispossession from the bedrock translation of this sentence, in other words, you grasp the fact that Baldwin means something more essential than material or economic loss, and then you grasp why it is that so many people are so anxiety ridden when confronted with the specter of Black suffering and their relationship to it; why there are so many Ronnie Kasrils and so few Heinrichs and Anitas. This is why I say that my relationship with my wife and my former commander present more problems than possibilities—because one can be seduced into holding beacons of a nauseating we-are-the-world hope for the future; and the redemptive denouement of White transformation will eclipse the *longue durée* of Black suffering. One starts believing in the redemption of the future the way one believes in a redeeming god. And one forgets that the future is what happens when one is not Black.

I'm reminded of a day in early June. The start of winter in South Africa; the day Heinrich was released from six weeks of torture by the apartheid regime for being part of an underground MK cell. He was one of my graduate students in comparative literature—his cover was that of a White nerd who liked to party. He and Tefu (another undergraduate at Wits, in the social sciences: both Heinrich and Tefu were trained operatives) and Bushy (Tefu's cousin and the MK commander of the West Rand) had bombed the Conservative Party headquarters in retaliation for the assassination of Chris Hani (allegedly orchestrated by Gaye Derby-Lewis, the Evita Peron of the Conservative Party).

(One thing that should not be dismissed, even though Heinrich plays it down, is that Bushy needed militant MK operatives to emerge and add their voices to those of the aboveground radicals who were voicing discontent at Mandela's sellout of all that we had fought for. The only way two really secret people could become public and gain legitimacy was for them to be captured by the police and tortured; and this is important because they had gotten away with it, but Mandela had immediately called in as many leaders as he could and threatened them with expulsion or with not securing a post in the new South African government when we came to power if they joined the over 600,000 lumpen and youth who were rising up to foment revolution after Hani was assassinated. The attack on the Conservative Party headquarters was to have been a catalyst or at least an accompaniment for that uprising. But Mandela's threats to highly placed notables in the movement helped quash this popular uprising. This is why, in my memoir, I write about how they went back to the rubble and left their identity documents there so that the police would burst into their dorm rooms and arrest them [Wilderson 2008].)

Heinrich had just been released from six weeks of torture. And now, the White grad students and faculty in comparative literature wanted to throw a party for him. The grad students and faculty in the comparative literature department lived in a world in which they had no connection to the most pressing struggle on the continent and perhaps in the world at that time; except for Dr. Ulrike Kistner, who had also operated clandestinely, and the two Black graduate students (one who had been a political commissar for the PAC [Pan Africanist Congress of Azania] in one of its guerrilla training camps). If memory serves me right, the Black students didn't come to the party—and no one seemed to miss them. White students drank too much and then began to chastise Heinrich for what he had done—it was subtle, lit crit chastisement; nothing so crass as to say, "We don't believe in violence, and we thought you were one of us." They would do things like quote someone like Deleuze, someone they just read who said capital was going to burn itself out, so, Heinrich, your efforts were wasted. The party turned out to be a really bizarre affair—I couldn't tell if they felt betrayed, embarrassed, or envious of Heinrich. It's hard enough being a White revolutionary and having this lot as your colleagues. Imagine what it's like to be Black and have to smile in these peoples' faces all day long. It's either your job or your sanity; and you end up choosing your job. The world is a ghetto.

That afternoon, before the party, Heinrich and I were standing in Yeoville. I was holding his wrists. I had genuine sadness about the marks of torture on his wrists, and I wondered if he was telling me the truth about everything that happened or if he was holding back some things. At the same time, the narrative of his torture was so different than Tefu's. Heinrich was tortured at the same time as Tefu, who is Black, but in separate chambers. Some people would say the important thing was that Tefu suffered more violence because the torturers jumped on his stomach and poured hot liquid into his ears, and Heinrich received less violence. But that's not what interests me. What interests me is the fact that the torturers assumed that Heinrich had a mother and a father. They worked that into the narrative of his torture. "Your father's dying. Your mother's going to be all alone," and so on. There was an empathetic relationship that was happening intuitively between torture victim and torturer. There was none of that with Tefu. In other words, they imagined themselves to be torturing some*one* with Heinrich, and with Tefu they imagined themselves to be torturing some*thing*. That's the most important dynamic that I don't think can be broken through political intervention, or interpreted adequately by way of political discourse. Afropessimism, had we had it as a lens of interpretation at the time, would have allowed us to understand this antagonism between Heinrich and Tefu, even though they were good friends and comrades who went up against the state together and in the same way. The antagonism is not in how they felt about each other. It is in the something to salvage that Heinrich (like Mailer) had and the nothing to lose that went with Tefu to his torture chamber.

Despite the fact that Heinrich and I were so close that people thought of us as one entity from time to time (when we taught in the English Department at Vista University in Soweto) and despite the fact that I'm sure that I come from more money than Heinrich comes from, our relationship to violence could not be reconciled.

I was only transposed into someone who was someone in those moments when White South Africans would hear my American accent. Before I spoke I was just a kaffir. They would hear my accent and make their apologies. "We thought you were one of our Blacks; but you're not." In other words, the degree to which I donned the accoutrement of Whiteness is the degree to which I approached Humanity. I became an exceptional kaffir. Just as here, in California, as a full professor at an R1 university, I am an exceptional nigger. But in his torture chamber, just as on the street, Tefu could not don the garment of Whiteness or its synonym, America. He was just Black; which meant he could not be seen or misseen as a quasi-relational being.

The Subaltern and the Slave

It was 1987, two years before I went to South Africa for the first time, and four years before I would go, for five years, to live there. I worked as a guard at the Walker Art Center overlooking downtown Minneapolis, and taught creative writing on the weekends and at night while I licked my wounds from eight ethically bankrupt years as a stockbroker. The first intifada had just begun in Palestine, and I had a dear friend from Ramallah who was also a guard at the museum. His name was Nabil. Nabil was a photographer who studied at the Minneapolis Institute of Art. But of most importance was the fact that we shared the same politics, revolutionary, and the same star sign, Aries: two people who were often wrong but never in doubt. "If we were in an airplane," Nabil once told me, "and we crashed in the desert and a survivors' detail was formed, some people would be tasked with finding water, it would be the job of others to forage for food and firewood, and we would need a team to build a shelter from what could be salvaged from the crash. But you, Frank, you would be one sitting back giving us orders." I didn't spoil the satisfaction he got from the dig by telling him he had mapped onto me traits that were just as applicable to him.

Most of the guards were either artists or writers or students. But only Nabil shared my politics of insurrection. We bonded early and kept our distance from the rest. I told him of my college dreams of going to Zimbabwe and fighting for ZANU/ZAPU (Zimbabwe African Union/Zimbabwe African People's Union) or to New York to join Assata and the Black Liberation Army. Nabil longed to return to Ramallah in order to make what he thought would be a more meaningful contribution to the intifada than the talks he gave to moist-eyed Minnesota liberals. He was twenty-five. I was thirty-one. In five years, I would be the same age Frantz Fanon was when he died in the custody of the Central Intelligence Agency. By the time Fanon died, he had fled Martinique, his native land, joined De Gaul's army, and been wounded fighting the Nazis; completed his internship in psychiatry and medicine; joined the FLN in the Algerian revolution; and penned four books on revolution and psychoanalysis. I had five years to catch him—a bar set high by my shame demon. Hubris at low places was where I lived. Much the same was true for Nabil. What a waste, he told me, photographing Scandinavians and loons when I should be back home making bombs. We had different shoulders but they bore the same chip. I was convinced of this one morning when he came to work smiling, despite the fact that his right eye was slightly bulbous and closed. Last night, he informed me, a friend of his from Palestine met these two gorgeous women ("White, of course," he said, under his breath, and I didn't bother to question the "of course" because I wasn't sure that he wasn't wrong). That White beauty goes without saying is the message one is fed all of one's life. To protest to the contrary is like being shortchanged and proclaiming to the person who shortchanged you, "This isn't about money." Nabil said that he and his friend could have taken them home if three rich Kuwaitis hadn't sauntered into the lounge. When one of the Kuwaitis made a move on the woman Nabil was talking to, Nabil told him, in a kind way, to go back to his booth. The man scoffed and said, "You don't even have your country." But he went back. As the night wore on, the Kuwaitis sent champagne to Nabil's table. Then all three of them approached. They offered to take the women to an exclusive after-party at a penthouse suite in the suburb of Edina. "Just you two," the one Nabil had sent packing said, "not the stateless ones." Since they were three and Nabil and his friend were two, they accepted Nabil's offer to discuss the details of the party in the parking lot. Nabil waited for the teeth of the time clock to pierce his employment card, then put on the blue museum blazer that we all wore, and I followed him into the main gallery. As I passed him to take up my position on the mezzanine he smiled: "We beat those Kuwaitis until we were tired." It wasn't as much bucked horns locked over pride of possession of two forbidden females that sparked the dustup in the parking lot—though that was surely part of it. What seared the flesh on his skin most was the Kuwaitis' riddle of Nabil's landlessness. I felt it too. And thought my loss (whatever I thought was my loss) was analogous to his. "I would have beaten them too," I said.

In those days a high, grassy knoll abutted the building that housed the Walker Art Center. The knoll is gone now. Dug out and scraped clean like a root canal. Nabil and I often took our lunch there. In springtime, when the cold breaks and the skies clear, it commanded a view of white swans lacing the surface of the lake at Loring Park, and distant cars in downtown streets sparkled like sequins in the sun, and from that knoll you could see the Basilica of St. Mary's copper dome corroded by melted snow and driving rain to a blue-green brilliance that once made me think that ruin was the true object of love. The knoll was also the vantage point from which death in the making would be seen. Just below it was the Bottleneck, an

FRANK B. WILDERSON III

intersection where three streets converged into one; a place where some of the most horrifying collisions occurred.

That hill was where Nabil told me about his cousin who, the day before, was killed in Ramallah—blown up while making a bomb. But he wasn't a suicide bomber. The Israeli occupation had yet to reach such levels as to push the insurgent populace to such tactics. It was an accident. Nabil blamed himself, the way that survivors often do, no matter how near or far in space and time they are from their dead. He survived by being here and not there. Nabil spoke openly as we watched the world below rush by without even looking up to pay its respects. At one point Nabil spoke of being stopped and searched at Israeli checkpoints. He spoke in a manner that seemed not to require my presence. I hadn't seen this level of concentration and detachment in him before. That was fine. He was grieving. The shameful and humiliating ways the soldiers ran their hands up and down your body, he said. Then he said, but the shame and humiliation ran even deeper if the Israeli soldier was an Ethiopian Jew.

The earth gave way. The thought that my place in the unconscious of Palestinians fighting for their freedom was the same dishonorable place I occupied in the minds of Whites in America and Israel chilled me. I gathered enough wits about me to tell him that his feelings were odd, seeing how Palestinians were at war with Israelis and White Israelis at that. How was it that the people who stole his land and slaughtered his relatives were somehow less of a threat in his imagination than Black Jews, the implements of Israeli madness, who sometimes do their dirty work? What, I wondered, silently, was it about Black people (about me) that made us so fungible we could be tossed like salad in the minds of oppressors and oppressed?

I was faced with the realization that the collective unconscious of Palestinian insurgents has more in common with Israeli state and civil society than it does with Black people. What they share is a largely unconscious consensus that Blackness is a locus of abjection to be instrumentalized on a whim (Marriott 2000, 2007). At one moment Blackness is a disfigured and disfiguring phobic phenomenon; at another moment Blackness is a sentient implement to be joyously deployed for reasons and agendas that have little to do with Black liberation (Marriott 2000). There I sat, yearning, in solidarity with my Palestinian friend's yearning, for the full restoration of Palestinian sovereignty; mourning, in solidarity with my friend's mourning, over the loss of his insurgent cousin; yearning, that is, for the historical and political redemption of what I thought was a violated commons to which we both belonged—when, all of a sudden, my friend reached down into the unconscious of his people and slapped me upside the head with a wet gym shoe: the startling realization that not only was I barred, *ab initio*, from the denouement of historical and political redemption, but that the borders of redemption are policed by Whites and non-Whites alike and in unison even as they kill each other.

It's worse than that. I, as a Black person (if *person*, *subject*, *being*, are appropriate since Human is not), am both barred from the denouement of social and historical redemption, and needed if redemption is to attain any form of coherence. Without the articulation of a common negrophobogenesis that relays between Israeli and Palestinian, the narrative coherence of their bloody conflict would evaporate. My friend's, and his countrywomen and -men's, negrophobogenesis is the bedrock, the concrete slabs upon which any edifice of Human articulation (whether love or war) is built. Degraded humanity can be frisked by exalted humanity and the walls of reason shake, but still stand. But when one is molested by a *thing* . . .

A mammoth pain swelled in my chest. Nabil and I were antagonists, not because as friends we were mismatched, and not because our politics were incompatible; but because the imago of the Black is "responsible for every conflictual situation" (Fanon 1967a, 146). For the libidinal economy that positions the Black imago as a phobogenic object saturates the collective unconscious; it usurps me as an instrument for, though never a beneficiary of, every nation's woes; even two nations at war.

For years I had seen myself as a degraded Human, seen my plight as analogous to the plight of Palestinians, Native Americans, and the working class. Now, I understood that analogy was a ruse. I was the foil of Humanity. Humanity looked to me when it was unsure of itself. I let Humanity sigh, in existential relief, "At least we're not him." To quote Saidiya Hartman, "The slave is neither civic man nor free worker but excluded from the narrative of 'we the people' that effects the linkage of the modern individual and the state. . . . The everyday practices of the enslaved occur in the default of the political, in the absence of the rights of man or the assurances of the self-possessed individual, and perhaps even without a 'person,' in the usual meaning of the term" (1997, 65).

Black people embody (which is different from saying are always willing or allowed to express) a meta-aporia for political thought and action. Blacks do not function as political subjects; instead, our flesh and energies are instrumentalized for postcolonial, immigrant, feminist, LGBT, and workers' agendas. These so-called allies are never authorized by Black agendas predicated on Black ethical dilemmas. A Black radical agenda is terrifying to most people on the Left because it emanates from a condition of suffering for which there is no imaginable strategy for redress—no narrative of social, political, or national redemption. This crisis, no, this catastrophe, this realization that I am a sentient being who can't use words like "being" or "person" to describe myself without the scare quotes and the threat of raised eyebrows from anyone within earshot was crippling.

I was convinced that if a story of Palestinian redemption could be told—its denouement culminating in the return of the land, a spatial, cartographic redemption—if a story of class redemption could be told—its denouement culminating in the restoration of the working day so that one stopped working when the labor was enough to produce use values, and surplus values were relegated to the dustbin of history, a temporal redemption, then there must be a story to be told through which one could redeem the time and place of Black subjugation. I was wrong. I had not dug deep enough to see that though Blacks suffer the subjugation of cartographic deracination and the hydraulics of the capitalist working day, we also suffer as the hosts of Human parasites, though they themselves might be the hosts of parasitic capital and colonialism. I had looked to the humanities (first as a creative practitioner and then as a critical theorist) to help me find and create the story of Black liberation—Black political redemption. What I found instead was that redemption as a genre was a parasite that fed on me for its coherence. Everything meaningful in my life had been housed under the umbrellas called "the humanities" and "radical politics." The parasites had been capital, colonialism, patriarchy, homophobia. And now it was clear that I had missed the boat. My parasites were Humans, all Humans—the haves as well as the have-nots.

If the disciplines that comprise the Humanities are to rid themselves of the parasitism that they heretofore have had in common with radical and progressive movements on the Left, that is, if our disciplinary labors are to face, rather than disavow, the discrepancy between Humans who suffer through an "economy of disposability" (Sexton 2015) and Blacks who suffer by way of "social death" (Patterson 1982), then we must come to grips with how the redemption of the subaltern (a narrative, for example, of Palestinian plenitude, loss, and restoration) is made possible by the (re)instantiation of a regime of violence that bars Black people from the imaginary of redemption.

Nabil and I didn't share a universal, postcolonial grammar of suffering. (Any more than Heinrich and Tefu could both be said to have kin.) Nabil's loss is tangible, land. When it is not tangible it is at least coherent, the loss of labor power. The paradigm of his dispossession elaborates capitalism and the colony. But how does one describe the loss that makes the world, if all that can be said about loss is locked within the world? In other words, how does one narrate an absence, the loss of loss? Baldwin came close when he tried to explain why his friendship with Mailer ended. The difference between something to save and nothing to lose. Nabil forced me to face the depth of isolation in ways I had wanted to avoid; a deep pit from which neither postcolonial theory, nor Marxism, nor the radical gender politics of unflinching feminism could rescue me.

* * *

For a year I took the antidepressants and the panic attack pills the doctor prescribed me, until I realized that that had not been an episode of madness because there was nothing to compare it to, no prior plenitude of sanity. Hadn't I always steeled myself against myself as a preemptive measure to secure their safety, even when, especially when, I was alone in my room with all of them? If the hospital episode was madness, then it was a clarifying madness; a lens of interpretation. That lens now has a name. Afropessimism. But it is not a lens of interpretation that comforts and cures, not at first. It explains the madness; accepts the timelessness of it; shows how sanity is, like a sanctuary from lynching, not a safe haven for my people. Where is the sanity in knowing that your death makes the world a decent place to live, that redemption dances on your grave? After a year, I flushed all the pills and made a refuge of the madness. I would make my home in the hold of the ship, embrace the antagonism, and burn it from the inside out.

Notes

The Alexander von Humboldt Foundation provided support for the year spent writing and researching in Germany. Parts of this chapter are from *Afropessimism* by Frank B. Wilderson III. Copyright © 2020 by Frank B. Wilderson III. Used by permission of W. W. Norton & Company, Inc.

1   An immanent critique is a method of discussing culture that aims to locate contradictions in society's rules and systems. This method is used in the study of cultural forms in philosophy and the social sciences and humanities.

FRANK B. WILDERSON III

2　　Ronald "Ronnie" Kasrils (born November 15, 1938) was minister for intelligence services from April 27, 2004, to September 25, 2008. He was a member of the NEC of the ANC from 1987 to 2007 as well as a member of the Central Committee of the South African Communist Party from December 1986 to 2007. The Sharpeville massacre radicalized Kasrils against the apartheid system, and he joined the ANC in 1960, becoming secretary of the Congress of Democrats in Natal in 1961, the same year he joined the South African Communist Party. In 1962, he received a five-year banning order prohibiting him from public speaking. He was a founding member of MK as a member of Natal Regional Command during the same year. He became the commander of Natal Regional Command in 1963. He underwent military training in 1964 in Odessa, USSR, and at the end of 1965 was sent to London to work for the movement there. During this time, Kasrils worked with Yusuf Dadoo, Joe Slovo, and Jack Hodgson, and they formed a special committee (1966–76) to develop underground activities in South Africa from the United Kingdom. During this time, he trained various people, including Raymond Suttner, Jeremy Cronin, Ahmed Timol, Alex Moumbaris, Tim Jenkins, and Dave and Sue Rabkin, with the aim of establishing underground propaganda units in South Africa. He served the ANC and was based in London, Luanda, Maputo, Swaziland, Botswana, Lusaka, and Harare. Kasrils eventually became a member of MK's High Command and was appointed chief of MK intelligence in 1983.

3　　To my knowledge, the term "antiblackness" was first named, as a structural imperative, by Lewis Gordon (1995) in *Bad Faith and Antiblack Racism*.

4　　I explore this assertion in more detail below.

5　　In Afropessimism, we might use the word "race" as a kind of shorthand, but it is inexact because oppressed nonblacks are secured in their coherence by a necessary antiblackness; so in a very real sense, Blacks are not only outside of Whiteness but are beyond, or excluded from, race.

AFRO-FEMINISM BEFORE

AFROPESSIMISM: MEDITATIONS ON

GENDER AND ONTOLOGY

IYKO DAY

The erasure of Black women is not purely a matter of missing facts.
AFRICAN AMERICAN POLICY FORUM, "Black Girls Matter"

Say Her Name

In *Blues\Blank\Black*, performance artist Dell M. Hamilton undoes Black womanhood (figure 3.1). Her descending metamorphosis is signaled through multiple costume changes, beginning with an evening gown, blond wig, and boa, shifting to a wedding dress, and later another floor-length gown. As the performance unfolds, Hamilton becomes progressively more disheveled, her body and gowns covered by the white chalk and charcoal she smears over herself. As she animates each new character—or versions of the same character—she addresses the audience: pontificating, singing, scolding, yelling. In the variety of personas Hamilton embodies, her act recalls and brings to life the provocative opening of Hortense J. Spillers's iconic essay, "Mama's Baby, Papa's Maybe: An American Grammar Book," in which the author recounts the many names of the

3.1 Dell M. Hamilton. Courtesy of Tiph Browne/Nerdscarf.

"marked woman": "'Peaches' and 'Brown Sugar, 'Sapphire' . . . 'Miss Ebony First,' or 'Black Woman at the Podium'" (2003, 203). Hamilton performs the many guises of the marked Black woman, her body too becoming a "locus of confounded identities, a meeting ground of investments" (Spillers 2003, 203). Symbolically overdetermined, "signifying property *plus*" (203), she is simultaneously unknown and unknowable within the existing semantic field—in the manner that Spillers conveys, "not everybody knows [her] name" (203). Thus it is the activity of naming that constitutes the central element in Hamilton's performance, at once evoking the collective force of being subject to both a literal and semiotic marking that nonetheless erases and renders her unseen.

Throughout this performative unraveling, Hamilton recites the many names of Black women and girls killed by the police, names that were not forgotten because they were never known. She writes their names in charcoal on vellum and distributes them to audience members; the murky translucency of vellum itself suggestive of human skin. Repeating, sometimes screaming the names, Hamilton reinforces the labor of grief, preservation, and documentation she commits to their memory. She evokes what Kimberly Juanita Brown calls a "repeating body": staging a "refusal to forget, a refusal to bend to the will of nearly two hundred years of fierce rhetorical denial" (2015, 11). In one act, Hamilton's performance joins the illegible grammar of Black femininity to the political invisibility of Black women's deaths, rearticulating the mission of the African American Policy Forum's Say Her Name project. By drawing together the concerns of Spillers's "Mama's Baby, Papa's Maybe"—an intervention that is now thirty years old—to the Say Her Name project, the repetitions Hamilton performs mime the temporal loop in which the legibility of Black women "remains opaque," as Saidiya Hartman underscores, "untranslatable into the lexicon of the political" (2016, 171).

To propose that "Afro-feminism" precedes Afropessimism in this essay is both to state the obvious and to mark a distinction in the role that Black feminism plays across the spectrum of contemporary race theory. On one hand, I aim to highlight the instrumental role of Black feminist thought for Afropessimist critical theory. In particular, the work of Hortense Spillers and Saidiya Hartman has provided an essential grammar and architecture for Afropessimism, a critical inheritance that is duly acknowledged by its adherents. On the other hand, my usage of Afro-feminism presents a kind of neologism or catachresis. It is a usage that marks a distinction in the trajectory of Black feminist thought when contextualized within the evolution of Afropessimist critical theory. The reason for exploring the intersection of Black feminism and Afropessimism is that while the latter is delivered from the rich critical legacy of the former, it wittingly or unwittingly transforms that inheritance into a staging ground of "articulation for men to write *through*" (Brown 2015, 7)—particularly in positioning Blackness outside of humanist material relations and as a condition of ontological death. Is this a disavowal of the mother? The purpose of this essay is to think with Afropessimism by reanimating the materiality of Black feminism by prioritizing the relations of power and domination that are constituted and reproduced through the capitalist value form. Value, in this sense, is less a reference to the intrinsic worth we assign to things or people than an index of time, specifically the temporality of social reproduction under capitalism. Reading into Afropessimism's rejection of orthodox Marxist categories for their inability to conceptualize Black fungibility and antiblack terror, I propose that a queer Marxist excavation of the threatening temporality associated with Black women's labor can open up new ways of engaging the social reproduction of racial capitalism and the queer, gendered excess it cannot contain.

Hamilton's performance raises questions about the cultural dynamics that render Black women unseen and unheard as political subjects. Connecting Spillers to Say Her Name, one finds in them both an incongruous dynamic. In both cases, they speak to the way Black feminist and queer interventions can evolve to produce political ambivalence at the level of gender, or, more problematically, to extend the abstract universality of Black male gender. How and why does this happen? As numerous debates over the core implications of Spillers's essay continue to take place, its Black feminist interventions are sometimes evacuated or redeployed for non-feminist ends. Reflecting on the origins of Black gendering processes in slavery, Hartman, too, observes the ensuing contradiction: "Depending on the angle of vision or critical lexicon, the harnessing of the body as an instrument for social and physical reproduction unmakes the slave as a gendered subject *or reveals the primacy of gender and sexual differentiation in the making of the slave*" (2016, 168, emphasis added). What I interpret from Hartman's evaluation is that the instrumentality of the slave's body as a reproductive, fungible commodity can be seen as either discarding the relevance of gender altogether or asserting its singular importance.

For some readers of Spillers's (1987, 80) work, then, the feminist implications of her argument for Black women to "gain *insurgent* ground as female social subject" fade in the glare of a larger ontological negation of Blackness itself. From this perspective, the ungendering of Blackness is ultimately a negation of a state of being rather than a reference to a particular gendered or sexual identity or practice. This view is in keeping with the general premise of Afropessimism, which understands the ungendered and undifferentiated fungibility of Blackness as the structural foundation of humanism. Blackness therefore serves as the basis of humanist ontology yet is excluded from it. Even though "Blacks are indeed sentient beings," as Jared Sexton clarifies, "the structure of the entire world's semantic field . . . is structured by anti-Black solidarity" (2016a, 12). Accordingly, as sentient beings who nevertheless lack being, the gendered experience of rape or physical violence should not be understood as instantiations of being. Rather, to assert the gendering features of antiblackness would impose what Frank Wilderson calls a "structural adjustment," whereby Blackness is "made to *appear* as 'man,' 'woman,' 'Proletarian,' 'child,' 'gay,' or 'straight,' and so on" (2010, 281) to make Blackness conform to the terms of humanism that is itself premised on Black nonexistence. Thus Spillers's deconstruction of normative gender assignment is here extended to make way for the wholesale rejection of the Black woman herself because she represents a "structural adjustment" that assimilates Blackness into humanistic categories.

Say Her Name confronts an analogous dilemma. The feminist and queer activist origins of Black Lives Matter notwithstanding, Say Her

Name emerged as a necessary corrective and supplementary resource to address the erasure of Black women from the almost exclusive media focus on police killings of Black men and boys. As proponents of the Say Her Name project, the African American Policy Forum reported that regardless of whether Black women's experiences with police violence are similar to men's or specifically informed by race, gender, gender identity, and sexual orientation, "Black women remain invisible" (Crenshaw et al. 2015, 3). Indeed, public outrage over the police murder of Breonna Taylor in her own home could only be summoned retroactively through the political injustice of George Floyd's killing by the police. In the following passage, Sexton confirms the seemingly inescapable collapsing of Black feminist and queer projects into masculinist and heteronormative discourse and optics: "How, then, did a black radical political-intellectual project generated largely by the labor of black queer women and centrally by the discourse of black feminist and queer theory become associated, again and still, with a masculinist and heteronormative popular reception? . . . Does it not make an *enunciative* difference when black queer women invoke the particular universal of their movement?" (2016a, 22).

For Sexton (2016a, 23), a more overarching question around the possibility of "lift[ing] up the intrinsic value of *any* black lives, let alone *all*" points to the answer. In other words, it does not make an enunciative difference until we deal first with the ontological problem of "the intrinsic value of *any*." This is one reason, according to Sexon, that Black feminist discourse currently operates on a "frequency whose transmission is too often broken up by interference or signal loss" (2016a, 30).

What else accounts for this interference and signal loss? Part of this communicative breakdown is clearly symptomatic of a distorted but frozen politics of Black gendered respectability contained in Daniel Patrick Moynihan's late 1960s Moynihan Report. As Spillers outlines in her critique, according to Moynihan, the "'underachievement' of black males of the lower classes is primarily the fault of black females, who achieve out of all proportion" (Spillers 2003, 205). In a society structured around normative heteropatriarchal domesticity, "Those persons living according to the perceived 'matriarchal' pattern are therefore caught in a state of social 'pathology'" (Spillers 2003, 205). In Moynihan's fictional Black family, Black men are thus the victims of Black women's pathological achievement. Working for white households and in their own, the Black woman is caught in a double bind whereby, as Hartman puts it, "She is the best nanny and the worst mother" (2016, 171).

A similar set of gendered assumptions structure the media's nearly exclusive attention on the deaths of Black men from policing. According to the African American Policy Forum (Crenshaw et al. 2015, 8), the vulnerability of Black men to police violence is often rationalized as a need to "'fix' individual Black men" or presumes the absence of Black male "mentors" as an index to causation. This critical framing reinforces the inherent vulnerability and victimization of Black men as the result of pathological mothering. When Black women leaders are brought into the spotlight, they are "often asked to speak only about their fears of losing their sons, brothers, partners, and comrades" (9) based on an underlying notion that political leadership and community stability are male. Here we see the way the feminist and queer origins of #BLM can be redeployed to implicitly reinforce the findings of the Moynihan Report.

Working at the intersection of queer theory and Afropessimism, Calvin Warren has attempted to highlight the gendered and sexualized specificity of antiblack violence. Acknowledging that Afropessimism becomes "uncomfortably silent when confronted with issues of sexism," Warren highlights the lack of an available grammar to engage the "uniqueness of this [gendered and sexualized] brutality, and it is *more* than antiblackness—a surplus violence to antiblackness" (2017, 401, 400). In order to avoid reinscribing the violent fallacy of "structural adjustments" that conceive of Blackness as ontologically equivalent with features of human difference, Warren proposes "onticide" as a procedure for addressing surplus violence that "highlights the *original death* of blackness as the center of humanism" and does not simplify the particularity of the violence through recourse to intersectional analyses or any other critical mode that "seeks to understand blackness through forms of *equivalence* with human identity" (2017, 407, 409). While I appreciate Warren's attention to the way gendered and sexualized violence constitutes a "surplus violence" that is supplementary to antiblackness, his formulation of onticide casts "Black feminism" as a structural adjustment that capitulates to humanistic presumptions that "distort antiblackness and the violence of fungibility" (413). Through his rejection of intersectionality—because it "conceives of blackness as ontologically equivalent with features of human difference" (394)—he evacuates the political salience of Black feminism and the queer construction of gendered Blackness. To the extent that Warren draws on Black feminist theory—and Spillers in particular—it is ultimately to undermine that very project for its humanist presumptions and to foreclose Spillers's (1987, 80) call to rewrite "a radically different text for a female empowerment." The effect of this argument is to further render the existence of Black women fundamentally unknown and unknowable, the social reproduction of their political invisibility incomprehensible, and the relative valorization of Black masculinity irrelevant.

Taking stock, then, both the persistence of a cultural logic of pathological mothering and Afropesssimism's ungendered antihumanism account for some of the "interference and signal loss" to which Sexton alludes. But we should add a third layer of signal loss to Black women's visibility as political subjects. The occlusion of women and women's labor within a Marxist-oriented Black radical tradition, anchored by the political legacy of W. E. B. Du Bois and C. L. R. James, contributes to this signal loss. Looking to their work, the antecedents of the Moynihan Report are evident primarily in the gendered delimitation of what constitutes value-producing labor in slavery's afterlife. For instance, by transposing Marx's masculinist construction of the industrial proletariat into the context of Black labor, Black women's waged and unwaged domestic labor disappears. On this point, Hartman reflects on how the Black subject of politics has been inordinately shaped by a Marxist idealization of the revolutionary worker: "In two of the greatest works of the black radical tradition, W. E. B. Du Bois's *Black Reconstruction* and C.L.R. James's *Black Jacobins*, the agency of the enslaved becomes legible as politics, rather than crime or destruction, at the moment slaves are transformed into black workers and revolutionary masses fashioned along the lines of the insurgent proletariat" (2016, 166). In other words, a delimited, gendered construction of labor activism—modeled on the white proletariat—is cast as the only pathway to political relevancy. Extending the gendered constructions of labor through motifs of bourgeois respectability, Black women's domestic labor was either unseen or cast as a source of devaluation, an affront to the norms of heteropatriarchal domesticity and the basis of pathological mothering. As Roderick Ferguson notes of the morality attached to the liberal ideology of the family as a site of stability and civility, "the heteronormalization of African Americans [has been figured] as the primary resolution to economic devastation" (2004, 20).

For Du Bois, in keeping with canonical sociology, the solution for the injured Black family was to restore the breadwinning patriarch. The dangerous alternative of Black women's labor "made apparent the gender non-conformity of the black community, its supple and extended modes of kinship, its queer domesticity, promiscuous sociality and loose intimacy, and its serial and fluid conjugal relations" (Hartman 2016, 169). Efforts to restore Black women to the morality of marriage, motherhood, and family were forms in which the "borrowed institutionality" (Wilderson

2010, 127) of whiteness worked to thwart the development of politics that could account for the crucial role that Black women's labor played. Their labor could not be reconciled with the heroic construction of the Black male worker or the collective resistance associated with labor movements. And despite efforts of Black and women of color feminists to make the significance of gender, sexuality, and reproduction central to the constitutive features of slavery and its afterlife, value has not been an organic principle associated with the Black female laborer, even as this labor was instrumental to the creation of value and the accumulation of capital. Rather, as M. Shadee Malaklou and Tiffany Willoughby-Herard explain, the enduring common sense produced by the Moynihan Report suggests that not only is the Black woman figured as outside of value, but by virtue of "being unknowable, 'beyond redemption,' 'unruly,' and 'disorganized' in all stages and corners of her life—inside the womb, at the kitchen table, and out in the streets . . . the black matriarch produces an 'anti-property existence' that is a frontal attack on the concept of the family" (2018, 20). The political registers of Black women's antivalue existence seem to rely on their structural position outside of normative labor and kinship relations. Neither Afropessimism nor orthodox Marxism can address the reasons for the threatening devaluation that Black women represent in order to clarify what underpins the forms of surplus violence directed at them. Below I turn to a further exploration of Black women's deviant temporal relation to the capitalist value form before returning to questions raised by Dell Hamilton's performance. I conclude with reflections on maternal mourning and the limits of ontology.

The Libidinal Economy of Political Economy

A genealogical view of the internal relation between Black women's reproductive and productive labor offers possible insights into their political illegibility and pathologized construction. I suggest that the deviant pathology associated with Black women can be traced to a vexed modality of value under slavery that hinged on the temporality of their reproductive labor. As Grace Hong observes in her discussion of gendered inheritance under slavery, the "enslaved Black female was materially necessary to racial capital as the source of reproductive and productive labor" (2015, 103). By extension, Jennifer Morgan has delineated how white propertied generational inheritance in the Americas depended upon gendered assumptions of profit realization and capital accumulation. She notes that in assessing their property, "slaveowners supplemented the present value of enslaved persons with the speculative value of a woman's reproductive potential (Morgan 2004, 91). Building on these crucial insights, this analysis charts the libidinal economy of political economy by putting "the enslaved human *herself* at the center of our analysis of the commodity form" (Smallwood 2017, 80, emphasis added).

This analysis also responds to Frank Wilderson's bifurcation of libidinal economy and political economy, rooted in his argument that antiblackness is structured as a relation of gratuitous terror rather than a relation of capitalist hegemony. Under this logic, overcoming capitalism is not a conduit to Black emancipation, because civil society is structured around a fundamental antiblack antagonism rather than a conflict over the working day in a "society which does away not with the category of worker, but with the imposition workers suffer under the approach of variable capital" (Wilderson 2003, 226). For Wilderson, it is necessary to turn to a more urgent examination of the libidinal economy of antiblackness rather than the capitalist exploitation of waged labor. He puts it as follows: "the libidinal economy of slavery is more fundamental to its institutionality than is the political economy. In other words, the constituent element of slavery involves desire and the accumulation of black bodies and the fact that they existed as things 'becoming and being' for the captor. The fact that black slaves labored is a historical variable, seemingly constant, but not a constituent element" (2003, 239n4).

Chris Chen (2013) offers a helpful distinction on this point about labor, noting that "in contrast to a Marxist perspective that focuses on the struggle around the wage, or around the terms of exploitation, Wilderson identifies 'the despotism of the unwaged relation' as the engine that drives anti-black racism." Wilderson thus rejects Marxism's emphasis on work, production, and exploitation, and counters that the foundational irrationality of antiblackness precedes and exceeds the normative circuits of capitalism, "which prohibits the slave from entering into a transaction of value" (2003, 231). Among other implications, this view is a significant departure from contemporaneous positions within the Black radical tradition inspired by Cedric Robinson's *Black Marxism*, whereby the history of racial capitalism in the U.S. has its origins in Europe, was transposed into slave labor on plantations (rather than the factory system), and was continually resisted by a revolutionary Black consciousness. Advancing a theory of liberation, Robinson claims that "harbored in the African diaspora there is a single historical identity that is in opposition to the systemic privations of racial capitalism" (1983,

317). This is a reference to the Black plenitude rather than Afropessimism's positioning of Blackness as a condition of ontological death. Beyond the relations of redressable conflict, Robinson also approaches racial capitalism as an antagonism, but one that is never total nor without recourse.

I argue that Black women's labor is associated with a deviant form of value that poses a quantitative threat to the relations of white social reproduction. To be clear, my focus on value—which I develop below—is entirely consistent with Wilderson's rejection of orthodox conceptions of work, which are replete with moralistic, liberal assumptions that underpin civil society. Indeed, a traditional Marxist fixation on labor exploitation or class domination falls short of offering an explanatory framework that can account for the experience of Black social death. Traditional Marxism often ignores or casts the problem of slavery to the prehistory of capitalism. Among the important aspects I attribute to Wilderson's critique of Marxism is that he finds unexpected company with value-form Marxism, which similarly rejects an approach to the problem of capitalism primarily from the standpoint of labor. Analyzing capitalism as a system of social reproduction, this scholarship argues that a narrow focus on labor exploitation fundamentally neglects the abstract forms of social domination that are rooted in the value form. For Moishe Postone, the dehumanizing violence of a capitalist value regime is in the way it continually devalues social labor by accelerating time. Therefore, overcoming capitalism is not about abolishing labor exploitation but rather abolishing value as a social form of wealth. Unlike the wealth we associate with the accumulation of use values (money, property, etc.), value is a "self-mediating form of wealth" responsible for a form of domination "that cannot be grasped in terms of class domination" (Postone 2004, 59). It cannot be grasped because the social wealth associated with value is constituted through labor time, which is a "form of social mediation that moulds production, distribution, and consumption" (66). The end of capitalism therefore requires not the liberation of workers but rather the abolition of the worker and of labor's socially mediating activity.

Wilderson also registers a similar objection to traditional Marxism's retention of work, observing that "the mark of [Marxism's] conceptual anxiety is in its desire to democratize work and thus keep it in place, ensur[ing] the coherence of the Reformation and Enlightenment 'foundational' values of productivity and progress" (2003, 226). Echoing and extending this critique, Kathi Weeks affirms that "this tribute to proletarian labor and to the progressive development of productive forces replicates the fundamental attributes of capitalist society" (2011, 84). From Weeks's account, communism is merely a transformation of property relations that leaves intact the basic form of industrial production—and even the mode of capitalist command over production. As she puts it succinctly, "communism could be understood as the rationalization of capitalism, the taming and mastery of its processes" (2011, 85). So, postcapitalist society does not merely institute democratic ideals of collective ownership of the means of production but rather abolishes the entire mode of production. This objective is consistent with Wilderson's point that the slave demands that all "production stop; stop without recourse to its ultimate democratization" (2003, 230). This intersection between Afropessimism and value-form Marxism reinforces how the objective of anticapitalism requires the overcoming of the value form. This reframing raises questions about the status of humanism in Afropessimism's insistence that nothing less than an "'end of the world' [can] destroy humanism and its grammar" (Warren 2017, 407). Is it possible to conceive of the value form as constitutive of liberal humanism's competitive being, such that its destruction would constitute a radical break from existing social categories of time, space, and being?

If traditional Marxian discourse has been unable to "cope with the possibility that the generative subject of capitalism [is] the black body" (Wilderson 2003, 230), I want to pursue the gendering of this generative subject of capitalism and grapple with the assumptions embedded in Wilderson's rejection of labor as merely "a historical variable, seemingly constant, but not a constituent element." Does Black women's reproductive labor register only as a historical variable? In order to explore the interplay of value and antivalue in relation to Black women, I trace the vicissitudes of value production in slavery and its afterlife. The interplay of slavery and value is complex, and literature on the intersection of slavery and capitalism more broadly reveals strongly divergent views on the status of slavery in U.S. political economy. Among these, Cedric Robinson's *Black Marxism* is pivotal in seeking to rehistoricize and thus reconstitute the teleological arc of capitalist development as a series of successive stages, from feudalism to advanced capitalism. Other prominent Marxists have approached the volumes of *Capital* less on historical than conceptual grounds. For instance, in his *Companion to Marx's Capital*, David Harvey maintains the distinction between slavery and capitalism, arguing that Marx's labor theory of value was premised on free wage labor. Harvey allows that "slavery becomes more brutal under the competitive lash of market integrations into capitalism, while, conversely, slavery exerts strong negative pressures on both wages and conditions of work" (2010, 127). But ultimately, slavery "is not about the production of value in the sense that Marx means it. . . . [his] theory only works in the case of free labor" (126). Harvey sums up the incompatibility of slavery with Marx's labor theory of value by indicating that "there is no abstract labor in a pure slavery system" (127)

To begin to parse out what Harvey means regarding value "in the sense that Marx means it" and the absence of abstract labor in slavery, it is important to distinguish that Marx's labor theory of value is distinct from a theory of supply and demand, competition, or any other aspect of the "consciousness of the individual capitalist" (Marx 1976, 433). In the labor theory of value, the value of a commodity is an expression of its commensurability. As Gayatri Spivak notes, "value, simple and contentless, is just a form in use when things are made commensurable" (Hairong 2007, 445). But underlying its contentless form, value signifies a quantity of human labor: "commodities possess an objective character as values only in so far as they are all expressions of an identical social substance, human labour" (Marx 1976, 138). This human labor is not any kind of labor, but social labor. While specific human beings engage in the actual or "concrete" labor process to create any given commodity, the commodity's value is not determined by the time it takes specific laborers to produce it because, as Marx states mockingly, "it would be more valuable the more unskillful and lazy the worker who produced it" (129). Rather, value is determined by "abstract labor," which Marx defines as "socially necessary labor time." This is the labor time required to produce any commodity "under the conditions of production normal for a given society and with the average degree of skill and intensity of labour prevalent in that society" (129). Without a doubt, "normal" and "average" temporality is highly contingent on an array of social factors. But we can add that it is about the temporality involved in the social reproduction of the commodity-determined laborer, which is an entire organization of activities and gendered relations that are constitutive of life and labor. As Susan Ferguson explains, social reproduction refers to the "*internal relation* between reproductive and productive labour . . . compris[ing] 'the activities and attitudes, behaviours and emotions, responsibilities and relationships directly involved in the maintenance of life on a daily basis, and intergenerationally'" (2016, 48, 49). Workers must have the necessary means of social and material subsistence to survive and reproduce, which highlights the important spheres of social reproduction that exist beyond the site of so-called productive labor.

Harvey's objection to the association of "abstract labor" with slavery is that the quantification of units of social labor presumes a certain social equality of concrete labor facilitated by the generalized existence of wage labor. Harvey's relegation of slavery to precapitalism is shaped by Marx's discussion of social equality in Aristotle's time. In arriving at the concept of value, Marx reflects on Aristotle's inability to fully conceptualize the money form of the commodity, and the value it represents. Aristotle recognizes that "there can be no exchange . . . 'without equality, and no equality without commensurability'" (Marx 1976, 151). According to Marx, Aristotle is unable to identify the "homogenous element, i.e., the common substance" that the commodity represents, which is equal human labor of equivalent quality. Marx observes that Aristotle was unable to decipher this fact because "Greek society was founded on the labour of slaves, hence had as its natural basis the inequality of men and of their labour-powers" (1976, 152). Granting Aristotle's "genius" in discovering a relation of equality in the value expression of commodities, Marx posits the "*historical limitation* inherent in the society in which he lived" (1976, 152, emphasis added).[1] Harvey largely transposes the "historical limitations" of Aristotle's ancient Greek context into his conceptual rejection of slavery from capitalism's dynamics. Rereading Marx's assessment of Aristotle, we can conjecture that by the seventeenth century, the "concept of human equality had . . . acquired the permanence of a fixed popular opinion" in the U.S. colonies, even if it was reserved for white, propertied men. Indeed, the race- and gender-delimited ideal "that all men are created equal" was the political basis for the U.S.'s settler colonial independence movement. It is also important to recall that for the purposes of Marx's argument in *Capital*, volume 1, he allows for all labor power and commodities to exchange at their value, for an equilibrium in supply and demand, and for prices to correlate to value.[2] These are methodological distortions that similarly misrepresent the vast disparities across value-producing spheres of social labor.

Plantation-based slavery in the Americas was never the "pure slave system" that would approximate Aristotle's historical context, nor would emancipation represent a pure break from slavery. As Caitlin Rosenthal has demonstrated, plantation journals, quantitative practices of insurers, and accounting books before and after slavery remained noticeably consistent. She notes, "Planters continued to allocate labor of the freedpeople in much the same manner as they had allocated labor before emancipation" (2016a, 671). Further complicating the notion of freedom, Sexton (2015) notes how slavery could persist without any individual being lawfully held as a slave: "emancipation, far from providing a remedy for slavery, is actually a component of its form and function." Therefore, if we discard the idea that labor power ever functions "under normal conditions" or that there was ever equal or "identical human labour-power" (Marx 1976, 303, 129), we can accept that slave labor time was objectified into an abstract quantification of value that was "socially necessary." Slave labor was a principal source of commodity values that shaped and was shaped by technological innovation, international trade, corporate finance, insurance, and credit markets. In the manner that slavery instituted and manipulated technologies of efficiency that impacted "socially necessary labor time" in commodity production, it was perhaps the highest expression of the abstract domination of capital rooted in the value form that constantly seeks to reduce time through reconfigurations in social relations.

A consideration of technological innovation brings into focus the specific role that Black women's productive and reproductive labors played and their specific relation to value—socially necessary labor time—that would shape prices for raw and finished commodities in the U.S. and Europe. A focus on reproductive labor in particular can enable a reconceptualization of the social world. To reiterate an earlier point, socially necessary labor time is not just the so-called productive labor of agricultural work; rather, it refers to the entire social cost of reproducing commodity-determined labor—"the practical human activity that creates all the things, practices, people, relations and ideas constituting the wider social totality" (Ferguson 2016, 48). Indeed, as Rosenthal explains of slavery's "scientific management," planters took careful account of the impact of nutrition and medicine on productivity, "debat[ing] slaves' consumption . . . hypothesizing about what foods and beverages might expedite their slaves' labor" (2016b, 79). In contrast, outside of the American South, it was not always deemed socially necessary to sustain or increase slave populations through biological reproduction. As Maria Mies notes of Caribbean sugar plantations from 1760 to 1800, "The planters, as good capitalists, held the view that 'it was cheaper to purchase than to breed'" (1986, 91). Given the extremely high mortality rates, this mode of production evokes an especially vicious regime of violence and overwork. Therefore, even though Jamaica, Cuba, and Haiti imported vastly more slaves, by 1825 the Southern U.S. states held the largest slave population in the Americas by over one-third (Davis 2002, 109).

The mark of innovation in the American South was Black women's reproductive labor. By 1806–8, as legal barriers were placed on the importation of slaves while the expanding slave economies of the Southern states required more labor, this intensified the domestic slave trade and the role of Black women in reproducing the work force; their wombs condemned them to the legal doctrine of *partus sequitur ventrem*. This reproductive sphere is what Adrienne Davis aptly identifies as the "sexual political economy" of slavery: "It is this terrorizing aspect of enslaved women's lives that also distinguished their role in the political economy from that of black men, white women, and white men. At labor in the fields and in labor in the birthing bed—the enslaved woman was both a *mode of production and a mode of reproduction*" (2002, 113, emphasis added). While Black women's productive labor in the fields produced surplus value for the planter capitalist, the "mode of reproduction" should be understood as a technical innovation that was a source of relative surplus value.

Relative surplus value represents a temporary infusion of additional surplus value to the capitalist, often resulting from the implementation of new, more efficient equipment before competitors have a chance to introduce similar innovations. These efficiency measures function to reduce the socially necessary labor time to produce a given commodity, which, in turn, lowers the value of both the commodity and the labor power. As Marx puts it, this desire for greater efficiency is a central logic of capital: "it has an imminent drive, and a constant tendency towards increasing the productivity of labor in order to cheapen commodities, and by cheapening commodities, to cheapen the worker [herself or] himself" (1976, 436–37). For example, the introduction of Eli Whitney's redesigned cotton gin in the late eighteenth century dramatically increased the production of cotton by accelerating the productivity of slave labor, which resulted in lowering the cost of cotton and decreasing the value of each unit of labor time. Those plantations that first implemented this new technology would have generated a temporary relative increase in surplus value before the technology was generalized, shifting the socially necessary labor time required to produce cotton. Relative surplus value is thus inherently destabilizing because of its temporal impact on commodity values. In the case of the cotton gin, it decreased the value of labor time by speeding up production, thus reducing the overall value of cotton.

From this standpoint, enslaved women's reproductive labor becomes identifiable as a continual rather than temporary source of relative surplus value. Particularly as cotton production grew in the American South, displacing eighteenth-century tobacco, rice, and indigo crops, the demand for slaves grew. Thus, in their potential to expand the slave population, slave owners identified female slaves as "increasers" (Morgan 2004, 82), associating their reproduction with temporal acceleration. As Rosenthal notes, Thomas Jefferson referred to this as a "silent profit": "He estimated that the enslaved population would increase at approximately 4 percent per year and that this increase, combined with rising prices, would result in a large profit [5–10 percent annually] beyond what was earned in the sale of commodities" (2016b, 83). With the power to accelerate production through population increase, women's reproduction was the technology that could generate relative surplus value and decrease the value of commodities and the labor expressed in it.[3] There is thus a double inheritance that the enslaved female passes on. First, through the logic of partus sequitur ventrum, the child inherits from the mother a disinheritance, or the lack of claims or rights. Second, through the generation of relative surplus value made possible by expanding the population of slaves as a technology of labor acceleration, enslaved females passed on a diminished form of value. By cheapening commodities and the laborer through reproduction, she passed on a devaluation—in addition to a disinheritance. This connects to Hong's important point that "the enslaved Black female was materially necessary to racial capital as the source of reproductive and productive labor, but in that reproductive role, she threatened to simultaneously undo and reproduce the epistemological separation between social life and social death" (2015, 104). To extend her argument: as the source of value, surplus value, and relative surplus value, the enslaved Black female's reproductive power held within it the ability to mediate time, its acceleration or suspension.[4] Of course, Marx failed to acknowledge the role of women's reproduction as a means of increasing productivity. As Sylvia Federici concludes, "Marx never acknowledged that procreation could become a terrain of exploitation and by the same token a terrain of resistance" (2004, 91).

If enslaved Black women were a continual source of relative surplus value under slavery, the aftermath of slavery dramatically reconfigured the inheritance of this value regime. While Black men "touched . . . by the mother" (Spillers 1987, 80) inherited a disinheritance under slavery, in its afterlife this disinheritance was recast as a devaluation of wage labor (as the enduring effect of temporal acceleration). However, for Black women, their association with acceleration was recast as temporal excess and a threat to the entire system of social relations mediated by capitalist value. No longer exclusively a source of white wealth as relative surplus value, the power of Black women's reproduction was redirected toward Black social reproduction. Thus the value tied to the temporal acceleration associated with Black women's reproductive labors under slavery was reconstituted as a deviant excess that threatened the social reproduction of white supremacy upheld by the value regime. Ceasing to function as the hidden hand that sutured the economic foundation of state and civil society under slavery, in slavery's afterlife Black women's reproduction was figured as a dangerous excess that threatened to undo that foundation. As LaShonda Carter and Tiffany Willoughby-Herard lay out, "the crux of the antagonism between Black mothers and the state interest in Black reproduction is that the state wishes to translate all the result of Black reproduction (social and biological) into currency" (2018, 96). Black women's transformation into labor evoked an illegible and dangerous embodiment of antivalue, threatening the social reproduction of racial capitalism. And in Black women's misinterpellation into the heteropatriarchal sphere of liberal domesticity, they thwarted the disciplinary logic of possessive individualism and instead occupied a sphere outside the property relations that governed the nuclear family. As M. Shadee Malaklou and Tiffany Willoughby-Herard assert, "the black matriarch produces an 'anti-property existence' that is a frontal attack on the concept of the family" (2018, 20). As a figure of antiproperty and antivalue, the Black woman exceeds the very conception of the possessive individual.

Returning to the question of what accounts for the signal loss that prevents the violence against and deaths of Black women, girls, trans*, and nonbinary people from registering as an ethical crisis, I propose that one possibility is related to the notion that Black women's reproduction is figured as a source of antivalue, and social relations are a threat to possessive individualism. By extension, by participating in alternative, horizontal, and extended modes of kinship outside the proprietary logics of the heteropatriarchal family unit, the sociality of Black women disrupts the hierarchical order of capitalist social relations. Black women's antiproperty existence is a threat to a value regime that supports the social reproduction of white wealth and Black death. As such, Black women do not register as individuals, nor are their deaths individualized. This is not an argument for restoring Black women to the ranks of the possessive individual with a life to lose; rather, it is a recognition of Black women's political power over the value form, from slavery to its afterlife. Asserting an affirmative pathologization of Black women's destructive relation to racial capitalism, Carter and Willoughby-Herard declare, "we are embracing the accusation that our motherhood is deadly" (2018, 100).

This transformation of Black women's relation to value evokes what Grace Hong and Roderick Ferguson (2011) call a "strange affinity" between Black women and Chinese men. In the late nineteenth century, a perception of the excessive efficiency—or temporal acceleration—of Chinese labor projected a temporal and quantitative racial essence onto

Chinese bodies. Later, as their labor threatened white labor, the excessive efficiency of Chinese labor became increasingly associated with social degeneracy and sexual vice. The temporal excess associated with Chinese bodies through their higher rate of exploitation combined with the perversity associated with the nonreproductive spheres of Chinese homosocial domesticity. This rendered Chinese labor a quantitative, temporal threat to the qualitative and normative temporality of white social reproduction. In other words, the temporally excessive and fungible character of Chinese labor was the foundation upon which Asians have been associated with a destructive value regime. This threat was ultimately grounds for over half a century of Chinese immigrant exclusion. Alternatively, Black women's association with temporal acceleration and relative surplus value under slavery was in its afterlife transformed into an association with disordered surplus populations and a threat to white social reproduction and wealth. On this point, Malaklou and Willoughby-Herard offer that "this m/othering makes something that profoundly exceeds the terms and conditions placed on the mother's reproductive functioning—something intangible and occult and world-destroying" (2018, 23). In addition, by practicing modes of sociality that depart from normative institutions of the nuclear family, Black women's autonomy from patriarchal gender norms represented an assault on property relations that rely on a hierarchical gender binary. Therefore, what is revealed in the deviance ascribed onto Chinese male and Black female bodies in the late nineteenth and early twentieth centuries is how threats to the value form are constituted through the sphere of reproduction. The deviant homosociality of Chinese men registered an unnatural form of social reproduction that was embedded in the value form. Their very nonreproductivity was associated with an excessive efficiency that devalued the social reproduction of white labor. For Black women, enslaved Black women's reproductive power to mediate value through time was, in slavery's afterlife, associated with a destructive, quantifiable threat to the socially necessary labor time required for the social reproduction of white wealth.

To return to Afropessimism's critique of Marxism in light of this consideration of Black women's relation to value, the gendered contours of the value form reconfigure several points. First, it is less "the despotism of the unwaged relation" that Wilderson refers to than the despotism of the value relation whose racialized and gendered efficiency passes on a devaluation. Specifically, the general fixation on the wage/nonwage relation obscures central questions about the gendered racialization of the value form. The wage is only one expression of a more expansive, gendered, and sexualized scene of commodity-determined labor. As producers of value and relative surplus value through reproduction, the exploitation of Black women plays a socially mediating role that exceeds the scope of the wage relation. Second, Black women's labor and reproductive labor was precisely a "constituent element" of slavery and its afterlife. Therefore, responding to Sexton's question about whether "it is possible to lift up the intrinsic value of *any* black lives, let alone *all*" (2016a, 23), the intrinsic value of any and all Black lives is constituted through the inheritance of Black women's threatening relation to value. If Black men represent a devaluation that is nevertheless grievable, Black women represent a threat to the entire value regime that renders her gender unknowable, nonindividualized, and un-grievable. Sexton asks, "What economies—political, libidinal, symbolic—must be destroyed or negated, what others forged or affirmed?" (2016a). In racial capitalism, the political, libidinal, and symbolic economy of the capi-talist value form must be destroyed; what must be forged and affirmed is the lives, horizontal sociality, and gender nonconformity of Black women. The refusal to see or hear the struggle of Black women is to capitulate to racial capitalist ideology borne out of and thus threatened by Black women's re-productive and socially reproductive labor. The social reproduction of Black life is pathologized because it is a violation of the value form, a violation of the socially necessary reproduction of possessive whiteness. Recognizing the power of Black women's ability to create, produce, sustain, and trans-form on terms that disrupt the reproduction of racial capitalism, we might envision new conceptualizations of work that further that disturbance. As Angela Davis affirms, drawing on Marx, "'labor is the living, shaping fire; it represents the impermanence of things, their temporality'" (1983, 11).

Ontology and Idealism

I conclude where I began this essay, with Dell M. Hamilton's *Blues\Blank\ Black*, and consider how her performance of repetition, despair, and nam-ing orients us toward a Black feminist politics of mourning. In making the choice to stage the illegibility, nonconformity, and erasure of Black women in connection to the Say Her Name project, Hamilton reflects that her performance "comes out of a lot of rage/heartbreak, most of which I don't know what to do with" (personal communication, 2017). This buildup of frustration and grief echoes Spillers's own "feeling of hopelessness" about the fact that "no one wants to address [Black women]. . . . I mean we really are invisible people" (2007, 308). Among other affective registers, these comments evoke the labor of mourning. Honing in on the relationship between African American motherhood and mourning, Jessica Millward states, "Mourning . . . accompanies every aspect of African American history from slavery through its afterlife" (2016, 162). Indexing a long tradition of grieving mothers that extends from Mamie Till Mobley (Emmett Till) to Lezley McSpadden (Mike Brown), Hamilton's focus on Black women and girls offers a framework for thinking about the performativity of mourning.

From the public mourning of grieving mothers to the performance of mourning, these enunciations of grief are an extended, surplus mode of reproduction. As Joshua Chambers-Letson proposes, "If women's work has been scrubbed from the history of capital's reproduction, performance can function as a means of recovering this absent presence, allowing us to restore the scene of 'women's work' to an account and analysis of the reproduction of capital" (2016, 133). In this manner, performance appropriates what he calls "the mother function," becoming a "means of maintaining and reproducing the absented present of the loss object within the time and space of the spectator's present (137). In Hamilton's performance of this "mother function," she not only reanimates and reproduces what Chambers-Letson refers to as the "trace" (138) of the lives of women, girls, and nonbinary people who have been murdered by the police, but she "restores the scene of 'women's work.'" Hamilton's performance of Black women's gender nonconformity through the labor of mourning highlights how mourning itself becomes a site of recovery of trace lives, a temporal confusion and extension beyond life, and a revelation that locates Black women's labor at the center of racial capitalism. Through her shifting personas and physical movement inside and outside the performance space, she evokes the unruly space and time of mourning that turns on the irreconcilability of the past in a stance toward the future. As R. Clifton Spargo delineates as an "ethics of mourning," he states that "unresolved mourning becomes a dissenting act, a sign of irremissible ethical meaning" (2004, 6). It positions the mourner in an alternative, nonlinear time of the other, a fugitive temporality that Black women inhabit in the production of Black social life.

Hamilton's unruly performance of maternal mourning evokes the queerness of Black female subjectivity that, as Terrion Williamson delineates, "attains meaning by way of an amoral social order" (2017, 19). Hamilton thus defies the logic of normative patriarchalized female gender—which, as Spillers reminds us, "is the *only* female gender there is" (1987, 73)—and instead offers a vision of queer Black gender that is reducible to neither the heteropatriarchal codes of white civil society nor the structural coherence of humanism. Her confrontation with gendered and sexualized erasure is ultimately illegible within a rigid Afropessimist frame, in which history and politics are collapsed into a metaphysical plea for the end of the world. In the latter's ontological realm, the possibility of resistance is effectively foreclosed, as David Kline observes, as "there is not much left in which to appeal than a kind of apocalyptic messianic, and contentless eschatological future space defined by whatever this world is not" (2017, 61). This blank utopianism registers what Victor Li describes as a form of "necroidealism," in which utopia and death are linked by an "impossibility of representation" (2009, 277). Here the death or disappearance of the subaltern "enables the subaltern to fulfill the role of the resistant and inappropriable other" (Li 2009, 277). This figure of the dead or disappeared subaltern is similar to the ontologically dead Black subject of Afropessimism. But, as Li cautions, "such an immortalization of the subaltern involves a disturbing necroidealism that abandons the messiness and ambiguity of actual struggle for the reassurance of a political ideal" (280). Against such a necroidealism, Hamilton's militant mourning rejects such abstract political reassurance.

Hamilton's mourning is foremost an accounting of the terrible loss of gendered Black social life. These are not losses that are reducible to the terms of Black social death. As Williamson emphasizes, Black social life "coheres, accumulates its sociality in the wild. . . . The *outside* of value is *its* tabula raza" (2017, 18). From this standpoint, there is no beyond to Blackness—no Blackness that is uninhabitable or demands an end of the world. What stands before us in Hamilton's maternal provocation is the demand "to contend with the unthought black subject who destabilizes 'civil society' and, consequently, the very notion of civility itself" (Williamson 2017, 19). Against a position of totalizing, irremediable abjection, the queer Black gendered subject of Black feminism stands for the legion who confront the struggle on the ground against disappearance, disposal, and erasure in an antiblack value regime. Political rather than metaphysical, this is a struggle that always occurs somewhere, not nowhere.

Notes

I am grateful to Dell Hamilton, Kimberly Juanita Brown, The Dark Room: Race and Visual Culture Studies Seminar, Asha Nadkarni, Jane Degenhardt, Peggy Lee, Moon-Kie Jung, and João Costa Vargas for valuable feedback and conversations. I am also thankful for generous commentary from audiences at the University of Minnesota, Princeton University, Dartmouth College, and the University of Illinois, Urbana-Champaign.

1   Marx writes, "The secret of the expression of value . . . could not be deciphered until the concept of human equality had already acquired the permanence of a fixed popular opinion. This however becomes possible only in a society where the commodity-form is the universal form of the product of labour, hence the dominant social relation is the relation between men as possessors of commodities" (1976, 152).

2   A significant rationale for Marx's adherence to a methodology based on market equilibrium is rhetorically driven, insofar as his critique of bourgeois political economy required that he incorporate its utopian market logics in order to debunk them.

3   See Sylvia Federici's discussion of the removal of women from wage labor in nineteenth-century England, which shifted to a mode of production that relied on women's unpaid reproductive labor as a source of relative surplus value: "Its development (following the passage of Factory Acts limiting the employment of women and children in the factories) reflected the first long-term investment the capitalist class made in the reproduction of the work-force beyond its numerical expansion. . . . Marx spoke of it as a shift from 'absolute' to 'relative surplus,' that is, a shift from a type of exploitation based on the lengthening of the working day to a maximum and the reduction of the wage to a minimum, to a regime where higher wages and shorter hours would be compensated with an increase in the productivity of work and the pace of production" (2004, 99).

4   Space constraints limit me from engaging more fully in debates over the slave's relation to value. In Cedric Robinson's account, the "capitalist world system appropriated Black labor power as *constant* capital" (1983, 309)—a position that I suggest is incomplete. The issue of constant, or fixed, capital in *Capital*, volume 2, is itself the subject of intense debate but generally refers to machinery, production sites, or "beasts of burden" that do not generate value but have the capacity to generate surplus and relative surplus value. The fact that the appreciation or depreciation of slaves was meticulously calculated suggests that planters assessed their slaves on terms similar to the fixed capital represented by railroad cars and tracks (Rosenthal 2016b, 83). In this essay, I approach slave labor primarily as human capital—variable capital, in Marx's terms—that was a producer of value but whose human value evolved over a lifetime. One implication, as Rosenthal observes, is that "the valuation of slaves vividly displays their dual status as humans and as salable commodities that could be reduced to a price" (2016b, 84).

TOWARD A GENERAL THEORY OF ANTIBLACKNESS

ANTHONY PAUL FARLEY

Slavery is death, death only, and that continually. Slavery-to-segregation-to-neosegregation is not progress; it is only death repeating itself, white-over-black to white-over-black to white-over-black. What we cannot remember, we repeat. Race is the endless repetition of our unremembered death. Our unremembered death is the navel of the modern era. Local theories, small acts, microresistances, diversities, identities, intersectionalities, and all the other names for all the myriad ways in which we are not one, are all, in the end, repetitions. Each repetition is an abdication of the right to philosophy. If the unexamined life is not worth living, then our abdication of the right to philosophy is also an abdication of life itself. We have been naught, we shall be all. We are in need of a general theory of antiblackness. A song to gather harmonies from all around:

> At the round earth's imagined corners, blow
>
> Your trumpets angels, and arise, arise
>
> From death, you numberless infinites
>
> Of souls, and to your scattered bodies go
>
> **JOHN DONNE,** "At the Round Earth's Imagined Corners (Holy Sonnet 7)"

Speculative philosophy is a right asserted in and through grand narrative, and it is the vessel within which our memories may be usefully gathered. Our memories are the harmonies of our "numberless infinities of souls." The rising requires us to understand that we shall be all. The general theory of antiblackness is that understanding.

A wind crosses the world and unfolds in white. A sail appears on the horizon, crossing the far points of memory and speculation. And everything that is solid melts into air. Middle Passage, Manifest Destiny, New World Order, American Century, Infinite Justice, Enduring Freedom, War on Terror; Make America Great Again, so it goes, endless accumulations, endless enslavements, the endless sovereignty of capital. For some to own, others must first be owned.

"The wealth of societies in which the capitalist mode of production prevails appears as an immense collection of commodities" (Marx [1867] 1990, 125). Marx's words mark our present situation, and thus the past marks our beginning and our destination as we go back to the primal scene. The general theory of antiblackness begins with the slaves. The general theory of antiblackness begins with the commodity that speaks. The general theory of antiblackness begins at the zero hour of exploitation. That moment, the moment of capture, was the moment we were marked as black. Thus classified, marked as black, we became a class, white-over-black. That moment, the moment of white-over-black, is the moment in which we were constituted as a race, as white-over-black.

There is no race, save as hierarchy, as white-over-black. White-over-black is a desire and a pleasure. White-over-black is the desire for hierarchy and the pleasure of hierarchy. The will to classify is the sadistic form of the desire for hierarchy. The will to be classified is the masochistic form of the desire for hierarchy. The will to classify is a desire of the flesh, for there is no classification that is not first written on the body. White-over-black in the nonrevolutionary situation means that all have come to an agreement regarding the satisfactions and dissatisfactions that will coordinate the passage of bodies marked as white and bodies marked as black through institutional spaces or scenes. Sadism and masochism (s/m) are the terms of the social contract, the rule of law, governing the color-lined, nonrevolutionary situation.

Race and class, the two beginnings of the general theory of antiblackness, are the far points of memory and speculation for the sentient commodity and its system, the system of capital. We are all still within that moment's endless unfolding. Emancipation did not take place. Emancipation's place is beyond the juridical horizon. Every attempt to go back will be haunted by the concerns of the present, just as the present is itself haunted by the concerns of the past. We are haunted by the specter of the one big union, the general strike, and the end of slavery. We are haunted by the specter of communism. Recall the words set to the tune of "John Brown's Body" and "The Battle Hymn of the Republic":

> They have taken untold millions that they never toiled to earn. / But with-out our brain and muscle not a single wheel can turn. / We can break their haughty power; gain our freedom when we learn / that the Union makes us strong. / In our hands is placed a power greater than their hoarded gold; / Greater than the might of armies, magnified a thousand fold. / We can bring to birth the new world from the ashes of the old, / For the Union makes us strong. (Chapin [1923] 2003, 25–26)

What does a general theory of antiblackness look like? The questions have the same answer. Law, as critical race theory has seldom recognized, is the monopoly on violence that is used to keep white-over-black; recall the primal scene of accumulation. The monopolists of violence force us all to look at our feet as they beat us about our heads. The idea that emerges amid the stars that swirl about the broken and bowed heads of the dispos-sessed is, ironically, the idea of the rule of law.

The beaten slaves imagine that the next blow will not come, and the next, and the next, and the next, and soon these imaginings, and these blows, become a pleasure, an ecstasy, a closeted expectation, and a fun-damentalism. These imaginings are juridical strivings for equality of right and due process, basic elements of the rule of law. The beaten blacks, heads bowed, white-over-black, form prayers to the monopolists of violence, prayers for legal relief from the violence of dispossession. These prayers create a false god, the state, whom the defeated hope to appease with ever more sickening displays of fidelity to the rule of law and to the future fair-ness of their masters. Without the prayers of the defeated and traumatized dispossessed, there is no monopoly, no legal system, no market, no private ownership of the source of life (e.g., the means of production), no white-over-black, no false god, no earthly master. Without the prayers of the dispossessed, there is anarchy and communism. That is the future that is beyond the place we are now. Anarchist communism is the future beyond the primal scene of accumulation.

How came we to this terrible present? The primal scene of accumulation is always traumatic. We recall the trauma of the inaugural accumulation—a trauma too great to be borne, a moment that seems to vanish like the wind—only in the mode of repetition.[1] Our traumatic repetitions—our knowing nonknowledge of what happened—unfolds in our struggle for equal justice under law.[2] Not-knowing is not emancipation.

c-m-c.[3] Someone with only labor to sell chooses to sell it to an owner in exchange for a certain sum of money. If that sum is a living wage and if there is a market, then the labor seller will be able to buy the commodities required to live and, perhaps, to produce again, out of his body, more labor to sell, and then more, and then more. The choice is death or sale. The commodity sold is not labor. The commodity sold is the laborer, treated as a thing to be sold. Death is the only freedom of the market. Death is what happens when some have everything and others have only the skins that they are in. Marx stated, "What is in fact brought to market is not labour, but the labourer. What he sells to the capitalist is not his labour but the temporary use of himself as a working power. This is the immediate object of the contract which the capitalist and the worker conclude, the purchase and sale which they transact" ([1863] 1975, 113).

m-c-m. Someone with money purchases commodities in the form of labor and the means of production. If all goes well during production, then the new commodities produced by those who labor will be exchanged for an amount of money in excess of the amount of money with which the process was begun. That the dispossessed are dispossessed of that value m' may also be expressed as $m + \Delta m$, or surplus value. Some or all of that surplus value, Δm, may find its way back into the next cycle, m'-c-m'', and the next, m''-c-m''', and so on and on to infinity. "The complete form of this process is therefore m-c-m', where $m' = m + \Delta m$, i.e. the original sum advanced plus an increment or excess over the original value I call 'surplus value'" (Marx [1867] 1990, 251). The owners regard the capitalization of Δm as a sign of their abstinence, as a virtue, and as a justification for their lordship over the earth and all that is in it. Surplus value is, in fact, the sum and substance of their rule.[4]

These processes require a market. A market requires certain rules. Promises must be kept and commodities must be bought and sold according to agreement, not simply taken, or there is no free market; no buying, no selling, only grabbing and getting.[5] Buyers and sellers must meet as if they were free and as if they were equal. One buys, one sells; there are only sellers and buyers; and all exist in the free market only as buyers and sellers, as entities-without-other-qualities, as monads. There can be no outside of the market. The market must therefore become the world (Marx [1867] 1990, 729–30).

The colorline appears as a flaw in the seemingly crystalline perfection of the market. The crystal is neither flawed nor perfect; its flaw is its perfection. The colorline is the constitutive contradiction of the market. Without the colorline there is no market. The market requires ownership, and this ownership is an ownership of people that is displaced onto an ownership of things. What are these things other than the crystallized labors of laborers past, other than accumulated, dead, labor? The Middle Passage is the primal scene of accumulation that became these United States. As we follow the mark of the black, it leads backward along the timeline, as do all marks, to a primal scene. The scene is played out at the far points of memory and speculation; in this case, our case, the primal scene of accumulation is the Middle Passage and the marking of the body as white-over-black.

The bearers of the mark do not meet as equals in the market; rather, they meet as white-over-black, white-over-black only, and that continually, thus continuously disrupting the flows of exchange and production. The colorline is itself a pleasure and a commodity. The fact that the pleasure dares not speak its name does not make the fact of desire any less palpable. White-over-black is a desire, an orientation. It is the result of training. In our color-lined situation, that is, within the folds of the primal scene of accumulation that is the concern of this essay on the general theory of antiblackness, institutions are white-over-black, white-over-black only, and that continually. Were it otherwise, we would have no need to speak of the color line, save as a line that was broken. The line has not been broken. Desire and imagination extend that line to infinity, through all space and time. Bodies find their way through all institutional spaces by orienting themselves vis-à-vis each other, white-over-black. We can orient ourselves because we have the capacity to desire and the faculty of imagination. A person's orientation is an ability as well as a desire. It is the ability to desire, and it is an actual desire. White-over-black is an orientation that is the result of training desire and imagination in white-over-black.

This training in white-over-black is the spirit of the law that closes the gaps, resolves the conflicts, and clarifies the ambiguities. This training is what enables those who are successfully trained to see the law as a system of rules that magically operates without desire—as a dance of sugarplum fairies or as a machine—but not as the brutish grabbing and grasping and gobbling of as much as possible that it is in reality. The real only appears to us as the primal scene of accumulation. The reality of that primal scene is screened by fables such as the rule of law. This training in white-over-black is what allows the trained to see white-over-black as the North Star and thus orient themselves and everything else that would otherwise be a blooming, buzzing confusion. The relation between white-over-black and the rules through which that pleasure is realized may seem more or less direct, as with yesterday's segregation, or it may seem more or less indirect, as with today's neosegregation.

The movement from slavery to segregation to neosegregation is not up from slavery, it is toward slavery. The passage from slavery to segregation to neosegregation is the form in which the perfection of slavery appears and masks itself. Slavery is perfect when the slaves themselves willingly become things. The perfect slave makes itself a slave by bowing down before the rule of law, and this it can do only after its so-called emancipation. Perfecting slavery is what the slave does when it bows down before the law and prays for relief. Slavery was white-over-black. Segregation was white-over-black. Neosegregation is white-over-black. White-over-black to white-over-black to white-over-black: the cycles do not simply begin with slavery, they end in slavery, or they end in revolution. Anarchy is the end of race, the end of property, the end of the rule of law, the end of the prehistory of humanity. Anarchy is the one big union, the general strike, and the new world within the shell of the old.

The manifest content of a legal interpretation, like the manifest content of a dream (Freud [1900] 2010, 157), always and everywhere represents a latent wish. Wherever that wish or desire is distorted—as it always is in a law-governed situation, for law is only distortion of conflict and contradiction—there is a conflict or contradiction. Lenin, quoting Engels, noted that the existence of law or "the state" is itself an admission, albeit coded, that "society has become entangled in an insoluble contradiction with itself, that it has split into irreconcilable opposites which it is powerless to conjure away" (Lenin [1917] 1976, 9). Furthermore, "The state is a product and manifestation of the irreconcilability of class contradictions. The state arises where and when and to the extent that class contradictions objectively cannot be reconciled. And, conversely, the existence of the state proves that class contradictions are irreconcilable" (Lenin [1917] 1976, 9).

That conflict or contradiction is constitutive, for without the white-over-black, without the original accumulation, the state machine never begins its work of condensation, distortion, displacement, and secondary revision. Without the successful monopolization of violence that is the state, the original accumulation never takes place. Without the original accumulation, that is to say, without the violent marking of the dispossessed, there is no market and no need for the rules that reframe dispossession as the meeting of minds under conditions of freedom and equality. Without the constant and distorting black presence, there is no faculty with which to imagine equality. The Black is capital's faculty of imagination. The Black, the slave, has as its profession the fabulation of equality. This is the work of dreams. The dream, like the law, is the disguise of the wish, and that disguise takes work. It takes the work of distortion, displacement, secondary revision, and much else besides these things.

A rule cannot determine the circumstances of its own application: "This was our paradox: no course of action could be determined by a rule, because any course of action can be made out to accord with the rule" (Wittgenstein 2009, 201a). There are always "gaps, conflicts, and ambiguities" (Kennedy 1997, 219). Legal rules, when well crafted, appear to us as locomotives traveling on to infinity on rails of necessity. This craft, jurisprudence, is an alchemy. There are desires and lived relations that we disavow or repress. For example, we establish the rules of the market, rules of freedom and equality, and these rules are supposed to repress the impulse to slavery and exploitation. We know this impulse well; it is the impulse of the entire market and all the life within; it is the primal scene of accumulation. The instrument of repression is the vehicle of return. The desires we repress through the rule of law are the desires that return to us upon that selfsame vehicle. Pleasure makes us pursue our desire, and imagination enables us to pursue our desire to infinity. We project our desires—our disavowed or repressed relationship of white-over-black—across the entirety of time and space and then judge our laws against these ideal forms of our own making. Laws are always interpreted against these uncanny and unearthly forms. We judge our laws from within the cave of our own unknowing and according to the standards of our own disavowed desires.

The rules regarding equality and freedom would not be required were the dispossessed not marked for dispossession. But for the omnipresent and perpetual desire for and habit of repeating the original dispossession of the dispossessed, the dispossessed would have no motive to imagine rules for equality and freedom. Rules for equality and freedom are nonsensical where all is held in common; they are imaginable only from a situation of dispossession. The omnipresent repetition of the original dispossession means that it has become an orientation, a way of being and a way of training for one and all. If the habit of hatred were not widespread and institutionalized, then the dispossessed would not need to imagine rules for equality and freedom; one need not imagine what one already is in fact.

ANTHONY PAUL FARLEY

However—and this is vexing—the fact of habitual and institutionalized hatred means that the rule, any rule, will be read in the direction of the hatred that has become habit and institution. The rules, recall, are always available for any reading whatsoever because nothing in the rules themselves can permanently fix their meaning or application. The line flowing out into infinity, into the mystic, is our own desire. Logic is the form taken by repressed desire. Only trained desire fixes the rules in any particular direction or meaning. Thus the dispossessed produce the illusions by which they themselves are deluded. These are the laws of equality and freedom on which the market depends. The dispossessed produce rules fitted for each situation, for each crisis—and there are many crises. Each crisis is averted, and the system, the market, is saved for tomorrow because tomorrow there will be equality, and tomorrow and tomorrow and tomorrow, world without end. The slave thus builds a mansion for the future goodwill of its master and, at the same time, a cage for itself.

These endless cycles—C-M-C and M-C-M—appear to us to be without beginning as well as without end. Our memories of a before-time, of a time-before-time, seem as unreal as a time before breathing. Our imaginations are compassed by the seeming lack of other possible worlds. All that is, all that can be, all that can ever be, all that has ever been, all, now appears to be only that which can be accounted for on this timeline, a timeline that has left us, in the words of the great Jamaican poet Claude McKay, "hunted and penned in an inglorious spot" ([1919] 2004, 1007).

A commodity is exchanged for money, and the money is exchanged for more commodities. Money is exchanged for commodities, and the commodities are exchanged for money. The owner owns the means of production—a factory, a forest, an entire world—and offers money in exchange for labor power of a certain time and intensity and direction. The owner is not one. The owner is legion (Mark 5:1–20; Luke 8:26–39). The legion makes the offer.

The offer cannot be refused. The means of production are owned, and that means that they are owned by some and not by all. Those who do not own the means of production—a factory, a forest, an entire world—either die or accept the offer. Hunger, thirst, and the elements prey upon those without sustenance and shelter. Moreover, as people do not live by bread alone, there are many things besides these bare necessities that are required to keep the miseries at bay, roses, for example.

Consent is the offspring of the weapon and the flesh. The offer of a labor contract presupposes a world that is owned by some but not by all.

The offer presupposes a world of property. The world of property is one in which violence sustains the class relation whose avatar is the legal relation that is expressed by the offer-acceptance-consideration of the contract.

The social contract negotiated by the subaltern's struggle for law is a Faustian bargain. Nonknowledge of the fact that the devil always takes his due is the most certain hell. The subaltern creates its own hell. The subaltern unconscious speaks in a Faustian voice through its struggles for equal justice under the law. Recall the words of Mephistopheles: "I'd give myself over to the devil, if I were not he himself" (Goethe [1808] 1985, lines 2809–10).

Some own and some do not. Once upon a time, beyond the time out of mind wherein social contracts are said to have been drafted and signed, there was cooperation and a forest full of wonderful things to be found or cultivated or gathered. There were various inventions and enchantments that helped in making life more and more wonderful, and there was as much and as good for all to have and hold as each desired, and work that was not the expression and fulfillment of desire was unknown. Once upon a time, but neither now nor on any now-imaginable timeline. No, none of these things are to be found within the original accumulation's domain of possibilities. There is the original accumulation, and there are its endless repetitions; the collected veils our lived relations wear to hide themselves from our eyes, the uncanny, the self-deception that is the rule of law, is endless. Within the illusions of the primal scene of accumulation there are meetings of the mind that result in contracts; there are offers and acceptances and considerations, there are Malthusian spurs and invisible hands guiding all toward some ultimate end that we are told is for the best in what we are told is the best and only possible world.

What is to be done? Not knowing is not emancipation. We have a knowing nonknowledge of the primal scene of accumulation. The original accumulation is a universe complete unto itself, a monad, and the monads have no windows. What follows is the unfolding of the Middle Passage.

Tooth and talon, iron and steel, blankets and smallpox, free trade and helicopter gunship; all manner of instrumentalities, natural and not, have been used in the performance of the initial accumulation, in the marking of bodies, in the primal scene, in the primitive moment of accumulation. The scene of the inaugural dispossession is untimely, always untimely. It is the emergence of time. The unfolding of this dispossession, its endless unfolding, is the timeline—present/past/future—that the dispossession itself establishes.

ANTHONY PAUL FARLEY

The trauma of the mark—the dispossession or negation—cannot be borne. Who can bear it? Who can bear being nothing? How can nothing be? The duration of this impossibility, this negation that limits us, that closes us in, that horizons us, this unbearable world that we shoulder, is something we ourselves have projected in order to make sense of the unthinkable negation—in order to make it intelligible, in order to bear the unbearable burden of objecthood, death. Lost in the labyrinthine ways of our own minds, we mistake symptoms of trauma for the laws of nature and nature's god.

Time, space, and the concepts and categories of the understanding are not innocent. They are symptoms of hegemony. They are the always-belated appearances, apparitions, avatars of the traumatic primal scene of accumulation. They are the forms taken by our unacknowledged disavowals of our lived and exploitative relations. Law, political economy, culture, and so on seem to tumble out history requiring the equilibrating metaphysicians with their nets to sort things out and set things right. They imagine starry heavens above, moral laws within, and a goal toward which all history must move. All their imaginings are naught but disavowals of the lived and exploitative relations that give these imaginings the form of logical certainties.

Space, time, causation, and all of the categories and concepts of the understanding; all of these come from original accumulation. They are the big bang of the original accumulation. The original accumulation is the unseeable frame of all possible events, of all space and time. It is repeated in the endless enclosures. The enclosures are not real in themselves; the rationality they seem to represent is only the dream that disguises the desire for perpetual exploitation.

In nonrevolutionary situations, that is, in situations of unbroken state-monopolized direct or indirect violence, the exploiter and the exploited, together, and each secret from the other, desire to perpetuate their exploitative relationship. The exploiter and the exploited are both possessed by a desire for exploitation. The exploiter loves exploiting the exploited, and the exploited love being exploited by their exploiters, and these desires—inculcated and shaped by the lived relation between the top and the bottom—are sublimated in rules of order or laws. These sublimations are no more vivid than in the rules that manifestly declare that all are equally protected by and subject to the laws of the land. The achievement of this sublime state of perpetual peace is a constant struggle.

The slaves struggle for equality. They do so, however, within the unfoldings of the primal scene of accumulation. Their struggle occasions the unfolding of the primal scene. They struggle for equality of right. The slaves' struggle is the struggle for law. The rule of law is nothing other than the endless unfolding of the primal scene of accumulation.

The slaves dream of rights equal to the ceiling of their ambition, the paradise of ownership just above the black forest of their outstretched arms. Recall:

> The more productive capital grows, the more it extends the division of labour and the application of machinery; the more the division of labour and the application of machinery extend, the more does competition extend among the workers, the more do their wages shrink together. In addition, the working class is recruited from the higher strata of society; a mass of small business men and of people living upon the interest of their capitals is precipitated into the ranks of the working class, and they will have nothing else to do than to stretch out their arms alongside of the arms of the workers. Thus the forest of outstretched arms, begging for work, grows ever thicker, while the arms themselves grow ever leaner. (Marx [1891] 1978, 47)

The forest is enchanted by rights. In the dark, a black planet imagines ways in which the opportunities of its substitute sun, for which it yearns in all of its myriad branches, are compromised by a color line, and then it imagines that the compromise could be otherwise. Equal rights are imagined by the slaves, the ones who bow down before the law and by bowing lend their spirits to the law. All of it is magical thinking.

Race is a mark on the body. Before the mark there can be neither ownership nor class. Before the mark there can be no division of labor, no hierarchy, no law. Hierarchy only occurs within the space and time occasioned by the accumulation that was, in the primal scene, organized around the mark. Space and time and the concepts and categories of the understanding are nothing in themselves; hence, the many paradoxes of so-called pure reason, space, and time are rather and merely the traumatic unfolding of the primal accumulation.

Accumulation marks the transition from violence to right. The mark is the inaugural violence of right. Class formation is racial formation, and racial formation is class formation. The mark must be made on the flesh. The mark must be made on the flesh because before the property relation there is only the skin we are all in. It is within that skin that we all begin. Hierarchy must therefore be written on the body before it can be reified or sublimated as property. Before the mark there is only the one. After, there are legion. Before the mark there is only the flesh we have in common. After the mark there are races and sexes, powers and principalities, deaths and possessions. The mark divides the whole into the many. The mark divides all into haves and have-nots. The name of the former is legion. The latter are possessions. Everything after the mark becomes death and possession.

Death and possession, twins born of the same mark, twins born of the union of the legions and their possessions, thus make their appearance in the world. The have-nots are themselves the possessions of the haves. The haves are possessed. They must accumulate ever more, or they perish in capitalist competition. Their possessions are the have-nots.

The mark is the end of violence and the beginning of right. The mark is the end of right and the beginning of violence. Violence is the beginning and the end of right. Right is the beginning and the end of violence. The violence is unto death. The violence transforms life into object, into possession, into property, into death. The right transforms this transformation, but only in appearance. The right makes death appear to be life. The science of right is the deceit of death—"All these things will I give thee, if thou wilt fall down and worship me"—and also the secret of its sovereignty (Matthew 4:9 and Luke 4:7).

Not knowing is not emancipation. Ignorance is not freedom. Repression is not liberation. What is enlightenment? *Having the courage to know!*: "Enlightenment is man's release from his self-incurred tutelage. . . . Self-incurred is this tutelage when its cause lies not in lack of reason but in lack of resolution and courage to use it without direction from another. . . . 'Have courage to use your own reason!'—that is the motto of enlightenment" (Kant [1784] 1981b, 3). Per Kant, knowledge of the "universal laws" governing the phenomena brings with it the "hope that if we attend to the play of freedom of the human will in the large, we may be able to discern a regular movement in it, and that what seems complex and chaotic in the single individual may be seen from the standpoint of the human race as a whole to be a steady and progressive, though slow, evolution of its original endowment" (Kant [1784] 1981b, 11).

What is the original endowment but the primal accumulation? The evolution of capital—M-C-M′ to M′-C-M″ to M″-C-M‴ and so on and on and on—is the demise of the human. This is fitting for capitalism, because capitalism is the rule of death over life—living laborers are made to serve accumulated, dead, labor, and they become their labor. They become the death that calls them to labor. They become the death that is the slave's calling.

The struggle for liberty, equality, and fraternity, the struggle for these things on the terrain of law, folds back upon itself. Each instrument of repression becomes another vehicle by which the passion for inequality returns, and so it goes, white-over-black, again and again and again. Within the event horizon of the juridical, nothing is possible and resistance is futile.

The slave creates its master. This is the secret of the world. Slavery is perfected only after emancipation. This is so because only emancipation allows the slave to fully and completely choose enslavement. The slave chooses enslavement when it bows down before the state to pray for legal relief. The slave bows down and thus perfects its own slavery. This is the true alchemy of race and rights: "The devil showed the witch the way, but the devil cannot stoop to brew the potion" (Goethe [1808] 1985, lines 2809–10). The slave struggles for equality under law, "a watery beggar soup" (Goethe [1808] 1985, line 2392).

Patricia Williams writes,

> To say that blacks never fully believed in rights is true. Yet it is also true that blacks believed in them so much and so hard that we gave them life where there was none before; we held onto them, put the hope of them in our wombs, mothered them and not the notion of them. . . . The making of something out of nothing took immense alchemical fire—the fusion of a whole nation and the kindling of several generations. (1992, 163)

Williams writes of the alchemy of race and rights as if it were a form of progress. It is not. It is the tragic repetition of the primal scene of accumulation. Generations of slaves threw themselves into the fire. The many thousands gone, in Williams's (1992, 163) words, "the kindling of several generations," have been burned in a hell of their own creation. The white-over-black of the primal scene of accumulation remains the same, and the slaves are no closer to emancipation; worse, with every new equality, with every new equation, they lose consciousness of just how put down they are and by whom:

WITCH: See how it's done!

Make ten from one

The two must go,

And three is so,

When four is lost,

You earn the most.

From five to six,

By the witch's tricks,

Come seven and eight

In excellent state!

And nine is lame

And ten is tame—

All in the witch's numbers-game

GOETHE (1808) 1985, lines 2553–57

"All these things will I give thee, if thou wilt fall down and worship me" (Matthew 4:9 and Luke 4:7). The drama continues:

FAUST: I think the witch is running a high fever.

MEPHISTOPHELES: You've barely heard the half of it. I know it well—it is the tenor of her book; I used it once and wasted time with it.

GOETHE (1808) 1985, lines 2553–57

The slave bows down before the law when it prays for legal relief. The slave's prayer for equality of right, for due process, for the rule of law, is always already granted. The rule of law is the slaves' own creation. It is the sigh and submission of the oppressed creature. The slave imagines a world in which it is not made to bear the mark. It imagines a world in which rights are equal, and it fashions its prayer in the form of a rule. And then it gives that rule to its rulers. Its rulers, of course, rule against it. And so the slave must begin again and again and again, ever into the mystic. The slave creates the law, the monopoly of violence that keeps white-over-black, by bowing down in prayer for legal relief. The slave's fundamentalist faith in the future goodwill of its master makes unnecessary the general strike of tomorrow and tomorrow and tomorrow. Thus is the immortality of the original accumulation and its avatars, law and property, assured.

Rules do not determine the circumstances of their own application. Rules regarding the application of rules do not determine the circumstances of their own application (Wittgenstein 2009, 201a). Furthermore, a rule for the application of rules cannot solve the problem of indeterminacy for that rule; the rule for the application of rule will also be incapable of determining the circumstances of its application, and so on. The rule of law is an idea produced in the slave by the unbearable suffering occasioned by the dispossession, by the original accumulation. The rule will always be directed against the slave, and the slave has knowing nonknowledge of that fact. If the habit of directing all against the slave were not general and institutionalized, then the slave would never have imagined the rule. Since the habit of directing all against the slave is general and institutionalized, the rule will be read against the slave. A rule, as Wittgenstein observed, cannot determine the circumstances of its own application. Its meaning is a result of our training.

Our institutions show us the sum of our training. Our institutions, under the color line, are color lined. The rule formulated by the slave to repress the desire for white-over-black becomes the vehicle for the return of that same desire. The slave formulates the rule, pursues the alchemy of race and rights, and chases after phantoms in order to hide from its own shameful desire for the perpetuation of slavery. The slave, like the master, has been trained in white-over-black. Recall Faust's fright at a peculiar dog that enters his laboratory where he pursues his alchemical experiments: "I think he's softly weaving coils of magic for future bondage round our feet" (Goethe [1808] 1985, lines 1158–59). Faust dismisses his own fright: "I cannot find a trace of any ghostly thing. It's all his training" (Goethe [1808] 1985, lines 1172–73). Faust heeds the words of his friend Wagner: "A simple dog well-trained to heed commands may even earn a learned man's affection. Yes indeed, he quite deserves your favor as a student and a fellow scholar" (Goethe [1808] 1985, 1174–77). The slave's pursuit of the juridical form is its own coded desire for continued slavery. What dedication! "Wavering forms, you come again; Once long ago you passed before my clouded sight. Should I now attempt to hold you fast? Does my heart still look for phantoms? You surge at me! Well, then you may rule" (Goethe [1808] 1985, lines 1–5).

The word for world is forest or plain or valley or mountain or something else that is forever. And then the forever of the world is smashed into then and now and tomorrow and tomorrow and tomorrow. And then the world of forever is smashed into mine and yours, his and hers, theirs and ours, possessor and possession. These broken bits, the relationships, are taken to be elemental, constituent parts of a whole. But the whole that they appear to constitute is not the same whole that was smashed to make them. It is not the original whole but rather a false unity pulled over our eyes to blind us to what has been and what might be.

The mark is and then all else is not. The mark is and then all else is for naught. The mark is and all else becomes nothing, for nothing can come before the mark. The mark produces its own past and its own future and

ANTHONY PAUL FARLEY

its own present. Possession becomes the world's past and its future and its present. Death thus becomes the world. The mark is the end of the world.

The mark is a wound. Those who would own must gather together as one in order to mark the others for dispossession. The mark of dispossession must be written on the body because that is where the dispossessed are to be penned. The dispossessed are the prisoners of their bodies. The mark appears as the key. Race is the mark of dispossession; it is written on the skin or found there ready-made. The dispossessed Other is never allowed to stray outside of the prison of the skin (e.g., a Black doctor, a Black criminal, a Black). The mark changes the skin and that within into a thing, a possession, a commodity.

Prior to the mark, the skin we are in holds us all in common. We are all flesh. Flesh is one. Flesh is each and everyone in common. The violence of the mark is directed against the common, the commons. The violence of the mark aims at the transformation of the commons into the property of some and not others, into mine and yours and neither his nor hers. The violence of the mark means that ours becomes not theirs. Property follows the mark. Law is the repressed memory of this deathly injury and its mode of repetition.

The dispossessed reproduce the mark through their struggle for law. The rule of law is the traumatic repetition of the mark. Those who would own gather together as one, as Leviathan, as a corporate body, in order to oppose those soon-to-be-marked as Other to the owners. One who would own must first become one with others who share the desire to own. One person cannot own another because any such slavery, with its Jacobins and Maroons, murders sleep for any would-be master. When sleep comes to the master, freedom comes for the slave. While the master sleeps, the captive may overwhelm or escape. To overcome the terror and Marronage of sleep, the one who would own must first become many, and the many must then become as one. The many become one through the mark. The many become one in order to own. Ownership of things presupposes ownership of people and the transformation of people into things, which amounts to the same thing, and such ownership requires violence.

Property requires slavery. Ownership of things is first of all ownership of people. The institution of property requires the institution of property relations. Property relations are relations between people that are looked upon as if they were relations between people and things.

The would-be owner enters the commons and says, "This is mine!" The statement "This is mine!" is only sound and fury until its signification is fixed by violence. Such signifying violence, no matter how strong its individual perpetrator may be, may always be returned or evaded by its victim while its originator sleeps, and thus come to naught. And sleep does come. Thus, the one who would own must first become the many, and then the many, the ones who would own, must become as one. The many become as one through the mark. They must do so in order to own because ownership of things is first ownership of people-turned-into-things, and such ownership requires a violence that does not fade with the sleep of its author. The violence of ownership is a fire that must be constantly tended. Leviathan, the monopoly of violence, the state, does not sleep. Leviathan is a jealous and punishing god. The dispossessed are its chosen people. Leviathan exists only as a result of their prayers.

Property relations are relations between people, between owners and nonowners, in which the owners come to own the nonowners' labor power. This power resides only within the skin of the nonowners, as if that power were a thing separate or separable from its fleshy host and therefore alienable. One owns a thing, for example, land, and some other does not own that particular thing. The property, land, is a relation between owner and nonowner that is treated as if it is a relation between each and the land. The owner and nonowner exist in a hierarchical relation to each other that may be observed through the lens of the property said to be the possession of the former and not the latter. The relation, the dominion of the owner over the nonowner vis-à-vis that land, is set in place by violence directed against the nonowning class by the owning class. The violence is a special violence that performs its task by indirection; it is directed against the nonowning class as if it were directed against everyone, and it is directed on behalf of the owning class as if it were directed for the property. The property right, and its place in the matrix of class relations laid down in law, is protected as if such protection were the protection of the peace of all through the protection of some mysterious quality residing within the property. The owning class is protected as if such protection were the protection of all people and not merely the protection of a master class residing within and above the dispossessed, a master class that dares not speak its name.

Ownership is enclosure. The commons is divided—smashed and then fitted—into endlessly varied enclosures. Everything comes to be owned, even the conditions required for life itself. Some own only the skin that they are in. Under conditions of general ownership, that is, where ownership has expanded to the point at which the maintenance of life itself requires submission to the rule of ownership, the force of circumstances leads those

ANTHONY PAUL FARLEY

who own nothing but the skin that they are in to sell that which resides only within their skin, their labor power, their bodies, themselves. This force of circumstances is capitalism. Capitalism is enclosure. This is mine or ours and not hers or theirs. Enclosures presuppose an original accumulation, a Middle Passage or a Manifest Destiny, to give two examples. The original accumulation presupposes a marking of the flesh, Black and Red, to give two examples corresponding to those of the preceding sentence. The original accumulation creates past, present, and future out of the ruptured timelessness of the commons.

When the means of production are not owned by all, when life is not lived in common, when life is not lived according to the maxim "from each according to her abilities and to each according to her needs"; when there is possession and dispossession, then some are necessarily left without the means by which to reproduce their lives. And this lack, this force of circumstances, this dispossession, leads the dispossessed to sell themselves on the market. In this moment, the original capture, the original accumulation, the original dispossession, is represented as freedom, freedom of contract, freedom of choice, freedom. Dispossession is death, but the dead do not always know that they are dead. Revolution is an awakening back into life, but that is to take a great leap forward from this point in this exposition. Those who have been dispossessed of all but the skin that they are in have, in fact, also been dispossessed of that skin, but not of the (false) idea that it (that skin) is (still) theirs in which to dwell. They have been dispossessed of themselves, and the mark of dispossession is what they bear on their skins. They, the marked ones, are made by the force of circumstances represented in the mark to experience dispossession and death as choice, as life, as subjectivity, as freedom. These, their so-called freedoms, are experienced when they, seemingly as an act of choice or of will, join in the workers' commonwealth of toil. They join the commonwealth of dispossession by entering into agreements with their masters. This is the great acceptance, the slaves' affirmation of slavery. These are all the days before the general strike.

The owners offer the dispossessed the opportunity to work. The dispossessed bargain with owners for certain wages, hours, and working conditions. The dispossessed compete against each other to become the possessions of the owners. And this feels like freedom to the dispossessed, who have nothing other than dispossession, the death they already died, to compare to this shadow of another shadow. The dispossessed do not know that they are already the possessions that they will become. This is the way that the eternal, the totality, is smashed into a past, a future, and a present of capital.

The dispossessed and the owner reach an agreement, a shadow of the social contract, the shadowy source of the social contract, and under its terms the dispossessed agree to perform a task for the owner for a certain value. The value that the owner provides to the dispossessed will be less than the value that the dispossessed provides to the owner. This is not an exchange; rather, it is an exploitative relationship that is represented and treated as an exchange between the owner and dispossessed alike.

The dispossessed works for an owner, and the owner derives a value therefrom. Part of that value is absorbed by the production to yield the new value (such as consumption of the materials used in the course of production). Part of that value is promised to the dispossessed in exchange for labor power. Time appears as a measure of value: if the dispossessed works from 9 a.m. to 5 p.m., then it may be the case that the dispossessed has generated a value from 9 a.m. to 11 a.m. that accounts for the value of whatever other instruments of production are involved in the work performed. It may be the case that from 11 a.m. to 2 p.m. the worker has generated an additional value in the amount of the value that the owner has promised to provide the dispossessed in exchange for the labor performance. The performance of labor, the performance of dispossession, however, does not end at 2 p.m.; it continues until, let us say, 5 p.m. A question appears: What happens to the surplus value generated by the worker between 2 p.m. and 5 p.m.?

The dispossessed is dispossessed of that value. That surplus value, its accumulation by the owner, is the expression of the disavowed relation of the owner to the possession; the dispossessed is the possession of the owner. Dispossession, then, is the relationship between the owners and the dispossessed. The dispossessed are not free. This, their lack of freedom, however, they disavow. The dispossessed are property, but this, too, they disavow. The dispossessed disavow their dispossession. The struggle for law is their (failed) dispossession of their own dispossession.

The dispossessed work for free, but they are not free. Their free work can never make them free. The dispossessed do not freely perform their free work; rather, they perform according to the force of circumstances, the force of the original dispossession, within the fold of the original or primal accumulation, all of which is a tale foretold in the hieroglyphic of the mark that designates those who are to have nothing but the skin they are in.

In the beginning, the mark must be made or found ready-made on the skin. In the beginning, there is the one; all flesh is as one, undivided, undifferentiated. The one becomes the many after and through the mark. The mark is forced upon the flesh that it divides into owner and owned. The

ANTHONY PAUL FARLEY

mark, its violence, the force of circumstances, the original or primal accumulation, is traumatic. It is, therefore, unremembered or repressed. The trauma of the primal scene, the original accumulation, is unremembered in the mode of repetition.

The owners are the inheritors of the primal accumulation. The dispossessed are the inheritors of the primal dispossession. The primal accumulation is accomplished through the marking of others for dispossession. The line between owner and owned, between person and thing, is fixed by the mark. On one side are things (fixed and variable capital), and on the other side are owners, capitalists.

The primal scene of accumulation is the beginning of the class contradiction between markers and marked. As on a darkling plain, ignorant armies clash over equal rights and rule of law. Rights cannot be equal. There is no rule of law save as the disguise for the rule of one group over another. What is called class is not class. What is called race is not race. Slaves chase after shadows of their original dispossession. Slave criticisms, including most critical race theories, are but reenactments of the original dispossession by those inhabiting the universe created, bound, and bounded within the horizon of dispossession. White-over-black to white-over-black to white-over-black, world without end.

The slave pretends to itself that it has captured its tormenter:

FAUST: You my prisoner? Well I'll be damned! It seems I've turned a handsome profit!

MEPHISTOPHELES: The dog knew nothing when he first jumped in; But now the tables have turned; The devil's caught and he cannot leave the house.

FAUST: Why can't he slip out through the windows?

MEPHISTOPHELES: A hellish law stands in the way: Wherever we steal in we must steal out. We're free to choose the first, but the second finds us slaves.

FAUST: So Hell itself has its legalities.

GOETHE [1808] 1985, lines 1406–13

The slave pretends that it has turned the tables on Mephistopheles. The slave thinks it can bargain with the devil for a social contract. The slave mistakes the part that it plays in the drama. The slave is itself the devil to whom it offers up its soul. The slave is caught within the windowless monad of its soul, the soul it surrenders to fashion the very system by which it is tormented. Hell itself has its legalities. The spirit is surrendered. The slave gives up the ghost. The specter begins its haunt. The system of capital acquires a spirit. The slave leaves its marked flesh behind, but it can never get far enough away from the skin it is in. Indeed, all it has is that selfsame skin which, by force of necessity, it must alienate in the market. And it is that very market that the slave maintains through the enabling fictions of freedom and equality, legality and rule of law that it is its profession to produce. The master feels freedom in the seemingly frictionless transit of his thoughts through the subaltern classes at his command. The slave feels its freedom in and through its seeming escape from the flesh to the noumenal world as it universally legislates for the kingdom of ends, a kingdom that is always coming but never comes. So the instrument of repression is the vehicle of return, and desire has its way. The desires of the master become flesh and that flesh begets thought and that thought is naught but the thought of the flesh, its pleasures and its chastisements, forever and ever and ever.

It all stops when we remember. What is to be done? Two hundred years ago, when the slaves in Haiti rose up, they, of necessity, burned everything: "They burned San Domingo flat so that at the end of the war it was a charred desert. Why do you burn everything? asked a French officer of a prisoner. We have a right to burn what we cultivate because a man has a right to dispose of his own labour, was the reply of this unknown anarchist" (James 1989, 19). The slaves burned everything because everything was against them. Everything was against the slaves, the entire order that it was their lot to follow, the entire order in which they were positioned as worse than senseless things, every plantation, everything. "Leave nothing white behind you," said Dessalines to those dedicated to the end of white-over-black. "God gave Noah the rainbow sign. No more water, the fire next time." The slaves burned everything, yes, but, unfortunately, they only burned everything in Haiti. Theirs was the greatest and most successful revolution in the history of the world, but the failure of their fire to cross the waters was the great tragedy of the nineteenth century.

At the dawn of the twentieth century, W. E. B. Du Bois wrote, "The color-line belts the world." The color line continues to belt the world. Indeed, the slave power that is the United States now threatens an entire world with the death that it has become, and so the slaves of yesterday, today, and tomorrow, those with nothing but their chains to lose, must, if they would be free, if they would escape slavery, win the entire world.

Notes

1   Reform is a mode of repetition: "Revolution within a modern industrial capitalist society can only mean the overthrow of all existing property relations
and the destruction of all institutions that directly or indirectly support existing property relations. It must include the total suppression of all classes
and individuals who endorse the present state of property relations or who
stand to gain from it. Anything less is reform" (Jackson [1972] 1990, 7–8).

2   George Jackson's historical observations were prophetic: "The mass psycho-
social national cohesiveness has trembled on the brink of disruption and
disintegration over the last fifty years, threatening to fly apart. . . . But at
each crisis it was allowed to reform itself; with each reform, revolution became more remote. This is because the old left has failed to understand the
true nature of fascism. We will never have a complete definition of fascism,
because it is in constant motion, showing a new face to fit any particular
set of problems that arise to threaten the predominance of the traditional-
ist, capitalist ruling class. But if one were forced for the sake of clarity to
define it in a word simple enough for all to understand, that word would be
'reform'" ([1972] 1990, 117–18).

3   As described by Marx: "The direct form of the circulation of commodities is
c-m-c, the transformation of commodities into money and the re-conversion
of money into commodities: selling in order to buy. But alongside this form
we find another form, which is quite distinct from the first: m-c-m, the transformation of money into commodities, and the reconversion of commodities
into money: buying in order to sell. Money which describes the latter course
in its movement is transformed into capital, and, from the point of view of its
function, already is capital" ([1867] 1990, 247–48).

4   Accumulation begets accumulation: "The more the capitalist has accumulated, the more is he able to accumulate. The surplus-value that makes up
additional capital no. 1 is the result of the purchase of labour-power with
part of the original capital, a purchase which conformed to the laws of
commodity exchange and which, from a legal standpoint, presuppose[d]
nothing beyond the worker's power to dispose freely of his own capacities,
and the money-owner's or commodity-owner's power to dispose freely of
the values that belong to him; equally, additional capital no. 2 is merely
the result of additional capital no. 1, and is therefore a consequence of the
relations described above; hence each individual transaction continues to
conform to the laws of commodity exchange, with the capitalist always buying labour-power and the worker always selling it at what we shall assume
is its real value. It is quite evident from this that the laws of appropriation or
private property, laws based on the production or circulation of commodities, become changed into their direct opposite through their own internal
and inexorable dialectic. The exchange of equivalents, the original operation

with which we started, is now turned round in such a way that there is only an apparent exchange, since, firstly, the capital which is exchanged for labour-power is itself merely a portion of the product of the labour of others which has been appropriated without an equivalent; and, secondly, this capital must not only be replaced by its producer, the worker, but replaced together with an added surplus. The relation of exchange between capitalist and worker becomes a mere semblance belonging only to the process of circulation, it becomes a mere form, which is alien to the content of the transaction itself, and merely mystifies it. The constant sale and purchase of labour-power is the form; the content is the constant appropriation by the capitalist, without equivalent, of a portion of the labour of others which has already been objectified, and his repeated exchange of this labour for a greater quantity of the living labour of others. Originally the rights of property seemed to us to be grounded in a man's own labour. Some such assumption seemed necessary, since only commodity-owners with equal rights confronted each other, and the sole means of appropriating the commodities of others was the alienation of a man's own commodities, commodities which, however, could only be created by labour. Now, however, property turns out to be the right, on the part of the capitalist, to appropriate the unpaid labour of others or its product, and the impossibility, on the part of the worker, of appropriating his own product. The separation of property from labour thus becomes a necessary consequence of a law that apparently originated in their identity" (Marx [1867] 1990, 729–30).

5   Marx observed, "Commodities cannot themselves go to market and perform exchanges in their own right. We must, therefore, have recourse to their guardians, who are the possessors of commodities. Commodities are things, and therefore lack the power to resist man. If they are unwilling, he can use force; in other words, he can take possession of them. In order that these objects may enter into relation to one another as commodities, their guardians must place themselves in relation to one another as persons whose will resides in those objects, and must behave in such a way that each does not appropriate the commodity of the other and alienate his own, except through an act to which both parties consent. This juridical relation, whose form is the contract, whether as part of a developed legal system or not, is a relation between two wills which mirrors the economic relation. The content of this juridical relation (or relation of two wills) is itself determined by the economic relation. Here the persons exist for one another merely as representatives and hence owners, of commodities" ([1867] 1990, 178).

PART II

GROUNDINGS

LIMITED GROWTH: U.S. SETTLER SLAVERY, COLONIAL INDIA, AND GLOBAL RICE MARKETS IN THE MID-NINETEENTH CENTURY

ZACH SELL

Samuel Tayler was one of over one million enslaved people sold through the internal slave trade in the United States. Tayler was sold away from his family in Georgetown, South Carolina, to Mobile, Alabama, in 1835. In 1838, following the Panic of 1837, the price of cotton had crashed, and Tayler's "price" dropped in relation (Baptist 2010; Lepler 2013). In a letter to Elizabeth Blyth, the slaveholding rice planter who sold him, Tayler wrote that declining prices made it possible for him to rejoin his family and for Blyth to profit by repurchasing him (Tayler 1945, 339).[1] "My mind is always dwelling on home, relations, and friends which I would give the world to see." He closed his letter, "Remember me also to Sarah, my mama, and Charlotte, my old fellow servant, and Amy Tayler."

The reality of slavery in the United States created conditions where enslaved people such as Tayler were systematically and serially separated from kin (Byrd 2008; Hartman 2016). Tayler writes, "I beg you will tell me how all my relations are" while stating he would be "happy" "to serve" Blyth and her descendants. The form of address to Blyth, who had earlier separated

Tayler from his family, is part of the everyday, persistent interpersonal racial violence that defined settler slavery in the United States. Reading Tayler's letter itself introduces the violence of slavery's archive: What was the relation of Tayler's current owner to the letter and its content?

Tayler's lifeworld was structured in relation to settler slavery's position within the global economy. The systematic movement of enslaved people through the internal slave trade was driven by the rapid settler expansion of cotton plantations in the United States. The internal slave trade enabled Upper South planters in states like South Carolina to profit through speculation in enslaved people along with rice, cotton, and other plantation staples. This allowed slaveholders to live through the trading of enslaved people while profiting from plantation agricultural enterprise, a form of life that W. E. B. Du Bois (1935) noted had "curious psychological effects" upon whites.[2] Global commodities markets intersected with the valuation of Black life and were at the same time structured by the systematically controlled mobility of enslaved people. The unique qualities, prices, and volumes of commodities exported from the United States, particularly cotton, tobacco, sugar, and rice, shaped the internal dynamics of settler slavery expansion and the character of the global economy simultaneously. An 1852 handbill directly connected enslaved people and the production of plantation commodities, advertising the sale of a "gang of 25 Sea Island cotton and rice negroes" in Charleston, South Carolina, purchasable through a combination of money and mortgages.[3] Such trading was the product of valuations that economically rendered enslaved people as laboring, exchangeable, and accumulable commodities whose value was backed by the legal regulation of U.S. slavery.

Cotton was the export commodity emblematic of the mid-nineteenth-century U.S. slaveholding economy, tied to global industrial transformation. Rice was also a significant export commodity, situating U.S. settler slavery within the global economy. Rice from South Carolina began to be exported to England in the early part of the eighteenth century. While cotton surpassed rice in significance in the nineteenth century, Carolina rice persisted as a significant export commodity in the mid-nineteenth century through the American Civil War. In Liverpool markets, Carolina rice, grown extensively in the low country of South Carolina and Georgia, served as the benchmark for all mid-nineteenth-century rice staples.

Mid-nineteenth-century British demand for Carolina rice was accompanied by a series of projects to introduce Carolina rice cultivation in colonial India. Upon visiting the United States, a former East India

Company official argued that the British Empire had access to colonial labor through peasant smallholding cultivators beyond anything possible through settler slavery in the United States (Fullilove 2017, 77). As Francis Bonynge wrote, "It may be supposed that a poor man in that condition could not contend with the planter of Carolina with his hundreds of slaves, but that is not the case; the naked Indian has the advantage through the combination of all the planters in a district" (1851, 45–46). Such a perspective reflected a belief in the colonial possibility of enforcing export agricultural cultivation according to metropolitan demands. However, colonial projects to introduce Carolina rice in India did not reflect a direct competition between labor in colonial India and the United States in the ways Bonynge imagined when making such comparisons. Instead, such projects were part of the interrelationship between U.S. settler slavery and colonial India, which made it possible to understand colonial transformation in India through plantation slavery in the United States. The economic dynamism of U.S. plantation slavery, as imagined through its commodities, particularly U.S. cotton staples, Virginia tobacco, and Carolina rice, depended upon an antiblack fetishism of commodities that enabled projects for colonial transformation beyond the Atlantic world, conditioned by commodity possibilities revealed through U.S. slavery. In the United States, white settler antiblack racism existed through enslavement and land grabbing backed by the U.S. empire-state in a form buttressed by an export-oriented economy. Projects to introduce Carolina rice cultivation in colonial India were informed by the possibilities of colonial agrarian transformation that could be understood in relation to the realities of U.S. slavery and through interpretations of U.S. slavery's position within the North Atlantic economy.

This chapter begins with an examination of the role of Carolina rice within North Atlantic markets. It then considers the transforming realities of enslaved people who cultivated Carolina rice in the mid-nineteenth century, situating enslaved lives in relation to Atlantic world transformations in rice milling. The chapter concludes with a series of colonial projects to introduce Carolina rice cultivation in India between 1830 and 1870. Through these overlapping histories, this chapter situates the social, cultural, and economic production of Carolina rice as part of a global colonial and slavery-based project that exposes the reach of slavery and antiblackness within nineteenth-century capitalism. Together, enslaved cultivation of rice in South Carolina and Georgia, the transformation of milling, and colonial projects to introduce Carolina rice into India reveal overlapping realities where racial slavery in the United States, wage labor in Britain, and multiple sets of agrarian relations across colonial India converged. The convergence of different realities through global capital reveals divergent social relationships and experiences. Across these overlapping worlds, the experience of Tayler had no equivalent. The British colonial pursuit of Carolina rice in India was itself the result of imaginations about an export economy made possible through interpretations of future economic possibilities imaginable through slavery-produced commodities.

The Demand for Settler Slavery

The mid-nineteenth century was characterized by the persistent demand for slavery-produced plantation commodities including not just sugar, tobacco, and cotton but also rice. Brazilian, Carolina, and East Indian rices were among the most common staples sold in British markets from 1830 through the Civil War. Rice staples from Brazil were also the product of slavery and were exported to Britain and continental Europe (Carney 2004). Rice from British Burma would become increasingly important for importation to British and European markets, especially after 1850, with further impetus following the American Civil War (Adas 1974; Coclanis 1993; Siok-Hwa 1968). Yet until Black emancipation in the United States, Carolina rice served as the benchmark for rice staples consumed in England. Carolina rice was, in general, in the highest demand, sold in high volumes, and with the highest prices until the disappearance of the staple from British and European markets following Black emancipation. The post–Civil War collapse of Carolina rice and the disruption of the slavery-based rice plantation complex were entwined.

The very name Carolina rice located the staple as a product of U.S. slavery. In *Household Words*, Charles Dickens (1856, 8) offered observations upon the fetishism characteristic of demand for Carolina rice in European markets:

> It must not be supposed by European readers, that rice, in the larger acceptation of the word, is represented by "the finest Carolina," or even "the best London Cleaned Patna." There is no more affinity between those white artificial cereals, and the "real, original" staple food of India and the East, than there is between a sponge-cake and a loaf of genuine farm-house bread.

The truth is, people in this part of the world, have no conception of what good rice is like. If they had, there would not be such a lively demand for the produce of the Southern American States. But such is prejudice, that if a merchant were to introduce into any port of Great Britain, or Ireland, a cargo of the real staple food of orientals, he would not find a purchaser for it, so inferior is it in appearance, in its colour, shape, and texture, to the better known and tempting looking grain of South Carolina.

Dickens's account brought together and compared global rice staples according to racial and colonial logics. Dickens at once observed that the demand for the produce of enslaved people in the United States had no basis in reality while at the same time noting its persistence.

While widely consumed, rice was not the principle staple of English households. In England, rice might be used as an ingredient in puddings, flours, rice cakes, fritters, custards, and ground rice milk (A Lady 1840). In an 1863 survey of working-class households (conducted at the moment of Black emancipation in the United States), the surveyor noted that rice was most commonly consumed in working-class households in winter "to supply the place of vegetables" and that small quantities of rice were consumed in 58 percent of cases in almost every county (Public Health 1863, 241).

The supplementary position of rice within the mid-nineteenth-century English diet was a product of both a demand for what was filling with the most economical way of reproducing labor power at the lowest rate possible. This was part of social relations between enslaved people and the English beyond the world of textile production alone. When formerly enslaved people visited England, they took note of the difference in experiences between English laborers and enslaved people bound to rice plantations. In 1855, the Black abolitionist William Wells Brown wrote that he had often been told that "the English labourer was no better off than the slave upon a Carolina rice-field. I had seen the slaves in Missouri huddled together, three, four, and even five families in a single room not more than 15 by 25 feet square, and I expected the same in England. But in this I was disappointed" (1855, 101). Analogies between English workers and enslaved people distorted fundamental differences in lived experiences, differences highlighted particularly in Black abolitionist thought.

The demand for Carolina rice in England brought together disparate global commodities of enslaved and colonial produce, enabling English consumers to make decisions about preferences in relation to the perceived character of these commodities. The British abolitionist George Thompson, who would travel to both the United States and India, observed of England, "Ask the frugal housewife, who prepares the dish of rice for her household, or her guests. These are the buyers, the rewarders, the upholders of Slavery" (1839, 5). Beneath such appearances was a world of global capital where labor processes in the United States, Britain, and India came into relation through exchange. North Atlantic shipping networks facilitated the dominance of U.S. slavery–produced commodities within British and continental European commodities markets (Beckert 2014, 113–14).

U.S. slaveholding rice planters such as Edward Heriot realized their globally dominant position in plantation production was the product of the singular value that commodities produced by enslaved people in the United States had within British and European markets. At the 1851 Great Exhibition in London, Heriot's Carolina rice received an award for the best rice staple. Judges praised the rice as "magnificent" and compared it against the "slovenly character of the native commerce" of colonial India (Committee of General Literature and Education, 1854, 107, 109). Such comparisons were ideological and did not describe the intrinsic character of rice. At the same time, such comparisons contributed to the perpetuation of Carolina rice's unique valuation within British and European commodity markets. Heriot argued that if U.S. slavery was destroyed,

> the agricultural productions, and the whole civilized world would be shook to its very center—Europe would feel it much more than we would—the manufacturing interests would be overturned, and destitution and nakedness of the working classes would amount to famine. Think of the cotton, rice, sugar, Indian corn, wheat, and other exports from the country consumer in different portions of the world, and the manufacturing of some of them giving employment to millions of people, what if all were cut off— and recollect that free white labour cannot be substituted—it is a monstrous question. . . . It is now interwoven with the relations of the world.[4]

Heriot's observations did not reflect the complex political-economic relations that made settler slavery persist within the global economy. Yet the persistence of this belief was based upon the ability of planters such as Heriot to realize themselves globally through their relationship to slavery as slaveholders and to land as settlers. The commodities produced through settler slavery in the United States accounted for nearly 75 percent of U.S. domestic exports by 1860 (Inikori 2002, 193).

The Transformation of Carolina Rice

Throughout the nineteenth century, the demand for Carolina rice persisted. However, as this demand persisted, the relations of rice production and export transformed. This transformation intensified the violence constitutive of the labor process, particularly worsening enslaved people's work experiences through confining enslaved people increasingly to plantation labor in the process of rice production. Throughout this era, the practice of milling Carolina rice relocated increasingly to Liverpool, London, and continental Europe, incorporating the work of British and continental European workers in the process of rice production.

Rice cultivation was the most complex and differentiated process of plantation agriculture in the U.S. before the Civil War. Enslaved knowledge of rice planting practices shaped to the pace and character of rice cultivation and milling. In the eighteenth century, rice milling through pounding was among the most labor-intensive processes of plantation production on the low-country plantations of South Carolina and Georgia. The patterns and pace of enslaved labor were regulated in part by enslaved people while also dictated by the demands of slave owners (Berry 2007: 32–34). Manual pounding, beating rice with a mortar and pestle, relied particularly upon enslaved women's work and provided the basis for the milling of Carolina rice. Pounding rice yielded four products: market rice, small rice, rice flour, and chaff. Flour, chaff, and small rice were partially allocated as provisions for enslaved people (Clifton 1978a, 106).[5] Small rice was distinguished from Carolina rice and classified as the "imperfect grains" that emerged from the pounding process.[6] In daily struggles over rice, enslaved people reappropriated some of this rice, selling it or consuming it to supplement deficient plantation rations (Dusinberre 1996, 141; Wood 1995, 92–93).

Low-country rice cultivation was often but not exclusively organized according to the task system, with considerable variation in cultivation practices between individual plantations (Morgan 1982, 563–99). Rice fields could be made from drained swamps, surrounded by ditches for irrigation. The digging of these ditches was brutal work that freed people often refused to perform following emancipation (Bailey 2017, 123). In cultivating, enslaved people would first chop the ground, mixing layers of soil roughly two to three inches deep. After chopping, the ground would again be hoed. In March, seed planting commenced. Enslaved people would quickly and evenly trench a field with great precision and evenly distributed rows. On some plantations, enslaved women would then cover seeds using wooden beaters (Bryan 1832, 530). Enslaved men and women would then plant a field in a single day so that it could be flooded for the first time. This first flooding would last for a period of between one and two weeks. The water was drained from the field and enslaved people would weed and hoe before a second flooding. Planters and drivers demanded unrelenting and physically destructive work from enslaved people (Q.E.D. 1832, 630–31). During the second flooding, enslaved people would be forced to wade through flooded rice fields, picking volunteer rice, an inferior rice that reduced the staple's market value. Meticulous attention to staple quality as demanded by slave owners was characteristic of U.S. plantation slavery more generally (see also Johnson 2013).

Following the final draining of rice fields, enslaved people cut rice with sickles, then placed cut stalks out to dry in stacks (Olmsted 1856, 471–75). In harvesting, overseers placed different demands for cutting on enslaved people, exactions that varied based upon the distance cut rice stalks would be carried and the requirements of individual planters. Ben Horry, enslaved as a youth, remembered that cutting rice was an "awful job" and that he was assigned to cut half an acre per day (Horry 1938). Sometimes twice as much was demanded. When an assigned task was not finished, overseers and drivers deployed direct physical violence against enslaved people (James 1936, 35; Kemble 1863, 134).

Enslaved people would then tie rice in bundles (Claiborne 1828, 311; Munnerlyn 1828, 220–21). Enslaved people struggled to place limits on planter demands and regulate the work process in all stages, including cutting. As one planter complained, Black rice cultivators were "cunning enough to remember that what they are harvesting they will have to thresh, & will tie as small sheaves as they can" (Clifton 1978b, 8–9; House 1954, 60). Such efforts were part of the daily struggle over the intensity of plantation extortion managed and maintained by planters, overseers, and drivers.

Carolina rice production rested not only upon the labor of enslaved people but also on the knowledge of enslaved cultivators in South Carolina and Georgia, which was turned into commodities uniquely valued when sold for export, a form of valuation that reflected back upon enslaved people themselves. Black knowledge and skill in rice cultivation emerged through the African diaspora and the pathways of a productive process that tied the rice-producing South Carolina and Georgia low country to practices of West African rice production in Upper Guinea (Carney 2007).[7] Enslaved people knew more not only about the process of rice cultivation, but also about the daily management and day-to-day operation of plantation work, knowledge that could produce intense oppositions between Black drivers and field laborers (Clifton 1978a, 104–10; 1981, 331). Planter anxiety was pronounced in rice cultivation because it depended upon enslaved people working without direct supervision. Rice planters often knew little about the daily practice and process of rice cultivation, leaving plantations sometimes for up to six-month periods beginning in spring or early summer out of fear of the climate and returning in November after the rice harvest (Brewster 1947, 7–9). Often, Black drivers were relied upon for their knowledge about rice cultivation (Clifton 1981, 335). As one planter responded when asked about rice-planting techniques, "[I] will barely suggest, (and in this instance only) the propriety of your consulting the driver, being an old rice planter" (McBride 1830, 238). The response put to words the known but rarely stated (see also Stuckey 2013, 304).

The threshing and milling of rice underwent significant transformations during the first half of the nineteenth century. These transformations occurred across the North Atlantic world, with implications for the British imperial world. After cutting, rice was threshed, winnowed, and pounded. Threshing relied particularly upon bondwomen's labor and entailed flailing rice stalks with a wooden staff that had a second wooden staff bound to it (Olmsted 1856, 475; Phillips 1929, 115–17; Schwalm 1997, 27). This process separated the rice from the stalk. Flailing was among the most labor-intensive processes within rice production, which limited the capacity for expanded production (Elliot 1851, 306). By the 1850s, on the largest plantations, threshing might be done by enslaved people using a threshing machine, introduced in the 1830s. Yet often throughout this period, threshing continued to be performed by hand. As the once-enslaved Maggie Black remembered of threshing, the process of rice cultivation was accompanied by songs. Such songs in part regulated the pace of work on rice plantations (Black 1936, 59).

If threshing was the most labor-intensive part of rice processing, its milling placed consistently high demands on enslaved labor. Throughout the nineteenth century, the labor-saving mechanization of milling enabled expanded theoretical possibilities for accumulation by slaveholding rice planters. In the early nineteenth century, the mechanization of rice pounding became increasingly common (Chaplin 1993, 227–74). This mechanization first took place directly upon South Carolina and Georgia plantations. This was supplemented by several mills including two in Charleston, which each claimed over seventy enslaved people. The West Point Mill claimed ownership in eighty-nine enslaved people (Lander 1954, 61; Starobin 1970, 20–21). Steam engines and millstones for some of these rice mills were manufactured in Britain and shipped from Liverpool to South Carolina.[8]

Elizabeth Blyth, who sold Tayler away from his family, would sometimes send her rice to be milled at the mills of Jonathan Lucas in Charleston.[9] The Lucas family had accumulated considerable capital through slavery, the construction of mills, and the milling of rice. The Lucases were also involved in the Atlantic world transformation of rice milling. From 1817, the milling of Carolina rice transformed, with Carolina rice now exported from the United States in unmilled, paddy form. In 1819, the South Carolina slaveholder Jonathan Lucas partnered with London merchant Henry Ewbank to obtain a patent for a rice cleaning machine in Britain ("Patents Lately Enrolled" 1819). In the early 1820s, Jonathan Lucas Jr., of South Carolina, was involved in the construction of rice mills in England capable of processing over 300,000 bushels of rice ("Industry of the Southern and Western States" 1848, 288; Lucas, Jr. and Norton, 1824, 133). Lucas Jr. facilitated the construction of three rice mills in Liverpool and one in Rotherhithe near London. In 1822, during the trial of Denmark Vesey, Bram and Richard, two enslaved people owned by Lucas, were acquitted of involvement in a conspiracy that shook Charleston's white supremacist planter class (Egerton 1999). In 1823, the first shipment of rough rice (known as unmilled or paddy rice) was exported from the U.S. to Britain. In 1828, a slave-owning Southern rice planter could assume that paddy rice would be exported more often than milled rice because England had its own mills ("The New Trade in Rough Rice" 1828, 460). By 1850, most rice exported from the United States was paddy rice. Transformations in rice milling relocated a crucial part of the work process, long conducted by enslaved people across the Atlantic, expanding the circuit of rice production to envelop, create, and rely upon wage laborers in the English cities of Liverpool and London as well as mills in continental Europe. This also enabled further containments upon plantations, particularly potent given fears about enslaved flight and insurrection made particularly possible outside of the plantation. As John Hope Franklin and Loren Schweninger (1999) note, one rice mill owner experienced a near shutdown after five enslaved people fled from the mill. The relocation of rice milling to England and continental Europe structurally concentrated enslavement in rice production to plantations.

The Atlantic world transformation of milling was calibrated according to increasing profitability, shipping logistics, consumer desires for fresh

ZACH SELL

Carolina rice, and the perpetuation of U.S. slavery. North Atlantic shifts in milling practices made the expanded exportation of Carolina rice to British and continental European markets possible. One South Carolina rice planter noted that continued dependency upon enslaved labor for rice milling would have made it impossible to produce and "prepare for market anything like the number of barrels now produced. But, by the application of steam, and improvement of Machinery, the Rice-mill has been introduced into Europe, paddy exported there in the rough, and offered freshly prepared to consumers, thereby enhancing its value and increasing its consumption" (R.W.R. 1846, 466). A British observer who traveled between South Carolina and London reflected, "I have frequently, since my return, eaten rice managed in this way by Messrs Lucas and Ewbank of London, as fresh in taste and in appearance as any I met with in South Carolina" (Hall 1830, 165). These transformations enabled the persistence of slavery on rice plantations in the South Carolina and Georgia low country.

Mechanization reduced the ratio of enslaved labor on colonized land, making the profitable production of Carolina rice part of an intensification of the labor process for enslaved people. Through tariff policy, Britain further encouraged the exportation of unmilled rice from the United States while offering a reduced tariff for the importation of rough rice from West Africa. Tariff disputes were resolved in 1846, just as the proslaveholder Walker tariff in the United States and the repeal of the Corn Laws in Britain established a proslavery free trade policy between the United States and Britain (Jones 1958, 76; Polk 1888, 64). Slaveholding mill owners and family members moved between South Carolina and England with ease, writing one another about their thoughts about both countries, discussing diasporic families while Atlantic relations of production in rice milling and consumption shifted in proslavery ways.

Some Carolina rice planters feared the movement of milling to England, stating that such a movement would ultimately enable the displacement of Carolina rice from European markets by South and Southeast Asian staples (Bonynge 1851, 513). Other planters saw this as only enhancing the advantage that U.S. slaveholders had over India and Southeast Asia because the increased weight of unmilled Carolina rice enhanced the shipping advantages of South Carolina over colonial India (City Rustic 1828, 351). Meticulous control of the process of production exacted through slavery enabled a competitive advantage. The demand for slavery through the consumption of Carolina rice continued through the Civil War.

The concentration and extension of Carolina rice milling in Liverpool, London, and across Europe enabled a racialized transnational and transimperial organization of labor. This organization was part of global market fluctuations, concentrating enslaved people who produced rice for export to work in rice fields. The Atlantic shift of milling enabled the degradation of plantation labor for enslaved people, reduced the amount of labor required on land, and made it further possible for rice planters to profit through the internal slave trade.

The labor process transformed through the intensification of work itself for enslaved people even as the elementary components of the work process remained unchanged in plantation cultivation. Laboring in rice swamps had singularly negative impacts on the health of enslaved people (Dusinberre 1996, 50–51). The hand milling of rice was exacting and demanding in the process of rice production and relied particularly upon Black women's labor. Yet the machine milling of rice expanded the territorial domain of rice cultivation on transatlantic and imperial scales, enveloping workers from London and continental Europe. This enclosed Black people to the particularized work of plantation slavery, in the plantation low-country rice fields of South Carolina and Georgia, also making planters able to speculate upon enslaved people for expanding cotton plantations, especially in the lower South.

The introduction and expansion of mechanical milling transformed the winter season on plantations, recentering Black work toward maintaining rice fields. One white plantation observer stated that "humanity rejoices" because of mechanization. He continued that mechanization transferred to water and steam work that was "exhausting to the human as well as to the animal frame—and in this feeling we are confident every planter deeply sympathises" (Elliot 1851; Gray 1933, 731). Despite proclamations of sympathy, which simultaneously degraded enslaved people through the "zoological" language of the white supremacist settler (Fanon 1963, 7), the introduction of milling technologies freed up enslaved labor time for the slaveholder rather than for those enslaved. Technological innovations in rice milling enabled planters to place new demands upon enslaved people. Ned, an enslaved man who labored in a mill upon a Georgia plantation, attributed his own relative health to not having labored in rice fields (Kemble 1863, 151). While Ned reflected upon his own relative health, as rice milling became the work of wage laborers in Britain and continental Europe, this transformation confined enslaved people to labor in rice swamps and maintained their enslavement. The mechanization of rice milling appropriated and concentrated enslaved labor to field and plantation maintenance, to clearing land and preparing manure, while extending the workforce to include English factory workers (Q.E.D. 1832, 634). This meant that those enslaved upon rice plantations would work longer in swamps, which planters imagined would lead to death from the very act of being in such places. The physically destructive nature of plantation labor upon white bodies characterized dominant planter imaginations of plantation work in the nineteenth century (Asaka 2017, 47, 49).[10] In the mid-nineteenth century, "premature death" in the global circuits of Carolina rice plantation production and consumption had an antiblack character (Gilmore 2007).

The Colonial State of Carolina Rice

In 1840, the *British India Advocate* described a vision of emancipation through the free market wherein the world's commodities would be placed in competition with one another. Commodities produced through slavery would be forced out of the market because of price: "Produce a sufficient quantity of the same commodities at as cheap a rate, or at a cheaper rate, by means of free labour, and American slavery will receive its death blow" ("Objects of This Journal" 1841, 2). Throughout the nineteenth century until Black emancipation in the United States, the cultivation of Carolina rice through U.S. slavery was driven by British consumption and unimpeded by such a logic. The mid-nineteenth-century world, within which slavery had been abolished across the British Empire but remained present in the United States, Brazil, and Cuba, continued to be dominated by a global plantation system that Sylvia Wynter described as characterized by a rhetoric of "liberal free trade . . . which freed the slaves, compensated the masters and set the slaves free in a world dominated by market relations, to fend naked for themselves, [which] was the first sketch of monopoly capitalism." This plantation dominance, as Wynter continues, also demanded the disciplining of Indian peasants, as occurred in the colonial planter suppression of the Indigo Rebellion of Bengal in 1859. For Wynter, it was in this world that peasants who resisted "growing indigo as a commercial crop for the English, had to be taught a lesson. The world had to be kept safe for the market economy" (Wynter 1971, 100–101). In this analysis, forms of domination introduced through Atlantic-world plantation slavery established principles for imperial and colonial domination through capitalism characterized by unmediated exposure to the violence of capitalism, temporally after slavery and spatially beyond the Atlantic. The movement of indigo cultivation itself from Saint-Domingue and Carolina to colonial Bengal during the late eighteenth century sketched out earlier histories of this relation. In the mid-nineteenth century, colonial projects to introduce Carolina rice cultivation in colonial India exposed colonial interconnections between U.S. slavery and peasant- and plantation-based agrarian production in colonial India that existed according to a disciplinary logic that depended upon liberal principles of free trade that did not operate against slavery but were made in relation to it.

Projects to introduce Carolina rice into colonial India emerged sporadically, with greatest frequency in the Bengal and Madras presidencies, and during an era marked by Atlantic emancipation within the British Empire and the end of slavery in the United States, depending upon lessons of market dominance that were informed by colonial ideas of imperial market making that interpreted colonial possibilities in relation to the unique role that the U.S. played in the export of agricultural commodities. Projects to introduce Carolina rice in colonial India entailed the movement and reformulation of practices that emerged through plantation slavery in the United States to colonial contexts where the status, meaning, and practice of agriculture existed differently. In India, the colonial state pursued export agriculture under the belief that the export trade was crucial to capital accumulation (Robb 2007, 80). However, colonial projects to introduce Carolina rice did not depend upon the replication of U.S. settler slavery even as they emerged through slavery and reveal dynamics within the coconstitutive structuring particularities of antiblackness and U.S. settler colonialism in relation to British colonial agrarian projects in India. Such colonial projects in India expose ideologies of British imperial liberalism drawn to the economic dynamism of U.S. settler slavery. As one colonial official observed, "The statement frequently appears in the history of our attempts to acclimatize this [Carolina] rice, that the people would not eat it even if they could grow it. I take the liberty to doubt this; but were it even true, and the grain grown for export only, the experiment is of great importance. The people do not eat jute, but they are glad to grow it for all that."[11] This perspective depended upon peasant smallholding cultivators disciplined according to the logic of market relations and production for export. Yet the dependence of such projects upon the options or decisions of cultivators to pursue or not pursue the cultivation of Carolina rice also revealed emerging differences between U.S. settler slavery and the articulation of a nonenslaving colonial liberalism characterizing colonial agrarian projects in India that were also attended by exposure to capitalist and agrarian crisis, particularly the severe colonial famines of the nineteenth century, a reality that projects for export rice production only exacerbated. The abstract belief in introducing structures of choice through the colonial economy that would make the cultivation of rice inevitable existed in the same historic conjuncture as U.S. settler slavery enforced enslaved cultivation of Carolina rice. While in British India the colonial state struggled to induce the expanded cultivation of Carolina rice among smallhold peasant cultivators, in the South Carolina and Georgia low country, asymmetrical struggles between enslaved people and planters occurred over the labor process and the realities of enslavement upon plantations where Carolina rice cultivation was entrenched.

The United States, a settler and enslaving empire-state, supported slaveholding white supremacy and power until the American Civil War. Within the British Empire, the Slavery Abolition Act of 1833 legally declared the end to the centuries-long history of direct British slavery. Former slaveholders were compensated with £20 million; formerly enslaved people experienced postslavery rule characterized by continued colonialism (Draper 2013). In metropolitan Britain, the pursuit of free trade policies enabled continued profits through slavery in the United States, Cuba, and Brazil. Not only did Lancashire textile manufacturers depend upon U.S. cotton produced through slavery, the equalization of sugar duties enabled the expanded consumption of slave-produced sugar imported from Brazil and Cuba, something that itself led to a decrease in demand for North India–produced sugars (Amin 1984; Bosma 2013; Huzzey 2010; Williams 1994 [1944]).

The power of white slaveholders in the United States and of former slaveholders in Britain did not characterize slaveries in colonial India. The 1833 Emancipation Act exempted India and Mauritius. However, the Indian Slavery Act of 1843 legally declared the end of slavery in India. Despite this, British colonial law was often indifferent to caste-based bondages that did not, as Rupa Viswanath writes, directly depend upon or emerge through colonial legislation but were instead reproduced through "local power and state authority." The colonial state protected the relationship between landed caste elites and Dalit laborers as something that was "mutually beneficial," even as Dalit laborers sought means to challenge and escape caste oppression (Viswanath 2014, 25–26).

Despite variation across diverse agrarian relations characterized by multiple forms of plantation and peasant smallholding production, no agrarian relations in nineteenth-century colonial India resembled U.S. settler slavery. The British Empire pursued forms of European planter and merchant power but did not enforce a regime of accumulation predicated upon white planter permanent settlement coinciding with racial slavery. Indigo and tea production was defined by violent relations and had European planter classes. The tea gardens of Assam existed through what Jayeeta Sharma (2006) has usefully termed an "extractive economy" undergirded by violence and colonial racializations. At the same time, as Rana Behal and Prabhu Mohapatra (1992) have noted, plantations in India had no history of production through slavery. Outside of tea and indigo, the colonial state's power was often "shallow" or limited in its ability to create and sustain production for export (Robb 2007, 291). Global commodities markets produced and enabled formations of South Asian peasant smallholder structured indebtedness, particularly through the rise of foreign demand for Indian primary products (Bose 1991, 6; Washbrook 1990, 41). Peasant options and choices, alongside landholders' decisions, interests, and investments, often limited the colonial state's ability to reorient agrarian relations toward the export trade in a form capable of supplanting U.S. settler slavery.

Instead, the location of U.S. settler slavery in an export-oriented North Atlantic economy influenced mid-nineteenth-century British economic aspirations for colonial India to match this capacity through export, through different colonial configurations of labor and land. This made the introduction of Carolina rice into India at once connected to broader liberal colonial projects of agricultural "improvement" (Arnold 2005; Kumar 2013) and at the same time structurally distinct. Experimental projects occurred on the landholdings of Bengali *zamindars* (landholders), in jails in the Madras presidency, and at colonial gardens. When efforts to introduce Carolina rice relied upon coercive institutions such as the jail or figures such as U.S. overseers brought to India, the extension of these projects also depended upon decisions made by cultivators and landholders. This diverged from the realities of U.S. settler slavery, where bond people could struggle over the process of production yet had no control over the staples cultivated. The project to induce demand was about the liberal structuring of economic coercion intended to create economic forces that would make the extensive production of Carolina rice for export inevitable.

Despite projects that demanded Carolina rice, colonial officials and invested zamindars proved unable to introduce Carolina rice. This inability was also attended by distance from the realities of enslavement in the United States, and of enslaved people, that made the growth of Carolina rice possible. The Bengali zamindar Radhakanta Deb was a leading voice within the Agricultural and Horticultural Society of India (AHSI), a British colonial–dominated agricultural institute that included members of Bengal's Zamindari Association (Bhattacharya 1975, 56–65; Sengupta 1990).[12] Deb's observations on rice cultivation in Bengal reflect a belief that the introduction of different staples in India could emerge from drawing upon techniques and seeds from the United States and reformulating these practices in relation to "native process." According to Deb, "European experience" would introduce "the methods of culture" while "taking so much from the native process adopted in this country as will serve the objects of science").[13] Projects to transform the colonial economy toward expanded exports, to introduce U.S. staples, entailed systematic efforts to introduce U.S. overseers, seeds, gins, implements, and modes of assessment—in some instances, direct physical violence. While the structuring dynamics that characterized U.S. settler slavery were never replicated, demands for the extension of the relations of economic dynamism that characterized the North Atlantic slavery with which colonial India experimented throughout this period were conditioned by the possible futures offered by the profits gained through plantation slavery–produced commodities.

Rice cultivation and consumption had deep cultural, economic, and social significance within India during the mid-nineteenth century, serving as a principle food grain in many parts of the subcontinent. Radhakanta Deb's "On the Culture of Paddy in Twenty Different Districts" represents an inquiry into these practices with support from the colonial AHSI. When sold in Liverpool markets, the staples cultivated in Bengal and exported to England were considered "rough and inferior," sometimes valued at less than half Carolina rice ("Report from the Society of Arts" 1839, 120).[14] In colonial India, focus upon the export-based cultivation of Carolina rice emerged through the cultural and economic implications that plantation slavery in general and U.S. settler slavery in particular introduced.

Projects to introduce Carolina rice cultivation in colonial India according to British consumer demands reveal part of the structural location of U.S. settler slavery within the global economy. The AHSI would write the South Carolina Agricultural Society as early as 1831 inquiring into the purchase of Carolina rice, frequently orchestrating the shipment of Carolina rice from South Carolina to Liverpool and from Liverpool to Kolkata.[15] As the East India Company and AHSI tried to grow Carolina rice in India, neither the deeper Black diasporic relations nor the contradictions that defined U.S. settler slavery and made Carolina rice uniquely valued in the North Atlantic were reproduced.

At times, colonial officials believed that their inability to grow rice was the result of the climate and location where Carolina rice cultivation was pursued. In the Sundarbans, mangroves in the Bay of Bengal, colonial officials repeatedly sought and were unable to introduce Carolina rice.[16] When one project failed, an official wrote, "I feel confident that this failure cannot be attributed to want of care on the part of the Ryots [cultivators]."[17] The language of agrarian failure itself offers insight into the projects made in relation to colonizing visions of successful agricultural transformation as defined by colonial officials (Birla 2016). In Odisha, another colonial observer stated that he believed it would be difficult or impossible to introduce Carolina seed there:

> Those who have grown the seed refuse to eat the grain, and besides, there is no local demand for it, and until such demand arises cultivators will never be introduced to substitute the cultivation of Carolina rice for their own staple crop. If the Carolina mode of cultivation is absolutely necessary to ensure good results, the Ooryas will not adopt it, and will, therefore, never succeed in raising a crop which will secure for them the large profits that are anticipated.[18]

Such a perspective, even as it was based upon export cultivation, also recognized existing colonial dependence upon peasant smallholder cultivators' decisions and practices of consumption, a deep problem for the colonial state. The implication in such observations was often an argument for direct intervention through force.

In Bihar in 1840, an indigo planter reflected upon projects over the previous decade to introduce Carolina rice. According to the planter, he distributed Carolina seeds within the district with results that were largely satisfactory. The amount "far exceeded anything the Ryots had ever been accustomed to witness from their ordinary crops." The planter suggested that zamindars in the district should introduce Carolina rice on an "extensive scale amongst the ryots." After four years, he believed it had been cultivated to a considerable extent, noting that with "efficient machinery under proper management," the staple could compete with Carolina rice sold upon the European market and "command a much higher price than any of the best descriptions hitherto imported from Bengal." This made him advise zamindars in the region of the efficacy of introducing the staple also for increased yields.[19] However, despite these observations, this project was not pursued.

Between 1839 and 1849, an extensive project focused particularly upon the introduction of U.S. cotton and rice staples centrally entailed relocating U.S. plantation overseers to colonial India (Florio 2016; Hazareesingh 2013; Logan 1974; Olmstead 2017; Sell 2016). In 1839, an East India Company official named Thomas Bayles traveled from Bristol to New York en route to the American South, where he would recruit overseers and planters knowledgeable about the process of plantation production, focusing upon both rice and cotton cultivation. Bayles first visited South Carolina where he examined Carolina rice plantations, observing methods of cultivation. Bayles reported confidently that he would be able to introduce and reproduce these techniques across India. In Savannah, one of the largest cotton markets in the South, Bayles met the wealthy plantation owner Charles Harris, who owned Upland and Sea Island cotton plantations in Georgia and in Jefferson County, Mississippi (Woodman 1968, 15). Bayles would send not only cotton seeds and implements but also 250 bushels of Carolina rice to India.

In general, white planters and overseers involved in the rice plantation economy were reluctant to relocate with Bayles, partially because of the lucrative nature of their livelihoods in the American South. One overseer who would have been willing to relocate requested from Bayles an annual salary of $2,500, an amount Bayles could not provide.[20] In such instances, planters and overseers valued their own knowledge of the production process according to global coordinates and made demands in relation, positing white supremacy as a commodity. Because Bayles could not pay as demanded, he took extensive notes on the process of rice cultivation, stating that he was "particularly struck" by the advantages of introducing South Carolina styles of rice cultivation to India. Because of this, he recorded the "whole process" of enslaved rice cultivation in South Carolina and Georgia.[21]

Despite difficulties securing the relocation of white planters and overseers involved in the rice economy, Bayles recruited two overseers who claimed knowledge about cultivation, John Blount and James Morris. Blount would be placed in the Bengal presidency while Morris would be located in the Madras presidency. Morris's efforts to introduce the so-called American system of rice cultivation at Erode in the northwestern Madras presidency reveal cultivators' choices disrupting the colonial pursuit of Carolina rice in India, even when directed by white plantation overseers from the United States.

Morris, an Arkansas-born cotton planter, arrived in Madras on October 20, 1840. While the majority of Morris's attention focused upon cotton, he was also involved in a failed attempt to introduce rice cultivation between 1841 and 1843 at Erode. In 1841, Morris described the failure of his rice field as "certainly the most provoking and discouraging of any thing I have ever met with in the whole course of my life."[22]

The East India Company Board of Revenue, along with local revenue collectors, sought to inquire into the cause of the project's failure. While Morris believed he could have been successful, the district *tehsildar* (revenue collector) Rangasamy Naik disputed any such claim, reporting, "The American mode of cultivation is unprofitable in every respect. The American ploughs are too large and heavy to be of any use and cattle of sufficient strength to work them with are not procurable in this part of the country. This difficulty may be overcome by the employment of additional coolies but as the system itself is not in any way advantageous, the ryots of this talook (revenue district) are not willing to follow it."[23] The refusal of peasant cultivators to follow Morris's method of rice cultivation was part of a set of already existing colonial agrarian relations in India that simply could not accommodate the introduction of forms of rice cultivation emerging from U.S. settler slavery. The capital investment required for the purchase of implements used in the cultivation of the so-called American system seemed too great for the Erode district to meet the revenue demands of the colonial state.[24] The structure of colonial contradictions and the contradictions of U.S. settler slavery were not the same. The possibility to refuse to follow the demand for the growth of rice had no equivalent in the United States even as slaveholders and enslaved people engaged in oppositional struggles.

Morris accounted for his economic and agricultural failure through the language of white supremacy. Morris wrote that the people of Erode were a "treacherous indolent race of beings."[25] In the face of Morris's white supremacist commitments, without the relations of U.S. settler slavery, he failed to introduce any comparable form of export rice cultivation in India. He knew nothing about it and did not possess the means of violence and expropriation that characterized the South Carolina and Georgia lowcountry plantation economy. In 1845, Morris wrote his brother stating he was in "good health." In 1846, Morris died in Ballari from cholera. His grave reads, "cotton planter of Natchez, Adams County, Mississippi, U.S.A." Morris was neither a cotton planter nor from Natchez, Mississippi.

In addition to relying upon U.S. overseers, projects to introduce Carolina rice drew upon practices of colonial incarceration, particularly following Black emancipation in the United States.[26] These projects continued to occur in colonial India. On July 30, 1868, several barrels of U.S. rice seed were forwarded to the director of the Chengalpattu jail, located in the northern part of British India's Madras presidency, part of a plan for introducing Carolina rice to the region developed by the jail's superintendent, Dr. Thompson. Thompson's experiments were rooted in a belief that Carolina rice would be easily grown by a "great body of convicts" in the jail.[27] When free, Thompson believed former convicts would bring positive reports of Carolina rice to their villages and proliferate its growth. The jail was meant to be a node for introducing the cultivation of rice in villages across India based upon the decisions of once-jailed cultivators to continue to grow Carolina rice.

Thompson and other colonial administrators believed this model was generalizable in jails across India and could fundamentally transform rice cultivation. Some also believed such a project could be self-sustaining. For Thompson, a large-scale system for the introduction and proliferation of Carolina rice cultivation could also lessen the cost of colonial jails by forcing prisoners to grow their own food. Containment and the transformative effects of incarceration were intended in such perverse imaginations to reform smallholding cultivators into adapting Carolina rice through prisons.

Plans to introduce Carolina rice cultivation through jails were intended to transform the practices of prisoners and depended upon the fortification of jailing practices and simultaneously seizing control over the biological functions and social reproductive capacities of prisoners. The Chengalpattu jail would need to be expanded from 177 to 450 prisoners for such purposes. This jail expansion, Thompson calculated, would be funded through a single crop of Carolina rice. Thompson further sought to understand how control over the biological functions of prisoners would facilitate expanded rice cultivation, adding up the "average quantity" of human excrement that would be used to fertilize land. Despite both Thompson's recommendations and enthusiastic interest among colonial administrators, the plan was not generalized after a season of experimentation.

While the project to proliferate Carolina rice cultivation through the transformation of prisons and prisoners did not advance in 1868, Thompson's interest in introducing Carolina rice to the Madras presidency was part of the continued iteration of colonial agrarian projects that drew culturally and economically from the possibilities represented by U.S. settler slavery's position within global capitalism while at the same time unfolding according to market relations within colonial India that depended upon a different configuration of colonial space and the carcerally enforced disciplining of prisoners to a postincarceration life characterized by subordination to the demands of the global economy.

* * *

In his overview of slavery and the Atlantic slave trade, C. L. R. James noted that slavery triumphed through the "negative recognition" of enslaved people "in every work sphere" (James 1970, 151). For James, negative recognition characterized the impossibility of white acceptance that enslaved people could also be gifted artisans. The constitutive violences of slavery went far beyond work alone, a reality that makes the structuring violences of slavery unrecognizable (Hartman 2016). The negative recognition James outlines was part of a generalized antiblack hostility toward enslaved people that defined the nineteenth century with implications for capitalist social relations, characterized by the emergence of global capital through antiblackness.

In the U.S. South, social, cultural, and economic connections made through the world of rice cultivation created situations where U.S. slaveholders racially imagined differences between peasant smallholding cultivators and enslaved people. These imaginations produced contradictory conclusions about capitalist markets and were characterized by the state of "negative recognition" James described. One U.S. rice planter recalled the arrival of Bayles in the U.S., describing ways that the settler economy of rice cultivation seemed to emerge from thin air against a colonial imagination of India outside of history. As the planter wrote, "Here, then, was an embassage from the banks of the Ganges—a spot where rice has been cultivated probably for twenty centuries, to inquire into the method of cultivation and preparation of a people amongst whom the grain had no existence one hundred and sixty years ago" (Elliot 1851, 307). Such a racialized territorial imagination was ignorant of the "deep roots" (Fields-Black 2008) of rice cultivation through the African diaspora while also reproducing a settler slaveholder myth of North America as *terra nullius*. While projects to transform staples existed across colonial India, the ability to transform the British imperial economy through U.S. settler slavery exposed differences between expressions of colonial power in South Asia and the relations of power constitutive of U.S. settler slavery within the global economy. The antiblackness that dominated settler slavery in the United States was not reflected in the contradictions that structured colonial agrarian relations in South Asia, even as colonialism in South Asia had a racial character. The "negative recognition" of enslaved people within the growth of Carolina rice in the mid-nineteenth century, along with violent histories of dispossession that characterized settler slavery, made this reality unrecognizable for those who sought to transform the economy and remake themselves through Carolina rice. The global implications of antiblackness within projects to introduce Carolina rice are located in the Atlantic particularities of racial slavery, which introduced possibilities and imaginations for social, cultural, and economic transformations that extended far beyond the Black Atlantic. In projects to introduce Carolina rice, colonial visions for free market economic transformation within India were formed through, rather than removed from, plantation slavery in the United States, experimenting with carceral logics while at the same time dependent upon the exposure of smallholding peasant cultivators to the unmediated violence of the capitalist economy.

Notes

1   Tayler had been sold to Mobile for $1,900. He believed he could be repurchased for between $1,000 and $1,100.

2   In 1859, the largest single sale of enslaved people in the U.S. occurred when 436 enslaved people were sold by the rice and cotton planter Pierce Butler (Bailey 2017).

3   Louis D. de Saussure, 1852, "Gang of 25 Sea Island Cotton and Rice Negroes," Schomburg Center for Research in Black Culture, Manuscripts, Archives, and Rare Books Division, https://digitalcollections.nypl.org/items /510d47df-a25f-a3d9-e040-e00a18064a99.

4   Edward T. Heriot to Cousin, April 1854, Edward T. Heriot Papers, Rubenstein Library, Duke University.

5   "Notice of the Agricultural Society of South Carolina, on the Profits of the New Trade of Rough Rice," October 16, 1827, Minutes of the Agricultural Society of South Carolina, South Carolina Historical Society.

6   "Notice of the Agricultural Society of South Carolina, on the Profits of the New Trade of Rough Rice," October 16, 1827, Minutes of the Agricultural Society of South Carolina, South Carolina Historical Society.

7   Experiments with cultivation techniques from India, China, Egypt, and Spain also occurred within South Carolina. E.g., 1 October 1825, Minutes of the Agricultural Society of South Carolina, South Carolina Historical Society.

8   Thomas Naylor to William Lucas, October 9, 1823, Jonathan Lucas Papers, South Carolina Historical Society.

9   Elizabeth Blyth Papers, Rubenstein Library, Duke University.

10 Charles Pinckney, *An Address Delivered in Charleston before the Agricultural Society of South Carolina at Its Anniversary Meeting*, 9, 14–15, qtd. in Asaka 2017, 47.

11 R. Knight, "On the Cultivation of Carolina Paddy," General, August 1873, 9–14, State Archives of West Bengal (Kolkata).

12 The AHSI was based in Bengal and dedicated to agricultural improvement throughout India, especially through the introduction of new staples and cultivation techniques.

13 Deb 1836a. Deb made these observations within the context of cotton and tobacco cultivation. For his views on rice, see Deb (1836b).

14 On Bengal cultivation efforts, see AHSI (1842), 8, 12.

15 "Minutes, 18 October 1831," Agricultural Society of South Carolina, South Carolina Historical Society.

16 Cecil Beadon to James Hume, November 11, 1846, Minutes of the Agricultural and Horticultural Society of India, 1843–46, Agricultural and Horticultural Society of India (Kolkata).

17 Beadon to Hume, November 11, 1846.

18 Experimental Sowing of Carolina Paddy, 30 September 1874. Financial Department, Agriculture, Produce and Cultivation. State Archives of West Bengal.

19 "Successful Introduction of American Rice into the District of Purneah," *Transactions of the Agricultural and Horticultural Society of India, 1839 to 1842*, July 8, 1840, Library of the Agricultural and Horticultural Society of India (Kolkata).

20 T. Bayles to James Cosmo Melville, June 1, 1840, "Return of Papers in the Possession of the East India Company Showing Measures Taken since 1836 to Promote the Cultivation of Cotton," House of Commons Parliamentary Papers (1847) 42, 15, p. 19. Hereafter HCPP 42.

21 Bayles to Melville, June 1, 1840, 28.

22 James Morris to J. V. Hughes, No. 2 [December 22, 1841], HCPP 42, p. 329.

23 Urzee from Rangasamy Naick, September 13, 1842, "Rice Cultivation in Coimbatore," British Library, IOR/F/4/2025/91369(BL), http://www.bl.uk/manuscripts/FullDisplay.aspx?index=64&ref=IOR/F/4/2025/91369.

24 Videe Sen, *Mahazurnamah* (Memorandum), September 21, 1842. Coimbatore Rice. IOR/F/4/2025/91369 (BL). Available online at http://www.bl.uk/manuscripts/FullDisplay.aspx?ref=Ior/f/4/2025/91369.

25 James Morris to Brother, December 1842, James M. Morris Papers, South Caroliniana Library, Columbia, South Carolina.

26 Another project was explored at a jail at Ranchi.

27 Carolina Paddy, Bengal, General, P.N 171–73, Sept. 1869. (SAWB).

FLESH WORK AND THE REPRODUCTION

OF BLACK CULPABILITY

SARAH HALEY

Black feminist thought delineates the reproductive character of antiblackness. Kimberly Juanita Brown (2015), Angela Y. Davis (1971), Thavolia Glymph (2008), Sara Clarke Kaplan (2007), Saidiya Hartman (2016), Tera Hunter (1997), Jennifer Morgan (2004), Dorothy Roberts (1997), Christina Sharpe (2010, 2016), and Hortense Spillers (1984, 1987) are among the scholars whose interventions have demonstrated that Blackness and antiblackness are made and remade in the wombs and reproductive labors of Black women; their work elucidates the reproductive life of antiblackness under slavery and in its afterlife. Under the heavy influence of this tradition of Black feminist thought, this essay revisits histories under discussion in *No Mercy Here: Gender, Punishment, and the Making of Jim Crow Modernity* (Haley 2016), to further consider the relationship between reproduction and Black criminalization, conceptualizing social reproduction as central to the maintenance of the carceral regime; carceral social reproduction conscripts labor in the service of a social constituted by Black exclusion, dispossession, and violation. If the afterlife of slavery resides in "skewed life chances, limited access to health and education, premature death, incarceration, and impoverishment," the ongoing regime of carceral *partus sequitur ventrem* operates by positioning criminal culpability in the

Black womb and by compelling daily activity that reproduces captivity (Hartman 2007, 6).

A prison archipelago. This was the plan crafted by John T. Brown, the head of Georgia's prison system in 1875, to prepare for a class of Black prisoners who he believed would surely emerge from the ashes of emancipation in which Black women's maternal capacity lay buried; he argued that, deprived of maternal moral instruction, "these young vagrants will get out of their long shirts and into 'Georgia Stripes'" (Brown 1875, 12). He envisioned a carceral island plantation, located just off Savannah, for the production of "sea island cotton, rice and sugar cane." To Brown (1875, 12), the island was ideal because its "liquid walls" prevented escape, thereby easing the hardship of managing so-called convicts. Although the prison isle of maternal deviance never came to fruition in Georgia, the construed relationship between Black maternal abjection and carceral state building held.

As scholars including Angela Y. Davis, Dorothy Roberts, and Christina Sharpe have noted, the idea of Black women's inherent role as the re/producers of criminals has rationalized mass incarceration. Christina Sharpe argues that through the disfiguring of Black maternity, the Black womb has been turned into a factory "producing blackness as abjection much like the slave ship's hold and the prison" (2016, 74). As she writes, *The belly of the ship births blackness; the birth canal remains in, and as, the hold. The belly of the ship births blackness (as no/relation). . . . Birthing in the belly of the state: birthed in and as the body of the state"* (2016, 74). This project of disfiguring Black maternity as a mode of entrenching slavery and mass incarceration has been a consistent, performed, repeated process. This is historical continuity but, as Kimberly Juanita Brown and Avery Gordon gracefully argue, this is also the temporality of repetition and haunting; Brown identifies "the repetitive qualities of the black Atlantic that hover somewhere between the past and the present" (2015, 13), while Gordon illuminates the "endings that are not over" (1997, 195).

In 1900, Martha Vines found herself among the multitudes of Black mothers for whom slavery was an ending not yet over. In municipal court she was charged with cursing at several of her children; she was even accused of cursing at the child who was serving time in a convict lease camp, the state's castigation of her treatment of a child who daily faced battering and bruising and privation under its own command. Her case was the subject of a 1900 *Atlanta Constitution* article and graphic titled "Lively Scenes from the Police Matinee." The judge presiding over the case was certain that the charges were severe because "what Darktown can't stand must be intolerable enough."[1] Her status as a blighted mother of disorderly progeny was at the core of the judicial decision, according to the press account. After asking Vines to verify how many children she had, the judge chastised her for disturbing the neighborhood with her numerous "offspring." He advised her to send some of them to another locality before asking whether she knew the story of the old woman who lived in a shoe, and, in case she didn't, he recited it for her. "Here was an old woman who lived in a shoe. She had so many children she didn't know what to do. She gave them some broth without any bread, then whipped them all soundly and put them to bed." The judge again advised that she send some of her children away so that she could more easily deal with the others, the bonds of Black maternal affection either irrelevant, invisible, or impossible. Before she was taken to jail, the judge commented, "I really believe it would be worse punishment to send her back to her children."

Black women's perceived excessive reproduction of nefarious Black children was a divergence from their primary function, maintaining the white domestic sphere. The *Constitution* captioned the article's accompanying cartoon with a revision of the nursery rhyme: "There was an old woman who lived in a stew; and cussed her young brats till she made the air blue; she was so very wroth and they so badly bred; that the fussy old woman to the chaingang was led."[2] This depiction, which centers Black women's reproductive labor as the source of criminality, a source so powerful as to be atmospheric, exemplifies carceral social reproduction's role in the toxic ecology of antiblackness.[3]

In the foreground of the illustration was a depiction of Martha Vines whipping her daughter, a girl who represented the dangerous class who would be created by Vines's maternal iniquity and who, presumably, would then go on to reproduce a subsequent generation of Black vagrants. The judge fined Vines $5.75 and was impervious to her complaint that she didn't have a cent. The Jim Crow carceral state enforced one of the most consistently stable presumptions of American history, mobilized continuously for the justification of draconian racial institutions—that Black women's inherent deviance reproduces (and thereby produces) Black cultural pathology, necessitating legal and extralegal control.

Importantly, the nineteenth century reveals a long history of associations between Black maternal turpitude and the necessity of captivity in discourses of liberal reform. In her foundational 1901 book *Experimental Sociology*, sociologist and progressive reformer Frances Kellor recounted her observation of a Black woman who dwelled in a "cell of infanticide"

(106); According to Kellor, the woman had been convicted of infanticide, and during her imprisonment a "strange desire for dolls possessed her." The unnamed woman of Kellor's narrative had been convicted of killing her child and was now, as she described it, holed up in a prison cell, refusing any social contact; when she was not working, she spent her time making, playing with, and caring for dolls in her cell. An illustration of the woman was published in the *Chicago Tribune* in 1900. Black maternal social reproduction is here rendered by Kellor, a foundational figure in the American progressive social work movement and Chicago school of sociology, a thing of insanity or fantasy and existing only in the space of captivity.[4] Black maternal iniquity and naturalized captivity here ground one of the founding texts of social work—the field established to address the question of the social.

The gendered afterlife of slavery as Black criminal culpability is characterized by the continued unfolding of what Stephanie Smallwood, Jennifer Morgan, and Christina Sharpe have discussed as the disfiguring of Black maternity (Morgan, Sharpe, and Smallwood 2017). The condition of the criminal follows that of the mother, culpability brought forth from the womb of Black women. While judges, reformers, journalists, and prison administrators portrayed Black criminality as a process of Black biological and social reproduction, the carceral social regime was actually being socially reproduced by the forced labor of imprisoned Black women; their unremunerated work compelled by the waged brutality of prison guards. Social reproduction designates activity primarily carried out by women to sustain the production of the waged worker, rendered invisible by its primary location in the domestic sphere, its lack of compensation, and the general naturalization of capitalist economic relations from the nineteenth century onward; Marxist feminists encourage a recognition of such labor as the condition of possibility for most forms of capitalist accumulation and urge an attendant reconceptualization of the political, economic, and social that accounts for the material realities and relations of power contained in the realm of reproductive labor (Dalla Costa 1972; Davis 1981; Federici 2004; James, 2012). This essay questions the character of the daily activities coerced and performed by white historical actors that make and sustain conditions of Black captivity. The carceral, presented as a natural fact of modern political and social life, has required and continues to depend upon the reproductive labor of antiblackness.

Black women's reproductive labor was both criminalized and coerced for the fortification of nineteenth-century carceral capitalism. Black

SARAH HALEY

women who worked as cooks, laundresses, and caregivers were accused of theft for using the materials in white homes for their own subsistence; they were convicted of stealing employers' clothes they were in the midst of washing and sentenced to months of hard labor for using such things as a plate or chair for their own meals; in a city without an adequate sewage system, they were sent to municipal chain gangs for dumping dirty water from their homes.[5] Meant to reproduce white life at the detriment of their own, social reproduction was both Black women's core economic function in the industrializing Southern economy and the source of their obliteration. Such enforcement of criminal law deemed Black women's own social reproduction as theft, placing them in a unique position as responsible for the social reproduction of whiteness and white economic stability, charged disproportionately with and maligned for the reproduction of Black life and labor, and outlaws in their own self-preservation.

Such sentences meant months or a year in Southern convict lease camps or chain gangs where guards performed socially reproductive violence to entrench the carceral social. From the 1870s through 1906, criminalized Black women in Georgia worked in convict lease camps where they laid railroad lines, made brick, cut trees, and performed grueling agricultural labor under conditions of rampant medical neglect and disease, and under the force of the whip and the persistent daily terror of rape; in the second and third decades of the century, they were sentenced to chain gangs where they constructed county roads under similar circumstances (Haley 2016; LeFlouria 2015). Convicted in municipal court of public-order crimes such as cursing in the company of a white woman, they were forced to break rocks in city streets. In the 1880s and 1890s, Black women in Atlanta were between five and six times more likely than white women to be arrested and were far more likely to be sentenced to convict labor than their white counterparts (Fulton County 1871–86). Statewide, between 1870 and 1900 there were never more than ten white women in Georgia's felony and misdemeanor convict camps combined, that is, in the entire state prison system; the numbers for Black women ranged between 129 and 345, and they constituted between 5 and 10 percent of the overall prisoner population. From 1908 until 1936, approximately two thousand Black women were sent to chain gang camps in comparison to four white women (Haley 2016).

As a consequence of convictions for charges often related to social reproduction, they were made to socially reproduce the carceral state—an essential function. In every convict labor camp in Georgia, at least one

Black woman was assigned to captivity-sustaining labor under the threat of the gun, the bloodhound, the lash, and the sexual entitlements of white prison guards. Cooking, cleaning, and mending for the entire prison labor force was their work, performed before, after, and in addition to the other labor required of all prisoners. "Apportioned Promiscuously" throughout the convict lease system to serve as cooks and washerwomen, imprisoned Black women were required to wake up in the middle of the night to cook and then distribute food for a prison population of up to 150 (Principal Keeper, 1874, 9–10). Pearl Black was one of the few women in the Sumter convict camp in 1908, having been sentenced to a year of hard labor for adultery. She was pregnant when she was arrested and was still "on her feet cooking" until at least a month before she was due, despite complaining to prison camp officials that she was suffering great pain.[6]

This was a specific form of reproductive labor—the forced work of calibrating human ephemera for the marginal/temporary reproduction of Black life: imprisoned women were tasked with preserving their own bodies and those of their captive counterparts only to the extent and only for so long as the necessary labor could be extracted from them. Priced for expiration, once their bodies were so damaged that they were no longer usable, convict industrialists were able to replace them for a nominal cost (Mancini 1996). In slavery's afterlife, Black women were forced to manage intensified Black fungibility through basic provision. But imprisoned women were impelled to the cooking, cleaning, and mending tasks of carceral social reproduction, by socially reproductive assault. That is to say, the daily activity of force required to compel the labor of basic human need provision is also part of the work of carceral social reproduction. If, as Marxist feminists argue, capitalism derives its power, in part, through the erasure of social reproduction as a critical element of capitalism, recognizing the role of socially reproductive violence in establishing and reestablishing the social life of antiblackness and its attendant regimes of captivity is also imperative.

The ledgers tell the story. The 1885 Old Town Camp whipping reports show that women routinely received thirteen lashes for idleness, slowing down, and other work performance infractions; in 1909, the Southern Lumber Company's ledger cites the imposition of six lashes for Black women's disobedience; other women were whipped for "being filthy about cooking."[7] Hospital ledgers and annual prison reports documenting sickness and pregnancy reveal that sexual access to Black women was disbursed as an entitlement and benefit to prison guards; at one camp, 30 percent of women gave birth to children fathered by prison guards; at other camps, women had

SARAH HALEY

multiple children as the result of sexual assault by guards.[8] Women who made and remade the convict camp as a space of capitalist productivity and Black liminal life for both Black women and men did so under terroristic coercion; both this specific force and the labor it compelled was central to the project of Southern capitalism, as each of the convict-leasing industries was critical to urban and regional modernization.

In at least one convict camp, Black women were forced to reproduce both white social life and Black detention. The first all-female convict camp was built in Atlanta in 1885, for women convicted of both municipal and state crimes. This camp was located on the property for Fulton County's brand-new almshouse for paupers and the elderly. Prior to 1885, the almshouse was deemed inadequate and uncomfortable.[9] The Fulton County grand jury recommended that the facility be moved closer to the city and that a "brick building [be] erected capable of more accommodations and conveniences for the better care and attention to the unfortunate poor and helpless of our county." The city's captive Black female labor force weathered the heat with little shelter and made the brick so that the county poor could be transferred from "rude hovels" to a brand-new building that would keep out the cold. The superintendent of the almshouse and female convict camp verified that all of the bricks used in the almshouse construction were made by imprisoned women; eighteen women were so employed, assisted by five men and two brick molders.[10] Women who had been convicted in city court for crimes related to their economic precarity were forced to build and serve, constructing the infrastructure for their future captivity while attending the needs of indigent white women and men in a new building that would be the pride of progressive reform.

Like the men and women who labored for the Chattahoochee Brick Company, the women who made the almshouse brick had to shovel wet clay and transport it back to a plant. There they had to push the clay through rectangular molds, then fire the bricks in coal kilns, where one or more of the brick makers would have to stand near the kiln, enduring the blistering heat in order to toss batches of bricks into the top of a large oven. The predominantly female crew made forty thousand bricks in Georgia's summer heat in 1884. They were forced to rush to complete the job before winter interfered with the construction of the new facility. During their sentences, which ranged from six to twelve months, they were required to perform domestic and agricultural labor, cooking and cleaning for the residents of the almshouse, farming, and planting cotton. In 1885 they produced hundreds of bushels of corn, potatoes, peas, and onions, and 2,400 pounds of meat—provisions for the almshouse residents. As if that was not work enough, they were also assigned to grade the roads surrounding the almshouse. By 1897, several other counties, including Chatham, Laurens, Glynn, and Richmond, had county or almshouse farms that worked female misdemeanor prisoners, while some women convicted of misdemeanors in these and other counties were sent to all-female camps where servitude meant serving, farming, and industrial labor for the development of gendered racial capitalism.[11]

This work of maintaining the camp and the labor of enforcing this work is activity that constitutes a form of perverse social reproduction, activity that maintains the barest life not for long-term sustenance, but for the maintenance and naturalization of the category of Black prisoner and the maintenance of a system of captivity that extracted industrial and agricultural labor to the point of human expiration. If the reproduction of the worker has been the domain of the domestic and a central domain of women's unremunerated labor for the production of labor power, reproductive labor has similarly been critical to the persistence of carceral power. Marxist feminism has sharpened understandings of how, with the development of industrial capitalism, the "reproduction of labor-power carried out in the home and its function in the accumulation of capital became invisible" and feminized (Federici 2004, 75). Yet the character of Black women's forced reproduction represents a distinct positionality produced by particularized violence and the predicament of laboring at the nexus of invisibility and elimination. As Saidiya Hartman argues, "It has proven difficult, if not impossible, to assimilate black women's domestic labors and reproductive capacities within narratives of the black worker, slave rebellion, maroonage, or black radicalism, even as this labor was critical to the creation of value, the realization of profit and the accumulation of capital" (2016, 167). The reconciliation of Black women's labor within the domain of women's work has proven similarly challenging. She is tasked with the daily activity of what might be called flesh reproduction, the simultaneous reproduction of the Black worker and the figure of the Black criminal, both fungible and subject to bodily disintegration, under the specific conditions of perennial criminalization, familial estrangement, sexual violation, and potential death.[12]

The belly of the ship births Blackness (as no/relation). This relation of socially reproductive labor to the carceral regime, more than the use of prison labor for private corporations, is the facet of nineteenth-century convict labor that is most prototypical and enduring. The system that has

SARAH HALEY

and continues to depend upon socially reproductive and disproportionately Black labor severs the relationship between many Black women and
their children. As Dorothy Roberts notes, "one-third of women in prison
are black; one third of children in foster care are black and most have been
removed from black mothers who are their primary caretakers"; she calls
this statistical overlap "evidence of a form of punitive governance that perpetuates social inequality" (Roberts 2011, 1477). Through the imposition
of deadlines for determining and securing parental rights that incarcerated
parents often cannot meet, the obstacles to financial stability that incarceration imposes, and the decline and denial of public benefits, the loss of
parental rights for imprisoned women is often permanent (Roberts 2011,
1480–81). The carceral state, then, represents the theft and redistribution
of the means of Black social reproduction—the denial of Black parental
affective and material reproductive capacity in kinship networks and the
reallocation of such emotional and physical resources to the carceral state
itself.

This dynamic was recognized by men at Folsom Prison who issued a
manifesto in 1970 with demands for scale wages, union rights, and the
right to "support their own families" since "at present thousands of welfare
recipients have to divide their checks to support their imprisoned relatives
who without the outside support could not even buy toilet articles or food.
Men working on scale wages could support themselves and families while
in prison" (Davis 1971a, 58–60). These represent only a few of the thirty
demands of a brilliant manifesto that explicates how captivity doubly bur-
dens Black social life and reproduction by extracting resources from those
on the outside and depriving those inside of the capacity to help sustain
the lives of loved ones left behind; men at Folsom also requested adequate
family visitation time and facilities and sentencing limits to ameliorate the
inherent violence of estrangement that caging imposes and which could
not be addressed by the wage.

Influential prison abolitionists including Ruth Wilson Gilmore, Craig
Gilmore, and James Kilgore have emphasized the fact that most work
performed by imprisoned women and men takes place in public rather
than private prisons and consists of maintaining the prison itself rather
than labor for private industry or commodity production (R. W. Gilmore
2015, 2019; C. Gilmore 2019; Kilgore 2015). The prison abolition organization Critical Resistance has called this the housework of prisons. The
vast majority of imprisoned women and men work "regular prison jobs,"
that is, the work of maintaining captivity itself: food service, maintenance,

laundry, and so on. In Georgia, Arkansas, Alabama, and Texas imprisoned women and men earn exactly $0 for this work (Sawyer 2017). In 2010, prisoners across the state withheld the socially reproductive labor that is the basis for the accumulation of carceral capital; such capital resides in the finance-backed expansion of the prison population and attendant expansion of prisons themselves (see Gilmore 2007). They demanded a wage, better nutrition, and educational programs before they would resume reproducing the prison, and in response authorities violently denied the means of their subsistence, shutting off heat and hot water (Hing 2010); the standoff elucidated the inherent tensions in the carceral regime's dependency on limited social reproduction and weaponizing of the means of social reproduction in defense of itself. Popular discussions of the Georgia strike (and prison strikes after 1971 in general) place them in genealogical relation to the Attica rebellion and generally describe the predicament of imprisonment as a continuation of slavery. The afterlife of slavery in the carceral present is animated by the specificities of ungendering—that is, slavery's inauguration of the forced social reproduction of white life and capital by Black women cast out of normative gender; the carceral formation of gendered racial capitalism has been executed through the rendering of Black female bodies as flesh, or perhaps socially reproductive and ideologically productive flesh workers. This economic arrangement, inaugurated under slavery and continued in nineteenth-century carceral industrialism through predominantly Black female labor, now persists in the current incarnation of late carceral capitalism, in which economic value derives from captivity itself rather than the production of goods.

As racial capitalism has proceeded through the alternate specificity and fungibility of racialized gender, it is not altogether surprising that what began as a system conscripting Black bodies excised from the category "woman" but forced to perform specific forms of labor and subject to particularized sexual violence is now disproportionately performed by captive Black male workers and a disproportionately Black queer and trans labor force.[13] Slavery haunts the carceral contemporary, both requiring and enshrining racialized gender.[14]

Forced to make and serve undesirable food with inadequate nutritional content, imprisoned people then must use the wages of their reproductive labor to purchase food and other basic necessities such as hygiene supplies, nonprescription medical supplies, and household goods in prison commissaries. Less often, but significantly, some prisoners perform the work of physically maintaining (or, one might say, saving) the home. For decades, imprisoned women and men in California have contended with the domestic disaster of blazing wildfires; the prison fire camp program pays imprisoned firefighters less than $2 per day and saves the state $100 million (Vasquez 2018). State violence continues to be the waged force behind this compulsory heroicism. This makes a recognition of the long history of Black women's performance of this labor all the more urgent in apprehending antiblackness and the specific continuities in conditions experienced by incarcerated people, 40 percent of whom are Black (Sawyer and Wagner 2019). The invisibilization of this work naturalizes the prison as a self-perpetuating social institution. This naturalization in turn isolates imprisoned people from the realm of concern for those analysts and activists who focus on late capitalist forms of immaterial and affective labor. Under antiblackness as a gendered regime of economic, social, and epistemological power, Black women have long been tethered to service and immaterial and affective labor and have also been interpolated in the normalization of Black captivity, seen as both producing and reproducing the criminalized. Importantly, the flesh work that Black women have historically performed represents a template for a mass system of captivity in which men and nonblack prisoners are currently bound to work.

Carceral capitalism is grounded in and reliant upon daily activity that reproduces the injured and caged life upon which the carceral state accumulates value. Notably, as in previous incarnations of prison history, this is the reproduction of ephemeral rather than sustained life; each year in prison reduces a person's life expectancy by two years (Widra 2017). The managers of that labor are also engaging in activity that reproduces a social world structured in antiblackness broadly and racial capitalism specifically. Routinely erased and effaced, the carceral state has long been entrenched through a gendered regime of antiblack social reproduction and continues to be haunted by the historical life of Pearl Black.

Notes

1   "Lively Scenes from the Police Matinee," *Atlanta Constitution*, August 29, 1900, 5.
2   "Lively Scenes from the Police Matinee," *Atlanta Constitution*, August 29, 1900, 5.
3   On antiblackness as weather, see Sharpe (2016).

4   On Kellor as a leader in social work, sociological theory, and progressive reform, see Allison D. Murdach (2008), Fitzpatrick (1990), and Lengermann and Niebrugge (1998).

5   Susan Conyers, clemency petition, 1894, Applications for Clemency 1858–1942, Convict and Fugitive Papers, Record Group 1-4-42, Georgia Archives, Morrow, Georgia; Fulton County Recorder's Court Dockets, 1871, 1872, 1878, 1879, 1885, 1886, uncatalogued, Atlanta History Center.

6   Pearl Black, clemency petition, Applications for Clemency 1858–1942, Convict and Fugitive Papers, Record Group 1-4-42, Georgia Archives, Morrow, Georgia.

7   Punishment Reports of individual camps, 1885–1908, Corporal Punishment Monthly Reports (Whipping Reports), 1884–89, Record Group 21-1-11, Georgia Archives, Morrow, Georgia RG Record Group (GAA).

8   Anonymous, "The Life Story of a Negro Peon, Obtained from an Interview with a Georgia Negro," in *The Life Stories of Undistinguished Americans, as Told by Themselves*, edited by Hamilton Holt (New York: James Pott, 1906), reprinted in Gerda Lerner, ed., *Black Women in White America: A Documentary History*, 150–55 (New York: Vintage, 1972).

9   "Grand Jury Presentment," *Atlanta Constitution*, May 3, 1882, 5.

10 R. L. Hope, "A Glimpse into the Life of Fulton County's Poor," *Atlanta Constitution*, January 6, 1895, 11.

11 "The County Almshouse," *Atlanta Constitution*, August 28, 1884, 7.

12 On flesh, see Hortense J. Spillers's (1987) transformational theory in "Mama's Baby, Papa's Maybe: An American Grammar Book."

13 In a national study of juvenile detention facilities, 40 percent of incarcerated girls and 14 percent of incarcerated boys identified as LGBT; also, 85–90 percent of incarcerated LGBT youth are youth of color (Movement Advancement Project, Center for American Progress, and Youth First 2017). One in two Black transgender people has been to prison sometime in their lives (Lambda Legal 2012). As of 2014, 9 percent of Black transgender women were incarcerated in the previous year, ten times the rate in the general population (National Center for Transgender Equality 2018).

14 This formulation is drawn from Ruth Wilson Gilmore's (2015) argument that "capitalism requires inequality and racism enshrines it."

"NOT TO BE SLAVES OF OTHERS": ANTIBLACKNESS IN PRECOLONIAL KOREA

JAE KYUN KIM AND MOON-KIE JUNG

At a photo op in 2015, the delivery of heating coal to the poor in Seoul, the chair of South Korea's ruling Saenuri Party made a racist joke at the expense of one of the volunteers: "Your face color is the same as the briquettes' color." Leading the presidential polls at the time, Kim Moo-sung was addressing a Nigerian national, one of some forty exchange students from twenty-seven countries taking part in the event. A social media backlash and a quick apology ensued, and public interest dissipated (Bahk 2015; "S. Korean Presidential Frontrunner" 2015; Yoon 2015).

In a different but related register, North Korea had also attracted international attention, and an uncommonly public denouncement from Washington, the year before. In the immediate wake of President Barack Obama's visit to South Korea, the Korean Central News Agency published a pair of articles that Caitlin Hayden, the spokesperson for the White House National Security Council, reproved as "particularly ugly and disrespectful." In the English-language version, the state organ of North Korea referred to Obama as "a wicked black monkey" and "a crossbreed with unclear blood." The Korean-language edition elaborated in even less restrained rhetoric. Nevertheless, in its analysis of the rant, the *Washington*

Post somehow found "some clear contradictions in North Korea's stereotyping," noting that "the North maintains active ties with several African countries and just signed a cooperation agreement with Nigeria" (Fish 2014; Harlan and Goldfarb 2014; "North Korea Media" 2014; Saul 2014).

The differences between the two episodes are telling, if unsurprising: offhanded remark versus deliberate agitation; prompt public regret versus unapologetic defiance; anticommunist governing party of a democratic state versus communist single party of a totalitarian state. In this chapter, we focus on a rarely noticed, underlying parallel and examine its origin. Even a casual perusal of the internet or, increasingly, academic writings would show that Kim's remark is hardly a rare expression of antiblackness in contemporary South Korea. To a lesser degree of transparency and certainty, the same goes for North Korea; it is revealing that the North Korean state assumed its diatribe would be intelligible to and would resonate with its populace. Is there a common genealogy to the two Koreas' antiblackness? Given that there are very few Nigerians or other Black people in either Korea, how do we make sense of this manifest antiblackness?

The prevailing answers to questions of race in Korea point to the recent influx of migrant workers, the postwar influence of the U.S. military and mass media, or Japanese colonialism. We do not dispute their partial value. However, the current literature does not go back far enough, and it does not address the persistent antiblackness. In this chapter, we argue that the construction of imagined racial inferiors, including foremost people of African descent, centrally shaped Korean identity formation, tracing it to and focusing on the precolonial era. First, with the concept of the *colonially vulnerable*, we call attention to the positions and outlooks of peoples and states that were susceptible to foreign rule in the age of empire, the late nineteenth and early twentieth centuries. Second, drawing on the crucial insights of W. E. B. Du Bois and James Baldwin, we explain the overlooked but insistent presence of Black people, as well as American Indians and other Indigenous peoples, in precolonial Koreans' racial discourse: imagining their racial inferiors fundamentally shaped how Koreans took in and took on the treacherous modern world. Third, the subsequent empirical sections of the chapter illustrate our argument for three precolonial periods leading up to Japanese annexation. Our evidentiary base is a comprehensive survey of Korean newspapers, "unrivaled" as "a medium for producing national knowledge" in general and in precolonial and colonial Korea in particular (Schmid 2002, 6).[1] Finally, peeking into the colonial era and beyond, we conclude with a racial analysis of the Declaration of Independence of 1919.

Antiblackness of the Colonially Vulnerable in the Age of Empire

Until around the turn of the present century, to characterize race as a marginal topic in the sociology and history of Korea would still have been an overstatement (Eckert et al. 1990; J. Kim 2015; M. Shin 2003). The notion that Koreans as a people were and have always been homogeneous was so widely and unquestioningly accepted as to render race seemingly invisible and immaterial. In South Korea, an influx of foreign laborers and brides in the past few decades, along with a dramatic decline in "Korean" birth rates, unsettled this state of affairs. From 1990 to 2015, the number of foreign-born persons rose from fewer than 50,000 to nearly two million and is projected to constitute 10 percent of the population by 2030 (Moon 2015, 2–3).

Discriminatory practices and negative attitudes toward the migrants—most of whom hail from Asia, particularly Southeast Asia, and work in the 3D (dirty, dangerous, difficult) industries—have increasingly drawn the attention of the news media, human rights organizations, and academics (Ahn 2013; Amnesty International 2009; Kang 2009; A. Kim 2009; S. Kim 2012; Y. Lee 2009; Moon 2015; Poon 2016; J. Shin 2009; G. Shin 2013; I. Watson 2012). The explanation, both lay and scholarly, for South Koreans' manifest racism has centered on what had previously been taken for granted—Koreans' deep sense of racial homogeneity and distinctiveness—and its clash with the new multiracial reality. The more sophisticated versions recognized the self-perception of racial purity not as a veridical reflection of a millennia-old historical fact but a fairly recent invention born of anticolonial and postcolonial nationalism.

The conventional wisdom possesses a measure of cogency, but the puzzle of antiblackness remains. For instance, why would a survey of South Korean college students find that they are most biased against Black people as well as Southeast Asians and at comparable levels (as cited in Kang 2009; G. Shin 2013)? Racism against Southeast Asians may track their increased presence in South Korea, but with no similar growth in numbers or concentration in low-status positions, how do we make sense of the high levels of antagonism toward Black people (Han 2015; Kang 2009; N. Kim 2008; B. Park 2010; G. Shin 2013)? Again, the dominant ideology of racial homogeneity may play a significant role, but if it is engendering a general nativism, it cannot explain why Koreans hold whites, also seen as foreign, in much higher regard than Black people, in fact even higher than Koreans themselves. As Bang Hee-jung, the principal investigator of the survey study, concludes, "While [Koreans] feel superior to black people and Southeast Asians, they feel inferior to Caucasians" (as quoted in Kang 2009; see also Han 2015; N. Kim 2008; G. Shin 2013). Some scholars attribute South Koreans' antipathy toward Black people to the powerful postwar influence of the U.S. military and mass media (N. Kim 2008, 2015; Moon 1997). This explanation certainly obtains but begs the question of why South Koreans, from the moment U.S. soldiers began landing in 1945 or Hollywood movies commenced entertaining the masses, were so readily able and willing to receive and reproduce such an apparently alien worldview. And if North Koreans are similarly disposed against Black people, and no less sure of Koreans' racial purity, as they appear to be, the explanation there could not be the hegemonic sway of the United States (Hitchens 2010; Myers 2010; G. Shin 2006, 2013; Young 2013, 2015).

We trace Koreans' construction of their imagined racial inferiors, including people of African descent but also American Indians and other Indigenous peoples, to the precolonial era. In his study of the German overseas empire, George Steinmetz (2003, 2007, 2008), following Edward Said (1978) and others, alerts us to the importance of precolonial discourse of the colonizer-to-be in shaping the colonial state's subsequent "native policy." In other words, he argues that how the colonizer had conceived of and described the colonized before colonization pivotally influenced how the colonizer would later rule the colonized, "ranging from genocide to efforts to 'salvage' precolonial cultures" (Steinmetz 2008, 589; see also Goh 2007; Lowe 1986).

The colonized are not looked upon as passive victims, in this view, but their agency is seen narrowly through the lens of reaction to colonial domination: "responses by the colonized, including resistance, collaboration, and everything in between" (Steinmetz 2007, 2). We expand the scope of the agency of the colonized or, more accurately and less teleologically, the colonially vulnerable. We conceptualize it as more than reactive, as preexisting colonization (if it were to pass), and in relation not only to would-be colonizers but also other colonially vulnerable, colonized, and otherwise oppressed peoples around the world.

Eric Hobsbawm refers to the period from the last quarter of the nineteenth century through World War I as "the age of empire." Symptomatically, the sheer number of heads of states referring to themselves as "emperors," and being recognized as such, hit its peak then; the monarch Gojong was a part of this global trend, declaring Korea to be an empire (Daehanjeguk, 大韓帝國) and himself the emperor in 1897. More meaningfully, colonial empires engulfed the globe, as "most of the world outside Europe and the Americas was formally partitioned into territories under the formal rule or informal political domination of one or other of a handful of states" (Hobsbawm 1989, 56–57). Reaching colonial saturation, the age of empire was a profoundly different world than the so-called age of discovery. More likely than not, the *colonially vulnerable*, peoples and states susceptible to loss of sovereignty to foreign states, were consciously aware of their precarious condition and strove to make sense of and make their way in the perilous world.

For all concerned, race was central. Here, W. E. B. Du Bois proved peerlessly perceptive and prescient. As we all know, he proclaimed famously that "the problem of the twentieth century is the problem of the colorline." Less known, this color line did not stop at the borders of the United States. It signified nothing less than "the relation of the darker to the lighter races . . . in Asia and Africa, in America and the islands of the sea" ([1903] 1965, 221). Writing in the age of empire, Du Bois understood in real time what is now belatedly being acknowledged—and too often being misrecognized as newfound and cutting-edge: "the color line belts the world" ([1900] 1996, 48; [1906] 2005, 33).

The historical study of East Asia long appeared to be exceptionally inhospitable and resistant to serious analysis of race, but since the 1990s, it has gained traction.[2] An early proponent, Frank Dikötter argued, "the importance of racialised identities in East Asia has so far been deliberately ignored. However, far from being a negligible aspect of the contemporary identities, racialised senses of belonging have often been the very foundation of national identity in East Asia in the twentieth century" (1997b, 1–2). No exception, recent historiography has firmly established the centrality of race to Korean identity formation and sovereignty struggles, from the late nineteenth century onward (Em 2013; Pai 2000; N. Pak 2001; S. Pak 2003; Schmid 2002; G. Shin 2005, 2006, 2013; Tikhonov 2010, 2013; J. Watson 2007).

We accept the broad arc of the prevailing narrative. From Korea's perspective, the late nineteenth century in East Asia was a time of tumult: encroaching West, waning China, strengthening Japan. Rising to influence in the 1880s, reformers continually tried to map out Korea's survival as a

sovereign state in this new world through the overlapping racialized discourses of enlightenment (*gaehwa*), civilization (*munmyeong*), and social
Darwinism. With Japan's imperialist intentions toward Korea made unequivocally clear by 1905, a pan–East Asian racial outlook gave way to one
that asserted Koreans' racial distinctiveness, derived from a common pri-
mordial origin and purity of blood. Further developing and evolving during
and after Japanese colonialism, variations of this racialized nationalism
have been dominant among Koreans, in both the North and the South.

That race was crucial to Koreans' precolonial, as well as colonial and
postcolonial, history is no longer controversial. What lingers, however, is
the implicit and explicit assumption that Koreans' *racial* nationalism was
"originally an anti-imperialist and anti-colonial ideology" that is only now,
confronting a novel multiracial reality, finding *racist* expression (G. Shin
2013, 371). In this chapter, focusing on the precolonial era, we argue that
racism, in the form of imagining racial inferiors, has, at least since the
late nineteenth century, been vital to Koreans' sense of themselves and
their place in the modern world. Alongside Koreans' preoccupation with
whites, Japanese, and Chinese, we find incessant fixation on African Americans and other Black peoples and on American Indians and other Indigenous peoples, whom Koreans have consistently believed to be inferior to
themselves.

To explain the persistent presence of Black and Indigenous peoples
in the Korean imaginary, despite their physical absence in Korea, we return
to Du Bois, the preeminent contemporary theorist of the age of empire,
and turn to the passage in *The Philadelphia Negro* discussed in the present
volume's introduction:

> And still this widening of the idea of common Humanity is of slow growth
> and today but dimly realized. We grant full citizenship in the World-
> Commonwealth to the "Anglo-Saxon" (whatever that may mean), the Teuton
> and the Latin; then with just a shade of reluctance we extend it to the Celt
> and Slav. We half deny it to the yellow races of Asia, admit the brown Indi-
> ans to an ante-room only on the strength of an undeniable past; but with
> the Negroes of Africa we come to a full stop, and in its heart the civilized
> world with one accord denies that these come within the pale of nineteenth
> century Humanity. (Du Bois [1899] 1996, 386–87)

This was the world Koreans, and other colonially vulnerable peoples
and states, navigated at the twilight of the nineteenth century and the
dawn of the twentieth. For Humanity, the "civilized world," the polestar

JAE KYUN KIM AND MOON-KIE JUNG

by which it charted and policed its boundaries in an absolute, "full stop" sense was antiblackness, the unconditional exclusion of "the Negroes of Africa." Less unconditionally, the exclusion of "the brown Indians." Even less unconditionally still, the exclusion of "the yellow races."

Writing much later, and hence underscoring the idea's durable and disheartening validity, James Baldwin similarly described the core significance of antiblackness, which he also frequently related to anti-Native racism in his writings, in ordering the world:

> Try to imagine how you would feel if you woke up one morning to find the sun shining and all the stars aflame. You would be frightened because it is out of the order of nature. Any upheaval in the universe is terrifying because it so profoundly attacks one's sense of one's own reality. Well, the black man has functioned in the white man's world as a fixed star, as an immovable pillar: and as he moves out of his place, heaven and earth are shaken to their foundations. (1962, 20)

For the colonially vulnerable Koreans, a variation of the same racial logic held. They could admit their partial denial from, and partial acceptance into, "civilization," and they could aspire to fuller acceptance and despair at setbacks, all without collapsing into existential chaos. Their imagined status relative to whites, Japanese, and Chinese could be and was in dynamic play. What stood still was their abiding belief in the racial inferiority of Black people and American Indians, the imagined fates of whom Koreans loathed, feared, and had to avert, and as the impending doom of colonialism neared, the specter of Black enslavement, above all, haunted their imagination. In this nontrivial sense, antiblackness has been the fundament, the bottommost bedrock, of Korean identity formation, one that lives on.

Facing the Age of Empire

Although Western battleships started to appear off Korean shores in the 1850s, the outcome of the Second Opium War in 1860 made palpable the likelihood of China's decline and the West's encroachment, which was reinforced by the advancing presence of Russia at Korea's northern border the same year. In response, Korea, under continuous rule of the Joseon dynasty since 1392, enforced a policy of seclusion. Though fighting off France and the United States in 1866 and 1871, respectively, Korea gave in to the mounting pressure and signed treaties with various empires, beginning with Japan in 1876, followed by a number of Western states and China. With the opening came "Western ideologies and thought such as the theories of civilization and enlightenment [munmyeong gaehwa], social Darwinism, nationalism, and liberalism . . . (often through Japan)," according to Gi-Wook Shin (2006, 25). The literal name in Korean for the bloody 1871 war with the United States, Sinmiyangyo or Barbarian Incursion, hinted at both a certain syncretic compatibility of the new ideas with the preexisting Sinocentric schema of civilization/barbarity and the revisions to come (Chang 2003, 1332).

In the 1880s, the major task at hand for Korean elites was the invention and advancement of the "nation" through "foreign," or Western, ideas and technology (Yi 1969). Reasoning that gaehwa could not be successful without enlightening the masses, the reform leaders of the Gaehwa Party, or Gaehwapa, determined that the newspaper was the most powerful means of reaching them, following Japan's example. With continuing efforts from gaehwa leaders, the Office of Culture and Information (Bangmunguk) published the first modern Korean newspaper, *Hanseongsunbo*, in 1883. The only formal channel available to Koreans to learn about the unfamiliar world beyond their borders, it communicated the importance of distant and novel ideas and events. Not surprisingly, *Hanseongsunbo* was the first to introduce the concept of race to the Korean public, in an 1883 article titled "Speaking of Continents and Oceans":

> Speaking of race, there are approximately three: yellow, white, and brown. Since human beings' appearance and physique vary by locations, however, race is further divided into five kinds—first, Mongol race, so-called yellow race; second, Caucasus race, so-called white race; third, Ethiopia race, so-called black race; fourth, Malay race, so-called brown race; fifth, American race, so-called copper-colored race. . . . In the case of Asia, China, Japan, Joseon, and Siberia fall into yellows; India and Arabia fall into whites; East India Islands fall into browns. This is because the kinds of species are already different, and thus their colors are different, although different foods and climates are also aspects of the difference. As time changes and [different races] marry each other, the races are gradually mixed. Therefore, nowadays, it is difficult to distinguish which people belong to which color race.[3]

As with other Western ideologies noted by G. Shin (2006), ideas about race made their way to Korea via Japanese, as well as Chinese, sources and influences. Although all of its editors and reporters were Korean,

JAE KYUN KIM AND MOON-KIE JUNG

Hanseongsunbo often cited Japanese and Chinese newspapers and was closely advised by a Japanese counselor. Inoue Kakugoro, the Japanese advisor, was a pupil of Fukuzawa Yukichi, one of the first scholars to import the concept of race to Japan by translating numerous books from the West and an avid supporter of racial improvement through eugenics (Chung 2002). The racial taxonomy in the *Hanseongsunbo* article bore particular resemblance to Fukamauchi Motoi's *Geography for Elementary Schools*, published in 1874, which was, in turn, based on Western works by authors such as William Huse, Ogustin Michel, and Gold Smith, all of which drew on the "five-race theory" of German physician and anthropologist Johann Friedrich Blumenbach (Sun 2012).

In contrast to the matter-of-fact, neutral tone of *Hanseongsunbo's* inaugural piece on race, a pair of articles published a month later took on another aspect of Fukamauchi's book: its articulation of race to a normative understanding of civilization. Discussing peoples of the Americas and Africa, the newspaper found in them the antitheses of the civilized. American Indians were "savages" who were losing their land to Europeans:

> Since early people of the European empire did not recognize the existence of land in the middle of the Atlantic Ocean, they [Europeans and American Indians] could not exchange with each other; thus only aborigines lived together. They are the so-called copper-colored race and fall into the category of savage. . . . Columbus finally discovered the whole continent of America; thus Europeans gradually migrated and flourished to amass their present wealth. Copper-colored race members have hidden themselves in forests and would never again build a nation and stand on their own feet. Alas, the guest is strong, and the host is weak—sad that they are losing their ancestors' land and cannot recover it.

Africans were "savages" with ruthless customs who enslaved and sold each other:

> The race belongs to blacks and cannot escape from the category of savage. . . . Seen from the view that they even kill people for religious rites, it is needless to say how lowly their custom is. Their political system is the despotic dictatorship; their custom is brutal and atrocious, and thus every village invades and plunders each other, capturing people into slavery and often selling them in markets. Even worse, they bury the living with the dead at the funerals of lords, vassals, and their families. They always sacrifice human life in rituals for rain and prosperity; many even decorate

their houses and furniture with human skulls; the word savage is for these people.[4]

At first glance, these early articles on race, few in number, could be dismissed as insignificant, perhaps reflecting an indifferent public; in similar fashion, Pak Jeong-yang, a Gaehwapa leader and Korea's ambassador to the United States in the late 1880s, mentioned Black people and American Indians only peripherally, once or twice, in his travel reports (N. Pak 2001, 279). With time, however, the *Hanseongsunbo* articles proved to be a harbinger, prefiguring the discourse on race that would soon proliferate. A decade after the paper's initial foray into racial discourse, Yu Gil-jun, another reform leader and diplomat, published the widely popular and influential *Observations on a Journey to the West* (*Seoyugyonmun*). Informed by an intellectual voyage to the West, by way of China and Japan, that preceded the literal one, the multivolume book not only featured race prominently but depicted American Indians as "hopeless" and "soon-to-be extinct" and Black people as incapable of making use of their resources (Yu [1895] 2004, 85, 101). Such ideas would take firm hold as Korea, buffeted by imperial forces, struggled to hold on to its sovereignty.

Entering the Age of Empire

Hanseongsunbo did not last long. In 1884, Gaehwapa attempted an overthrow, known as the Gapsin Coup, that was quickly put down. Radical Gaehwapa elites and their families fled to Japan, killed themselves, or were killed. Bangmunguk burned down during the violent upheaval, and *Hanseongsunbo* perished with it. With conservatives gathering strength, and Gaehwapa defeated and dispersed, one might have predicted pessimistic futures for munmyeong gaehwa and the newspaper. Instead, the conservatives in power decided not only to revive the publication, under the new name of *Hanseongjubo*, but to devote more resources, increasing Bangmunguk's workforce threefold, and to reach out to the masses, publishing in Korean and mixed script rather than in Chinese. Although it, too, had a short lifespan, owing to Bangmunguk's ballooning deficit, the paper signaled that munmyeong gaehwa had become, in some irreversible sense, the dominant ideology by the 1880s (Yi 1969).

Precipitated by the ultimately failed Donghak peasant rebellion in southwestern Korea, the Sino-Japanese War of 1894–95 ended the post–

JAE KYUN KIM AND MOON-KIE JUNG

Gapsin Coup rivalry between China and Japan. The very first article of the Treaty of Shimonoseki that concluded the war, decisively won by Japan, insisted on China's recognition of Korea's complete independence, terminating their long-standing tributary relationship. It formally commenced the decentering of China in Korea (Schmid 2002). Following a burst of Japan-sponsored reforms, collectively known as the Gabo Reforms, Japan's influence and imperial ambitions in Korea were quickly checked by Russia, which, with the backing of France and Germany, intervened to successfully change the terms of the Treaty of Shimonoseki, effectively wresting control of Liadong Peninsula, including the coveted Port Arthur, from Japan. Japan's standing, in Korea as well as among Western imperial powers, took another hit after the 1895 assassination of Queen Min, plotted by Japan's minister to Korea. The ensuing decade was one of keen imperial rivalry between Japan and Russia over Korea and Manchuria. With Korea's sovereignty hanging in the balance and in continual jeopardy, munmyeong gaehwa in this period became more oriented toward resolving crises and securing independence.

The first privately led and Korean-only newspaper in Korea, *Dongnip-sinmun* reflected the times, as evidenced by its name, *dongnip* (independence, 獨立). After the Gabo Reforms, a Gaehwapa member who once fled to Japan and then the United States, Seo Jae-pil (hereafter Philip Jaisohn, his legal name upon acquiring U.S. citizenship), came back to Korea and founded the newspaper in 1896. Publishing exclusively in Korean, his goal was to attract the widest public support for munmyeong gaehwa, as he reasoned that the Gapsin Coup had failed for its lack of popular backing (Yi et al. 1993).

According to *Dongnipsinmun*, the most important thing for the "wretched people" of Joseon Korea was education, Western education to be specific.[5] By pursuing new knowledge as Japan did—in contrast to China, which continued to center Chinese classics—they could one day achieve a level of munmyeong gaehwa comparable to Japan or even the West. On its face, the assumed superiority of the West in the logic of munmyeong gaehwa could be interpreted as temporal and developmental, not racial, since civilization and enlightenment were attainable by any nation through education (Schmid 2002). However, Koreans presumed that the possibility of advancement was not equally available to everyone or every "race." Although enlightenment entailed education, the West's success had also depended on race.[6] On this score, Koreans surmised they would fare well: "If we compare Joseon people with the many peoples of the East, we are smarter and more diligent than Chinese people and have bigger and stronger bodies than Japanese people. Thus, if we are educated well and behave with knowledge, we would become the best race in the East. Then, we would become the best country in the world."[7]

Koreans frequently compared themselves to other East Asians, particularly the Japanese and the Chinese, but the discourse of Koreans' racial distinctiveness was not yet hegemonic. It coexisted and competed with a pan–East Asian understanding of race that was more prevalent (G. Shin 2006). Identifying with the "yellow" or "East race," *Dongnipsinmun* cast its gaze not only upward to whites, the imagined racial superiors, but also downward to Africans, American Indians, and other peoples imagined as racial inferiors:

> In the world, there are so many different types of humans like blacks, yellows, reds, and whites. People of Northern Europe have white faces and soft hair, but some have dark faces. However, usually European people have white skin, straight and soft hair, clear face lines, straight nose, and large eyes. The East race people have yellow skin, black and stiff hair, slanted eyes, and protruded teeth. Blacks have black skin, curly hair like sheep, a protruded jaw, and a flat nose. Blacks are stupider than the East race and very inferior to whites. American Indians have a reddish face similar to the East race. However, in terms of their size and the degree of enlightenment, they are less than the East race. . . . Among all the races, since whites are the most brilliant, diligent, and courageous, they have gradually defeated other inferior races all around the world and acquired land and forests. Therefore, some races among the inferior, who cannot learn whites' knowledge and customs, should be gradually extinct. In a country like America, the natives never learned the whites' knowledge and enlightenment. By not doing so, millions of a race have died within two hundred years, and only a few thousands are left nowadays. They climbed into the mountains or moved into the bushes and fed on the food from the American government. Their numbers are decreasing every year, and they will be extinct within several years. The Australian natives are similar to blacks and no more enlightened than blacks, and thus their lives are not much different from animals. Among these savages, some of them do not even know how to use fire.[8]

Carrying on the racial project begun by *Hansungsunbo* and *Seoyugyonmum*, the paper constructed essentialized and fixed images of hopeless Black people and American Indians whom education could not rescue while exhorting Koreans to follow the path of munmyeong gaehwa.[9]

A three-tier typology prevailed, with Korea firmly in the middle stage of enlightenment (Schmid 2002): "England, France, Germany in Europe and the United States in America have become the best enlightened nations, and the rest of the nations have been gradually becoming enlightened. Japan in the East has been treated as enlightened since thirty years ago. Korea, China, and Thailand have become half-enlightened. However, Africa and the rest still cannot escape from savagery."[10] European colonization of Africans and American Indians was justified by their inability to develop their abundant natural resources, which, intimating the growing influence of Protestant missionaries at the turn of the century, was characterized as a sin warranting punishment:

> Africa is famous for its wealth. It has precious forests, glittering diamonds, other jewels, ivory, gold, and silver everywhere. However, African natives never knew how to use these treasures and died with gold in their hand. Finally, as God punishes their vice, people from many European nations have shared the continent of Africa and made many useful goods in the world with the treasure. The continent of North America has fertile lands, various creatures, gorgeous rivers, and mountains. However, the natives known as Indians have lived there for thousands of years and made all the riches useless with their savagery. After it became the land of England's race, the country finally became the strongest and richest country in the world. Indeed, people are stupid if they don't understand how God punished the Indians' sin.[11]

Koreans, as "yellows," belonged to an intermediate category, but the categories were not equidistant, and their trajectories were divergent:

> There are five races of human beings. First is Mongolian, second is Caucasian, third is African, fourth is Malay, and fifth is American. . . . If we see these five races, they are all the same human beings in the world in spite of their complexions and appearances. All have joy, love, and hatred. However, some races have much knowledge and assets and are thus treated with respect everywhere, while some races have no knowledge and talent and are thus treated with contempt. . . . There are also many nations, such as the savage nation, preenlightened nation, semienlightened nation, and fully enlightened nation. The savage nation, the so-called worst, has no knowledge and thus cannot live like humans. . . . Koreans fall into the yellows. . . . As we have roughly explained, blacks and reds are no less than human beings. However, they are not worth talking about. Also, savage and

preenlightened nations are no less than nations, but they are not worth talking about. However, since Koreans are yellows in the East, thus not a bad race at all, let's become an upper nation among the East and West.[12]

Civilization and enlightenment were about acquiring knowledge, but they were also about "assets" and "talents." As "yellows," Koreans had the requisite racial potential to become a "fully enlightened" nation. "Blacks and reds," "savage and preenlightened nations," were beyond the pale. In this post-Sinocentric world, whites' place at the top of the civilized/savage scale was taken for granted as much as China's and Korea's paramount position on the civilized/barbarian continuum had been mere decades before. But Koreans could take solace in believing that they were racially far above Africans and American Indians and therefore could aspire to full enlightenment, however bleak their present circumstances might be.

In this way, feelings of solidarity with Black people were out of bounds. Describing the deaths of European colonizers in Africa, one article stated, "The black race viciously killed the Europeans in Africa. Wherever you go, a vulgar and ignorant race obliterates foreign people with barbaric law. How can they not be treated with contempt in the world?"[13] Although those Africans might have been fighting for their land, just as Koreans were trying to defend against Western domination, Koreans, blinded by Black people's imagined backwardness, could not draw the parallel. On the same day, another article informed its readers of how miserable their fellow Koreans' lives were in Japanese-owned factories in Korea: they were treated worse than "black slaves." The point of the comparison was clearly to generate outrage for their own, not empathy or sympathy for Black people.

In addition to *Dongnipsinmun*, Jaisohn also founded, in 1896, the Independence Club (Dongnipyeopoe), which attracted an enormous following across class lines. Joseon continued with efforts toward munmyeong gaehwa as Gojong, with the encouragement of the club, declared himself emperor and his realm an empire. Evolving from the club's public forums attended by thousands, the People's Assembly (Manmingongdonghoe)— something like "street parliaments"—was organized and achieved a level of political influence (Em 2013, 74). However, swayed by conservative factions that falsely accused Dongnipyeopoe of wanting to replace the monarchy with a president-led republic, Gojong cracked down on its leaders and shut it down for good in 1898. Under government pressure, Jaisohn returned to the United States the same year, and *Dongnipsinmun* discontinued publication in 1899.

Encouraged by the success of Dongnipyeopoe and *Dongnipsinmun*, how-ever, many newspapers sprang up in its place. Most of the new publica-tions were short-lived, but one of them, *Hwangseongsinmun*, lasted until Japanese annexation in 1910. The newspaper was launched in 1898 by Namgung Eok, a Dongnipyeopoe member, upon his release from jail, with help from other reform leaders such as Na Su-yeon and Yu Geun. Different from *Dongnipsinmun*, it was oriented more toward intellectuals, written in Korean mixed script as well as classical Chinese. This approach limited the paper's reach, but it did show how these intellectuals made sense of race after *Dongnipsinmun*.

Despite the shattered dreams of Dongnipyeopoe, *Hwangseongsinmun* maintained a similar racial ideology and sense of hierarchy. According to one article, if "natives" are not enlightened, they will become extinct according to natural law, just "as grass cannot be tall in a dense forest."[14] In keeping with Lamarckian environmentalism, proper education and patriotism provided the path toward civilization.[15] Stemming from regret for an uncivilized and barbaric past, the possibility of advancement for Koreans was a stressed theme of munmyeong gaehwa. However, a narra-tive of Korean redemption was not enough. Koreans' finding their bearings seemingly required securing a firm footing on who they were not: "blacks" and "reds." Blaming the colonized and euphemizing the colonizers, one article stated, "Those blacks there [in Transvaal], who are stupid savages, are deprived of sovereignty by guests."[16] Here and elsewhere, recurrently described as peoples being on the verge of extinction, "blacks" and "reds" were practically interchangeable with "savage race" and "inferior race."

The writers of *Hwangseongsinmun* also viewed the world as a racial battleground. In contrast to *Dongnipsinmun*, which tended to show only admiration for whites, *Hwangseongsinmun* often saw them as adversaries, who could annihilate "yellows" as they had exterminated Black people and American Indians.[17] But there was a distinction. The reason for the ex-tinction of Black people and American Indians was their essential racial traits. They were peoples without history.[18] Marked by their unchanging racial inferiority, they did not qualify as combatants in *Hwangseongsin-mun*'s racial war: "reds and blacks are not even close to being powers in the world."[19] By contrast, the current backwardness of Koreans—and, inversely, the supremacy of the West—was a matter of munmyeong gae-hwa or education: "The reason the West is called the civilized is not [because they are] innately a special race but [because they have] built schools and educated the talented in their country."[20] Koreans could suffer the fate of Black people and American Indians, but not necessarily. They were a people of history. Their suffering, unlike that of Black people and American Indians, was historically contingent. Koreans' being "yellow" was a necessary, though insufficient, condition for future progress. They were of a "race" that had belonged among "the civilized in the past" and, as "the government and people work in their duties," were again "soon to be advanced."[21] The newspaper encouraged Koreans to inspire fellow "yellows" who might be giving up.[22]

"Yellow" solidarity was the dominant racial theme, but Japan as a colonial threat loomed, a tension illustrated by an exchange between *Hwangseongsinmun* and *Chosonsinbo*, a Korea-based Japanese newspaper.[23] When Japan urged Korea to enforce its law allowing the free entry of Japanese, *Hwangseongsinmun* related the issue to what it saw as an eventual Japanese settlement plan that would "drive out Koreans and gradually lead to extermination" and "definitely turn [Koreans] into American reds."[24] As translated and published in *Hwangseongsinmun*, *Chosonsinbo* responded with condescending accusations of unwarranted self-hatred and self-doubt:

> In general, when an inferior race interacts with a superior race, it is clear that the real examples of gradual extermination are not only the reds in America but also the Ainu race in Japan. However, is it not too much self-hatred to conclude that Koreans are an inferior race that is to be defeated in the racial competition? In our opinion, we cannot even momentarily believe that Koreans would be an inferior race that would lose its procreative power on the field of racial competition. And when we inquire into the recent case of [the city of] Incheon, as the population in Incheon grows alongside the foreign settlement, it proves that there is a group [Koreans] who can endure the competition with a superior race.[25]

Hwangseongsinmun replied that Koreans did not doubt themselves to be an inferior race but, rather, sincerely believed in and desired peace.[26] In a more elaborate rejoinder three months later, the paper reminded the Japanese that Japan's advancement started merely thirty years before and that Korea had once taught civilization to Japan, while rejecting the assumed racial dichotomy between the two peoples.[27] Historically based bluster notwithstanding, Koreans' sense of insecurity was real. Different from the rather hopeful perspective of *Dongnipsinmun*, *Hwangseongsinmun* allowed that Koreans could potentially fall into a situation similar to those of Black people and American Indians. The paper worried that Koreans' devotion to the pen rather than the sword disadvantaged them in the social Darwinian contest of survival of the fittest.[28]

Still, despite anxieties provoked by Japan, and the West, "yellow" racial identity predominated. When South Africa allowed the entry of Japanese workers, *Hwangseongsinmun* gave a racial explanation: physically big but without substance, Black workers there were no match for the superior Japanese "yellows."[29] In a similar vein of "yellow" pride, racial discrimination against Japanese and Chinese workers in Hawai'i and Australia triggered outrage.[30] "Yellows" shared a common destiny after all. Even the Russo-Japanese War of 1904–5, which would eventually turn Koreans against the Japanese and the idea of a pan–East Asian "race," generated initial, if wary, support for Japan, as the war could demonstrate the racial superiority of "yellows."[31] *Hwangseongsinmun* called for solidarity of the "yellow" peoples behind Japan to drive back the "white" Russians: "If Russia emerges victorious and Japan is defeated, then the East will be rent asunder and the yellow race will be finished."[32] Perhaps hoping against hope, Japan was seen as a protector rather than a violator of Korean sovereignty, and therefore advocating such a racial alliance was not at odds with Korean nationalism. First and foremost, the enslavement and extinction of "yellow" peoples by whites had to be stopped (Schmid 2002, 88, 93). On the brink of potential disaster, a writer for *Hwangseongsinmun* feared, loathed, and beseeched:

> America once belonged to reds, but they are not seen anywhere. After seeking the reason, [I found out that] they lived like beasts . . . then lost their beautiful and fertile lands. What caused their loss, beggar-like lives, and gradual extinction? . . . The peace treaty between Japan and Russia could be the moment that Korea might be ruled by Japan or become a nonaligned country. . . . The situation of those pathetic and pitiful reds is my situation of today. People around the world would look at me the way I insulted reds. How painful and pitiful it would be. . . . Hence, . . . please act now—not to be the same as reds.[33]

Succumbing to the Age of Empire

Upon its decisive—and, to the world, racially shocking—defeat, Russia recognized, in the Treaty of Portsmouth, Japan's preeminence in Korea. In separate treaties, the United States and Britain likewise endorsed Japan's supremacy there. Unfettered by rivals, Japan promptly claimed Korea as a protectorate through the Eulsa Treaty in 1905. Step by step thereafter, Japan infringed on Korea's sovereignty, culminating in formal annexation in 1910. With Japan's colonial intentions evident by the conclusion of the Russo-Japanese War, Korea's hoped-for "yellow brother" turned into the greatest threat to the survival of the Korean "race." Koreans' destiny seemed to be following those of their imagined racial others, Black people and American Indians, by becoming "slaves," not unlike "cattle," of foreigners.[34] This final precolonial period saw the start of Korean nationalist historiography, reimagining, according to Henry Em, "the history of Korea as the history of the Korean *minjok*," a category that thoroughly conflated race, nation, and ethnicity (Em 2013, 79; see also Em 1999; Robinson 2007; Schmid 2002).

As seen above, "slave," and its cognates, was already a recurring, if intermittent, motif in how Koreans perceived their predicament in the age of empire. In the half decade after the Eulsa Treaty, however, its usage soared. During the paper's entire existence, from 1896 to 1899, *Dongnipsinmun* contained only fourteen items that used the word.[35] For the later *Hwangseongsinmun* (1898–1910), the number was 384, of which only seventy, or less than 20 percent, were from before 1905. The other popular newspaper of the period, *Daehanmaeilsinbo* (1904–10) published 616 pieces with the word during its run.[36] In this regard, perhaps the most prototypical and widely read—as well as, in retrospect, a canonically nationalist—text of the era was "I Wail Bitterly Today" ("Siillyabangseongdaegok," 是日也放聲大哭), a 1905 editorial in *Hwangseongsinmun* by the paper's editor-in-chief, Jang Ji-yeon. Written in reaction to the Eulsa Treaty, it bemoaned "the splitting asunder of the three nations of the East"—the paper's heretofore vaunted but elusive pan–East Asian alliance of China, Japan, and Korea. "Alas, four-thousand-year-old territory and five hundred years of sovereignty were given over to the other, forcing twenty million souls to become *slaves* of others. . . . Alas, bitter. Alas, resentful. Our twenty million brethren, *enslaved* brethren!"[37]

While munmyeong gaehwa and independence were the major themes of the entire gaehwa period, the sudden surge in the use of the term "slave" reflected Koreans' sinking outlook as their colonial vulnerability intensified. They sensed the real and impending danger of colonial takeover but, with Joseon having been a sovereign state since the fourteenth century, had no firsthand or recent experience and no ready-made language to make sense of it directly. It was both intensely near and abstractly removed. Enslavement, usually associated with Black people, and extinction, usually associated with American Indians, were the key metaphors through which Koreans grasped this unfamiliar threat. As being colonized became palpably imminent, slavery, especially, found a particular resonance. Through the schema of slavery, loss of the sovereign state was repeatedly likened to loss of the sovereign self: "If a person depends on another, he loses his freedom, his status plunges, and he cannot avoid slavery. . . . If a nation relies on another, it threatens its independence, loses its national face, and also cannot avoid slavery."[38] Slavery was something—the worst thing—imaginable and yet relatable as a form of domination. Only in the previous decade, in 1894, was slavery outlawed in Korea as a part of the Gabo Reforms.[39] Almost everyone had living memory of the institution. At the same time, although both Korean terms for "slave" were used, *noye* (奴隷) predominated over *nobi* (奴婢). Nobi referred to enslaved people of Korea, while *noye* was reserved for enslaved people in other contexts, such as Africans in the Americas; with enslavement and colonization so semantically linked, both Black people and American Indians were frequently invoked in reference to slavery, but, as suggested by the terms "black slave" (*heungno*, 黑奴) and "red savage" (*hongbeon*, 紅番), Black people were much more closely identified with it. Noye was thus both familiar and foreign, and as a metaphor for colonialism, it familiarized a doubly foreign form of domination—foreign to Korean history and enacted by a foreign power. Yet slavery was always a metaphor, not a synonym, for colonialism. Koreans did not believe they were or would be literally chattel. However fervently they represented themselves as "slaves," there was always this buffer between the figurative and the literal, reinscribing the color line between themselves and their imagined racial inferiors, Black people in particular, even as they rhetorically erased it.[40]

The overriding imperative was not to be colonized, not to "become slaves of others." According to Pak Eun-sik, one of the prominent Gaehwapa elites who, like many of his colleagues, later participated in the independence movement during the colonial era, survival of the fittest was the natural law. After humans vanquished all other animals, the world became more connected, and competition turned to the next chapter: the struggle between human "races," wherein the superior "race" with superior intelligence and power viewed the inferior "race" as "savages" and was not afraid to annihilate them. Pak thought that examples of inferior "races" were African "black slaves" and American "red savages." He then argued that fellow Koreans were about to lose their superior status—that is, on the verge of "becoming slaves of others" and being killed.[41] According to this social Darwinist logic, inferior "races" would become "slaves" of others through their inability to work as a group, religious disunity, or lack of education.[42] For *Hwangsungsinmun*, the reason "blacks" and "reds" became "slaves," not unlike "cattle," of foreigners was because "they have no intelligence and thereby no competency" as "intelligence gives rise to the right to freedom." Unlike them, Koreans could retain their right to freedom by pursuing the "new learning."[43] The slogan "not to be slaves of others" pressed Koreans not to suffer the same fate. According to another writer, losing one's freedom was the greatest "sin," which would result in enslavement. To those who would doubt him, he pointed to the extinction of the American "copper-colored race" and the collapse of the African continent.[44]

At times, Koreans dared to compare themselves unfavorably to Black people. For example, learning that Koreans were displayed as animals at an exhibition in Japan, *Daehanmaeilsinbo* desponded that Korean "yellows" had become worse than Black people who had been sold into slavery.[45] But in these moments, Koreans were not identifying with Black people or actually admitting that they were as inferior as, or inferior to, Black people and American Indians. The purpose was to incite fellow Koreans into action, to collectively, patriotically elevate the "four-thousand-year-old nation." Relaying reports from the United States, Pak Eun-sik wrote about "an American Ph.D., Dr. Stone[, who] extolled Korean workers as far superior to American workers." Likening Koreans to "American ancestors from England," he supposedly ranked Koreans "the highest among the races in the world in intelligence." From this Western, and thus tacitly authoritative, assessment, Pak concluded that Koreans' "original traits were in fact superior to others." However, this "good people became stupid, ignorant, vulgar, and inferior, turning . . . into animals without spirit and vigor, thus at last experiencing the humiliation of slaves."[46] Still, the fall was a *historical* process and, given Koreans' superior traits, could be reversed. In contrast to "African savages" who were unable to progress, lived with wild animals and insects, and remained enslaved, Koreans with their sacred history and incomparable patriotism could overcome their temporary enslaved status.[47]

The idea of a distinctive Korean "race" had not fully taken hold, and the notion of a pan–East Asian "yellow race" lingered, which only deepened the sense of betrayal toward the Japanese: "How could Japanese call Koreans savages and even worse than dogs and pigs? If you despise and insult the same race in the East, you do not deserve to be human."[48] For some, the decisive struggle would still be between "yellows" and "whites," the only two "races" that mattered; "blacks," "copper-coloreds," and "reds" were not worth considering.[49]

Time and again, Koreans buoyed themselves by denigrating Black people and American Indians: "In America, blacks and reds have become slaves to whites and were violated by them. The reason they have reached the verge of extinction is natural selection, because the brain power of the races is indeed inferior to whites." Koreans were different, smarter.[50] "Blacks" and "reds" were predestined to enslavement because of their innately inferior nature, while Koreans' inherent and cultural superiority would lead them in the opposite direction. In these final precolonial years, Koreans recognized their decline, but even as they feared and perceived a closing distance between themselves and their imagined racial inferiors, they never lost their racist faith that there would and should always be a gap.

Conclusion

In the history of Korea, the significance of the March First Movement, in 1919, could hardly be overstated. "A shining moment of national unity during the long dark night of Japanese rule," according to Michael Robinson (2007, 47), "it placed the plight of the Korean people briefly on the world stage, precipitated a major shift in Japanese control policies, and was a public relations disaster for the Japanese." A decade into Japan's harshly coercive occupation, as many as a million people took to the streets in marches and demonstrations, starting on March 1, 1919, and extending into the summer, despite a notoriously bloody crackdown.

At the outset, befitting this high moment of nationalism, a declaration by a group of thirty-three activists—"The Declaration of Independence"—proclaimed "Korea . . . an independent state" and "Koreans . . . a self-governing people." The document's words and sentiments have been familiar to generations of Koreans ever since, but in light of our arguments above, we would like to call attention to the unnoticed racial subtext. For instance, the sentence "The enslavement of twenty million resentful people by force does not contribute to lasting peace in the East" drew on countless other such utterances about slavery, since the precolonial era, that had formed the condition of its intelligibility and resonance. Likewise, consider the statement, "We do not intend to accuse Japan of infidelity for its violation of various solemn treaty obligations since the Treaty of Amity of 1876. Japan's scholars and officials, indulging in a conqueror's exuberance, have denigrated the accomplishments of our ancestors and treated our civilized people like barbarians" (H. Kim 1989, 2–3). The more direct translation of the final predicate would be "treated our *minjok* of culture like *ignorant natives*."[51] With the interpolating modifier *mae* (ignorant), the word *tomaein* (土昧人) was a variation of *toin* (native), which had long been used to refer to Black people (African toin), American Indians (American toin), and other so-called inferior and savage natives; according to the first comprehensive Korean dictionary, compiled during the colonial era, "toin" denoted "unenlightened savages fixed to a certain land."[52] This momentous proclamation for Korean freedom, then, was not only an explicit "affirmation of the principle of the equality of all nations" and "the demand of our people for justice, humanity, survival, and dignity" but also an implicit assertion of unquestioned superiority over those beyond the pale of justice, survival, dignity, and, indeed, Humanity (H. Kim 1989, 2–3).

The construction of imagined racial inferiors would persist through the colonial and postcolonial eras, variously structuring and inflecting Korean history. Black people and others Koreans deemed to be their racial inferiors would remain as critical to Korean identity formation as peoples they viewed as their equals or superiors. In their bid for inclusion, Koreans would continually endorse the global accord denying that Black people come within the pale of twentieth and twenty-first century Humanity.

Notes

An earlier version of this chapter appeared as "'The Darker to the Lighter Races': The Precolonial Construction of Racial Inferiors in Korea," *History of the Present* 9, no. 1 (2019): 55–83.

1   No doubt, the reach of newspapers was severely limited, favoring the literate in a predominantly illiterate society, which we should always keep in mind (Kimura 1993, 642). They nonetheless constituted the most popular means of mass communication, particularly as they began to publish in Korean and mixed script (combining Korean and Chinese) rather than, as traditionally, exclusively in Chinese (Choi 2000; Lee and Ch'oe 1988; Schmid 2002).

2   For examples, see Chow (1997), Chung (2002), Dikötter (1992, 1997a), Koshiro (2003), Kowner and Demel (2013, 2015), Oguma (2002), Sautman (1997), Shih (2013), Sullivan (1994), Tajima and Thornton (2012), Takezawa (2005), and Weiner (1995, 1997).

3   "Juyange Daehae Nonham," *Hanseongsunbo*, October 31, 1883, 10. Unless otherwise noted, all translations are our own.

4   "Apeurikaju," *Hanseongsunbo*, November 30, 1883, 13.

5   "Ronsyeol," *Dongnipsinmun*, April 25, 1896, 1.

6   "Ronsyeol," *Dongnipsinmun*, June 24, 1897, 1.

7   "Ronsyeol," *Dongnipsinmun*, May 2, 1896, 1.

8   "Ronsyeol," *Dongnipsinmun*, June 24, 1897, 1.

9   This view did not preclude intermittent expressions of sympathy or even empathy. A report on the United States, for instance, could lament the ill treatment of both "blacks" and "yellows." See "Ronsyeol," *Dongnipsinmun*, October 16, 1897, 1.

10 "Doragan Illyoil Gyeongsyeong Hakdangesyeo Gwangmu Hyeopoe Yeonsyeol (Jyeonho Yeonsyok)," *Dongnipsinmun*, February 19, 1898, 1. For three-tier typology, see Schmid (2002).

11 "Mollayossiui Uigyeon," *Dongnipsinmun*, August 31, 1898, 1.

12 "Injyonggwa Namnaui Bunbyeol," *Dongnipsinmun*, September 11, 1899, 1.

13 "Oeguk Tongsin," *Dongnipsinmun*, April 9, 1896, 2.

14 "Ryanghoesuham," *Hwangseongsinmun*, October 19, 1898, 2.

15 "Segyee Yabeon (Sokchingyaman) Ira," *Hwangseongsinmun*, April 14, 1899, 1.

16 "Yeonggilliwateuranseubal Ryanggukgane Gaeheuni Iguhaya Jeongi-ga Sabakameun," *Hwangseongsinmun*, October 25, 1899, 1.

17 "Geumjisegyesange Yuiljongbulpyeonghwadogihani Gijiri Eumjihago Giseongi Gangpokago," *Hwangseongsinmun*, December 2, 1899, 3.

18 Of course, we borrow from Eric Wolf's (1982) *Europe and the People without History*.

19 "Honghwangui See Hongsuui Hwa-ga Mimansoyanghaya Maengsuui Hae-ga Chungillyeonsuhamae," *Hwangseongsinmun*, May 24, 1899, 1.

20 "Buhakgyoneun Gaejinmunhwahaneun Ildaemunnora," *Hwangseongsinmun*, July 5, 1899, 1.

21 "Seoini Yumuneohaninwal Gwigugi Cheojaedongyanghaya Gigihuwa Tomaewa Injongi Yeohahan Guginyo," *Hwangseongsinmun*, May 30, 1899, 4.

22 "Sigungnyonguigagwan," *Hwangseongsinmun*, January 25, 1900, 2.

23 Unrelated to an earlier newspaper with the same name that had also been founded by the Japanese, in Busan, Korea, *Chosonsinbo* (朝鮮新報) was based in Incheon, Korea.

24 "Byeonjayudohan," *Hwangseongsinmun*, October 7, 1901, 2.

25 Translated in "Iljakbonboronseore Ilboninjayudohaneul Byeonnonhayatdeoni," *Hwangseongsinmun*, October 12, 1901, 2.

26 "Jaebyeonilboninjayudohan," *Hwangseongsinmun*, October 14, 1901, 4.

27 "Byeonjoseonsinbobyeonmangjiryu (Sogi)," *Hwangseongsinmun*, January 29, 1902, 2. Titled "Argument on *Chosonsinbo*'s Absurd Fallacy," the second rejoinder was a series of four articles published between January 28 and 31, 1902.

28 "Minnyaktoechukpiljangjeolmyeol," *Hwangseongsinmun*, October 16, 1901, 2.

29   "Irinijuui Heoga," *Hwangseongsinmun*, August 21, 1903, 1.

30   "Dongyangnodongjaui Baecheok," *Hwangseongsinmun*, September 11, 1903, 1.

31   "Pak Jang-hyeon Giseo." *Hwangseongsinmun*, August 19, 1904, 2.

32   "Panhang Seoljiryu," *Hwangseongsinmun*, June 23, 1904, 2, as quoted and translated in Schmid (2002, 92).

33   Yi Jeong-rae, "Migukaningongnipyeopoe Yi Jeong-rae," *Hwangseongsinmun*, October 28, 30, 31, 1905, page 1 in each issue.

34   "Yeollyeonhwaseolbeop," *Hwangseongsinmun*, August 23, 1905, 2.

35   The term "slave" appeared in seventeen articles in *Hanseongsunbo* and seven articles in *Hanseongjubo*.

36   The paper was founded by an English journalist, Ernest Thomas Bethell, with help from Korean nationalists such as Yang Gi-tak, Shin Chae-ho, and Pak Eun-sik. Because the publisher was English, the newspaper was free from Japanese censorship until formal colonial annexation.

37   Jang Ji-yeon, "Siillyabangseongdaegok," *Hwangseongsinmun*, November 20, 1905, 2, as quoted and translated in Schmid (2002, 95), emphases added.

38   "Daesejibulgabulbyeon (sok)," *Hwangseongsinmun*, June 3, 1907, 1, as quoted and translated in Schmid (2002, 61–62). Of course, in this time of deteriorating monarchy and emerging nationalism, "sovereignty" itself was undergoing radical redefinition.

39   On slavery and Korea, see Campbell (2005), B. Kim (2003), K. Kim (2003), Patterson (1982), and Peterson (1985).

40   This "color line" between the literal and the metaphorical—between the actual enslavement of Black people, above all, and the rhetorical use of it in nonblack discourses of freedom—was not unique to precolonial and colonial Korea but has long been one of the defining features of the modern world (Buck-Morss 2000). In relation to China, see Karl (2002, 120–24).

41   Pak Eun-sik, "Gyoyugi Bulheungha-myeon Saengjoneul Budeuk," *Seou* 1 (1906): 8–10.

42   Jang Ji-yeon, "Jimaesam (Sok)," *Daehanjaganghoewolbo* 5 (1906): 23–27; Pak Eun-sik, "Daehanjeongsin," *Daehanjaganghoewolbo* 1 (1906): 56–58; Ra Seok-gi, "Minjokjuuiron," *Seobukakoewolbo* 8 (1909): 39–40; Won Yeong-ui, "Jonggyojigubyeol," *Daedonghakoewolbo* 3 (1908): 20–23; and Yi Gap, "Ronhakoe," *Seou* 4 (1907): 24–30.

43   "Yeollyeonhwaseolbeop," *Hwangseongsinmun*, August 23, 1905, 2.

44   Seol Tae-hui, "Pogijayujawisegyejijoein," *Daehanjaganghoewolbo* 6 (1906): 18–23.

45   "Cheokjigeumseong," *Daehanmaeilsinbo*, June 5, 1907, 4.

46   Pak Eun-sik, "Gihoe," *Seou* 4 (1907): 1–3. As they believed munmyeong gaehwa originated in the West, Koreans often saw the gaze of the West as a yardstick with which to measure themselves.

47   Cho Hae-saeng, "Cheongnyeonui Deugui," *Taegeukakbo* 19 (1908): 1–4.

48   "Sisapyeongnon," *Daehanmaeilsinbo*, August 22, 1907, 2.

49 "Dongseomundap," *Daehanjaganghoewolbo* 3 (1907): 69–70.

50 "Aporakgwanjeoksasang," *Hwangseongsinmun*, January 22, 1910, 2.

51 Emphases added. The whole sentence in the original Korean mixed script reads, "學者는 講壇에서 政治家는 實際에서 我祖宗世業을 植民地視하고 我文化民族을 土昧人遇하야 한갓 征服者의 快를 貪할 뿐이오."

52 *Hanguel Hakoe Jieun Keun Sajeon* 6 (1957): 3167. Begun by a group of Korean scholars in 1929, *Hanguel Hakoe Jieun Keun Sajeon* (한글 학회 지은 큰 사전) was confiscated by the Japanese in 1942. With funding from the Rockefeller Foundation, the first volume was published in 1947, and after the interruption of the Korean War, all six volumes found their way to print by 1957.

PART III

CAPTIVITIES

"MASS INCARCERATION" AS

MISNOMER: CHATTEL/DOMESTIC WAR

AND THE PROBLEM OF NARRATIVITY

DYLAN RODRÍGUEZ

Introduction: The Story of Mass Incarceration

As the phrase "mass incarceration" spreads across scholarly, activist, jur-isprudential, policy, popular cultural, and governmental venues, a relatively coherent narrative process has attained increasingly wide political-ideological traction.

First, there is an uneven though identifiably growing acknowledgment that a contemporary, half-century statecraft of gendered racial terror has intensified the broader social formation's institutional-cultural capacity and will to profile, criminalize, incarcerate, and denigrate targeted bodies, places, and populations. These are assumptively Black geographies, though they are not always explicitly identified as such.

Quickly and slowly, alarmed responses spill forth through journalis-tic, testimonial, activist, and (empiricist) social scientific revelations that confirm the suspicion that the martialing of domestic war (against drugs/gangs/border crossers/terror/gender and sexual counternormativity/etc.) has misidentified and/or exceeded the operational objectives of an otherwise entirely intentional, juridically supported, and strategic (national-to-global) process of human dysselection (Wynter and Scott 2000, 119–207).

Next, there are spreading, dense accounts of degradation and suffering that traverse individualized tragedy to collectively, communally voiced, insurgent outrage (it becomes clear, however, that many of these accounts actually preceded the growing, increasingly generalized acknowledgment of the crisis).

A protracted skirmish ensues, as organized political blocs, cultural institutions, and emergent grassroots-to-virtual/social media collectives attempt to make sense—that is, to definitively narrate—this turmoil.

Entering the skirmish (at the same time that they are formed by it) are multiple coalescences of organic and professional intellectuals—of the racial state, nonprofit/foundation regimes, and liberal cultural industry, including think-tank and corporate-commissioned academics, writers, and artists—who collectively strive to restore a paradigmatic liberal faith in the virtues and possibilities of righteous national reform against this state-sanctioned climate of atrocity. From a *New York Times* op-ed, April 2016: "Reform is imperative, not just for its economic or budgetary benefits, but for individuals who deserve a second chance and the families and communities who stand beside them" (Furman and Holtz-Eakin 2016).

In response to the catchphrased problem of mass incarceration, there grows a definitive, outraged rhetoric of liberal humanist alarm that strives for a sense of shared moral grievance: "The scale and the brutality of our prisons are the moral scandal of American life," asserted *The New Yorker* (Gopnik 2012), while the Soros Foundation announced a $50 million grant to the ACLU by proclaiming "America's bloated prisons are an appalling and expensive failure, the politics of fear overwhelming common sense and human decency" (Stone 2014).

Morality, common sense, decency: these are the rhetorical signals of an institutionally (and state-) sanctioned cultural-political momentum to renarrate the fatal, miserable, gendered-racial-colonial asymmetries of suffering, misery, and carceral displacement as atrocious scandals, corruptions, miscalculations, and racially (antiblack) disparate criminological militarizations of a misled and misdirected political and social formation, originating with the War on Drugs and culminating in 2.5 million people held captive by the state.

If there is such a massive problem, it can be fixed, if we bring rational heart to mind in another adventure of humanist reform, if we follow the stories into the tragedy and insist over and over again that such harrowing details are not the intended outcome of this state, this nation-building epoch, this policy-formed martialing of cultural and domestic military force, then solutions are imminent, the threads of a racial modernity to again be pulled taut around the jagged, always-disarticulating edges of the civil underside, where statecraft unfolds on the intimate geography of the flesh. (Such narratives reaffirm the permanent suspicion some of us hold of the assumptive national-historical "we.")

I offer this working thesis: that mass incarceration is not only an increasingly institutionalized narrative regime with sprawling scholarly, intellectual, and cultural-political (that is, activist) consequences, but is also a condition that thrives on the cultural-political fallout of antiblack state and extrastate violence, the damage of which cannot be contained by universal promises of futurity or life (postracial or otherwise).

(To be continued.)

Prestory: Antiblack Criminalization as Precedent/ Antecedent/Paradigm

The formation and geographic metastasizing of gendered-racial criminalization is both premised on and actively shaped by the dynamic, systemic historical forces of antiblack criminalization. To invoke common notions of criminality (behavior, bodily comportment, dress, gender presentation, alleged predisposition to violence, etc.) is to draw upon a historically vast reservoir of materially accessible images/imaginations of Black and Afro-descended "criminals." In fact, African indigeneity was a focal point for the genesis of modern hemispheric criminal justice and criminological apparatuses and is traceable to the transatlantic slave trade as well as the earliest stages of the diasporic African presence in North America: Rediker writes that the slave ship was "a mobile, seagoing prison at a time when the modern prison had not yet been established on land" (2007, 45).

Lerone Bennett Jr. describes in the classic text *Before the Mayflower* how "the African brought [their] mind and [their] ethos to America with [them]. . . . The first generation of African-Americans were carriers of an African world view." This collective embodiment and practice of diasporic African life continuity was central to the earliest iterations of racial criminalization as antiblack political-cultural repression: "In 1680 the Virginia Assembly said that 'the frequent meetings of considerable numbers of Negroe slaves under pretence of feasts and burials is judged of dangerous consequence'" (1984, 42–43). In continuity with Virginia's founding patriarchs, American physician Samuel Cartwright infamously crystallized the link between the chattel institution and the precursors of criminological (hence social) science in his 1851 coining of the medical diagnosis "drapetomania" to describe "the disease of mind" that "induces the negro to run away from service" (1851, 707). According to Cartwright, this criminal act could be corrected through modest improvements to the housing, clothing, and nutrition of the enslaved. He emphasizes, however, that if such white benevolence fails to quell the enslaved's inclination "to raise their heads to a level with their master," then "humanity and their own good require they should be punished until they fall into that submissive state which it was intended for them to occupy in all after time." It is useful to consider the white academic invention of drapetomania as a conceptual-methodological blueprint for the rising, complexly institutionalized connection between the Black-racialized figure of the criminal, gendered antiblack criminalization, and the rise of a modern white civil society consistently cohered through criminological/social science, criminal law, and physiologically directed racist state violence.

This is to say, well over 150 years before the term "mass incarceration" was coined in a moment of liberal racial crisis, the United States academic-state-cultural nexus was actively constituting the juridical, discursive, apparitional, fantastic, and journalistic premises of carceral criminalization in the Black "masses," enslaved and nonenslaved, pre- and post-Emancipation.

Writing in 1895 amid the Southern renaissance of lynching that unfolded over a full half century, antilynching activist Ida B. Wells-Barnett deepens the critical archive on gendered antiblack criminalization by illuminating the sociality produced in the creation of a paradigmatic criminal figure: the Black (cisgender) male rapist/sexual predator of white women:

> Humanity abhors the assailant of womanhood, and this charge upon the Negro at once placed him beyond the pale of human sympathy. With such unanimity, earnestness and apparent candor was this charge made and reiterated that the world has accepted the story that the Negro is a monster which the Southern white man has painted him. And today, the Christian world feels, that while lynching is a crime, and lawlessness and anarchy the certain precursors of a nation's fall, it can not by word or deed, extend sympathy or help to a race of outlaws, who might mistake their plea for justice and deem it an excuse for their continued wrongs. (Wells-Barnett 1895, 60)

Wells-Barnett concisely addresses a crucial facet of the long historical production of the criminal in gendered Blackness: that the complex
entanglement of criminalization with the layered, state-sanctioned, and
white supremacist civility of racist, colonial, and antiblack dominance—
in their varying scales and forms—compose a criminological social totality in which extralegal (and fatal) violence against criminalized beings is
sanctioned by the state, systemically condoned by a racist heteropatriarchal juridical order, and valorized by a national-cultural order that thrills
in the waging of domestic/continental and global warfare. She continues, "The entire system of the judiciary of this country is in the hands of
white people. To this add the fact of the inherent prejudice against colored
people, and it will be clearly seen that a white jury is certain to find a Negro
prisoner guilty if there is the least evidence to warrant such a finding"
(Wells-Barnett 1895, 87). Wells-Barnett's study of lynching demonstrates
that it is frequently the case that not even the threshold of "the least evidence" is required for either criminal conviction or state-sanctioned (extralegal) punishment of Black people under the cultural reign of U.S. white
supremacy and its proliferations of violence.

Dorothy Roberts, echoing the work of Angela Y. Davis, Hortense Spillers, Saidiya Hartman, and a long genealogy of Black feminists, builds on
Wells-Barnett's era-specific work by offering a historical analysis of the
unique criminalization of Black (cisgender) women and girls. Working
from the well-documented fact that "America has always viewed unregu-
lated Black reproduction as dangerous," Roberts's classic study *Killing the
Black Body* locates Black motherhood and Black women's biological capacity to bear Black children at the nexus of the U.S. criminal justice regime,
from the chattel period onward.

> For three centuries, Black mothers have been thought to pass down to their
> offspring the traits that marked them as inferior to any white person. Along
> with this biological impairment, it is believed that Black mothers transfer
> a deviant lifestyle to their children that dooms each succeeding genera-
> tion to a life of poverty, delinquency, and despair. . . . Disparaging stereo-
> types of Black people all proclaim a common message: it is the depraved,
> self-perpetuating character of Blacks themselves that leads to their inferior
> social status. (Roberts 1997, 8–9)

Roberts identifies the biological nexus of racial dominance that not
only provides a framework for gendered human differentiation, but also
enacts a logic of transgenerational and immutable criminalization that

preys on notions of genetic as well as cultural heredity. Sarah Haley's (2016) close examination of multiple penological and criminological archives in the U.S. South spurs a critical elaboration of this gendered antiblack technology, illustrating how the policing and incarceration of Black women is not only central to the formation of an apartheid "Jim Crow Modernity," but also structures the post-Emancipation construction of the U.S. criminal law apparatus in and of itself. Black women—which is to say Black people—are projected into law and national culture as subjects of gender-racial deviance (criminal, sexual, and otherwise) in the process of cohering a modern infrastructure of jurisprudence and everyday cultural intercourse.

These and other gendered antiblack forms of racial criminalization suggest that a logic of social neutralization, terror, and communal liquidation (via law enforcement, state-condoned extralegal violence, and civil/social death through incarceration) animates the modern criminological enterprise, which encompasses academic, legal, and hegemonic cultural institutions. The figure of the criminal is originated, structured, and dynamically reproduced in antiblack, anti-African, gendered chattel relations of racial and civilizational dominance.

Brennan Center Blue Ribbon: The Fallout of Unintended Consequences

Notions of criminality and criminal threat can only be understood as deeply historical cultural-political productions: they are generated in and across multiple discursive layers, including visual signifiers of incorrigible Black sexual endangerment of white civil society (e.g., the prominent, notorious exploitation of Willie Horton's mugshot in George H. W. Bush's 1988 presidential campaign), populist rhetorics of indecency and criminal social deviance (Barry Goldwater's 1964 "law-and-order" campaign against the Black and domestic U.S. Third World and anticolonial rebellions and freedom movements; Hillary Clinton's 1996 coining of "superpredators" as a catchphrase reference to since-debunked imaginaries of spreading Black youth criminal behavior), and popular cultural forms (including video games, television and film entertainment, social media, corporate news programs, and politically themed radio shows and podcasts).

At the crux of the historical criminological and proto-criminological enterprise is a differentiation between what Wynter identifies as the

8.1 Black man with "End Mass Black Incarceration" sign at San Francisco Bay area protest, c. 2015.

Renaissance Era distinction between the "saved" and the "cursed," the Enlightenment and scientific era distinction between the "selected" and the "dysselected," and the fatal racial and racial colonial distinction between bourgeois Man and a global field of "natives" and "niggers" (Wynter and Scott 2000).

Against this long historical prestory, the more recent liberal-progressive reformist critique of mass incarceration (while sometimes rearticulated by abolitionist, antiracist, and Black radical practitioners as "Mass Black Incarceration"; see figure 8.1) lends itself to the quiet absurdities of a multiculturalist, postracial lexicon: the discourse invokes soundbite analyses and activist rhetorics that rest on notions of unfairness, systemic bias, racial disparity, and institutional dysfunction that in turn demand vigorous reforms of the racial state, to be conducted through internal auditing, aggressive shifts in law and policy, and piecemeal rearrangements of state infrastructure.

Exemplifying the institutionalization of this political-analytical position is the advocacy of NYU Law School's influential Brennan Center for Justice, founded in 1995 by the family and former clerks of Supreme Court Justice

William J. Brennan. A nonprofit policy think tank seeking "to improve our systems of democracy and justice" in order to "hold our political institutions and laws accountable to the twin American ideals of democracy and equal justice for all" (Brennan Center for Justice 2018), the Brennan Center held a conference in 2014 titled "Shifting Law Enforcement Goals to Reduce Mass Incarceration," with panels populated by an array of federal prosecutors (from New Jersey, Maryland, Kansas, Alabama, Louisiana, and the U.S. Department of Justice, among others), district attorneys, a former president of the National Rifle Association and American Conservative Union, police officials, and criminal defense litigators. Headlined by U.S. Attorney General Eric Holder (whose keynote speech i examine later in this chapter), the conference mission statement references the criminological policing logic driving the emergence of a postracial mass incarceration reform bloc:

> This conference offers an opportunity to assess the way federal prosecutors can shift priorities. It will allow us to hear how state and local law enforcement can innovate so that safety does not come with the high costs of unnecessary incarceration. And it will gather the nations' top budget experts to explore how economic incentives can steer policy—wisely or unwisely—throughout the system.
>
> We are deeply grateful to U.S. Attorney General Eric Holder for his encouragement for this work and his presence today. We are appreciative, as well, to the law enforcement leaders who will speak out in this conference. . . .
>
> The Brennan Center works to reform the systems of democracy and justice. We seek to ensure that American institutions follow core values. *Thus we are committed to ending mass incarceration as a mission for our organization.* (Brennan Center for Justice 2014, i, emphasis added)

The conference spurred the publication of the blue-ribbon Brennan Center report *Federal Prosecution for the 21st Century* (foreword by former U.S. Attorney General Janet Reno), which recommends "concrete reforms to federal prosecution practices to support 21st century criminal justice policies. This new approach would reorient prosecutor incentives and practices toward the twin goals of reducing crime and *reducing mass incarceration*" (Eisen, Fortier, and Chettiar 2014, emphasis added).

It might seem significant that in the span of a year, the Brennan Center reneged on its initial commitment to ending mass incarceration by revising its mission to merely reducing it, with no clarifying remarks. Upon closer scrutiny, however, there is no substantive difference between these apparently contradictory objectives: the notion of ending mass incarceration does not provide any semblance of aspiration (much less a policy agenda) to facilitate a systemic downscaling or elimination (abolition) of prisons, jails, or detention centers; to the contrary, it suggests an invigorated, neoliberal antiracist-to-postracial rationalization of incarceration that rationally, fractionally downsizes the captive population (largely by way of decarcerating "nonviolent offenders" and those convicted of "victimless" War on Drugs crimes) and, by extension, attempts to alleviate some of the systemic racial asymmetries that produce Black carceral subjection as an essential feature of contemporary U.S. jurisprudence and social formation. "It is truly remarkable how much safer the country has become since the crime wave of the 1980s and 1990s. . . . *But the policy response to the crime epidemic has yielded an unintended consequence.* The United States has more than tripled its incarceration rate over the past four decades (Eisen, Fortier, and Chettiar 2014, 13).

Reproducing the now-canonical criminological assumption that the expansion of gendered racist incarceration at such a pace and scale is in fact and unquestionably an "unintended" outcome of the last half-century or so of U.S. criminal justice statecraft, *Federal Prosecution for the 21st Century* seamlessly cites criticisms of mass incarceration from prominent right-wing figures like Senator Rand Paul and New Jersey Governor Chris Christie, while quoting California Attorney General Kamala Harris's advocacy for "a third way forward: smart on crime" and New York City Police Department Commissioner William Bratton's 2014 pledge (borne of a laughable deficit of self-awareness) to engage in "collaborative problem-solving with the community." On the back of these implicit endorsements, the report outlines a strategy that incentivizes prosecutors to "address the root causes of violence or unethical behavior . . . [and] focus on prevention strategies . . . in an attempt to prevent crimes rather than just punish offenders after they commit them" (Eisen, Fortier, and Chettiar 2014, 14).

The critical premise of the Brennan Center's effort is the liberal belief that antiblackness and racial-colonial state violence are not fundamental and systemic (or otherwise intended) productions of the U.S. state in its local to global iterations. As the Brennan Center reconsiders the mission and method of criminal prosecution for the new millennium, it heavily invests in the prospect of a more balanced symbiosis of preemptive policing, preventative criminology, and punitive incarceration within the statecraft of postraciality. Thus, *ending* mass incarceration is tantamount to—which is to say, functionally synonymous with—*reducing* mass incarceration: neither goal provides a rigorous differentiation or definition of its key terms or modifiers. In this collapsing of purpose, the Brennan Center turns toward reliance on a corporate approach to neoliberal organizational change, expounding rhetorics and methods of institutional leanness, agility, and more efficient management of organizational waste and disciplining of ineffective or underachieving personnel.[1]

Appealing to the "unique authority" of prosecutors, the report's recommendations rest on the Brennan Center's model of "Success-Oriented Funding," in which government resources and grant opportunities are linked "as tightly as possible to clear, concrete objectives that drive toward the twin goals of reducing crime *and* reducing mass incarceration." "Grounded in basic principles of economics and management, Success-Oriented Funding provides incentives to achieve . . . priorities, thereby changing practices and outcomes. It can be applied to all criminal justice agencies, actors, and funding streams" (Eisen, Fortier, and Chettiar 2014, 14, 4).

Rearticulating the neoliberal cultural-disciplinary structure that mystifies notions of individual responsibility in the context of downsized state capacity, Success-Oriented Funding foregrounds the prosecutor as the personification and organic leader of a top-down, state-led autoreform, guided by the rituals and management metrics of personnel reviews: "As noted by the Blue Ribbon Panel, US Attorneys can help move the country away from overreliance on punishment and incarceration. They should begin with implementing Success-Oriented Funding in their own offices, turning inward to evaluate their own policies and their staff's performance" (Eisen, Fortier, and Chettiar 2014, 45).

Within this worldview, economic costliness, bureaucratic inefficiency, government bloat, and juridical irrationality require vigorous correction and redirection toward the goals of criminological precision (of which fractional decarceration is one part) and maximum prosecutorial operativity. In this context, *Federal Prosecution for the 21st Century* is as much a cultural text as it is a policy document.

Narrating the prosecutor as a fetishized, bureaucratically ascendant figure, the reformist telos rests on a conception of the prosecutor as the primary historical agent of a potentially momentous institutional change. Portrayed as something approximating a law-and-order superhero, the district attorney is not only charged with the grave and otherwise overwhelming (for ordinary humans) responsibilities of protecting civil society and enforcing (criminal) justice, but is also a figure of moral

DYLAN RODRÍGUEZ

gravity, actively reshaping the hegemonic common sense of the martial racial state:

> Federal prosecutors play a distinct and significant role in combating crime. . . . [They] are the protectors of federal criminal and civil law, charged with investigating cases and seeking justice in challenging circumstances. They handle cases large and small, complex and simple, violent and petty. . . . They ensure that offenders are held accountable for crimes committed. They are charged with serving justice and keeping the public safe. . . .

> Members of the Blue Ribbon Panel overwhelmingly believed prosecutors could play a leading role in rethinking prisons as the central tool for fighting crime, *either through the bully pulpit* or through other means such as alternatives to incarceration. (Eisen, Fortier, and Chettiar 2014, 13, 27, emphasis added)

The measures advocated by the Brennan Center report would almost certainly institute a significant shift in contemporary criminal justice culture, protocols, electoral platforms, and intentional prosecutorial outcomes: if the prosecutorial paradigms and methods inducing mass incarceration are akin to criminal justice saturation bombing, *Federal Prosecution for the 21st Century* argues for the sociological and criminological merits of high-yield prosecutorial precision strikes, focusing policing, juridical, and carceral state capacities "on fewer but more significant cases, as opposed to fixating on sheer volume" (Eisen, Fortier, and Chettiar 2014, 20). The report intends to offer an ambitious, far-reaching blueprint for national reform: it signifies ambitions toward bipartisan, hegemonic political traction by vesting credibility in a blue-ribbon panel overwhelmingly populated by prosecutors (of fifteen members, eleven were current or former district attorneys, one a former associate deputy attorney general at the U.S. Department of Justice, and one was deputy director of the Executive Office for U.S. Attorneys).

Departing from the Brennan Center's privileged example, it may be worth raising several questions addressing the substance, significations, and sociogenic consequences (per Fanon's and Wynter's discourse on sociogeny[2]) of such and related mobilizations of mass incarceration as a reformist rubric:

- How does the mass incarceration reform bloc differentiate between mass incarceration and justly administered, righteous, democratic, and/or *nonmass* incarceration?

- Is ending or reducing mass incarceration a matter of attaining a numerical threshold, and if so, what is the threshold, and what determines the methodologies of this prospective carceral downsizing?
- What is the political and cultural logic shaping the collapsing of a proto-abolitionist mission—ending mass incarceration—into a reform program that focuses entirely on improving the protocols and funding priorities for the statecraft of policing, criminalization, and carceral domestic war?
- If we consider the conceptual framework (as differentiated from the funding base and political infrastructure) of the Brennan Center effort as both symptomatic and productive of a potentially hegemonic reformist ambition, what can be deduced about the implicit, imputed, and overt meanings of mass incarceration as a facilitating rhetoric?
- Who are the presumed subjects (historical agents) and anticipated/assumed constituencies of the mass incarceration reform rubric (e.g., elected officials, liberal middle class white suburbanites, college-educated activists, incarcerated political educators/organizers, evangelical Christians, philanthropic foundations, former Obama voters)?
- What if the seemingly canonized, liberal commonsense assumption of *unintended consequences* is false?

In Defense of White Life: Mass Incarceration Reform as Police Subsidy

Considered from another position, *Federal Prosecution for the 21st Century* reflects the dense brainstorming of a reconfigured post-1960s antiblack and racial-colonial domestic war—a rigorously, dynamically planned and executed regime of state strategies for addressing the overlapping economic-geographic-political crises cultivated by cresting and overlapping Black radical, anti-colonial, feminist and queer liberation struggles, deindustrialization and its racially structured displacements and abandonments of working people, the rise and decline of neoliberal/global capitalism, complex and always-resurgent white nationalisms (including liberal variations), and the absolute persistence of collective, creative human praxis that counters the hegemony and armed dominance of White Life (McKittrick 2015; Rodríguez and Goonan 2016; Weheliye 2014). The context and substance of the Brennan Center's convening of police, district attorneys, and liberal academics is structured in a collective state of denial that the prior and contemporaneous half-century of martial-juridical planning generated relatively well-anticipated, systemically predictable, and paradigmatically asymmetrical casualties—including the consistently evident, transparent, and tediously orchestrated decades-long construction of the misnamed condition of mass incarceration.

Studied and reread as such, *Federal Prosecution for the 21st Century* proposes to withdraw the ground troops of gendered antiblack carceral war (that is, the war machine of astronomical Black captivity) for the sake of a reconstructed approach to community occupation and redirected, tactically intensified policing. As the prosecutorial paradigm is a central and formative dimension of the envisioned refurbished, more sustainable carceral state, the reconstruction fixates on the repression of illicit behaviors as empirically identifiable, correctible, and containable pathologies, inscribing criminalized acts as scalable deviations from proper liberal citizen subjectivity.

Such an approach reproduces and enhances the long historical technologies of criminal profiling—a methodology of policing as well as a morbid and magical antiblack statecraft with roots in criminological eugenics and the early twenty-first-century racial-economic crises of U.S. industrialization. The technology of the criminal profile actively imagines as it (simultaneously and immediately, concretely) apprehends and narrates the particular profiled being as cultural figuration, physical comportment (including gesture, fashioning, and skin-blood-bone physiology), and potential domestic enemy combatant.

The reform of mass incarceration, in this instance, endorses an expansion of carceral policing logics beyond the discrete institutional-spatial sites of prisons, jails, detention centers, and juvenile facilities. This expanded regime of control, containment, and intensified policing of particular profiled beings (bodies, spaces, communities) is to be implemented through weaponized, high-efficiency state surveillance and the ramping up of ostensibly extracarceral state violence, resonating histories of border rangers, frontier war, slave patrols, and punitive industrial and agricultural labor discipline. Thus, while the reform of mass incarceration declares a counter- or anticarceral intention, its reconstructionist vision proliferates an invigorated logic and refurbished technology of carcerality in the reproduction of gendered antiblack state violence.

Further, the cultural-political narrative of mass incarceration rests on a pair of overlapping political-analytic insistences: first, that the primary fallout of the carceral epoch—that is, the rigorous institutional and cultural militarization of law, civil society, and the martial state against Black life and the potentially transformative insurgencies of Black futurity—is the morally reprehensible and historically tragic, though also largely unintended or accidental, outcome of a compartmentalized moment in the life of U.S. criminal justice policy and carceral domestic war; second, that ending or reducing mass incarceration presumes the ahistorical absoluteness of police, criminal jurisprudence, and incarceration as permanent conditions of sociality, statecraft, nation building, citizenship, public safety, and democracy. To end/reduce mass incarceration, in this narrative telos, is to reform and strategically refine the technologies of a revised/rationalized/just/democratic system of criminal justice rather than to address its roots in dynamic, historical racial-colonial regimes of surveillance, punishment, displacement, and carceral state violence. Black people generally, Native and Aboriginal people acutely, and multiple profiles and population categories identified by geography (e.g., U.S.-Mexico border, urban red light districts, housing projects, hypersegregated neighborhoods), physiology, religion, gendered-sexual presentation, citizenship status, and racial subjectivity are the peculiar and asymmetrical targets of a half-century carceral domestic war that has never remotely targeted the mass U.S. population.

Contemporary reformist rhetorics of mass incarceration avert confrontation with the long historical constitution of White (North American) Life as consistently, materially, and symbolically dependent on a militarized order of freedom that requires the subsuming of other forms of life and being to various antisocial formations of displacement, evisceration, and extinction. The social truth of the contemporary criminalization-policing-incarceration nexus is inseparable from the long historical power relations and densely normalized violence of chattel enslavement, Manifest Destiny genocide, U.S. apartheid, and colonialist and neocolonialist conquest. Gendered racial and racial-colonial technologies of human incarceration (herein understood as state-formed regimes and systems of capture and spatial confinement, not limited to jailing and imprisonment) traverse as they constitute the free-world institutions of the jail, prison, internment camp, reservation, school, factory, housing project, and asylum.

In the shadow of this always looming archive of carceral statecraft and genocidal nation building, the reformist vernaculars of mass incarceration have gradually resignified the bare facts of targeted, massive Black incarceration—and in various geographies, focused Brown and Indigenous incarceration—as a reformable racial dysfunction and fixable national moral problem, the gradualist execution of which is already accompanied by vindicating present-tense parables of postracialist Americanism triumphing over the new Jim Crow. Persistently challenging this emerging, aspirational reformist common sense is the well-worn recognition, supported by the consistently potent and altogether frequent convergence of cross-generational wisdom of experience and incisive historical scholarly-activist analysis, that the evident asymmetries of fatality and misery—which is to say the flesh-borne facts of asymmetrical domestic war—reflect the paradigmatic (hence unreformable) logics of U.S. statecraft in all of its dynamic, nuanced complexities.

This period-defining antagonism brings forward an older irreconcilable (nondialectical) contradiction: as the rhetoric of mass incarceration shapes a moment in the life of national political culture and inflects the signifying order of critical, progressive, and even leftist engagements with the contemporary carceral regime, it also tacitly reifies (that is, naturalizes) the long historical facts of white decriminalization, decarceration, and constitutive innocence. In so doing, the increasingly industrialized and institutionalized rubric of mass incarceration exerts an operational as well as an analytical and broadly cultural force that labors to deform, distort, and obscure other scholarly, theoretical, and insurgent (activist) languages of revolt, including those that invoke as they reinvent the feminist, queer, antiracist, abolitionist, anticolonial, and decolonial languages of domestic warfare, state violence, antiblack genocide, police terror, and settler colonial occupation, among others. These radical analytics, methods, and collectively produced knowledges identify and implicate the complex machineries of historical racial terror, and significantly predate the early twenty-first-century crystallization of a mass incarceration reform complex. In this sense, the reformist vernacular of mass incarceration can be recontextualized as a liberal multiculturalist and postracialist reaction to the various precedent forms of insurgent praxis that embody, envision, and collectively plan redistribution, reparation, liberation from police violence, and unmitigated decriminalization of body, being, way of life, and the soul itself.

The mass incarceration reform wave cannot summon the political will to commune with another kind of critical position: one that comprehends the allegedly scandalous dysfunction, brokenness, irrationality, and cruelty of the antiblack, racial-colonial state as its paradigmatic form, and which understands white multiculturalist civil society's vacillating tolerance, vindication, and reform of this fatal and miserable statecraft as the historical rhythm of U.S. nation building. Such a position is necessarily uncontained, as it is convened through a will to radical, transformative sociality deeply structured in abolitionist, liberationist, and (feminist, queer, diasporic) Black radical visions and traditions.

The next part of this chapter offers a concise and contemporaneous genealogy of the phrase "mass incarceration." At stake is the fabrication of an ideological consensus that has been massaged into the language of the racial state's organic intellectuals and simmers at the base of an emerging common sense of policing, criminalization, and human capture.

Mass Incarceration Narrativity: Origins and (Failed) Analogues

While it is possible to trace its origins to earlier historical moments, the contemporary iterations of the phrase "mass incarceration" surfaced with identifiable coherence in the mid-1990s, partly in response to the work of the thirty-four-member National Criminal Justice Commission. Funded by various nongovernmental sources, the commission was composed of such well-known antiracist activists, critical race theory scholars, and radical criminologists as Nils Christie, Derrick Bell, Charles Ogletree, Vincent Schiraldi, Eddie Ellis, and others. From 1994 to 1996, this group undertook an expository analysis of and comprehensive policy recommendations for what it described as "the largest and most frenetic correctional buildup of any country in the history of the world" (Donziger 1996, 31). The commission's work was far-reaching and global in scope, and its research and analytical labors culminated in the publication of *The Real War on Crime*, a widely cited report published in book form by HarperCollins publishers.

Coinciding with an early to mid-1990s groundswell of countercarceral and criminal justice reform initiatives spurred by scholars, grassroots, and (formerly) incarcerated activists/organizers, legal/civil/human rights advocates, and others, the National Criminal Justice Commission's high-profile critique contributed to a growing, counterhegemonic reframing of the alleged dysfunctions, corruptions, and (legal) irrationalities of the U.S. criminal justice cultural and policy infrastructure. Through the latter 1990s and early 2000s, an expanded left-progressive political spectrum of antiprison, carceral and penal abolitionist, prison moratorium, and human rights activisms proliferated across the U.S., encompassing (and producing) such organizations as Legal Services for Prisoners with Children (founded 1978), the Sentencing Project (1986), Critical Resistance (1997), Prison Moratorium Project (1998), and Justice Now (2000).

Notably, the term "mass incarceration" attained significant rhetorical traction in this period, surfacing in academic, activist, and progressive think-tank analyses and prominently appearing in such influential texts as Marc Mauer and Meda Chesney-Lind's (2002) *Invisible Punishment: The Collateral Consequences of Mass Imprisonment* and Michelle Alexander's (2010) widely read *The New Jim Crow: Mass Incarceration in the Age of Colorblindness*. Although a full, textured reading of the discursive life of the term "mass incarceration" exceeds the critical focus of this chapter, it should be mentioned that during this period, the phrase has been periodically appropriated by radical antiracist, feminist, queer, and abolitionist thinkers to amplify notions of targeted criminalization and juridically sanctioned domestic warfare. Yet while the nuances of mass incarceration rhetoric—and particularly, the variation in its political significations across moments, places, and subjectivities—belie simplistic ideological characterization, it is no less possible to identify how a proto-hegemonic, early twenty-first-century mass incarceration narrativity is attempting to articulate and convene a liberal (racial) common sense in the service of carceral reform.

Given the circulation and influence of Alexander's *The New Jim Crow* across communities and publics, from progressive Black church communities and abolitionist activists to public policy think tanks and elected officials, the book's narrative arc can be read as a crystallization of the key plot points and political implications of mass incarceration narrativity. Since numerous critics have incisively and rigorously outlined the book's analytical and methodological shortcomings, i will refrain from rehearsing those critiques here in exchange for offering a brief meditation on *The New Jim Crow*'s significance as a form of present-tense storytelling.

Lucidly illustrating a post–civil rights era marked by antiblack criminalization and targeted, large-scale incarceration, Alexander articulates her thesis through a historical analogy that posits the emergence of post-1970s Black incarceration as a "New Jim Crow." Strangely, the book contradicts its own narrative historical premises by asserting that the contemporary carceral condition actually cannot and should not be substantively equilibrated to (old) Jim Crow: "[although] the parallels between the two systems of control are striking," it is more important to understand that "there are important differences" (Alexander 2010, 195). Cataloguing the institutional, cultural, and political differences between the antiblack state regimes of Jim Crow segregation and post–Jim Crow racial incarceration, the book moves to compartmentalize the entirety of its own structuring historical analogy by asserting that "[the] list of the differences between Jim Crow and mass incarceration . . . might well be longer than the list of similarities."

In its penultimate chapter, *The New Jim Crow* compounds its own narrative contradiction by replicating an optimistic racial-historical telos that is abruptly incompatible with almost all of the secondary empirical evidence outlined in the previous two hundred pages. Alleging that the recent historical period (and onset of the Obama presidency) is marked by an "*absence* of overt racial hostility" among elected officials and other politicians, law enforcement officials, and within "the public discourse" more generally (Alexander 2010, 197), the book actively undermines the potential critical force of its own accumulated descriptions of mass incarceration. Alexander writes,

> Even granting that some African Americans may fear the police today as much as their grandparents feared the Klan . . . and that the penal system may be as brutal in many respects as Jim Crow (or slavery), the absence of racial hostility in the public discourse and the steep decline in vigilante racial violence is no small matter. It is also significant that the "whites only" signs are gone and that children of all colors can drink from the same water fountains, swim in the same pools, and play on the same playgrounds. Black children today can even dream of being president of the United States.
>
> Those who claim that mass incarceration is "just like" Jim Crow make a serious mistake. Things have changed. (2010, 197)

The New Jim Crow's assertion that the emergence of mass incarceration is accompanied by a generalized cultural-political decline in racist discourse and reactionary racist mobilization is distressing for both its overwhelming historical inaccuracy and potentially dangerous cultural, policy, and activist implications. On the one hand, this narrative contention grossly mis-estimates the post-1960s reawakening and expansion of organized white supremacist and white nationalist movements and ideologies, evidenced by the tripling of Ku Klux Klan membership during the decade of the 1970s (Marable 2007, 171), the numerical cresting of white reactionary hate groups in 2011, and the accelerated mainstreaming of white nationalism and overtly white supremacist ideologues during and after the 2016 presidential election (Potok 2017).[3] On the other hand, and perhaps more fundamentally, there is the deeper question of whether the Jim Crow narrative analogy provides an adequate critical prism through which to apprehend the formation of contemporary U.S. carceral regime.

DYLAN RODRÍGUEZ

Here, Alexander's failure to substantively engage a body of prior thinking and writing extends beyond citational negligence and leaks into complicity with historical-analytical illiteracy.

As the book and its author circulated widely among multiple reading publics in the years after its 2010 publication, *The New Jim Crow* catalyzed a turn in the life of mass incarceration rhetoric, veering into the counterabolitionist liberalism of racial state autocritique and self-instituted reformist assessment. What happens when the organic intellectuals of the racial state and discursive systems of the carceral regime actively absorb and rearticulate the plot points of mass incarceration narrativity? We can briefly consider three prominent examples spanning less than ten months.

Holder-Clinton-Obama's Law and Order: Three Speeches

U.S. Attorney General Eric Holder's keynote address for the Brennan Center in September 2014 provides one of the clearest, earliest examples of the racial state's engagement with mass incarceration narrativity. Addressing the problem of "over-incarceration" in the immediate wake of intense local and national protests over the police street assassination of Michael Brown in Ferguson, Missouri, Holder qualifies his gestures toward criminal justice reform through a valorizing depiction of an alleged period of progress in U.S. policing and prosecutorial practices. Holder's keynote tells a story of symbiosis between carceral streamlining and enhanced police capacity, suggesting it as the premise for an updated law-and-order paradigm:

> For far too long—under well-intentioned policies designed to be "tough" on criminals—our system has perpetuated a destructive cycle of poverty, criminality, and incarceration that has trapped countless people and weakened entire communities—particularly communities of color. . . .
>
> Perhaps most troubling is the fact that this astonishing rise in incarceration—and the escalating costs it has imposed on our country, in terms both economic and human—have not measurably benefited our society. We can *all* be proud of the progress that's been made at reducing the crime rate over the past two decades—thanks to the tireless work of prosecutors and the bravery of law enforcement officials across America. But statistics have shown—and all of us have seen—that high incarceration rates and longer-than-necessary prison terms *have not* played a significant

role in materially improving public safety, reducing crime, or strengthening communities.

In fact, the opposite is often true. (Holder 2015; see also Sullum 2013)

Holder's adaptation indicates the general compatibility between mass incarceration narrativity and the aspirational postracialist renovations of legitimated racist state violence. Guided by the mandates of institutional sustainability and liberal political respectability, the refurbishing of extracarceral domestic war becomes the militarized foundation for an overhaul of "well-intentioned" and accidentally, atrociously flawed criminal justice policy (aka the Reagan-Bush-Clinton–era War on Drugs). The particular positionality of the U.S. attorney general is paramount here: repeating the well-worn criminological critique of punitive, large-scale incarceration as a mode of production for antisociality rather than public safety, Holder is throwing a half century of U.S. criminal law and carceral expansion into the bin of American ill repute and liberal shame. Evidenced, then, is a political script of mass incarceration reform that not only leverages influence on the planning of the racial state's carceral infrastructure but also—inseparably—shapes the public discourse of its administrative overseers.

Seven months later, newly declared presidential candidate Hillary Clinton greeted recently appointed U.S. Attorney General Loretta Lynch with a resounding call for a new, aggressive era of criminal justice and police reform. In an ode to the recently resigned Holder, candidate Clinton made conspicuous use of the phrase "era of mass incarceration" in a platform speech to Columbia University's David Dinkins Leadership Forum. While urging the expanded use of police body cameras and decrying how "far too many people believe they are considered guilty simply because of the color of their skin," Clinton clings to one of the structuring, mystified, and disciplinary ambitions of white civil society: the fostering of affective connections between the militarized police and their implicitly Black subjects of occupation and imminent coercive exchange.

> We have to come to terms with some hard truths about race and justice in America. There is something profoundly wrong when African-American men are far more likely to be stopped by the police and charged with crimes and given longer prison terms than their white counterparts. . . . There is something wrong when trust between law enforcement and the communities they serve breaks down. . . . We must urgently begin to rebuild bonds of trust and respect among Americans between police and citizens. (Frizell 2015)

DYLAN RODRÍGUEZ

Hillary Clinton ✓
@HillaryClinton

End mass incarceration. Address inequality. Restore trust between law enforcement & communities. Read this & share: hrc.io/1beDAEy

9:19 AM · Apr 29, 2015 · Twitter Web Client

8.2 H. Clinton tweet, April 29, 2015 (screenshot taken February 2018).

Clinton's (2015) subsequent Twitter post captures the plot points of mass incarceration narrativity in shorthand: "End mass incarceration. Address inequality. Restore trust between law enforcement & communities" (see figure 8.2).

While Clinton's rhetorical turnabout on the matter of antiblack criminalization has been well noted, it is worth emphasizing that her mid-1990s grandstanding on the scourge of Black children "superpredators" (offered as a moral-panic endorsement of President Bill Clinton's 1994 crime bill) does not entirely contradict the substance of her 2015–16 campaign platform. In fact, there are overt narrative similarities as well as policy continuities between her now-infamous 1996 speech at Keene State University in New Hampshire and the propolice tenets buttressing the mass incarceration reform complex. It is possible to reread the words immediately prefacing Clinton's bestial call to "bring [superpredators] to heel" as the durable, long-resonating premise for the carceral reformist wager presented to a more recent electoral generation: "We have actually been making progress . . . as a nation, because of what local law enforcement officials are doing, because of [what] citizens and neighborhood patrols are doing. . . . because we have finally gotten more police officers on the street. . . . If we have more police interacting with people, having them on the streets, we can prevent crimes. We can prevent petty crimes from turning into something worse" (Clinton 1996).

Consider, then, how the organic intellectuals of the carceral racial state assume and adapt the very same vernaculars that are furtively purposed toward Black radical and abolitionist critiques of their policies, practices, and methods of civil pacification. Something wicked lurks beneath the state-appropriated narrative of mass incarceration reform that requires radical scrutiny.

President Barack Obama's remarks during a July 2015 address to the NAACP in Philadelphia echo and amplify candidate Clinton's message, sustaining the seamless narrative meshing of liberal criminal justice racial reform with strident propolice jingoism. On the one hand, Obama speaks the language of reformist civil rights antiracism when he stresses the need for a criminal justice apparatus that facilitates a restoration of Black and Brown boys and men (and to a secondary extent, girls and women) to positions of heteronormative racial respectability in multiculturalist civil society. Obama's explicit appropriation of the mass incarceration rubric further canonizes the liberal racial bildungsroman that guides the martial statecraft of postraciality:

> The bottom line is that in too many places, black boys and black men, Latino boys and Latino men experience being treated differently under the law.
>
> . . . This is not just barbershop talk. A growing body of research shows that people of color are more likely to be stopped, frisked, questioned, charged, detained. African Americans are more likely to be arrested. They are more likely to be sentenced to more time for the same crime.
>
> What is that doing to our communities? What's that doing to those children? Our nation is being robbed of men and women who could be workers and taxpayers, could be more actively involved in their children's lives, could be role models, could be community leaders, and right now they're locked up for a non-violent offense.
>
> So our criminal justice system isn't as smart as it should be. It's not keeping us as safe as it should be. It is not as fair as it should be. Mass incarceration makes our country worse off, and we need to do something about it. (Obama 2015)

Obama crystallizes the narrative logic of a Black neoliberal revision of African American community formation and survival, gathering vigorous applause from the NAACP audience in a hallucinating moment of historical fiction: "It is important for us to recognize that violence in our communities is serious and that historically, in fact, the African American community oftentimes was under-policed rather than over-policed. Folks were very interested in containing the African American community so it couldn't leave segregated areas, *but within those areas there wasn't enough police presence*" (Obama 2015).

　　　　　　　　　　　　　　　　　　　　　DYLAN RODRÍGUEZ

When the organic intellectuals and lead executives of the racial state begin to appropriate the ostensibly critical language of mass incarceration, it may be time to question whether the term has reached its point of explanatory and analytical obsolescence (that is, if it ever adequately explained and analyzed anything to begin with). The U.S. racial state—even in its momentarily postracialist and multiculturalist form—is both willing and capable of renarrating the story of mass incarceration as a call for better, that is, more tolerable and effectively racial consensus-building technologies of criminalization, policing, and incarceration.

It has become apparent that mass incarceration narrativity endorses (and is ultimately indistinguishable from) a statecraft of policing that skillfully links liberal post–civil rights racial sympathy and the long historical fact of racist and antiblack state repression to adamant demands for carceral downsizing and a kinder, gentler, expanded cultural and martial infrastructure of law-and-order policing. As a consequence, the sociality inhabits a vacillation—at the same time a generalized symbiosis—between broken-windows policing and compulsory police body cameras, stop-and-frisk harassment and community policing, and communal outrage over individualized episodes of (fatal) police violence and simultaneous demands for more and better policing, sometimes issued by ostensible spokespeople of police-occupied communities themselves. Further, if we follow the methodological and analytical schema offered by the late Stuart Hall and colleagues in their ever-durable 1978 study *Policing the Crisis*, contemporary policing can only be adequately conceptualized as a simultaneity of institutional projects: it is, at once, a militarized bureaucratic apparatus, a state and popular discursive regime, a far-ranging media and cultural production, and a dynamic state pedagogical project. *Policing is all of the above* (Hall et al. 2013).

The Mass (Back Then)

Who has become the "mass" of mass incarceration? If it is not the case that Euro-descended people and those racially marked white are subjects of criminalization en masse to a degree that remotely approaches the criminalization and incarceration of their Black, Brown, and Indigenous counterparts, then it may be necessary to accept that the term "mass incarceration" actually presumes casual and official white innocence, including the normative assumption of white bodily entitlement to physiological integrity and civil mobility.

On the other hand, a veritable library of scholars has traced the links between racial plantation slavery and the emergence of the modern American penal regime (Blackmon 2008; Childs 2015; Davis 1998; Dayan 2007; Hadden 2001; Haley 2016; Lichtenstein 1995; Mancini 1996; Muhammad 2011; Oshinsky 1996; Rediker 2007; Wacquant 2009). In its totality, this constantly growing archive of interdisciplinary and counterdisciplinary critical and radical thought illuminates how the unfolding of the modern U.S. carceral regime turns on the distended political legitimation and reinvigoration of slavery's antiblack racist statecraft and cultural production. That is, the historical ensemble of racial chattel violence has been persistently reformed (that is, not abolished) to fit the changing mandates of the postslavery, post–civil rights, and recent postracial and multiculturalist iterations of the American nation-building project: thus, the juridical designation of the convicted person as the bodily property of the state, eviscerated of civil existence (including alienation from the regimes of civil and human rights), composes an indelible (rather than historically compartmentalized or geographically isolated) power relation for cohering the modern U.S. state and constituting its (criminal) juridical apparatus across its historical and systemic modalities of growth, transformation, and reform. How might the historical force of antiblack carceral racial genocide and proto-genocide, formed in the power relations of transatlantic racial chattel slavery, be renarrated as an origin point for the modern U.S. racist state, including its contemporary criminalization, policing, and carceral apparatuses?

Consider, now, the storytelling implications of a radical racial chattel genealogy of the contemporary carceral regime, premised on the narrative techniques of historical continuity, transgenerational knowledge/wisdom, and the inhabitation of a permanent, physiologically activated condition of insurgency against U.S. slave coloniality (in and beyond western Africa, the Caribbean, and North America). The antiblack chattel relation forms as it facilitates the condition of modernity as well as modern (state) institutionality. This formation of power—as paradigm, method, and infrastructural template—structures the very coherence and preconceptual premises of modern institutions as and bureaucratic structures—including notions of order, administrative/labor hierarchy, disciplinarity/compliance, stability, and normative white civil subjectivity. As an antiblack, racial-colonial, genocidal and proto-genocidal project of white civilization building, the long historical construction of racial chattel and its emancipated rearticulation in racial criminalization permanently disarticulates any allegation of a New World mass: there is no mass; there are only differentiations of places, people, physiologies, subjectivities, and futurities.

> Neither slavery nor involuntary servitude, *except as a punishment for crime whereof the party shall have been duly convicted,* shall exist within the United States, or any place subject to their jurisdiction. (emphasis added)

Commonly valorized as the decree that abolished plantation slavery, the Thirteenth Amendment (passed by Congress in 1865) refurbishes the racist state by transparently recodifying the terms of bodily capture and subjection (aka slavery). Traced through the postplantation Emancipation sesquicentennial and beyond, the symbiotic cultural and state technologies of racial criminalization consistently inherit and actively weaponize the historical technologies of the slave ship, coffle, and auction block as the leverage points through which the duly convicted are made available for enslavement under the terms of criminal incarceration. In constitutional emancipation, the slave relation is not abolished but is reanimated through the imminent statecraft of criminal justice carcerality.

Given this genealogy of racial chattel and criminal justice, what are the consequences of a reformist mass incarceration narrativity that affirms the cultural-political legitimacy of a contemporary policing regime that cannot rehabilitate its reliance on a plantation/frontier methodology?

In a 2015 open letter that incinerates the American Civil Liberties Union for its sellout settlement with the Chicago Police Department on the matter of its notorious stop-and-frisk policies, Chicago-based grass-roots group We Charge Genocide embraces another kind of historical narrative. Densely excoriating the ACLU's bypassing of Black organizations and Black community leadership in its negotiations with the Chicago PD while refuting the ACLU's reductive understanding of stop-and-frisk policing, We Charge Genocide (2015) writes,

> We understand police violence to be rooted in historical and systemic anti-blackness that seeks to control, contain, and repress Black bodies through acts of repeated violence. Stop and frisk should be understood as a tool police use to punish Black people just for *being.* Police violence is always state-sanctioned violence, and further strengthening narrow supervision of police action by elites will never address that. This is why any legislative or law-based campaign to address police violence requires not just policy change, but an actual transformation of power relations between communities of color and the police.

We Charge Genocide is one of many sources of creative narrative genius that disrupt and transform liberal commonsense languages, contributing to a long-term critical and radical praxis that brings incisive and intensive attention to the long historical present tense of normalized social eviscerations and intimate encounters with global systems of power and fatality. This collective genius emanates from a complexly shared relationship to an indisputable fact: that the United States is an accumulation and reproduction of centuries of gendered-antiblack state violence, institutionalized dehumanization and ontological negation, and genocidal logics of domination.

Here, then, is another critical task, undertaken for the sake of disarticulating mass incarceration narrativity and offering a different, insurgent civilizational story against civilization: to define incarceration (and thus mass incarceration) against its juridical-cultural coherence as such.

Other Terms

Against the force of more commonly circulated languages and narratives, many in the (often overlapping) Black radical and anticolonialist genealogies have used other terms, even as far too many people actually inhabit their reality: annihilation, apocalypse, genocide, domestic warfare. Beneath, around, and actively overwhelming the sterile and increasingly state-sanctioned phrase "mass incarceration" there is institutionalized misery, collective anticipation of everyday racist state aggression, and the kind of creative radical and conspiratorial genius that might best be traced to the fugitive and plantation liberation praxis of the enslaved, alongside the historically colonized and occupied peoples around the planet who have figured out how to survive—and periodically disrupt or even overthrow—their own involuntarily inherited forms of occupation, policing, and spatial incarceration (Berger 2014; Burton 2016; Harney and Moten 2013; James 2007; Moten 2003; Stannard 1992; Vargas 2008; Woods 1998).

The discourse of mass incarceration in the early twenty-first century has, with some exceptions, been constituted and deformed by the overlapping ideological fields of white, multiculturalist, and/or civil rights liberalism: that is, the term tends to facilitate critical analyses that pivot on notions of unfairness, systemic bias, racial disparity, and institutional dysfunction; this generalized position, in turn, endorses and mobilizes around vigorous reforms of the state's incarceration and criminalization infrastructure, largely by way of internal auditing, aggressive legal and pol-

DYLAN RODRÍGUEZ

icy shifts, and rearrangements of carceral capacities and protocols. Such a reformist approach fails to critically address incarceration in and of itself, as a systemic logic and methodology of social formation that sustains the gendered racist power relations of chattel slavery, colonial conquest, and white supremacist nation building.

Consider what it means to inhabit the other side of a present-tense liberal-progressive common sense that seems inseparable from the white supremacist origins and logics of the modern humanist project. There is a possibility, at the very least, to remain uncompromising in the practice and theorization of radical terms, which translate into radical and transformative analysis, research, scholarship, and praxis. This is the dense reality of what some have begun to call "abolition" in the climate of twenty-first-century gendered racist state violence, within and beyond the United States.

Notes

1   While the literature on the management of corporate organizational change is vast, the particular inspiration for this reference is a short handbook distributed to administrators at the University of California, Riverside (Hiatt 2012).

2   In addition to the well-cited works of Sylvia Wynter and Frantz Fanon, see Marriott (2011).

3   According to the Southern Poverty Law Center's inventory of racist, nativist, and white supremacist hate groups in the U.S., there was a numerical historical peak in 2011, and a resurgence during the first years of the Trump presidency. Further, the SPLC notes that its inventory almost certainly underestimates the presence of organized white supremacy and white nationalism by virtue of its mainstreaming in local and national party politics and spreading presence online (Potok 2017).

GENDERED ANTIBLACKNESS AND
POLICE VIOLENCE IN THE FORMATIONS
OF BRITISH POLITICAL LIBERALISM

MOHAN AMBIKAIPAKER

The racial and state violence that Black women experience in Britain has never been recognized as an imperative of critical public-sphere issues of the day and thus has never achieved the significance or urgency needed to shape referendums, electoral outcomes, and public policies. And yet, Black women's everyday struggles against antiblackness in Britain are productive structural tensions that engage the ongoing dynamics of repositioning African-descended peoples into the zone of social death over the zone of social life (Patterson 1982). Understood through this foundational logic that constitutes Western liberal democratic social orders, Black women's lived experiences of historically continuous violation and dishonor and routine antiracist failures in seeking justice emerge not as individual aberrations but as naturalized and perverse modes of inuring antiblack coherence into British rule of law.

The structural and discursive linkages between the afterlives of slavery (Hartman 1997) and the dynamics of securing rule of law in Britain help to situate and contextualize the life story of Gillian, an African Caribbean woman who has spent decades fighting against police abuse in the East London borough of Newham. As a member of a community-based politically black antiracist organization, the Newham Monitoring Project (NMP, which existed between 1980 and 2015), I was Gillian's assigned caseworker in 2006 and worked with her on an incident that was not her first or last experience with police abuse.[1] In fact, Gillian had been at the center of NMP's Stop Police Harassment of Black Women in Newham campaign in the 1990s, which addressed issues from "police trivializing violence against women to the criminalizing of Black women" and attendant racial disparities in women's incarceration (Newham Monitoring Project 1993, 38–41).[2]

In order to make legible the ways in which Gillian and other African Caribbean women's lifetime experiences of racialization, violent racism, and state racism integrally constitute Britain's political liberalism, it is necessary to shift the current focus on theorizing antiblackness away from its psychologized dimensions. This move does not negate theorizing antiblack racism as an objective and cross-cutting libidinal economy that shapes the psychic and the political unconscious in relation to African diasporic peoples (Sexton 2010; Wilderson 2010). But psychologized frameworks of explaining antiblackness and relations of power inadvertently also make opaque the formal political logics and forces that are coextensive when deployments of gendered antiblack racism and violence within Westernized and juridified social orders occur. Gendered antiblackness and violence, I argue, are not simply gratuitous, but also logically coherent and reasoned as an everyday formal political consciousness whose raison d'être is to recursively reground Western liberal democracies in foundational distinctions between liberal subjects and nonblack bodies who are inscribed with popular sovereignty or the potential for popular sovereignty, and Black subjects and bodies who are rendered socially dead.

Western political liberalism's global legitimacy is based on its claims of creating a rights-based social order that is adjudicated through dispassionate and indifferent reasoning. Indifference to subjective experience is seen as a virtue in the traditions of Western legal formalism and a principle to be maintained in order to enact the impartiality of authority. However, it is the systematic-structural historical and contemporary indifference toward Black women who are ambivalently appropriated/excluded within such orders that actively underpins and reconstructs dispassionate rule of law. The ambivalent play of white recognition and repressive juridification that is aimed at submerging the pain, suffering, and violated personhood of Black women into exclusionary captive and colonial zones is necessary work required to continually reestablish the precepts of Western liberal democracy.

The recurrent deployments of dehumanized racializations, state violence, and violent racism against African Caribbean women reveal the continuum of gendered antiblack violence as a range of everyday political activities in which both white and nonwhite social agents engage, in order to reembed liberal rule of law and the antiblack alignment of the state. Hence gendered antiblackness is neither derived as a secondhand epiphenomenon of purportedly autonomous social factors such as the abstract conceptualizations of class or crises in the political economy, nor is it fully understandable as a subliminal and psychologized analysis of the "dispensation of energies, concerns, points of attention, anxieties, pleasures, appetites, revulsions, and phobias" (Jared Sexton, quoted in Wilderson 2010, 7). Another horizon needs to be regarded in order to understand the role that antiblackness and gendered antiblackness play in coextensively reconstituting and rearticulating Western liberal juridical rule.

A recent chapter in the history of violence against Black women, and in particular against African Caribbean women, whose mid-twentieth-century settlement in the metropole involves the mass migration of Commonwealth subjects from the Anglophone Caribbean colonies, primarily from Jamaica, Trinidad, and Guyana, but also from the smaller islands of Barbados, St. Lucia, Dominica, Antigua and Barbuda, Grenada, and others, has decisively shaped the character of the postempire British state. Such histories of struggles against gendered and racialized British state violence, however, are not recognized in official governance ideologies that have alternately stressed celebratory and neoliberal multicultural policies in the 1990s or repressive imperatives for harsh anti-immigration measures and counterterrorism-focused derogations of rights and civil liberties in the current period. Sustained social patterns of racialized and gendered violence against African Caribbean women that have cut across different ideological eras in British politics only appear in the public sphere through ahistorical or apolitical frameworks that register such violence as matters for liberal individual modes of antiracism, such as engaging British juridical institutions in order to find remedies and justice for individualized cases of police abuse or hate crimes, which are often referred to as racial harassment and attacks in Britain. Liberal juridical frameworks of justice are incapable of recognizing a lifetime of recursive victimization that is based on the everyday political logics of gendered antiblackness.

To make legible how gendered violence against African Caribbean women inures to contemporary British political liberalism, it is necessary to first provide a historicized narrative not only about oppression but also concerning the repression of the social-political efforts of African Caribbean women in contesting gendered antiblack violence in postempire Britain. Such a genealogy is necessary to situate the current social field within which it is possible to narrate contemporary African Caribbean women's personal and political stories as excessive stories that are too unruly for the frames of British political liberalism and yet constitutive of its racialized democratic norms.

Gendered Racialization of British Political Liberalism

As the work of Julia Chinyere Oparah/Sudbury (2016) has shown, the criminalization and the pathological representation and treatment of African Caribbean women in Britain are enacted through socially saturated gendered representations of African Caribbean women as members of illegitimate and unruly racial communities who possess strong, deviant characteristics that necessitate the state's and civil society's repressive securitization and violent containment rather than the application of equal personhood. These contemporary tropes of gendered racializations, however, do not emerge within historical vacuums. A usable genealogy of specific forms of gendered racialization can be located in the *longue durée* epistemic structures that are enveloped in the British history of slavery.

British political liberalism developed its ideal theories of liberal justice (Mills 2008) and the hegemony of private property–based rule of law in tandem with the historical positioning of African Caribbean women as enslaved chattel property in the colonies and directly in the metropole as well. The tensions around African Caribbean women's position within British slavery and colonial discourse are routed through productive white ambivalences and liberal anxiety with the prospect of enacting substantial equality and totally abolishing, not just the de jure laws that made the slave trade legal, but "a society that . . . could have slavery" and its affiliative rationalities (Harney and Moten 2013, 42). The diffusion of slavery and capitalist plantation epistemes (Quijano 2000; Robinson 2000), such as treating enslaved African women as economically incorporated labor and private property and therefore habitually alienated in natal and sociopolitical terms (Patterson 1982), has had an enduring influence in constructing anxiety and the illegibility around Black women's demands for justice within British legal traditions.

A key example of colonial political liberalism's nervousness about unrepressing the equal personhood of enslaved African women and abolishing their treatment as private property in British law lies in late eighteenth-century case of *R v. Inhabitants of Thames Ditton* (1785).[3] In this case, which was ruled upon by England's chief justice, Lord Mansfield, followed his earlier iconic decision in the famous *Somerset* case that is popularly understood as a shining moment in British abolitionist history as well as a push factor in prompting the American colonies to seek independence in order to preserve slavery and the property rights of settler colonials (Horne 2014). In *Somerset*, Mansfield had ruled that white masters could not forcibly remove slaves out of the metropole, even if they were still held as private property by white slave owners in the colonies. This decision, as T. T. Arvind (2012) argues, was based on making a choice between two contending strands of British legal standpoints concerning the institution of slavery at the time. The first viewed slavery as a form of bonded serf labor (villeinage), and the second viewed slaves as a form of chattel property. The Mansfield decision appeared to delimit the rights of slave owners to treat slaves as entirely chattel and minimally granted slaves some recognition as rights-bearing people within the metropole.

But the social and political anxiety produced by this decision, including its possible impact on the status of some 14,000 slaves who were kept by slave owners largely for domestic labor within the metropole itself, was a key factor in delimiting its scope in the subsequent *Thames Ditton* case, ruled upon by the same Lord Mansfield (Arvind 2012).[4] In this case, Charlotte Howe, an enslaved African Caribbean woman, had sought poor relief in the aftermath of the death of her master. Mansfield acted to deny any recognition of Howe's claim for justice because her original status as a Black woman slave was reaffirmed. He reasoned that poor relief was only granted to persons who were recognized by the law as having freely entered a contractual relationship, and Howe's origin as a slave from the colonies meant that she could not change her status as property into that of a free agent in the labor market.

As a Black woman, she was fixed in a zone of social death, irrespective of her physical location in the colony or metropole or changes in her working terms. Hence, contrary to his choice in the *Somerset* decision, Mansfield refused to expand Howe's claim to personhood rights in England. He elected instead to construct the meaning of liberal juridical dispassion as primarily determined by a greater common good that was vested in preserving white habitual social, political, and economic national interests.

MOHAN AMBIKAIPAKER

This was the common good that had to be protected against any moral imperative to recognize the free personhood or remedy the pain and suffering of Black women. The authorization of this liberal juridical antiblack logic, at the very historical moment that is celebrated as the beginning of the end of slavery in the British Empire, reinscribes the social death of Black women for the coming postabolition epoch.

Recently, Lord Mansfield's signature cases around slavery have entered contemporary popular culture through the movie *Belle* (2013), directed by the Black British director Amma Assante. The film focuses on the historical fact that Mansfield was raising a mixed-race Black niece, the progeny of his nephew who was a Caribbean planter, at the same time that he was adjudicating these landmark cases involving slavery. He is portrayed in the film as someone whose legal reasoning was positively influenced by his affection and in loco parentis relationship with his niece, whom he raised as an aristocratic subject, in spite of her skin color. The film also focuses on Mansfield's 1781 decision in the *Zong* case. In this civil case, a slave-trading corporation had thrown 122 slaves overboard in the Carribean Sea and then proceeded to make a claim for insurance compensation. However, as Arvind (2012, 116) has pointed out, while Mansfield is said to have personally found slavery an "odious" institution, he nonetheless cleaved to his dispassionate role as an English common-law jurist in upholding the commercial and economic order that relied on maintaining the status of Africans as goods and chattel private property.

> They justified this by invoking formalism—the principle of "decision according to rule," where the duty of a judge is to decide cases purely according to rules of law, unswayed by any other considerations no matter how compelling they may seem. And the law, they argued, left them with no choice but to uphold the existing order of things, however distasteful the result might seem to them. "Though it shocks one very much," Lord Mansfield said in the *Zong* [case], in law it made no difference whether the cargo thrown overboard was a cargo of slaves or horses. (Arvind 2012, 116)

Mansfield's construction of dispassionate reasoning with respect to the institution of slavery, both in the *Zong* case and in *Thames Ditton*, privileged liberal procedural norms over the recognition of enslaved Black women as subjects or bodies capable of experiencing pain and suffering. While these moments are celebrated in the film as progressive turning points in British history and heralding the abolition of slavery in the British Empire, it is nonetheless clear that the moment also changes and extends the form of gendered antiblackness into another liberal juridical modality that reinaugurates the social death of slaves.

This self-conflicted play of liberal juridical reasoning, however, is critical for constructing an objective and legitimizing effect on the hegemony of rule of law. Historical liberal-juridical procedures for repressing gendered and racialized claims for justice are important references for thinking about the ways in which contemporary claims for remedying Black women's lived experiences of violence in Britain are similarly constrained and repressed within juridified frameworks and traditions. The violated Black woman is both the trigger and the site through which the play of ambivalence/recognition and anxious repression of substantial racial justice is embedded with impunity as the norm.

The question of Black people's status as rightfully belonging within the ambit of popular sovereignty and hence as legitimate claimants to British justice has never been a settled affair. With the mass settlement of non-white Commonwealth subjects in the post–World War II era, white British racial nativist backlashes ensured that the status of Black people was kept within a permanent state of citizenship ambivalence as well. In 2018, the Windrush scandal erupted because of growing and undeniable evidence that many Caribbean migrants, most of whom were children of colonial subjects who at one time were themselves imperial citizens of the empire and Commonwealth, had been stripped of their lawful residency rights. This transpired in the midst of the ruling Conservative Party's efforts to construct a "hostile environment" against new undocumented immigration (Elgot 2018). As David Lammy (2018), an African Caribbean member of Parliament recounted, "The relationship between this country and the West Indies and the Caribbean is inextricable. The first British ships arrived in the Caribbean in 1623, and despite slavery and colonisation, 25,000 Caribbeans served in the first and second world wars alongside British troops. When my parents and others of their generation arrived in this country under the British Nationality Act 1948, they arrived here as British citizens."

And yet the lack of recognition of the inextricable relationship between African Caribbean migrants, slavery, and Britain is not aberrational. This forgetting and erasure is politically and socially necessary to enable the emergence and maintenance of a postcolonial white preferential British public sphere and liberal juridical order. The Windrush episode was but one recent example of the power of white British racial nationalism in shaping a rule-of-law regime that preferentially tends toward the logics of the ahistorical social liquidation of nonwhite Britons and the construction of a normalized consensus on the imperative to control non-European migration and to reduce and repatriate the Black presence. This antiblack ethic and popular consensus, however, is advanced on multiple interlocking and coded pretexts, such as white British cultural loss, social welfare state pressure, criminal predispositions of immigrants, non-European cultural and religious incommensurability, social incohesion, political extremism, and terrorism.

African Caribbean Women and Police Violence in Britain

With specific reference to African Caribbean women's experiences, studies have shown that the postimperial British state and society have constructed a violent, pathological and criminological relationship with Black women. Pioneering British feminist work surrounding violence against Black women in the 1980s conceptualized the violence faced by Black women as patterned through "racist sexual violence" (Hall 1985, 48).

Cases of sexualized assault against Black women by state agents such as police officers evidence contemporary contradictions in the purported ideals of British justice and liberal democratic governance. They occur in the broader historical context of the said ambivalence and anxiety necessary to simultaneously secure Black women's subordination and white British preferential rule of law. In 2007, Toni Corner, a nineteen-year-old African Caribbean woman with a history of epileptic seizures, was thrown out of a nightclub in Sheffield. As she attempted to make her way back in through a back door, police officers confronted her. One of them proceeded to punch her repeatedly until she was unconscious. Then they dragged her, with her trousers down, into custody. The chilling brutality was inadvertently captured by the nightclub's closed-circuit television and was discussed widely in the British media as reminiscent of the beatings of Rodney King in Los Angeles, or characteristic of racism in the U.S. deep South. The incident prompted Black journalist Hannah Pool (2007) to comment, "You cannot separate who Toni Comer is from what happened to her. Very little is ever said about the relationship Black women have with the police force. When the debate turns to police and ethnic minorities, it is almost always about white men versus Black men. You would be forgiven for thinking that the only time Black women and policemen came into contact with each other was at the Notting Hill Carnival." These structurally violent and gendered tendencies are continuous with the historic embeddedness of the dehumanized status of the African Caribbean woman's body in transatlantic slavery (Hartman 1997), colonial legal reasoning, and contemporary white nationalism.

The names Esme Baker and Jackie Berkeley are rarely remembered in contemporary Britain, but these African Caribbean women were the first Black women who dared to make official complaints of sexual abuse, rape, and assault against the British police. These were milestone cases in the 1980s that broke the silence and invisibility of Black women's experiences with policing. Ruth Chigwada-Bailey's (1991, 2003) classic studies on Black women and state violence in Britain presented four key reasons why Black women are likely to come into contact with and receive maltreatment from the police. First, there is the perception that Black women, as part of the poor and Black community in general, are likely to be engaged in criminally suspicious behavior. Second, it is due to the high rates of criminalization of Black male youth that Black mothers are also linked as potential accomplices. Third, their nonwhite racial difference sets them apart as potential targets for immigration checks and harassment. And fourth, Black women become targets for police violence when they are perceived as mentally unstable and dangerous. These key areas that Chigwada identified in the 1980s constitute the repertoire of racist criminological representations of African Caribbean women as morally suspect, potentially aggressive, and devoid of the respectable qualities of genteel middle-class white femininity.

These "controlling images" (Hill-Collins 2000) continue to inform mainstream public perception and are simply recognized as common sense for inner-city policing purposes. A 1989 story uncovered by Chigwada-Bailey also revealed both routine sexualized violations of Black women by the police and heteropatriarchal mobilizations of white male/police officer privilege and impunity as liberal juridical responses. The case involved a white policeman in Surrey who had been convicted of raping a young Black woman in his patrol car. He was sentenced to seven years in prison. However, upon appeal, his sentence was overturned on the grounds that the judge in the original trial had failed to direct the jury toward the good character of the police officer (see Chigwada-Bailey 1991, 141–45).

The outbreak of the Brixton uprising on September 28, 1985 (rendered as "riots" in the dominant discourse), and the mass protests at Broadwater Farm a week later were also events precipitated by incidents that involved

MOHAN AMBIKAIPAKER

the violent policing of Black women in London. In the first instance, Cherry Croce was shot and paralyzed during a raid of her home and, in the second instance, Cynthia Jarret suffered a heart attack following a police assault that also occurred in her home. Notably, in both cases, police aggressively broke into these women's homes to investigate alleged criminal behavior perpetrated by their sons.

In 1993, Joy Gardner, a Jamaican woman, was accused of an immigration infraction—she had overstayed her Commonwealth visitor's visa. Joy's mother had immigrated to Britain in the 1960s and had become a citizen. However, due to antiblack immigration politics and changes effected by the 1981 British Nationality Act, she could no longer sponsor her adult daughter, who now also had a five-year-old British-born son. At an earlier time, both women would have been considered British subjects or Commonwealth citizens, with rights to abide in Britain, but successive legislation had narrowed the conditions for eligibility. A newspaper report recounts what happened:

> It was early morning when five men and women burst into five-year-old Graeme Burke's home. They cornered and grabbed his mother, crashing through the furniture, forcing her face down on to the floor. They sat on her body, they bound her hands to her side with a leather belt and manacles, they strapped her legs together and wound yards of surgical tape round her head. At some stage, one officer took the boy into another room—but he could still hear his mother's cries. He never saw her alive again. (Mills 1999)

Three police officers from the Alien Deportation Group were tried for manslaughter. They were acquitted after telling a jury that Joy Gardner was the most violent woman they had ever dealt with and that the treatment she received was standard practice (Amnesty International 1995).

Black women's success stories have neither altered the habitual and abusive stereotyping of Black women in civil society, nor the violent protocols of how the British state and its police appear to treat African Caribbean women and, in particular, working-class African Caribbean women.[5] Brutal policing violence has continued, even as African Caribbean women have contributed greatly to educational social movements and have broken the glass ceiling in public life (Mirza 1992, 2009). There are now several high-profile politicians: Baroness Valerie Amos, a former Black British feminist academic, was the head of the House of Lords of Britain and a prominent UN diplomat. The long-standing East London MP Diane Abbot has also been a high-profile figure in Labour Party politics for decades, but she routinely endures mockery and "misogynoir" abuse in the media, social media, and the public sphere (Campion 2019).

In the following section, I offer a counter-storytelling narrative about how British society and its liberal democratic social order is experienced by Gillian Smith, an African Caribbean woman. She is both a victim of its gendered antiblack violence and an active resistor against that victimization.

Gillian's Story

Gillian Smith was born on the island of St. Lucia when it was still a colony and arrived in Britain in 1969 at the age of five, when her mother married a white English man and emigrated. They settled in her stepfather's residence in Hastings, a predominantly white seaside community in East Sussex. Gillian often recalled her childhood in idyllic terms and drew upon her memories of southeastern England's picturesque natural beauty as an inspiration for her own urban gardening.

"We came from good stock," she would say, "and didn't want for anything," referring to her stepfather's middle-class status as the self-employed owner of a gas station. She took great pride in her flawless elocution, a prized southeastern English accent, that to her was proof of the private school polish she had been privileged to receive, and her integration into respectable middle-class British society.

"People usually think that Black people have accents, but they hear me speak on the phone, and they don't think I am Black," she told me. She remembered that her stepfather would always correct her if she got too Cockney and began to drop her *o*'s and *h*'s. She did recall, however, switching into "a bit of Cockney" now and then, mostly in order to fit into East London and not appear as if she were putting on airs.

"I've always gotten into trouble for the way I speak," she said. "People are thinking, who the hell does she think she is? You've got other Black people coming along and speaking with accents, so they don't know what to do with me," Gillian continued, mocking a pseudo-African accent to express her antipathy toward new African immigrants in Newham.[6]

Gillian's stereotyping and resentment were situated in the context of the recent influx of highly educated professional migrants, principally from Nigeria. Gillian encountered many of these immigrants as the new frontline social and housing service officers of the borough. This shift in who was employed for these positions was one of the major changes that had taken place at the local municipal level in the past two decades. However, the diversification of personnel with frontline civil servants did not alter the fundamental structural logic of antiblackness and anti-immigrant treatment that the new diverse group of employees was expected to carry out.

The relationship was often tense between older and settled working-class African Caribbean and South Asian communities and the new civil servants who mediated state and municipal government policies. Gillian encountered few ethnic and racial minority state agents who were sympathetic to her plight. Lower-level local police officers, housing, and Homeless Persons Unit officers occupy a colonial-esque intermediary role between the state's law-and-order and austerity-based social services agenda and the working-class Black communities they help to govern in Newham, one of the most impoverished boroughs in London.

In spite of this downgraded treatment by the first-generation immigrant housing officers, Gillian asserted herself as superior in social status to the new arrivals. She mainly took pride in her tenure. She socialized widely with white British people and boasted of living a racially integrated everyday life. Gillian's long-term partner was a Jamaican man, James. Her brother had married a white British woman, and Gillian added that her son Mark primarily liked to date white girls. At present, he was dating a light-skinned, mixed-race girl. In her way of thinking, this life corresponded with what the British state had come to valorize as good civic behavior, or community cohesion, as opposed to the bad behavior of new immigrant groups who are perceived to self-segregate into separate ethnocultural enclaves and lives.

"He likes the white side of things," Gillian declared about her son Mark.

Gillian recalled her childhood in Hastings as her "happiest days," full of a quintessential seashore town "quiet life," something she felt to be the provenance of those lucky enough to be born white in Britain, and basically beyond the reach of most Black people who lacked kinship connections to rural England.

In the beginning I was a little uncertain about Gillian's self-presentation as a fully assimilated English and British person. I wondered about things such as internalized self-hatred and her lack of a strong racial consciousness. Before knowing the full details of Gillian's story, I hastened to judge her remarks as ideological expressions of an uncritical colonial Anglophilia.

In conversation I raised this matter with her one day.

"Yes, Black is beautiful. And I am a strong Black woman. Very Black. But sometimes you see what you go through. And you ask God, why is it that they have nice hair and I have to put things in mine? Why do they have a quiet life and are not bothered?" Gillian said.

Then, noticing my quizzical looks, Gillian started to relate experiences that stemmed from her childhood in Hastings. She told me a story that took place when she was ten years old. A white schoolmate named Kevin had been singling her out for racist name calling and bullying. He would call her a "Black this and that," Gillian told me.

One day when she was walking home from school, Kevin waylaid her and pummeled her with his fists. He left her unconscious and abandoned by the side of the road.

"He left me there for dead," she said.

Since Gillian was the lone Black girl in her East Sussex town, a passerby quickly recognized her and took her home. Outraged at what had happened to her daughter, Gillian's mother went to the boy's home to confront his parents. Kevin's parents, however, did not seem interested in disciplining or admonishing their child for what he had done.

The following day, Gillian took heed of advice her mother had given her. Her mother told her to defend herself by any means necessary. When, predictably, Kevin attempted to taunt and harass Gillian again, she grabbed his "willie" and squeezed hard. Yelping in pain, he ran off, and that was the last time he bothered her walk to or from school.

As she continued to grow up in Hastings, Gillian's own relationship with her white stepfather became increasingly strained as his marriage to her mother broke down. "It was fine when the love was there. When love was not there . . . there was lots of racism between them," she observed of her parents' interracial marriage.

Gillian's relationship with her stepfather was irreparably damaged when she became embroiled with the police as a young adult. By this time, she had moved to Newham and was living an independent life.

The incident occurred when she had been out shopping on Woodgrange Road near Forest Gate Train Station, a quiet residential neighborhood in Newham. She had run into an old friend there, and an unsettled misunderstanding between them turned into a heated argument. Gillian admitted that they were quarreling, perhaps a little loudly, but that it had not been a fight.

As she and her friend argued at the train station, officers from the Area 2 Territorial Support Group who were patrolling the area in a riot van stopped to investigate. An archived NMP report details what happened next:

On seeing the two women Gill and Ms. C arguing, two officers got out of the van and approached the women. One officer moved towards the back of the pavement, grabbing her hand and saying, "if you're not quiet, you're nicked." Gill explained that she was quiet and began to move to leave, but the officer blocked her path and forced her arm behind her back. The second officer returned after having spoken to Ms. C who had told him that there was no problem between the two women. The first officer said to his colleague, "we've got her on a Section 4" and forced Gill onto the floor. The two officers then handcuffed Gill, began to drag her towards the barrier at the edge of the pavement, and forced her over the barrier causing injuries to her stomach. At this point, Ms. C, witnessing the attack, began shouting to the officers to let Gill go and stop hurting her. The officers ignored her protestations and dragged Gill towards the van where she was lifted up by her arms and legs and thrown onto the floor of the van. As she struggled to get up off the van floor, the officers began racially abusing her, saying, "You Black dog, get on the floor" and "You bitch, get down, get down." One officer then grabbed Gill by the back of the neck and tried to push her to the ground. The other officer began to stomp on her legs and her back. During this ordeal, Gill suffered injuries to her body, had her jacket ripped and her jewelry snatched off. Gill was then taken to Forest Gate police station still lying on the floor of the van whilst the officers continued to abuse her racially and laugh at her discomfort. (Newham Monitoring Project 1993, 39)

The overwhelming use of force for a petty public disturbance was, at best, disproportionate. It was "for nothing, for nothing," Gillian said.

Unfortunately, Gillian's ordeal did not end in the police van. When she finally arrived at the police station, she was subjected to a strip search while the officers who had assaulted her watched from a distance and made lewd sexual comments. Gillian turned to the white female officer who was carrying out the search and asked that the search be stopped.

"Why are you doing this? You're a woman as well," she asked.

The question seemed to have some effect, and at this point the officer discontinued the search and brought Gillian to a cell.

Four hours later she was released, after having been charged with threatening behavior and interfering with the police in the course of their duties.

In response to the use of random excessive force and frivolous charges in Gillian's case, NMP launched a public mobilization and campaign for justice. Such campaigns against the police are fraught with danger for victims of the abuse, who fear that the police will retaliate against them. This concern would later turn out to be very real, as the local police began to target Gillian's young son through the use of stops and searches.

Gillian was aware of these dangerous possibilities but nonetheless decided to turn her individual experience into a broader community and political touchstone on the policing of African Caribbean and Black women as a whole. When Gillian arrived at One Love Centre on December 2, 1992, over a hundred people had gathered to hear her give her first-ever public speech. This public meeting in support of Gillian was the result of the work of an alliance of local activist organizations that had jointly mobilized around her case. Activists from NMP, the East London Black Women's Organization, Newham Asian Women's Project, and the Defend the Deane Family Campaign galvanized community-wide support.[7]

Though the immediate objective of the campaign was to get Gillian individual justice through the police's internal disciplinary system and the liberal juridical framework that regulated excessive force, the larger political goal was to bring attention to the "gendered racism" (Oparah/Sudbury 1998) that characterizes the state's routine, violent policing of working-class Black women's bodies. As NMP (1993, 40–41) stated at the time, Gillian's case "clearly demonstrates that it is not only young black men who suffer police racism and brutality."

Gillian delivered the following speech to address the community of activists and concerned residents that had gathered around her case at One Love. She was nervous and told me, "That was my first ever public speech. I must admit it was very nerve racking":

> Thank you for coming to support the campaign. My name is Gill as you all know. For legal reasons I personally cannot talk about the details of my case. I can say that on the 9th of October, 1992 I found out what being black meant in accordance to what the police did to me. The fear, the embarrassment, and the shame they made me feel on that day will stay with me forever.
>
> No woman should have to suffer such degrading treatment. After all, we are the women of today and fighting for the women of the future.
>
> Show Respect.
>
> This happened to me, it has happened to thousands of women before me, and unless we wake up, stand up, it will happen to thousands more.
>
> We must all remember our history and think back to how people reacted in the past to these same issues of harassment and racial harassment in our community, such as the Brixton Riots before. For as long as there have been

black people in this country, whether from Asian, African and West Indian origin, they have always had to fight for their rights and justice.

This campaign will go on not only for the men and women in this community who have suffered at the hands of the police but for our children.

I do not want my sons and daughters to be stripped naked by police officers, beaten and abused and sent to prison for being black in Britain.

This is an excellent public meeting; for every person in here there are ten more supporters outside. We are not alone.

There is a powerful organization, without any doubts in my mind, who can help fight the police in Newham. Personal respect to Hoss [Houssein] for the support and work of NMP.

No Justice, No Peace!

When Gillian's case came before the Newham East Magistrate's Court a year later, the campaign had generated enough local interest that eighty supporters packed the public gallery—an unusual show of interest and public monitoring for what otherwise would have been a routine magistrate's court affair. When I asked Gillian what happened, she searched through a folder of documents and produced a notepaper with her handwritten reflections on the events of that fateful day: "Finally we arrived at the Court House. We waited almost two hours for the arresting officers to arrive. Finally the police barrister stood up and asked the judge for more time. My barrister stood up and protested against the fact that this case should never have come to court. The judge stood up and said to the police barrister: 'No more time. Case is dismissed.'" In short, the arresting police officers had failed to show up to the court, packed as it was with community supporters, to present their evidence.

This victory was understood as a rare result of mobilized public interest and protest that had influenced what would otherwise have been a routine antiracist failure—a racially biased and typically propolice court process. Borough-wide leafleting, public meetings, and mass picket signs that packed the public galleries at Gillian's trial demonstrated that courts could be made amenable to racial justice outcomes only through public mobilization and pressure politics.

Despite this victory, Gillian's white stepfather never believed her account. He found her allegations to be incredible and preferred to retain his belief in the quintessential image of fairness in the British justice system and in the upstanding character of white police officers over the pain and suffering of his own Black stepdaughter. Like Lord Mansfield in the

Thames Ditton case, Gillian's stepfather was confronted face-to-face with Black women's pain and suffering. And like Mansfield he wrested a standpoint of liberal objectivity and dispassionate belief in the impartiality of white-dominated civic institutions through the very repression of the Black woman's claim for justice. This recognition/repression dynamic is critical not only in structuring the expulsion of Black women from the remit of liberal justice, but also from a sense of legitimate belonging to the popular sovereignty that underpins Western liberal democracy. It is through repressing Black women's pain and suffering, as was done during the time of slavery, that the abstract proceduralism underpinning rule of law is enacted and the believing liberal democratic subject is constituted.

"He had friends in the force," Gillian explained, and then added, "He always insisted that the police don't do that."

I had been working on Gillian's police complaint case for several months when suddenly I lost communication with her. She did not come by the office, as she often had, and her phone appeared to be out of service. But I knew where she lived and I had often popped over to her home to work on affidavits and other matters related to her case.

By now I knew a short route to her house and felt at home walking through the plane tree–lined streets of north Newham. The terrace homes, characteristic of the north borough, contrasted with the south, which was full of treeless tower blocks and dense housing projects.

I crossed Barking Road, which cut the borough into two and had once stood for a symbolic racial division between the white and nonwhite residential areas, although this had changed considerably with more Black people slowly moving south and more whites moving on to suburbs. Nevertheless, I would not have ventured on foot too far south to places such as Canning Town, Beckton, or the Royal Docks. I had absorbed the common sense conveyed to me by other Black people in Newham that these particular areas were no-go zones where the risk of racial harassment and attacks was high.[8]

As I walked, I thought of Gillian and her broken phone. Focused on my own good mood, I arrived at her home at an unfortunate social hour—the family was having dinner, or tea as working-class people in Newham called it. But in characteristic form, Gillian extended her warm hospitality.

"Join us for tea," she said.

I protested that I would come back later, but did not want to risk causing offense, as Gillian was already fixing a steaming plate of chicken stew and rice for me. As I began to enjoy this home-cooked meal, Gillian told me that in fact it was a wonderful time for my visit because the whole family was very happy.

"If you had come yesterday, you would have seen us all crying," she said.

I didn't know what she was referring to, but I smiled and continued to happily dig into my food.

"Six pounds and forty-five pence," Gillian said slowly and cryptically. "That's what they're giving us now."

"What do you mean?" I asked.

"Benefits," she explained.

I was startled and somewhat incredulous. At the time I was not at all familiar with how social welfare benefits in Britain worked, but surely they could not be that low. Newham has been ranked consistently as one of the most socioeconomically deprived boroughs in England with extremely high poverty rates (Newham Regeneration Planning and Property Directorate 2010, 7–12). There was no way the family could survive on such meagre amounts of local council support. As a field-worker at the time, I was trying to live as cheaply as possible, but I was certainly spending more than £6.45 a week on food and groceries. This was London, after all.

Slowly a story emerged. During the course of the previous twelve years, Gillian had been in and out of the welfare system and at various times received key benefits such as income support, housing, and child support. Most recently she had reentered the welfare system after she was suddenly laid off from a well-known builder's firm, where she had worked as a personal assistant to the supervisor. Her supervisor, a well-known white local who owned the business, had sexually harassed her. Gillian's protests and resistance against her boss resulted in a dismissal after a short seven weeks on the job. After she was laid off, she went to the local Newham Council welfare benefits office to get herself back on the rolls and received a rude shock when she was told that she was no longer eligible.

"They said that I needed to have a passport!" Gillian explained. "They said that during the seven weeks that I got that job, the law had changed and now anyone who signs on needs to show a marriage certificate or driving license or a passport! Well, I had a passport and I am legally in this country, but it wasn't up-to-date!" she exclaimed.

"But aren't you a British citizen?" I asked.

"Yes, I am," she replied.

"So why did you need to show a passport?"

What had happened was that during that seven-week period when Gillian was off income support, the British Parliament had passed another round of new laws and directives to implement a new "right to reside" test that scrutinized access to the benefits system (O'Neil 2011). This test was ostensibly introduced over media-driven political panics that the enlargement of the European Union (EU) to include ten new countries in Eastern Europe would presumably flood the benefits system in a matter of months. The government urgently responded within a Powellian border control mindset to assuage anti-immigration fears and introduced restrictive new eligibility requirements. Later, these rules were amended to allow new EU immigrants to access the benefits system after five years of residency. Under pressure from the European Union itself, almost thirty EU countries were subsequently granted exemption from the new right-to-reside rule. However, other countries outside the European Union, including all the Commonwealth countries, could not contest the new rules.[9]

With the new right-to-reside rule, Black immigrants already residing in Britain were suddenly burdened with providing documentary evidence of their legal status, regardless of their prior history of settlement or citizenship. Clearly, these new rules did not take into account the history of Black immigrants such as Gillian who had entered decades before from the Caribbean and who were once British Empire citizens or subjects. In fact, the new reforms reinforced the historical amnesia of those previous colonial relationships and the immigration flows that they had enabled. Gillian now was required to show documentary proof of her right to reside, which consisted of presenting a current passport (which cost £72 to renew), a British birth certificate, or a Home Office certificate granting citizenship.

Gillian's situation is representative of the thousands of ex-colonial British subjects—people from former African, African Caribbean, and South Asian colonies—whose lives become repeatedly entangled with laws made in response to new anti-immigration policies. Even though Gillian was not a new immigrant, her standing as a Black person in the social welfare state marked her immigration status and eligibility as suspicious. Documentary proof of residency was almost always the first line of gatekeeping before a British state agency would deign to provide a social service. During the year I was a caseworker at NMP, I had occasion to accompany victims of racial attacks and harassment to local agencies such as the Homeless Persons Unit, which was legally responsible for rehousing victims of racial attacks and harassment. These agencies almost always demanded documentary proof of residency, even in life-threatening situations.

Such abstract welfare benefits rules, however, are not color-blind. For example, while at these offices, I rarely observed white British people

MOHAN AMBIKAIPAKER

being asked about their legal residential status. They were assumed to be people who would "habitually" be residents in Britain, and hence the test was often waived (Fitzpatrick 2006). In Gillian's case, her physical appearance invariably triggered the need to prove that she was not a "person from abroad." She was repeatedly subjected to the new rules, even though Newham Council had been dealing with Gillian as an income and child benefit recipient for many years.

As we ate dinner together that evening, Gillian smiled cheerfully at me. "I made dinner for just £3.99," she said. Though I returned a small smile, I was feeling heavy inside.

"One pound fifty pence for chicken legs, £1.89 without skin. You put in some allspice, tomato, and stew for an hour in a good pot. If you have a pressure cooker, you could do it in half an hour."

Although I expressed my appreciation for the meal in the best ways I could, I really wished that I hadn't just popped in for dinner. I imagined the small pack of chicken legs that Gillian had purchased with the benefits money and looked around at the faces of Gillian and her two daughters enjoying the meal. There was nothing left in the pot.

On the walls of the living room in Gillian's home was a smiling picture of her ten-year-old son Mark, dressed in a scout's uniform. Adjacent to the picture were framed certificates that Mark earned for perfect attendance and punctuality. These certificates were part of the efforts of inner-city schools to recognize the successes of their pupils who were apt to be labeled as problem students. Gillian was very proud of these certificates and proud of Mark, and yet she spoke wistfully and nostalgically about that time when her son had been "a very happy normal boy."

These memories contrasted with the last years of Mark's secondary schooling, which had been almost consumed with fighting a series of detentions and exclusions that prohibited him from attending school. He had been expelled from Eastlea Community School in his last year of high school.

The image and certificates on the wall, awarded to a bright young boy, and the image of Mark as an adolescent troublemaker that Eastlea had constructed could not have been more disparate. According to Gillian, for the longest time Mark dreamed of becoming a barrister and had done well in the arts. He had even brought his school fame through an award-winning performance in a school drama that was staged at London's prestigious Royal Arts Festival.

Mark's decline in school performance and his conflicts with school authorities started when he fell victim to an assault by a parent of one of his white friends. This friend's father worked in the canteen of a local police station, and he did not like his son hanging out with Black people. One day while Mark was visiting his friend, the father punched Mark and told him to go away.

This racist attack was also taken up as a case by NMP, which sought to have the father evicted from his council flat for violating the anti–racial harassment clauses of his tenancy agreement. Mark and his family won the case, and the father was expelled from the borough.

Such hard-won victories over barrages of racial and police attacks, however, did not mitigate the damage that had been done to Mark's spirit and educational morale. Following the successful eviction, Mark started to develop a reputation in school as a troublemaker and found himself running afoul of hostile teachers and administrators. He was frequently sentenced to disciplinary exclusions from attending school. These interruptions in his schooling wreaked havoc with his education.

Once again with the help of NMP, Gillian tried to mount appeals against the school disciplinary system. She requested other forms of intervention, such as pastoral support services, to be used to address Mark's growing behavior issues, but she was repeatedly denied.

During the times Mark was expelled, most of his friends finished their schooling and moved on to college or the workforce. Mark, on the other hand, spent time in the local Territorial Army (Army Reserve) doing volunteer training as a way to pass the time and create some kind of structure in his life.

Eventually, NMP was able to overturn his school eviction, and Mark was readmitted to the school system. But when he returned to school, he was placed with a different cohort of students who were younger than he was. In his final year, Mark's academic performance suffered badly.

Gillian was devastated. "He's left school with no qualifications, nothing," she said.

After finishing high school, Mark immediately landed in trouble again. He was convicted of a charge of common assault and would spend a year appealing the conviction, again with the help of NMP. He did not often appear motivated to pursue his case and on many occasions threatened to derail his own chances of success by failing to appear for his hearings and missing his probation meetings.

As one of his caseworkers, I often had to scramble for doctor's notes to provide evidence that there were extenuating circumstances that justified his absence at his probation visits and to assist him in avoiding further arrests.

MOHAN AMBIKAIPAKER

The long shadow of police harassment on the family, repeated encounters with racism, and Mark's failed school experiences seemed to leave him resigned and cynical about the system. When I approached him to participate in an NMP antiracist workshop on police stop-and-search practices and the rights of people in those situations, he was barely interested. He brushed off any attempt I made to talk to him about further education options and the like.

"He's given up," Gillian declared to me.

In Mark's view, the long-running battle with the police had only brought rack and ruin on the family and had made him the target of police reprisals. Instead of developing a political, structural, and racial analysis of policing, he focused his resentment on his mother for her strong-willed challenges of police abuse at every instance. He interpreted her activism as the reason that his own personal dreams were unraveling. He even stated that he wanted to date and marry a white girl, "in order to breed the Black out" of his violated life.

In the process of filing numerous police complaints and listening to her life stories, I came to a deep recognition of how Gillian had been forced to experience and endure the behavior of white police officers and other white British males who had sexually violated her over the course of her life. Their collective actions were patterned forms of social action that recursively positioned a Black African Caribbean woman's body as a terrain for inscribing gendered and racialized subordination, in utilizing racial-sexual violence to constitute white supremacist and misogynistic desires and entitlements.

Such a socially and politically enabled declension of bodily integrity and sovereignty continued into Gillian's intimate family life. Gillian's family and home spheres were shaped not only by these external forces of racialized and gendered state violence, but also through domestic violence. Domestic abuse mirrored police abuse—where Gillian's body became the site to reproduce a cultural aporia between gendered African Caribbean identities and the normative ascription of a private-propertied, rights-bearing, and white-defined feminine individual.

One day Mark returned home in a maddened rage, trashed his room, and physically assaulted both Gillian and one of his teenage sisters. He had lost control, and Gillian felt she had but one choice.

"I called the police on him. Do you hear what Gillian is telling you, Mohan? I called the police on him!

"Inside my body I'm calm as you like, outside I'm shaking like a leaf. James [Gillian's partner] and Mark have been abusing me for years. I've been abused in my own home. I'm not such a perfect family after all. I've been with this man for twenty-three years, and I've been threatened and threatened. I've had to take so much shit for people around and from my own family."

This was the first time Gillian had confided in me of the long-term abuse she had suffered at home.

"Mark is so twisted and confused," Gillian said.

And glancing at her son's picture on the wall, she continued, "I've faced it for you, and why have you got an element of doubt?"

"I've got to hold it together for the girls. Thirteen years on, I'm up at six in the morning to see if the police are coming!"

Recently, Gillian had endured a home break-in. Members of a gang who were looking for Mark smashed their way in with guns, physically assaulted Gillian, and threatened her daughters.

Also, Gillian's revelation of domestic abuse by her son and partner shocked me. Her vulnerability to multiple modes of violence was beyond what I had imagined or what she had previously shared with me. And it was not a subject that she wanted to discuss in great detail with me.

In general, I was terrified for Gillian's safety. As a caseworker specifically authorized to work with her police abuse case, however, I was limited in my scope of intervention. I acted on trying to secure Gillian and her daughters in a location that would be safe from the armed intruders. I contacted Newham housing services to express the urgent need to have her rehoused at a safe address. This was the one concrete option for safety that I felt I could facilitate, now that I was aware of the danger that she faced from Mark's rages and embrace of criminal activity.

Ironically, when I was Mark's advocate, I now had to mediate the demands of the abstract proceduralism demanded by the local housing authority's urgent response team, which required that Gillian no longer house Mark, since he had by then reached an adult age. Mark's exclusion from living with the family was the council's condition for rehousing them to an adjacent borough. I communicated the council's ultimatum to Gillian. After some thought, Gillian finally agreed to the move, and she resigned herself to excluding Mark from the home in order to secure safety for herself and her daughters.

That was the last contact I had with Gillian until many years later, when, on a return trip to London, I chanced to meet her on the streets of Newham. She was making her way to the offices of the NMP, but this time she was doing so on an electric scooter. In the intervening years, Gillian had become disabled. It happened suddenly, and it wasn't clear what had caused the loss of her ability to walk or keep her balance. She reasoned that it was her body's reaction to the long years of struggling against everything she had gone through, all the violence.[10] She also let me know that Mark had recently spent time in prison.

Conclusion

The centering of Gillian's life story as an account of British society and its political liberalism at work embodies the ways in which gendered antiblackness emerges through a continuum of violence and recursive constructions of social death. Neither psychologized explanations of racism (as exceptional illiberal pathologies or even psychic norms) nor the histories of neoliberal economic, white British nativist and far-right political discourses can completely account for the liberal democratic political rationales that envelop the practices of violating Black women's bodies and rendering their resistance as incongruent to liberal justice.

As typologies and propensities of gendered antiblackness that circulate through the British social body, the forms of street-level racist attacks, police abuse, police retaliation for antipolice resistance, anti-immigration barriers, social welfare exclusions, sexual assaults, gendered retrenchment from accessing assault-free work, multiracial familial rejections, domestic interpersonal violence, and finally bodily disable-ization formed the continuum of violence that transmogrified Gillian's significance as an interloping presence in realms of national popular sovereignty, liberal-juridical justice, and dominant codes of femininity and inviolable personhood into the present/absent status of enslaveability and social death. Hortense Spillers (1987, 67) in her classic essay makes the conceptual distinction between how Black women are metamorphosed as subjectless "flesh" within regimes of Western enslavement and representation: "I would make a distinction in this case between 'body' and 'flesh' and impose that distinction as the central one between captive and liberated subject-positions. In that sense, before the 'body' there is the 'flesh,' that zero degree of social conceptualization." I would add that the process of turning Black women's bodies into bodies that have "zero degree of social conceptualization" and therefore signified as violable "flesh" is both a priori and an ever-ongoing process within Westernized liberal democracies that involves multiple interacting nodes and attracts multiple antiblack agents. This recursive process changes and shape shifts, not as distinctive and separate events, but as continuously interlocking forms of gendered antiblackness that are experienced within a lifetime.

Gillian's life was structured by manifold encounters and engagements where the persistent ontological vulnerability and dehumanization of her body, expulsions from national popular sovereignty, and the abrogation of liberal rights were simultaneously coarticulated. Hence, gendered antiblack violence must be read not only as the workings of libidinal and psychological dynamics but also as coexpressing formal political logics that draw upon and reinforce everyday racial positioning and system-structural tendencies in Westernized liberal democracies. These social relations, system-structural propensities, and the dis/alignment of the liberal state against Black women are in turn reproduced by grassroots and popular participation in the antiblack/political everyday. This founding-foundational loop in imperial and settler colonial liberal democracies[11] is intimately tied to the coterminous constructions of the interlinked zones of slavery/enslaveability, civil society (Harney and Moten 2013; Wilderson 2003), and state-specific liberal-juridical rights.

Hence it is not possible to understand the production of the norms of British political liberalism, especially its abstract proceduralisms, the systemic-structural construction of juridical indifference to Black pain and suffering, and the authority of its dispassionate legal formalism without reference to the coextensive logics of gendered antiblackness as a forceful civic and political activity. Contemporary Britain's social order that is white centered but multiracially inclusive is not only threatened by nativistic bigotry and white nationalism, it is also routinely coextensive with gendered antiblackness. Gendered antiblack violence is inured to British rule of law through longue durée and habitual violations of Black women's bodies and concomitant repressions of their claims and struggles for justice.

Notes

I would like to thank both Mariana Mora and Alix Chapman for reading and providing critical conversation and feedback for this chapter.

1   The concept of political blackness utilized by British social movements and Black British feminist discourse has traditionally encompassed African and African Caribbean women as well as South Asians, Arabs, and other oppressed and colonized women, although these formations are not

MOHAN AMBIKAIPAKER

socially naturalized and work disjunctively against more naturalized and contemporary modes of ethnoracial identifications and fissures (Alexander 2017; Ambikaipaker 2018; Mirza 1997; Mirza and Gunaratnam 2014; Reynolds 2002; Oparah/Sudbury 1998, 2001).

2 My relationship with Gillian and the ethnographic construction of her life story that I present arose from the context and limits of this caseworker/advocate-client relationship. But given that the NMP sought to politicize the channels of state-based social service provision, our relationship was marked not only by the concerns of her individual cases but by broad racial justice–based social movement questions in Britain as well.

3 See full text of the ruling in Roscoe, Frere, and Glenbervie (1831).

4 The estimate of the number of slaves kept in Britain itself during the time of slavery varies (12,000–15,000; see Arvind 2012, 136–38).

5 See Gargi Bhattacharyya's (1998) *Tales of Dark-Skinned Women* for an analysis of how success stories and exceptional achievements do not change negative racial stereotypes and cultural invisibility (see also Mirza and Gunaratnam 2014).

6 Foreigner-talk is a supposedly comical and stereotyping practice of constructing and mocking a nonstandard English accent (see D'Cruz and Steele 2000).

7 The Defend the Deanne Family Campaign involved an Indo-Caribbean minicab driver from the island of St. Vincent whose son was brutalized by the police at the Forest Gate police station (see Newham Monitoring Project 1992).

8 The everyday territorial control of London's urban neighborhoods through the deployment of white racial harassment and racial violence has been well documented as modes of British "neighborhood nationalism" (Back 1996).

9 Even the complaints framework was enveloped within the EU legal structure, and Commonwealth countries could not utilize that framework to contest the eligibility requirements for social security benefits (see O'Neil 2011).

10 Christen Smith (2016) has similarly researched the process of the long-lasting effects of antiblack violence on Black women and mothers in Brazil. As Smith explains, the concept of sequelae, or the long-term effects of gendered antiblackness, is part of the state's strategy for organizing Black life toward premature death. The wearing out and disable-ization of Gillian's body here is a result of the sequelae of British state violence and the necropolitical effects that compound direct physical violence and racial terror inflicted on her and her family.

11 See Ashraf Rushdy's (2012) account of how state-supported lynching in the Jim Crow era in the United States was an extension of the logics and demands of nonelite white citizenry who exercised democratic popular sovereignty and organized to align the state with their grassroots antiblack violence.

SCHOOLS AS SITES OF ANTIBLACK
VIOLENCE: BLACK GIRLS AND
POLICING IN THE AFTERLIFE
OF SLAVERY

CONNIE WUN

In September 2019, a six-year-old Black girl in Orlando, Florida, was hand-cuffed and arrested by a police officer in front of her classmates for previously kicking and punching her teachers. Her grandmother explained that Kaia Rolle, a first grader, struggled with insomnia and was often restless. A couple of school faculty questioned the need to restrain Kaia, but no one intervened upon the arrest. Unfortunately, stories of police officers arresting Black girls is not new. According to Morris (2015), there has been a long history of schools disciplining and police arresting Black girls.

Organizations including the Black Youth Project 100 and the African American Policy Forum have organized campaigns to highlight state violence against Black girls and women. According to the policy brief "SayHerName: Resisting Police Brutality against Black Women," by the African American Policy Forum and the Center for Intersectionality and Social Policy Studies at Columbia University (Crenshaw et al. 2015), Black women and girls in the United States are overwhelmingly subject to police violence in comparison to their non-Black counterparts. While most attention surrounding antiblack state violence has historically focused on Black men and boys, scholars and activists are also examining the ways that Black women and girls are affected by surveillance, harassment, and brutality (Crenshaw 2012; Morris 2012; Roberts 2011). According to Roberts (2011), Black women (and girls) are subject to criminalization and policing by a myriad of state institutions including the foster care system and schools. The African American Policy Forum (2014), Morris (2015), and NAACP and National Women's Law Center (2014) have examined the ways that schools have simultaneously overpoliced Black girls while neglecting their needs. Their studies demonstrate that, in addition to the criminal justice system, school discipline practices also criminalize Black girls. School discipline is only one example of the ways that the educational system in the United States has continuously inflicted and perpetuated violence against Black girls.

This qualitative study of Foundations High School (FHS), a suburban high school in northern California, examines the narratives of Black girls disciplined in accordance with school policies and practices. Drawing from the stories of six Black girls regarding their experiences with school discipline, the chapter provides narratives about race, gender, surveillance, criminalization, and punishment in schools. The girls' narratives provide important insight into the various ways that schools and school discipline affects their lives. Their stories and experiences suggest that the problem of antiblackness—through state violence—is not only with police officers and their departments but is also with everyday forms of school discipline and punishment. That is, school authorities, including those that have called police on their students, have helped to create a condition by which Black youth, and girls in particular, are subject to conditions of captivity in the afterlife of slavery.[1]

Layers of School Discipline

Foundations High School's discipline handbook outlines the school's mission statement including expectations and consequences for student behaviors. Every year, students are required to return a form to their school indicating that they and their parents are aware of the handbook's regulations and consequences. These listed regulations, however, are only a short inventory of rules that govern the school environment. In addition to the policies listed in the handbook, there are catalogues of Education Codes—state and federal—that regulate student behavior as well as dictate or legitimize consequences. Beyond school police officers, these rules are enforced by school authorities, including administration, faculty, and other school staff.

The handbook, which is a hybrid of federal, state, and district mandates, includes at least thirty policies. The codes that mandate suspensions and expulsions, which must be approved by the district school board, include several for weapons possession that can be traced to the federal Guns Free Schools Act of 1994 (Ayers, Dohrn, and Ayers 2001). This act is a federal policy created in the early 1990s by President Bill Clinton. Written into the Elementary and Secondary Education Act, the mandate requires that all federally funded schools expel students found with a weapon within one thousand feet from school grounds for at least one year. According to the mandate (Section 4141),

> Each State receiving Federal funds under any title of this Act shall have in effect a State law requiring local educational agencies to expel from school for a period of not less than 1 year a student who is determined to have brought a firearm to a school, or to have possessed a firearm at a school, under the jurisdiction of local educational agencies in that State, except that such State law shall allow the chief administering officer of a local educational agency to modify such expulsion requirement for a student on a case-by-case basis if such modification is in writing.

This federal mandate, school discipline scholars argue, has helped to shape several other state-based suspension and expulsion policies (Wald and Losen 2003). In particular, California Education Code Sections 48915, 48900, and 48927 expound upon the federal policy. There are over twenty-one offenses subject to suspension or expulsion listed throughout the California Education Code Sections 48915, 48900–48927. This list includes violent and nonviolent offenses. Violent infractions include causing physical injury, use of willful force, possession of weapons or imitation firearms, sexual assault or battery, witness harassment, hazing, physical, verbal and electronic forms of bullying, and aiding or abetting injury to another. If a student commits any of these violent enactments, authorities are required to immediately suspend or expel them. Students are also subject to criminal investigation if they commit any of the violent infractions.

According to the handbook, school discipline is about constructing a safe and effective learning environment. While the index of possible violent offenses is long, the discipline handbook also comprises a long list of nonviolent infractions such as drug-related and property offenses. FHS

CONNIE WUN

school administrators are authorized, as dictated by California Education Codes, to suspend or expel students for nonviolent infractions not limited to possessing controlled substances, property damage, theft, tobacco use, obscenity and profanity, drug paraphernalia, disruption, and receiving stolen property. The school handbook authorizes school administrators to police and discipline their students for numerous possible infractions. While much attention has been given to the ways that police officers have egregiously violated students, particularly Black youth, there has been less attention to the ways that school officials are also deputized to regulate and punish students for multitude of potential offenses.

The school also has strict policies about cell phone use and student attire. Students are mandated to keep phones "off and away" at all times. If students are found using phones in class, teachers are authorized to confiscate them and refer students to the principal. In this environment, once a student enters school grounds, they and their property are subject to surveillance and confiscation.

Students are also prohibited from showing their body parts. In particular, the handbook prohibits students from wearing "off the shoulder" tops or showing their "buttocks." These policies indicate that the school is not only interested in prohibiting drugs or violence, but also in policing and enforcing expectations about specific ways that students should dress and comport themselves. Students are also prohibited from displaying "obscene behavior" such as "prolonged kissing." These policies provide insight into the school's values regarding gender norms and their expectations for respectable performances of sexuality or sensuality. They prescribe the types of behaviors that are considered offensive, deviant, and subsequently rendered an offense (Foucault 1977). Importantly, the way that the students dress is not inherently bad or criminal but is characterized as such by these rules. In other words, student handbooks criminalize behaviors. They reinforce a particular set of cultural values that do not only dictate norms based upon a politics of respectability, they also authorize an entire population of adults to police young people's bodies. Put differently, the school policies and practices help to produce a hierarchy by which students are systematically undermined and policed. Students learn through these handbooks that they must behave in accordance to a particular set of (racialized and gendered) norms or risk punishment.

Based on the girls' narratives, despite the long list of rules, the nonviolent infractions applied most to their experiences with school discipline. They are more often disciplined for infractions labeled as "defiance" and "disobedience." In the students' experiences, characterizations of what constitute disobedience or defiance are often subjective (Chesney-Lind and Irwin 2008). Most of the trouble the girls got into was based on "talking back" to their teachers (Morris 2012; Sharma 2013). Despite the extensive list of discipline policies, only a few of them—particularly defiance and disobedience—typically affect Black girls.

Policed and Disciplined in School

During the 2013–14 school year, FHS was 22.1 percent Asian, 19 percent Filipinx, 32 percent Latinx, 7.8 percent White, 9 percent Black, 4 percent Native Hawaiian or Pacific Islander, and less than 1 percent Native American. Despite the diverse demographics of the campus, Black and Latinx students are more likely to be disciplined than their counterparts. According to the 2013–14 discipline data for all girls at FHS, Latinx girls constitute 37 percent of the population of girls who have discipline records (i.e., detention, suspension, or expulsion records). Black girls make up 26 percent and Filipinx girls constitute 12 percent of all girls who have discipline records. These numbers indicate that Latinx girls are overrepresented in the data and Black girls are even more disproportionately overrepresented. These large and troubling numbers, while extremely important to highlight, do not begin to tell us the breadth of antiblackness as it shapes the experiences of Black girls in schools. Their experiences with the antiblackness of school discipline include and extend beyond suspension and expulsion. Using school discipline as a primary example, this chapter examines the ways that schools, one of the many antiblack institutions in the United States, police and contain Black youth, particularly Black girls.

Overpoliced and Neglected

According to the girls, while all students were subject to school discipline, only some were subject to perpetual surveillance. In particular, Black girls in the study claimed that they often got into trouble for defiance and disobedience. They were often in trouble for having "attitudes," a "smart mouth," or "talking back." These behaviors, under the pretense that they disturbed the learning environment, were met with school-based consequences including referrals and suspensions. The consequences also included harassment, heightened surveillance, and jail. According to the girls, these behaviors, when committed by Black students, were criminalized and subsequently punished by school authorities. When their non-Black peers exhibited similar behaviors, they were either unnoticed or rendered normal. Similar to Ferguson's (2001) study on Black boys in elementary school, behaviors permissible for their non-Black peers, including wearing hats or talking to peers, became infractions for Black girls. The girls' narratives suggest that they were more likely to be policed, criminalized, and punished than their classmates.

While the girls acknowledged they were not suspended or expelled as often as boys, they felt they were under perpetual surveillance and incessantly disciplined. Their experiences with policing and discipline were more often with their teachers than with police officers. According to the girls, they were disciplined for "looking like they are talking," "chewing gum," or "getting up to throw paper away." For these other infractions, the girls explained that they were sent out of class for the entire period, or were yelled at, embarrassed in class, or left feeling constantly scrutinized. Historically, these informal types of punishment have not been documented as forms of discipline within school discipline research. Instead, there has been a greater emphasis on arrests, police violence, suspensions, and expulsions. Although formal discipline practices often take place, these "unarchived forms of discipline" were also commonly practiced, if not more so than encounters with police officers, suspensions, or expulsions (Wun 2014). These policing mechanisms also served to constrain and punish the girls' movements and behaviors.

Carla

Carla, a fifteen-year-old Black girl in the tenth grade, shared her experience of being suspended by school authorities and arrested by police officers on campus. Both institutions, she contended, placed her under observation and punished her for an infraction that she did not commit. According to Carla, the most difficult part of being suspended was that she tried most of her time in school to stay out of trouble, to escape surveillance from school authorities by being "under the radar." Understanding that Black students are more vulnerable to suspensions and expulsions than their peers, Carla tried to keep to herself to avoid conflicts with other students and to do well in her classes. She was deliberately quiet and reserved. She imagined that if she could avoid her teachers and administrators, she would be able to avoid getting into trouble. This also meant that she would often have to avoid asking for support and assistance from her educators. The objective was to minimize attention. In order to do this, Carla aimed to get good grades, stay silent in class, and avoid conflicts with students and adults. It also translated into a coerced version of isolation and containment in order to achieve some semblance of preservation.

Additionally, since she was living with her grandparents, she wanted to make sure that she did not burden them with any problems from school. This also meant "keeping to [her]self" and avoiding "bad crowds." At a young age, Carla created a plan to keep herself safe from the anti-black violence of the school, including its discipline policies and practices. Her plan, she hoped, would also serve to shield her family from the impacts that school discipline could potentially have on her home environment. Unfortunately, despite these efforts, she was still suspended and arrested. Carla was disciplined and punished for theft during the school year. "I was in the locker room and I had seen this girl at the other end. She was like going through people's lockers. I had witnessed that she was going through people's stuff. I didn't tell her to stop. I said, 'Don't touch these lockers cuz I know them'" (Carla, personal communication, April 5, 2013). Carla explained that she did not want to get involved, but she wanted to make sure that she helped protect her friends' belongings. According to Carla, after she made sure that the girl did not open her friends' lockers, she left the locker room. "She had taken an iPhone, a wallet, and I don't know what else. And I had walked out before her and she had walked out after me."

Aligned with her efforts to keep to herself, she did not report the incident to school officials. She explained, "It wasn't my business." Her decision was premised upon a particular common sense, which understood that "snitching" or telling on peers to school authorities could possibly initiate a confrontation between her, the other girl, and school authorities. Given this possibility, Carla avoided school administrators and the girl as a form of self-defense and protection. As Jones (2009) highlights in her study of "inner-city" Black girls, girls navigate complex layers of violence from their peers and state institutions (including schools and police). Many of their decisions can be understood as strategies for survival. Carla's mirror those of the girls in Jones's study. Yet, in spite of her efforts, she was unable to protect herself. Recalling the incident, she shared,

Somebody had said that they had seen me walk out with a wallet, but I didn't take anything. I got suspended and arrested for that. . . . The campus security came to my class. I thought it was because there was a boy who had gotten jumped and they wanted to ask me questions about that. And right when I got in [the office], they [the police] automatically said I was arrested for taking this, this, this. They read me my rights, said I had the right to remain silent. So I stopped talking. They asked me questions that I refused to answer. . . . They didn't handcuff [me] or anything. . . . It was just verbal. [The principal] said they wanted to ask me about what happened on Friday in the locker room. I was like okay. He said, "You heard there was an iPhone that came up missing?" [I said,] "Yeah, I heard there was an iPhone that came up missing." [But] I stopped talking. (Carla, personal communication, April 3, 2013)

When she was brought to the office by campus security, the police officers were there to greet her. They read her rights to her. She chose to remain silent and refused to answer any of the principal or police officers' questions. According to Carla's recollection, the police officers, an Asian male and a white male, were visibly upset by her refusal to speak. They responded to her by saying, "We don't have to deal with your attitude." Her decision to assert her right to remain silent to defend against self-incrimination or false charges was characterized by the police officers as having an "attitude." Carla was transported from school grounds to a holding cell at the city jail, which was located across the street from the high school. As soon as she arrived, she was taken into custody; the police officers took her picture and fingerprinted her.

CARLA: When I refused [to speak], they threatened to take me juvenile hall. [The white male police officer] got mad.

C: How do you know he got mad?

CARLA: He got red. He called my aunt, told her he was going to take me to jail. "We don't have time for this." They took me [to] jail, took my picture, fingerprints, asked me questions: How tall I was; How old I was. Put me in the holding cell until my aunt picked me up. (Carla, personal communication, April 3, 2013)

She was detained until the evening. No criminal charges were brought. Instead, she was mandated to attend a restorative justice program with counseling services. According to Carla, she was offered this alternative to avoid burglary charges. Since she did not clearly understand her rights and wanted to avoid court, she decided to accept the restorative justice option. This option included weekly check-ins with the restorative justice counselor for six months. She was also required to submit school progress reports from her teachers. While the latter helped her to stay on track in her classes, it also served to police her. She knew that she was being closely monitored for a crime she did not commit. In addition to meeting these court mandates, Carla was suspended from school for five days. She became known as "the troublemaker" in her family and among some of her peers. While she tried to be as minimal a burden as possible to her grandparents, school surveillance and discipline policies made her goal impossible. It did not matter to the police or the school that she had never been in trouble before the arrest. It also did not matter to them that she did not steal anything. More importantly, it did not matter to them that suspending and arresting her would cause harm to her and her family. Prior to the suspension and arrest, she was not considered a "problem child" for them. Following the disciplinary actions, she was stigmatized by her classmates and her grandparents. She tearfully recounted that for the first time in her life, her grandfather momentarily stopped talking to her.

Beyond the six-month probation, the punitive educational system and criminal justice system continued to have impacts on her emotions and relationships. She felt increasingly "lonely" because she needed to "keep to herself" even more than she did before the event. Determined to graduate from high school, she became even more quiet and withdrawn. Her story suggests that she was subject to punishment despite her efforts to stay under the radar and for how she chose to navigate complex conditions. It is almost as if the disciplinary policies and practices were inescapable.

Monica

Monica, a sixteen-year-old Black girl in the eleventh grade, explained that while she was a student who tried to do well in school and stay out of trouble, she was trapped by the antiblackness of school authorities. According to Monica, faculty did not understand her and refused to do so. Instead, they were more inclined to punish her for failing to meet their standards. She explained, "You're damned if you do, you're damned if you don't." Her experiences at school reflect Roberts's (1997, 2011) research, which demonstrates that Black women (and girls) are often simultaneously punished and neglected by state institutions, including child welfare services and the foster care system.

As the oldest of three children in a single-parent household, Monica was responsible for her siblings when her mother left for work in the evening. In addition to finishing her homework, her evening responsibilities included bathing, feeding, and putting her one-year-old and seven-year-old brothers to sleep. She explained, "I have a lot of responsibilities." The responsibilities she held and executed were demanding. This meant that she was often late to school because of staying up late with her brothers. Subsequently, she was often marked late to class, eventually leading to a truancy record. She shared, "I don't get much sleep." Although Monica previously explained to her teacher that she had extenuating circumstances at home, her teacher offered little sympathy. Instead, her teacher gave her several tardy referrals. Once during an argument with her teacher over a referral, Monica expressed her resentment and hurt by blurting out, "Whatever makes you sleep at night." Ironically, Monica had not slept. She imagined that her outburst would have alerted the teacher to her desperate frustrations about school and her life at home. Not only was Monica working to support her mother and her siblings, she was also struggling to do well in school. The school's policies and practices did not reflect or support the challenges and responsibilities she held at home. Instead, her teacher characterized Monica's behavior as "disrespectful" and gave her a referral for being late to class and disobedient.

Hartmann, Childers, and Shaw (2015) argues that family incomes and resources have greater impacts on children's lives than the makeup of family structures. This report, which was written on behalf of the Institute for Women's Policy Research, argues that Black girls are impacted disproportionately by the interstices of poverty, racism, and sexism compared to white boys and boys of color. These systemic conditions affect the girls' lives including their emotions. Monica shared, "For the past month, I feel depressed out of nowhere. I just get mad from lack of sleep. I have a lot of responsibilities" (personal communication, April 7, 2013). According to Monica's narrative, instead of recognizing and supporting her efforts to manage complex conditions and responsibilities, her educators and the discipline policies criminalize and subsequently punish her. Not only did her teachers and administrators discipline her with referrals and suspensions for needing to meet responsibilities that were out of her control and were a response to racialized and gendered economic disparities, they continued to neglect her needs for educational and emotional support. Their reactions created more frustrations, discord, and suffering.

Stacy

Stacy, a fifteen-year-old Black girl in the tenth grade, was suspended twice for fighting and, according to her, has multiple referrals for "disobedience." According to Stacy, the primary reason for her discipline record is because "teachers don't like Black kids." She witnessed teachers "disrespecting" Black teachers and contends that if adults can be disrespected, "imagine how [non-Black teachers] feel about students." Throughout Stacy's experience at FHS, she felt that Black students (and teachers) were often unsupported, policed, and disliked. In addition to her critique of the antiblackness of school discipline, Stacy shared that her discipline record was also a result of her induced "anger." Stacy explained, "I have a lot of anger."

Like Monica, Stacy believed that her anger emanated from trying to balance complex dynamics outside of school, including houselessness and domestic violence.

> STACY: We've been having problems at home. . . . Now we tryna see where I can stay. . . . I don't stay at home . . . [but] my momma doesn't want me stay with my granny [in Louisiana]. . . . I can't stay at home . . . cuz I don't get along with her baby daddy. . . .
>
> C: Why don't you get along with him?
>
> STACY: Sometimes he picks arguments. . . . Sometimes I be having arguments. Night before last, we got into an argument, cuz he pushed me.
> (Stacy, personal communication, February 21, 2013)

Stacy and her family moved from Louisiana to leave a domestic violence situation. Before her family was able to find housing in California, they lived in a domestic violence shelter, where she witnessed a mother who "miscarried right in front of [her]." Reflecting on this experience, Stacy shared that the experiences with domestic violence and houselessness impacted her experiences at school. Research has shown that experiences with traumatic events such as violence shape students' propensity toward depression, anxiety, and anger (Gillies et al. 2013; Kataoka et al. 2012). Stacy's narrative suggested a need for support services to help her cope with these painful experiences with premature death and gender violence. However, studies suggest that women and girls of color, particularly Black women and girls, are less likely to receive this support (Richie 1996). According to Stacy, not only was she able to identify the antiblack practices of her teachers, specifically in the ways that they treated their Black colleagues and students, she also experienced the school's ongoing neglect of her needs as a survivor of gender violence.

Studies demonstrate that women and girls of color, particularly Black women and girls, are more likely to live under conditions of poverty than their white counterparts (African American Policy Forum 2014; Hartmann, Childers, and Shaw 2015). Conditions of poverty render them more vulnerable to violence than their white counterparts. At the same time that they are more vulnerable to violence, including domestic and sexual violence, they are also subject to fewer protections and support services (Hartmann, Childers, and Shaw 2015; Richie 1996, 2012). For Black women and girls, when the institutions and their agents are antiblack, they are not only unprotected by state agencies, they are also vulnerable to state violence. In Stacy's case, she explained that in addition to her experiences with violence at home and with racist teachers, she also experienced physical violence from the school police officer.

The previous year, Stacy was involved in a verbal altercation off campus, which resulted in the police officer yelling and throwing her to the ground. He was accompanied by nine other law enforcement vehicles and a police dog (Wun 2014). She shared that the antiblack racism from schoolteachers and the physical violence from the police officer led her to emotionally withdraw from school. Her story demonstrates that she is not only a survivor of domestic violence and institutional violence from an antiblack school system, she was also a survivor of the violent criminal justice system. When asked if she spoke to any school counselor about the violence that she had experienced at home or at school, she referred to her experiences with the police officers and teachers to explain why she did not trust any adult at school. In response, Stacy explained, "I keep stuff in."

The decision to "keep stuff in" is a coerced response to a series of violent events as well as a response to a violent structure that is characteristically and foundationally antiblack. As Hartman (1997, 96) helps us to understand, it is a consequence of living under the condition of slavery and its afterlife, by which Black women and girls are not only assaulted but denied recognition of the potential to be injured, and the injury itself. Hartman (1997, 96) explained that "unredressed injury" is a condition of captivity for Black women. Instead of having the privileges and rights granted to whites, which include recognition of their susceptibility and experiences with pain, Black women and girls are positioned through institutional policies and practices to be structurally vulnerable to multiple forms of violence and without protection.

Charmaine

Charmaine, a fourteen-year-old Black girl in the ninth grade, explained that she gets into trouble because of things that happen outside of school. "Sometimes things happen outside of school." At the time of the interview, Charmaine had recently been given two referrals for disobedience and defiance. She explained the context of her behaviors at school: "There are five of us. Sometimes my mom doesn't eat so the rest of us can eat. Sometimes I don't eat so the little ones can eat. He [the teacher who recently gave her a referral] doesn't know that sometimes I have to walk one or two hours to school because my mom's car broke down. He doesn't know these things. They don't see these things" (Charmaine, personal communication, April 7, 2014). She believed that if her teachers understood her difficult experiences, they would be less punitive and more supportive.

During the exceptionally sensitive interview, she shared that she had been kidnapped and forced into prostitution. Studies suggest that although any person can be vulnerable to sex trafficking and that there are differences between consensual and coerced sex work, women and girls of color are more likely to be subject to forced prostitution than their white and male counterparts (NAACP and National Women's Law Center 2014). They are also more likely to be policed and punished for being in the sex trade (regardless of consent or coercion). She described her experiences of being forced into prostitution: "I got off the bus because it doesn't go up the hill and was going to walk to my friend's house. I was trying to call her but I dropped my phone. Someone grabbed me and threw me into a van. Next thing I know, I was in a hotel with a bunch of other girls" (Charmaine, personal communication, April 7, 2014).

She explained that she was subsequently forced to have sex with different men for nearly three months. According to Charmaine, the men who kidnapped her threatened to hurt her family including her siblings if she tried to contact them or the police. Although she was eventually able to leave, the impacts of the violence were ongoing. She found herself unable to focus in class. When asked about the type of support she received from school, she explained that school officials, who were made aware of the violence because of her excessive absences, had partnered with Child Protective Services (CPS) to monitor her and her family. In this sense, the school's response to Charmaine's experiences with sexual violence was surveillance and policing through an additional state agency, CPS. According to her, as a result of the partnership between schools and CPS, her mother was under police investigation for child neglect and abuse. This tripartite relationship between school administrators, police, and CPS did not only authorize policing of her mother, it induced Charmaine's anxieties and fears. Fearful of state punishment by schools, police, and CPS, including the possibility that she was going to be taken away from her family, she refused to talk to school counselors about the sexual violence she experienced. While educators shared that they were suspicious of the truthfulness of her claims, they recognized that they were also ill-equipped to support her. More importantly, some did not believe in supporting her regardless of the veracity of her story. Instead, they chose to dismiss and punish her for being a disruptive student.

Being subject to violence and having to fear that her mother could possibly be arrested impacted Charmaine and her experiences at school. She had a difficult time following directions. She admitted that she was easily angered and anxious. These emotions materialized as losing patience with teachers or refusing to complete tasks in class. Her teachers—particularly the white male who had given her two recent referrals—often responded with referrals and suggestions for suspension. According to Charmaine, she hoped that her teachers would learn about or consider the underlying reasons behind her difficulties at school instead of criminalizing and punishing her for disobedience and defiance.

Despite Charmaine's hopes, the author learned that most of her teachers, including the teacher who recently gave her referrals, had been notified about the kidnapping. In an interview with the teacher, he explained that he was suspicious about her narrative and believed that either way, Charmaine should not be "coddled."

While Charmaine may have been disobedient, her potential refusal to listen to her teacher or desire to interrupt class is reminiscent of Hartman's analysis of the importance of resistance under slavery: "The everyday practices of the enslaved encompassed an array of tactics such as work slowdowns, feigned illness, unlicensed travel, the destruction of property, theft, self-mutilation, dissimulation, physical confrontation with others and overseers that document the resistance to slavery. These small-scale and every-day forms of resistance interrupted, reelaborated, and defied the constraints of everyday life under slavery and exploited openings in the system for the use of the enslaved" (1997, 51). Put differently, Charmaine's responses, if they could be characterized as disobedience, were versions of resistance to a condition by which school authorities and other adults did not acknowledge the violence being committed against her and her injuries.

While she insisted on succeeding in school, before the end of the school year and this project, Charmaine had stopped showing up. Teachers believed that she had dropped out. According to the policy report by the NAACP and National Women's Law Center (2014, 20), "experiences of trauma correspond with decreased school engagement and reduced educational achievement. While not specific to African American girls, there is research linking children's reports to exposure to violence to poor academic performance." Although the school may not have been fully equipped to provide the services that Charmaine may have needed, the school discipline policies that her teacher used to send her out of class or to make her feel as though he or other teachers did not understand her circumstances speaks to the condition of constant surveillance and punishment without recognition.

Schooling in the Afterlife of Slavery

Hartman argues that our current period is affected by a longer history of antiblackness in which Black bodies are structurally and perpetually subject to premature death and ongoing captivity. In her analysis of the afterlife of slavery and Black women's subjectivities, Black bodies, she argues, are denied access to self-defense, privacy, or autonomy. Hartman (1997, 6) writes, "Black lives are still imperiled and devalued by a racial calculus and a political arithmetic that were entrenched centuries ago. This is the afterlife of slavery—skewed life chances, limited access to health and education, premature death, incarceration, and impoverishment." Further evidence of this condition can be found through police violence against Black communities and the simultaneous neglect of Black women and girls, including their experiences with sexual assault, domestic violence, and poverty. Richie (1996, 2012) and Roberts (1997, 2011) have written extensively about the ways that state institutions have systematically criminalized and neglected Black women and girls.

Through slavery and its afterlife, Black lives are imagined and constructed as captive, confined and subject to the whims of the master's fantasies. Hartman (1997, 8) further writes, "the enslaved were required to sing or dance for the slave owner's pleasure as well as to demonstrate their submission, obsequiousness, and obedience." Drawing from Black feminism's analyses of slavery and its afterlife, Dillon (2012, 121) contends, "Slavery's afterlife surfaces in the gaps between the recorded, the forgotten, and the never will be."

Informed by these frameworks, I contend that the educational system and school discipline in particular operate as instruments in the afterlife of slavery. Formal and informal disciplinary mechanisms position the Black girl as perpetually and involuntarily open to surveillance and control. In school and through school discipline, she is denied access to autonomy, which includes feelings and forms of self-defense. Empathy does not apply to her life and narratives. Her stories disappear and are disavowed. Through school discipline, she is made into a captive object, one that is constantly monitored but without recognition of her existence. In the afterlife of slavery, captive objects are not recognized as having access to injury, narratives of intersectional violence, suffering, emotions, or resistance. As the narratives of the girls suggest, they are also imagined and positioned as inured to pain or suffering. They operate to be watched, as criminals under observation, instead of as a subject/person with feelings to be recognized, defended, or supported. Importantly, this study does not believe that the girls are mere victims of the captive conditions created by school discipline policies and practices. Instead, their narratives demonstrate that they do not only resist but are survivors of antiblack state violence. As Sexton (2010, 33) writes, "This is why for Hartman resistance is figured through the black female's sexual self-defense, as exemplified by the 1855 circuit court case State of Missouri v. Celia, a Slave, in which the defendant was sentenced to death by hanging on the charge of murder for responding with deadly force to the sexual assault and attempted rape by a white male slaveholder."

By extrapolating the conditions of slavery and its afterlife, and its particular effects on Black women (and girls), Hartman (1997) provides insight into the underlying logic that informs the experiences Black girls have with schools and their methods of discipline and punishment. Black girls, this study demonstrates, are perpetually subject to punishment for infractions. The girls shared that they most often got into trouble for having attitudes or being disrespectful to their teachers or other staff. However, according to the girls' narratives, behaviors that were being characterized as forms of disobedience were their way of demonstrating that they had agency under captivity. It was also their way of demonstrating that they were suffering and resisting violence inside and outside of school. In other words, the girls were being disciplined and punished for the ways that they navigated and responded to antiblackness.

Conclusion

School discipline research has largely focused on the school-to-prison pipeline and its effects on boys of color (Advancement Project 2011; Ferguson 2001; Noguera 2008; Wald and Losen 2003). Although focusing on the school-to-prison pipeline and its impacts on boys of color helps researchers understand the disparities in discipline policies, these two approaches miss opportunities to examine the ways that school discipline does more than funnel students into prison. They render students captive in and through school. That is, schools are sites of captivity unto themselves. These studies also fail to consider the specific ways that schools and their discipline practices affect Black girls.

In particular, the school-to-prison-pipeline literature has paid particular attention to zero-tolerance policies (Ayers, Dohrn, and Ayers 2001; Greene 1999; Skiba and Knesting 2001; Skiba and Peterson 2000). According to these studies, schools funnel students into prison through exclusionary practices such as suspension and expulsion. These studies suggest that harsh discipline policies serve to drive students out of school. Students who miss classes are more likely to fall behind their peers and become disconnected from school (Advancement Project 2011; Kafka 2011; Morris 2015; Skiba and Peterson 2000). According to the studies, students who have been suspended or expelled drop or are gradually pushed out of school. Research suggests they are more likely to be exposed to the criminal justice system (Advancement Project 2011; Wald and Losen 2003).

School-to-prison pipeline researchers also contend that the increasing presence of police officers has translated into more criminalization and arrests of students at school (Kim, Losen, and Hewitt 2010). Behaviors such as being late to school, once considered school infractions, are now increasingly subject to arrests and citations. According to Kim, Losen, and Hewitt (2010), students are now more likely to be arrested not necessarily because they are committing more crimes, but because of the presence of police officers on their campus, who are authorized to criminalize and arrest students. These researchers contend that most of the primary problems with school discipline are with harsh discipline practices and the presence of police officers on campus. These arguments have propelled important campaigns and movements to remove police officers out of school.

Other scholars argue that schools are increasingly becoming militarized spaces that create punitive conditions for students of color (Nolan 2011; Saltman and Gabbard 2011). Within the context of a pervasive war on terror, militarized surveillance systems in U.S. schools help schools to categorize students, particularly those unable to pass the surveillance technologies, as potential terrorists. While such studies are important, they miss opportunities to examine the specific connections between the United States' structural and foundational relationship to antiblackness. Instead, they often use encompassing language of "students of color," "people of color," or "urban youth," thereby conflating Black students' experiences with those of their non-Black peers of color (Sexton 2010). This type of designation, while seemingly innocuous in the efforts to identify racial disparities in discipline policies, obscures the particularity of antiblackness and Black students' experiences.

As Black studies scholars including Sexton (2010) and Wilderson (2010) explain, antiblackness is without analogue. Such comparisons or conflations serve to undermine the specific centrality of antiblackness to U.S. society, its institutions, policies, and practices. While other non-Black students of color may be affected and othered by school discipline policies and militarized structures, Black youth—as they are with other forms of policing violence—are the "prototypical targets" of discipline policies (Sexton 2007b). Black communities are prototypical targets of all forms of policing across state agencies. This has been integral to the United States history, including in the afterlife of slavery. According to Hartman (1997, 97), "the law's selective recognition of slave personhood and subjectivity in regard to issues of injury . . . defined the identity of the slave female by the negation of sentience . . . and the negligibility of her injuries." Black girls in this study were prohibited from articulating their struggles, disagreements, or injuries. According to the girls, when they did, they were punished. School discipline policies and practices attempted to neutralize the girls' abilities to assert their agencies and subjectivities as humans, particularly within the context of the afterlife of slavery where they are structurally and institutionally rendered captive objects. The disciplining and punishment of these girls is a part of their condition of captivity. The latter is central to the social, political and economic foundation of the United States and its institutions. The outcome is that the girls and their needs are not only obscured, they are made possible by and through institutional neglect, disdain, and punishment. As a result, Black girls are coerced into feeling confined, misunderstood, and despised as they are subject to constant surveillance and control.

As the girls' stories indicate, they are up against multiple odds that are often, if not entirely, not of their doing. Their abilities to navigate these captive conditions may reflect more on their abilities to survive antiblackness than it does to the school's receptivity to Blackness (and Black resistance). When the girls resist these conditions or act out because of them, they are deemed defiant.

Instead of attempting to disprove the characterization that Black girls are defiant or disrespectful, it would be useful for school discipline and educational reform scholars to encourage the girls to be more defiant and more disobedient against an antiblack school system that characteristically punishes them, particularly because the behaviors being identified as deviant are enactments of the girls' injuries from surviving state, institutional, and interpersonal violence and their refusal to be silent about them. They should be resisting these conditions.

In order to best support Black girls within the context of the afterlife of slavery, there are a few suggestions. First, we should identify the role of antiblackness and, more largely, the afterlife of slavery in shaping school policies and practices and how they affect girls. Second, policy analysts, teachers, and students should be trained to identify the particularities of Black girls' experiences in order to develop policies, practices, relationships, and school cultures that support girls, including their efforts to resist conditions of captivity. Third, following the lead of Black feminist scholars, scholars and practitioners in the field of education should centralize students' narratives and needs, particularly Black girls' stories, surrounding their experiences inside and outside of school.

I also suggest that we adopt a Black feminist critique of schools by examining how schools are a part of a larger structure of captivity and antiblackness, how they intersect with other forms of violence and what this means for girls of color, and Black girls in particular (Crenshaw 2012; Roberts 2011). As Wilderson (2010) suggests, there is a condition of antiblackness that produces and perhaps relies on violence against Black communities throughout various social spheres and institutions. As we analyze schools and their relationship to Black suffering, it will be useful to explore Black suffering in schools as a condition within the afterlife of slavery where captivity is policy. It would also be imperative to create spaces for Black girls to feel supported as they resist captivity, to help dismantle institutions and conditions that are reliant upon their captivity, and to create a world that is instead premised upon their freedom.

Notes

Parts of this article have been previously published in Wun (2016).

1 While this study highlights the experiences of cisgendered Black girls, future research will need to analyze the relationship that antiblackness has on constructing gender through the educational system, and its impacts on Black gender nonconforming as well as transgender youth.

PRESIDENTIAL POWERS IN THE CAPTIVE MATERNAL LIVES OF SALLY, MICHELLE, AND DEBORAH

JOY JAMES

I smile rarely, but I am surviving.

DEBORAH DANNER, "Living with Schizophrenia"

Captive Maternals

Some variation of Deborah Danner's quote about schizophrenia might have been uttered by Sally Hemings or Michelle Obama, other women of African descent who have become historical markers for U.S. democracy while serving as Captive Maternals (CM) to presidents of the United States (POTUS). In "Introducing the Captive Maternal," I write: "Captive Maternals are self-identified female, male, trans or ungendered persons feminized and socialized into caretaking within the legacy of racism and US democracy. Captive Maternals are designated for consumption in the tradition of chattel slavery; they stabilize with their labor the very social and state structures which prey upon them."[1]

In "The Womb of Western Theory," I discuss how feminized caretakers of historically enslaved and disenfranchised Black communities become captive to a predatory democracy, one that denies Black freedom and female/child emancipation by redirecting the generative powers of caretakers from rebellion against predation to the reproduction of societies steeped in theft, trauma, and material consumption (James 2016).

In the eighteenth century, Sally Hemings became Thomas Jefferson's slave through his marriage to her half-sister, Martha. In the twenty-first century, Michelle Obama made history as the first official Black First Lady of the United States (FLOTUS) through her marriage to Barack Obama. Eight years later, the first Black president of an imperial militarist-capitalist nation, POTUS 44, passed his presidential mantle on to the twenty-first-century's first openly white nationalist POTUS, Donald Trump, 45. Deborah Danner never met Donald Trump. However, as a casualty of violent policing promoted by the presidential candidate who became 45, Danner materialized as a symbol of an anti-FLOTUS, and representative of anonymous subjugated, and combative, Black feminized caretakers—those most likely to die at the hands of violent policing. This essay theorizes from multiple sites linked to the function of the ungendered Captive Maternal. There is the past, the site of a revolutionary era owned by propertied white men, one in which pregnant Black teens soothed enslavers (and, in Paris and at Monticello, a future president). There is the contemporary era of "Black success equals Black power" in which a Princeton/Harvard grad metamorphosed from the stereotypical "angry Black woman" condemning racism into a charismatic FLOTUS mothering a color-blind nation. There is the current crisis of corruption which trashed democratic norms (which work best for the privileged) amid police violence in which an impoverished, medically fragile Black woman, in her bathrobe, was shot while clutching a baseball bat in her bedroom to ward off a white cop. Captive Maternals materialize in plantations, universities, public housing. Each site has the imprint of presidential power and policy, of forced Black intimacy, violability, and disposability.

Captive Maternals separated by centuries, privilege, and (de)privation, three women of African descent coexist as intergenerational connectors of antiblack racism, misogynoir, violence, and presidential powers. Enslaved "FLOTUS" Sally Hemings, official FLOTUS Michelle Obama, anti-FLOTUS Deborah Danner offer perspectives on the impact of antiblack racism on Captive Maternals. Miss Sally functioned as a "secret" concubine-slave/internationally sex trafficked child for Thomas Jefferson, POTUS 3, first in Paris as a chaperon for his daughters (her nieces). Ms. Michelle radiated the glamour of the Ivy-League liberal still mocked—due to her nonelite upbringing in Chicago—as "that ghetto girl" by the Vineyard's Black bourgeoisie. Dissociated from conventional beauty and decorum and intimacy with powerful (white) men, Ms. Deborah lacked the glamour, mystery, and alleged power of FLOTUSes 3 and 44. (Captive Maternals are also capable of inflicting violence upon themselves, kin, community, and external aggressors.)

Despite temporal distance and diverse access to presidents, the three women display kinship based on genealogies of vulnerabilities and disposability traceable to Black enslavement. The POTUS embodies the democratic sovereign who serves as the Commander-in-Chief of the police forces of a democracy built on wars against the Indigenous and Blacks. Miss Sally outlived the forced embrace of Thomas. Ms. Michelle tutored Barack's political career and cultural Blackness and with him became the first Black couple to preside over an imperial democracy. (Unlike Sally or Deborah, Michelle also became a multimillionaire and inspiration to the civic-minded.) Deborah became a target of policing that emulated authoritarianism if not proto-fascism. Each CM proved useful to the democracy. Privately addressing the neediness of presidents, they posed for the public as symbols of Americanization and "integration," "post-racialism," or victimization. Captive Maternals as prey, pleasers or combatants have been a staple in the American imagery.

Ms. Sally: When Your Rapist Is a POTUS

> I've never once ever heard anyone called a benevolent rapist.
> TITUS KAPHAR in "Are We Actually Citizens Here?"

Although Michelle Obama stated during the 2016 presidential campaign that sexual assault accusations against POTUS 45 had "shaken [her] to her core," such concern seems largely absent in discussions of his predecessor, Thomas Jefferson. POTUS 44's admiration for an author/scribe of the U.S. constitution whose three-fifths clause kept young Sally laboring to reproduce electoral votes for Jefferson's presidential victory fails to note that the founders' economy based on racial/colonial capitalism, from 1619 to 1865 created trillions of dollars of wealth for whites.

After the "Hottentot Venus" Saartje Bartmann, Sally Hemings appears to be the most historically fetishized Black sexual captive in the Western world. She functioned as the de facto third FLOTUS to widower Jefferson.

Racist law, codified by her enslaver, prevented her from marrying Jefferson to legalize her status as FLOTUS. However, it is likely that even if the 1967 Supreme Court ruling *Loving v. Virginia* had been passed centuries earlier, Virginia's most celebrated citizen would not have married the light-skinned Black. Law did allow Jefferson to free their children, but legal code constricted Miss Sally. Jefferson did not emancipate Hemings while he lived, perhaps from insight of the free-will of captive Black mothers who might resent his writing in the 1785 *Notes on the State of Virginia* that primates prefer Black females—a bestiality from which Jefferson spares Black males and the Indigenous. Thanks to DNA testing, Miss Sally now owns part of Jefferson's legacy. Say "Jefferson" as paragon of democratic virtue, and I will say "Hemings" as an illustration of democracy's barbaric deceptions. Say "Thomas" in reverence and hear "Sally" as satire.

As FLOTUS 3, Hemings functioned as Jefferson's muse and maternal caretaker. She was a political liability as a public political advisor, but it is highly likely that he talked about his duties and conflicts at home. During 1785–89, when Jefferson served as U.S. minister to France, he sent for Sally Hemings to serve as lady-in-waiting for his two young daughters. The fourteen-year-old Captive Maternal was "remade" by Jefferson as he dressed her for her role as escort for white ladies and for his own pleasure. An enslaved child worker transitions to sexual conquest, reproductive birth laborer creating more slaves for her owner. Thirty years Jefferson's junior, Hemings birthed and mothered his children while mothering an aging POTUS.

Some depict Jefferson as her chosen lover. Technically, the captive does not have the legal power to "choose." Emotional ties exist, but in a Stockholm syndrome situation, where coercion ends and desire begins is unclear. For some, the imaginary of Black acceptance through normalizing enslavement as endearment is essential. No one knows Hemings's agency and angst concerning her captivity. Jefferson's white progeny, specifically his daughter, namesake of his legal wife Martha, burned all papers referencing Sally Hemings. Academics and pundits research and postulate a relationship of reciprocity that transcends the reality of gender, race, caste, and captivity.

Artists and intellectuals can offer an emotional intelligence and insights that surpass academic skills. Barbara Chase-Riboud's 1977 *Sally Hemings: A Novel* creates fictional narratives that embrace Miss Hemings, her mother, and enslaved Black families with layerd interpretations of Jefferson's official life stories and lies, and academic and popular validations of his misogynoir. In the absence of historical documents, the oral history of Hemings's

Black family replaced the missing paper trail; their DNA resurrected her life. The meanings of her captivity, though, seem to be continuously (re)buried despite continuing excavations.

Titus Kaphar's painting *Beneath the Myth of Benevolence* depicts the partial image of an anonymous dark-skinned enslaved female painted underneath the famous portrait of Thomas Jefferson. The canvas peels back part of Jefferson's image to reveal the dark brown, bare legs, breast, torso, set features, and head wrap of a young African girl/woman seated at a table. In a public radio interview with Kaphar and historian Annette Gordon-Reed, author of *The Hemings of Monticello*, the artist stated that he painted *Beneath the Myth of Benevolence* after a conversation about Thomas Jefferson with a (white) high school teacher (Gordon-Reed and Kaphar 2017).[2] When the young artist referred to Jefferson as "complex" because he was both brilliant and enslaved humans, the AP history teacher qualified Jefferson's violence by stating he was a "benevolent slave owner." Coupling racial slavery with sexual terror, Kaphar responded with surprise that he had never heard of a reference to a "*benevolent* rapist?" The prolonged silence that followed his query prompted Kaphar to depart for his studio and paint *Beneath the Myth of Benevolence*. The unveiling of Jefferson superimposed atop the Black girl/woman, is the labor of a young, queer Black male, a CM who grew up in poverty and worked to protect his siblings from police and despair. Kaphar provides a critical function: he presents a window into the meaning of "Sally"; through that portal we can refuse to sanitize violence and presidential predation.

How is love differentiated from sexual captivity and torture? One's mind could ask Sally while parsing through the responses of those who seek to answer for her. Some argue that her light-skinned or "quadroon" status made her less Black and captured or more "free." That argument paradoxically suggests that as more "white" she was more capable of peerage, and a loving sexual relationship with a white POTUS enslaver. It's a racial argument against the significance of race which ironically makes whiteness the signifier for (unraced) human. Miss Sally cannot answer; but if she loved or respected her enslaved African mother (impregnated/raped by the "owner" father who sired two daughters with only Martha Jefferson as "free"), that argument is not well grounded. Even if classroom lectures pose FLOTUS 3 to whisper or shout that her enslaver was a lover and not a captor, by which metrics do you determine her speech to be (self)aware and free of deceptions? The ability to walk or run away from Jefferson came with penalties. Presidential powers are patriarchal and white supremacist powers. Law and custom limited the possession that Jefferson wielded over his first and only wife, Martha, who did not live long enough to perform the FLOTUS duties inherited by her younger, enslaved half-sister. Little inhibited Jefferson's patriarchal control over Sally Hemings and the hundreds of enslaved Blacks building his plantation and wealth.

One can trace Hemings's vulnerability to sexual predation and find a path that rethinks the trajectory of democracy and the impetus to the Revolutionary War as a war of liberation for white, property-owning males. In 1772, a British magistrate condemned chattel slavery and granted freedom to James Somerset, an enslaved Black man from the American colonies brought to England. Proslavery colonial Americans, such as Jefferson, could foresee Britain's future criminalization of slavery. The Revolutionary War resulted in the Articles of Confederation, the U.S. Constitution, and several centuries of POTUSes overseeing Black enslavement, exploitation and sexual violation as a national norm. The origin of U.S. democracy was not just about taxation without representation; it was also about codified racist control of humans without restraint.

The ultimate form of violation is to be reduced to disposable property, to be rendered a slave stripped of the rights and entitlements of humanity. The war of independence was also anti-abolitionist. Waged by counter-revolutionaries, the founding fathers simultaneously feared Britain abolishing slavery *and* African/Black-led violent rebellions in the Americas and formation of Maroons. In the supposed safety of the domesticated and enslaved home, controlling the CM would be the symbolic and material expression of executive power.[3] From Jefferson's presidential administration (1801–9) until his death in 1826, antiblack violence and enslavement were naturalized within the democracy.

The role of captive Black maternals in presidential antiblack powers is codified in Thomas Jefferson's defeat of John Adams in the 1800 presidential election. Jefferson prevails because Hemings, her children, and other enslaved people "voted" for POTUS 3. The three-fifths clause increased the electoral clout of slave-holding Southern states. Today, gerrymandering and the suppression of Black and brown voters is a form of violence that benefits white supremacy. (*Mother Jones*'s preelection polling, cited by Ta-Nehisi Coates [2017], tallied that if only white voters voted, Trump would have defeated Clinton 389 to 81 in the Electoral College.)

After the 2016 *Access Hollywood* tape release, candidate Trump briefly apologized for sexual predatory speech and acts. In late 2017, he recanted. (Trump never apologized for calling for the death penalty in a 1989 *New*

York Times advertisement for the DNA-exonerated Central Park 5; the 1989 rape was committed by Mathias Reyes; the falsely imprisoned youths received multimillion-dollar settlements from the city of New York decades later.) POTUS 45 referenced Jefferson in an attempt to condemn a critical press for "lying" when that press challenged his false claims that Barack Obama committed a felony by conducting illegal surveillance of the president-elect at Trump Tower. POTUS 45 inadvertently dragged Hemings into the fray with "fake news" accusations, reminding some that both 3 and 45 were engaged in sexual misconduct and assault (45's accusers could sue as free, white sovereign victims). Trump requoted Jefferson's denunciation of the press as "malicious and slanderous" when in actuality POTUS 3 lied to disparage journalists exposing his hypocrisy about his relationship with Sally Hemings. Jefferson's scholarly work reprinted violent racist-misogynist pornography that could have been buried in his private diary. The violence of his sexual imagination and predatory desires materialized as a reflection of the political-social order that he helped to engineer. This suggests that Jefferson thought himself above public censure and shaming, as does Trump. Some cite Jefferson's private (brief) contrition about slavery in a letter written to a powerful abolitionist priest in France as an example of a change of heart; given his acts and policies that missive seems more self-serving and playing to the public elites that condemned slavery.

Around the time Trump was born in 1946, Monticello curators turned Hemings's sitting room sanctuary, with its fireplace and potential solitude, into a "Whites Only" restroom or toilet. In 2017, when the new president took office, Monticello began renovations to restore the sitting room, transforming it into a museum or shrine. This "shrine" now exists as a conceptual space to reflect upon the limitations of POTUSes linked to CMs (but not the desire for rebellion for that aspect is stripped from Hemings's legacy).

Ms. Michelle: The Highs and Lows of Surrogacy

> When they go low, I go high. That's the choice Barack and I have made. That's what's kept us sane over the years.
> MICHELLE OBAMA, "Remarks by the First Lady at the Jackson
> State University Commencement"

During Barack Obama's 2009 inaugural celebrations, the descendants of Sally Hemings congratulated Barack Obama on becoming the forty-fourth president of the United States. Identifying herself as the great-great-great-granddaughter of Thomas Jefferson, Clara Lee Fisher's January 2009, "Letter to Thomas Jefferson about Barack Obama" is both atonement and reconciliation. Published in *Newsweek*, Fisher's letter embraced the presidential sovereign who enabled predatory capitalism through slavery and created its most consumed victim—the Captive Maternal: "Dear Thomas Jefferson, I would like to respectfully introduce myself as the great, great granddaughter of Madison Hemings." She references Jefferson's salacious *Notes on the State of Virginia*: "as if those unfortunate words express your definitive position on race." The Captive Maternal comforts her enslaving ancestor who became president: "If you have wrestled with the thought of these less than adept theories having found their way into history, be comforted in knowing that I have also read your letter of Feb. 25, 1809, in which your opinions concerning race had become quite progressive" (Fisher 2009).

Jefferson's "quite progressive" opinion is neither revolutionary nor advocacy for human equality; rather it reads as a peace offering to French abolitionists with whom Jefferson likely sought to establish his own stature as humanitarian and statesman. In the last months of his presidency, Jefferson sought recognition from French priest and abolitionist Henri Gregoire, who championed the humanity of enslaved Africans—something Jefferson emphatically did not do. The letter written by Miss Sally and Thomas's descendant does not mention the maternal line, only the paternal line. Understandably, prestige and power come from the presidential seat and seal, from which white males dominate over Captive Maternals and accumulate through their labor: "The nation you were so instrumental in establishing has become the greatest on the earth" (Fisher 2009). FLOTUS 44 would pronounce the same language of U.S. exceptionalism at the 2016 DNC Convention. Miss Sally's progeny asserts a claim that cannot be proven or disproven:

> The unfulfilled ideals of democracy which I am certain burdened your heart are closer to fulfillment. Slavery is ended and we the people in the year of our Lord 2008 have elected Barack Obama—an African American to our nation's highest office. The president-elect has said, "It is only in this country the United States of America that my story is even possible." You have begun a great work that in 200 years has not only survived but continues to become a more perfect union. (Fisher 2009)

Writing that Obama would "share the White House with his beautiful wife and two lovely daughters," Fisher offers praise: "It is my most sincere and heartfelt prayer that if any Americans harbor doubts or fears based upon race they will consider the position you so eloquently expressed, and recognize that our new president is not the fulfillment of a race but the culmination of the dreams of our founding fathers" (Fisher 2009). Fisher's optimism does not acknowledge, years before the election of 45, shared fantasies of white nationalism and female captivity across centuries.

As the first official Black FLOTUS, partnered to the first Black (male) POTUS, the issue of mental health for Michelle Obama stemmed from the extraordinary racist attacks she was forced to endure during the presidential campaigns and the Obama administration. Nearly all of the attacks synthesized her race, gender, and sexuality and generative powers as a Captive Maternal used by the administration to build populist or popularized bridges to communities whose material needs would be largely neglected by an administration in which the POTUS reminded that he was the first president *who happened to be Black*, not the first Black president who would lead/protect Black people from a white supremacy that he downplayed for political gain. As the icon for Black bourgeois success, the Obamas' confidence exuded that capitalism could work for everyone. Lacking the mixed-race hybridity (i.e., not having a white mother or a Kenyan father with a graduate degree from Harvard) Michelle embodied the "authentic" Black—the "problem" of the twentieth and twenty-first centuries.

At the 2016 Democratic National Convention (DNC) in Philadelphia, Michelle Obama stated to thunderous applause and cheers that she woke up every morning in "a house that was built by slaves." Forced and expropriated labor in a racist democracy built an icon of freedom. Her family/private achievements were ideologically aligned with global predatory capitalism; nonetheless past labor was to be celebrated as political transformation. With two beautiful Black daughters raised by herself, her mother, her husband (and servants and security) the FLOTUS signified a departure from the past: she was not Sally Hemings. However, the statement as a symbol of irrefutable racial progress should have precluded the possibility of POTUS 45. (No references were made to Black reparations or rebellions.)

During the eight years of the Obama administration, benefits accrued toward elites, those with Harvard, corporate, or military pedigree or adjacency. Black women rose in the ranks: Presidential Advisor Valerie Jarrett; National Security Agency Advisor Susan Rice; Attorney General Loretta Lynch. All with the ear of a president shepherded by a FLOTUS from Southside Chicago who sojourned into Princeton and Harvard Law but retained an anchor in Blackness that electrified the nervous system of white America seeking domestic service, surrogacy maternalism, and African animism. Black presidential powers in a racial democracy provide adjacency to whiteness: an expression of white power as imperial might. If, as leftist critics levied, Barack Obama was the first Black imperial POTUS, then Michelle Obama was the first Black imperial FLOTUS. Western empires were shaped by colonization and genocide. It's difficult to keep one's sanity if one plans to go against history and genealogy in a direction in which the nation does not wish to travel. No captive is exempt from the violence of racial or presidential powers or the temptation to share or wield them. That of course includes the POTUS and the FLOTUS. Presidential power works to stabilize structure, nation, political economy, policing, and social hierarchy. The FLOTUS works to stabilize the presidential powers of the POTUS. Whereas anonymity protected Hemings's experiences of predatory powers from being fully known, celebrity was considered to be a shield for Obama.

A 2017 poll ranked the nation's top four feminists, three Black women and one white woman: Michelle Obama, Oprah Winfrey, Hillary Clinton, and Beyoncé Knowles-Carter. Alongside an empress in business and a queen of entertainment, two FLOTUSes who built the political careers and steered the presidential ambitions of their husbands survived sexism and racism. When Bill Clinton was elected in 1992, Hillary Clinton boasted of a two-for-one bargain, while the nation chastised that it only voted for one white president, one who promoted draconian policing and imprisonment with the 1994 Omnibus Crime Bill and bogus science of Black children as "super-predators." Hillary Clinton wanted to be more POTUS than FLOTUS 42. That would have been unseemly for Michelle Obama, who did not seek a co-presidency, yet was viciously attacked by racists, including public officials.

Michelle had recruited and trained Barack when he was a political novice and community organizer; she introduced him to Chicago power brokers and Black elite communities and social networks. She mothered her husband, children, and eventually a nation. When POTUS 44 campaigned for Clinton (quietly in the primaries when she was challenged by Bernie Sanders and actively in the general election), his legacy to be protected by Clinton had been crafted by a Captive Maternal FLOTUS who addressed veterans' issues and childhood obesity, posed with a poster for abducted girls in Darfur, and promoted organic and healthy eating habits. The majority of whites, including white women, rejected Michelle's role model of ministrations when they voted in November 2016 for Donald Trump for president. Differentiating and distancing from Captive Maternals, their

"Great White Hope," with Melania Trump as standard bearer for white femininity plagiarizing the speeches of a Black predecessor, appealed not only to the leadership of white nationalist men but also to the desires of Identity Evropa (American Identity Movement) Volkmoms.

After the 2016 election, with the security blanket of POTUS 45, attacks against the Black woman with a Harvard JD who performed domesticity for the nation continued. A West Virginia white female director of a federally funded senior antipoverty program referred to FLOTUS 44 as an "ape in heels" on a Facebook post welcomed by her town's white female mayor. Following the public outcry, the director was fired based on the nonprofit's management and antidiscrimination compliance. The mayor apologized and resigned. In 2018, Roseanne Barr's *Roseanne* sitcom reboot on ABC was canceled after she referred to Valerie Jarret as an "ape."

In the *Atlantic*, Ta-Nehisi Coates (2017) argues that Donald Trump is the first "white president" because Obama was the first Black president. (The argument is complicated: one should seek out Coates's analysis.) Logically then, Melania Trump is the first "white first lady." The diminished achievements and white collar crime associates of those whites who followed the Black presidential power couple might distract from the fact that both administrations left the structures of white supremacy and predatory capitalism intact. POTUS 44 tended corporate hegemony with a subtlety, charm, care, and compassion lacking in 45. The POTUS with five (known) children by three different mothers is not the Black one, as late-night comics point out. Yet, even with the reversal of stereotypes, Trump's embrace of white supremacy still gave him superiority. Obama's ideological statements advocating color-blind stability and Black endeavor were not ideologically combative against white supremacy.

Whites' obsessive adoration of FLOTUS 44, who seems more popular than POTUS 44, reflects less a commitment to fight for social justice than a desire to "move on" with a promise that racial justice was within grasp. When the concept that the descendants of the slaves who built the White House were entitled to reparations, the admiration for FLOTUS 44 became clearly nontransferrable to antiracist political policy. From FLOTUS 45's campaign to end cyberbullying, Eleanor Roosevelt's work for civil and human rights, Jackie Kennedy's support for the arts, Hillary Clinton's forays into health care reform, Laura Bush's advocacy for literacy, and Michelle Obama's health initiative to combat childhood obesity, one senses that the range of causes could vary. Still, the foundation of every edifice concretized in exploited Black labor would not sway. The sanity that FLOTUS 44 spoke of in terms of going high or low is embodied in her May 9, 2015, Tuskegee University commencement address.

Listing a litany of assaults that Black airmen faced—menial labor, verbal abuse, police harassment, contempt from white soldiers—FLOTUS maintained that the "Airmen always understood that they had a 'double duty,' one to their country and another to all the black folks who were counting on them to pave the way forward. . . . The act of flying itself was a symbol of liberation for themselves and for all African Americans" (M. Obama 2015). FLOTUS 44 described her travails as a personal "tour of duty" where her body, speech, and policies were continuously scrutinized and satirized, misrepresented and derided—for example, a primary-win fist bump becomes "terrorist fist jab"; the New Yorker cover depicts her as a terrorist; a right-wing talk show host references her as "uppity" or "Obama's baby mama" (M. Obama 2015).

Inspirational speaking thus became a key FLOTUS duty. Going high to maintain stability, the FLOTUS asserted that spirituality and faith became her salve: "to keep my sanity and not let others define me, there was only one thing I could do, and that was to have faith in God's plan for me." Defining her primary role as a mother—her daughters as more important than her life—she rejected criticisms that she was not "bold enough" in the struggles for social justice and defined "Mom-in-Chief" as her primary job. Still, the FLOTUS claimed that she exercised agency in policy: "I worked with Congress on legislation, gave speeches to CEOs, military generals and Hollywood executives." She became a performer: to reach families, FLOTUS gardened, hula-hooped, did goofy dances and skits. Her "moral compass" offers no insights into capitalism, structural racism, the rise in childhood poverty, investment banks defrauding Blacks of homes, or foreign policy neglecting or destabilizing nations' Black populations. (She publicized #BringBackOurGirls for Nigerian girls and women kidnapped and raped by Boko Haram.) Presenting a guidebook of progress, FLOTUS 44 posited that U.S. history provided Americans with voting as a "better blueprint for how we can win . . . when we pull ourselves out of those lowest emotional depths, and we channel our frustrations into studying and organizing and banding together—then we can build ourselves and our communities up." This blueprint was advocated to offset insults that proved "insomnia-inducing"; the name calling; requests by white shoppers at Target to remove an item from a high shelf (despite her security detail) (M. Obama 2015).

In "The Pitfalls of Being the Best Black Surrogate a White Woman Could Hope For," philosopher Janine Jones (2016) uses Anita Allen's legal theory to argue that FLOTUS Michelle Obama functioned as a Black surrogate mother for white women (the predecessor would have been Oprah Winfrey, who was actually more of an empress). In theory, the best form of surrogacy that whites could buy or hope for would be theoretical and theatrical: a Black maternal protector or "mammy." For Jones, the 2016 presidential election positioned Hillary Clinton between two alleged sexual assailants, her presidential rival and her presidential husband. When H. Clinton's presidential candidacy faltered, Michelle Obama became her best surrogate. The moral negatives attributed to Black femaleness became political virtues of heroic suffering as Captive Maternals shielded Clinton by castigating Trump and the violent racist policing that sparked Black Lives Matter. The Black FLOTUS as political surrogate worked alongside the Black women organized into Mothers of the Movement (the DNC-supported group included the mothers of Trayvon Martin, Sandra Bland, Eric Garner, and others whose children were slain by racist policing). FLOTUS Obama and the Mothers of the Movement shared the DNC stage on separate nights. Their appearances demonstrated the political benefits of having Captive Maternal labor at one's disposal when seeking office. That FLOTUS 44 would provide a protective embrace toward FLOTUS 42 seemed to be an inverse of white power in the transfer of presidential power (Hillary Clinton was presumed to be the winning candidate after defeating Bernie Sanders in a procedurally flawed primary).

POTUS 45's farewell to the Obamas departing the White House following the January 20, 2017, inauguration included the presidential grab of Michelle Obama by Trump. Michelle was the only Obama to publicly criticize Trump's immorality and boasting of sexual assault. While Melania and Barack stood nearby, he pulled FLOTUS 44 into an embrace and kiss on the cheek while she attempted to lean away. As a white racist who heeded no boundaries, he temporarily expressed the shared condition of FLOTUS 3, hidden on a plantation, and FLOTUS 44, celebrated humanitarian virtuous mom: Blacks as Captive Maternals are actual or conceptual property who lack bodily autonomy and the right to rebel.

Ms. Deborah: Requiem for an Anti-FLOTUS

Many years ago, here in NY, a very large woman named Gompers
[sic; Eleanor Bumpurs] was killed by police by shotgun because
she was perceived as a "threat to the safety" of several grown men

who were also police officers. They used deadly force to subdue
her because they were not trained sufficiently in how to engage the
mentally ill in crisis. This was not an isolated incident.

DEBORAH DANNER, "Living with Schizophrenia"

In the 1984 Bumpurs shooting case, NYPD Stephen Sullivan was tried and
acquitted of second-degree manslaughter and criminally negligent homicide in 1987. On October 29, 1984, Sullivan first shot Miss Bumpurs in the
hand that held a kitchen knife before discharging a twelve-gauge single-
shot shotgun in the chest of the 260-pound grandmother who charged at a
team of NYPD officers sent to evict her due to unpaid rent from her $98 per
month New York City Housing Authority apartment. Then Police Commissioner Benjamin Ward revised NYPD guidelines for handling emotionally disturbed people: street officers wait for an onsite supervisor; police
create a safety zone around the individual. Thirty years after these protective protocols were printed, the life of an anti-FLOTUS—the noncompli-
ant, nondesirable Captive Maternal existing as state/social detritus—was
ended by the use of excessive police force against Deborah Danner.

Recalling Eleanor Bumpurs's October 29, 1984, killing by police, Deborah Danner wrote of her dread of being executed. A sixty-six-year-old
Black woman living in the Bronx with insufficient support from family
and society, insufficient care from the health industry, and hostility from
police expressed prescient fear of becoming a fatality to poorly trained,
indifferent, or hostile police. For Miss Deborah, "Any chronic illness is a
curse. . . . The nature of the beast is a complete loss of control—of your
emotions, of your intellect, your instincts, your common sense—basically
your sense of yourself, a really frightening aspect of this insidious disease"
(Danner 2012). Danner writes, "Even the smartest people/persons in the
world could not function in the realm of normalcy with that monkey on
their backs. . . . What if my medication fails me? I ask myself, will I know
if it does? Will the illness overpower its effectiveness? When? Where? . . .
Is that a delusion, I ask myself, my belief that I am worthy of respect and a
'normal' happy life?" (Danner 2012).

The U.S. Department of Housing and Urban Development (HUD)
oversees billions of dollars of housing that deteriorates from lack of re-
pairs, rats, lead, and mold, faulty elevators, aggressive police and gangs, and
unmet medical and mental health needs among its occupants. The New
York City Housing Authority overseen by HUD (which is in turn part of
an Administration's responsibilities), was Deborah Danner's home. The

month before the 2016 presidential election, Ms. Danner encountered NYPD who refused to wait in the grimy building hallway or living room for medical backup, and against protocols entered the private sanctuary of her bedroom without the support of mental health workers. Frightened and enraged, suffering from a schizophrenic episode, Danner threatened the officer with a kitchen knife. Rather than retreating or waiting for assistance to negotiate and de-escalate, he fatally shot her in the chest.

An unwilling domestic partner to draconian policing, Danner's death was part of the legacy of a war evolving from 1790s southern colonies' use of slave patrols to catch, cripple, or kill human fugitives. The POTUS powers of 45 fueled racially driven police violence. POTUS 44 caught off guard at the street insurrection following the murder of Freddie Gray, who died by severed spine while shackled in chains in a police van, called the protestors "thugs." Unlike Trump, he later retracted the pejorative and publicly mourned that he could not "federalize" or control local police malfeasance and violent criminality toward Black citizenry. In New York, POTUS 45's former home city, Miss Deborah became the imago for lethal police violence championed by Donald whose racist notions of law and order included calling for the death penalty, in a 1989 *New York Times* ad, for the exonerated Central Park Five (the standards for NYT concerning profit from advertisements steeped in racist animus and child abuse are unclear).

Deborah Danner had lived alone for thirty years. Estranged from her mother and sister, she mothered herself without birth family. Her Black and brown neighbors, who feared and worried about her, called police during her outbursts which occurred when she did not take medication. Deborah Danner received and administered emotional, psychological, and physical support to sustain herself. Ms. Danner had for years combatively resisted the attentions of police and paramedic. In fall 2016, Danner confronted the Forty-Third Precinct shift supervisor who chose his revolver over his Taser and refused to retreat and apologize for disturbing her. Responding to a domestic disturbance call, NYPD Sgt. Hugh Barry confronted a Captive Maternal with a family/community of one, a social isolate feared by others, one who feared herself. On October 18, 2016, after 911 calls from neighbors reporting her as "loud and disruptive," Sgt. Barry entered the apartment. The medical support team was already there but waiting at a distance for Ms. Danner to calm herself. Apparently Barry did not ask for information about Danner's health status, nor did he follow NYPD protocol for working with a mentally/emotionally disturbed person. New York State law grants the right to use deadly force to defend oneself against an able-bodied person attacking with a weapon. Barry was the only one in Danner's bedroom and so the only witness to his claim that Danner lunged at him with a baseball bat. According to his account, he persuaded Danner to drop a pair of scissors; but she picked up a baseball bat and tried to hit him; so, he shot her in the chest, twice. In June 2017, the Black female Bronx district attorney Darcel D. Clark, charged Barry with second-degree murder for the killing of Deborah Danner. Barry was acquitted in February 2018. In December 2018, New York City agreed to pay Deborah Danner's family a $2 million settlement.

Anonymous in life, Miss Deborah gained recognition in death. Her political persona became layered with identities targeted by excessive police force and execution: Blackness, femaleness, mental illness, poverty, rebellion, armed self-defense and "queer" (mental difference is a form of "queerness"). An impoverished Captive Maternal paranoid schizophrenic living alone in South Bronx projects, Deborah's struggles to mother and protect herself were terminated by white police, surrogates for POTUS 45, a loyal political base for the violence of presidential powers against disenfranchised communities.

Captive Maternals physically rebel against violent authorities protected by partial immunity. Few written records connect their community/ self-defense (read almost universally as aggression) to the president of the United States. Yet it is the executive branch that controls organized violence. Without proximity to or intimacy with a president, Deborah Danner nonetheless experienced and suffered the police power embodied in a POTUS. The antithesis of the attractive, attentive FLOTUS (Sally or Michelle) who functions as domestic surrogate for an imperial presidency, Ms. Danner was self-possessed and had severe medical needs. The negation of elite acquisition, polished possession, ceremonial pomp and circumstance—Danner's anti-FLOTUS signifies CMs whose lives and deaths are shaped by economic inequities, healthcare disparities, and policing.

Conclusion

The struggles of Sally Hemings, Michelle Obama, and Deborah Danner against antiblack violence and misogynoir reflect diverse representations of CM vulnerability in U.S. democracy. Their vulnerabilities and strengths influence our political imaginations, desires and fears in the absence of presidential powers used to combat antiblack racism.

The unofficial police acronym NHI, or No Humans Involved, refers to murder victims who are African Americans, prostitutes, or drug addicts. The acronym is also a political and electoral slogan. Police fail to find, notify, and grieve with the kin of a deceased NHI and inadequately investigate murders or rule "justifiable homicide"; they also function as executioners or perpetrators over whom the Black or Indigenous public has little control. Chants of "Blue Lives Matter" seek to dismiss "Black Lives Matter" and critiques of police violence. That political slogan embodies the Captive Maternal yet cannot represent the political autonomy of "Black Power."

The global conditions of vulnerabilities are revealed in Yemen, South Sudan, Somalia, Nigeria, Haiti, Brazil. The collective site of catastrophic suffering of tens and hundreds of millions of captives cannibalized and consumed as girls, women, boys, men, transwo/men under the watch of democracies and Presidential powers. It is inevitable that at some point and time they will recognize Frantz Fanon's "hence forward" moment, that point at which the CM moves suffering and trauma into mass movements, and movements into the Maroonage and war resistance in which community builds mutual aid and defense against police and presidential repressions.

Notes

Epigraph: Deborah Danner, "Living with Schizophrenia," January 28, 2012, https://assets.documentcloud.org/documents/3146953/Living-With -Schizophrenia-by-Deborah-Danner.pdf.

1   Joy James, "Presidential Powers and Captive Maternals," *Women in Philosophy APA Blog*, May 6, 2020, https://blog.apaonline.org/2020/05/06 /presidential-powers-and-captive-maternals-sally-michelle-and-deborah/.

2   Annette Gordon-Reed and Titus Kaphar, "Are We Actually Citizens Here?," June 29, 2017, https://onbeing.org/programs/annette-gordon-reed-and-titus -kaphar-are-we-actually-citizens-here-jun2017/.

3   Blumrosen and Blumrosen (2005) argue this position without addressing the diaspora and the agency of Blacks revolting against enslavement.

PART IV

UNSETTLINGS

ON THE ILLEGIBILITY OF FRENCH ANTIBLACKNESS: NOTES FROM AN AFRICAN AMERICAN CRITIC

CRYSTAL M. FLEMING

In *Resurrecting Slavery*, I demonstrated that commemorative discourses and events related to the transatlantic slave trade in France tend to mask the racial structure of slavery and its legacies (Fleming 2017). This obfuscation occurs through the asymmetrical racialization of the Afro-descended population in discourses about slavery as well as the avoidance and minimization of whiteness, particularly in representations and events sanctioned by the French government. Because commemorations of slavery orchestrated by French authorities typically ignore or downplay the existence of the white French majority, such discourses and events foster a superficial acknowledgment of the link between slavery and contemporary racial oppression and mystify the social realities of systemic racism in France. Thus, one of the central and ironic findings of my work concerns the fact that chattel slavery is not framed, even by many ordinary French Caribbeans, as linked to contemporary antiblack racism in the French context. This observation suggests that merely addressing or discussing the links between racism and slavery does not necessarily foster a *structural* understanding of antiblackness and white supremacy. This is because of the prevalence of superficial conceptualizations of racism and especially the persistence of the belief that racism is an individual rather than a collective, institutionalized phenomenon. The persistent denial of systemic and institutional racism in France also involves the specific denial of antiblack racism. Along similar lines, João Costa Vargas suggests that "while there seems to be an increasing social awareness of Blacks' experiences of discrimination, there is a denial of antiblackness as a foundational and structural fact" (2018, 1).

Reflecting on my experiences conducting and presenting research on French racism and engaging in public discourse online, this chapter explores individual and collective practices of denial and minimization that obscure antiblack racism in France. The central irony I wish to underscore is that commemorations of transatlantic slavery in France—which reemerged and accelerated after the 150th anniversary of the second French abolition of slavery in 1998—have both prompted antiracist mobilizations focusing on the experiences and suffering of people racialized as Black while also, in some cases, continuing to mask the social, political, and economic realities of French antiblackness and white racism.[1]

As an illustrative example, consider this statement rendered in a 2005 report of the Committee for the Memory of Slavery—an official commemorative organization organized by the French government. In this passage, the authors describe the legacies of slavery in French overseas departments and territories such as Guadeloupe, Martinique, and Réunion Island:

> Societies born of slavery and colonialism (against which they fought) remain marked by this legacy which includes . . . on the one hand, a legacy of inequalities, racism, the devaluation of the "Black" (individual) which served to legitimate their slave status, and by the legacy of a sense of shame attached to this infamous past . . . and on the other hand, by the creation of societies that are from their origin multicultural, multiethnic and multireligious. Situated in zones of diverse cultural and human contact (the Caribbean zone and the Indian ocean), they have remained lands of immigration.[2]

While the denigration of Blackness is recognized as directly tied to slavery, there is no recognition of Europeans or whites as agents and beneficiaries of antiblack racism. Moreover, the partial recognition of antiblackness as the "devaluation of the Black" demonstrated here does not reflect a robust understanding of antiblack racism as a structural, present-day feature of French society.

This nonrecognition of structural antiblackness specifically and racism more generally as constitutive features of the French social order illustrates

CRYSTAL M. FLEMING

what critical race philosopher Charles Mills (1997) refers to as the "epistemology of ignorance." For Mills, white supremacy requires the pervasive misrepresentation of the social world and the obfuscation of white dominance. Whereas slavery is very commonly recognized as linked to present-day racism in the United States context, this basic causal logic is very often undermined and outright denied by white French politicians and others who reject the existence of systemic racism in France. The sad, stunning reality is that mainstream antiracist organizations in France such as SOS Racisme and The Human Rights League (La Ligue de Droits de L'homme), still privilege individual conceptions of racism over structural accounts. Activist groups like the Representative Council of Black Associations (Le Conseil Représentatif des Associations Noires) and the Anti-Negrophobia Brigade (Le Brigade Anti négrophobie) are marginalized as radical for acknowledging the simple social fact that Black people are systematically disadvantaged by racism in France (Picot 2016). Commemorations of slavery and abolition have not yet destabilized the hegemonic denial of structural racism in France.

In the wake of Western colonialism and racialized enslavement, antiblackness has become a constituent feature of what it means to be modern, European, and French. Critical race theory acknowledges the role of colonialism and the transatlantic slave trade in establishing global white supremacy (Fleming 2017; Mills 1997; Weiner 2012). Through its sprawling colonial empire and practice of transatlantic slavery, France established itself as one of the world's most ruthless and prolific exploiters of Black and brown bodies. Yet despite centuries of colonial violence against Afro-descended people, the French state has managed to largely suppress and whitewash its ongoing history of antiblackness while maintaining a global reputation as a liberal democracy. This chapter asks: What discursive and political practices enable France to routinely disappear its violent subjugation of Black people across the globe, from the French overseas territories and departments in the Caribbean and Indian Ocean to former colonial possessions in South America, the African continent, and metropolitan France?

By linking my own observations as an African American scholar and critic of French (and global) racism to the experiences and knowledge of Black French observers, I hope to provide insight into the specific forms of misrecognition that sustain and reproduce the denial of antiblack racism and other forms of systemic racism in France. Extending my work on racial temporality and collective memory (Fleming 2017), I also draw connections between the Black Code and Police des Noirs—French policies that deployed violence and surveillance against Black people in the seventeenth and eighteenth centuries—and contemporary instances of antiblackness practiced by the French state and ordinary French citizens alike.

* * *

When Anna Julia Cooper, trailblazing Black feminist and social theorist, defended her dissertation on French attitudes toward slavery at the Sorbonne in 1925, her white male thesis advisor, Célestin Bouglé, accused her sober analysis of bias (May 2007, 111). It is unsurprising that Bouglé bristled at Cooper's scathing critique of French hypocrisy and racial oppression. Nearly one hundred years later, I experienced a similar form of epistemic violence in an exchange with a French scholar. I had been invited to speak about my work at an academic conference held in Europe. During my remarks, I pointed out that in France, the trauma of the Holocaust is often used to shut down demands for ethnic and racial statistics—data that a growing list of antiracist scholars and activists believe would be useful in the fight against racism. I also made what I took to be an obvious point—that the existence of interracial couples in France (and elsewhere) did not indicate the absence of systemic racism and white supremacy.[3] When I finished delivering my paper, the French scholar, who I would later learn identified as both white and multiracial, took great offense to several dimensions of my work—including my claim that France is a systemically racist society.

As we engaged in discussion and debate over the course of the conference, I was struck in particular by the French scholar's bewildering racial denial and paradoxical claims. At one point, she argued against the inclusion of race as an analytic category, while also gesturing toward a superficial acknowledgment of racism. Each time I pointed out patterns and proportionalities that provided clear evidence of white domination and antiblackness in France, she reacted with defensiveness. Over and over again, as I described forms of structural racism against Blacks and people of color globally, she retorted with references to cases where members of dominant groups were also mistreated. As an example, she pointed to the suffering of poor white opioid addicts in the United States as a rebuttal to my critique of white racism. At each turn, she crafted a false equivalence between the suffering of dominant and nondominant groups—"Men suffer too. Whites suffer too," she assured me. Remarkably, this woman somehow managed to both dismiss the data I cited on French racism and admit she

CRYSTAL M. FLEMING

hadn't, in fact, read the numerous empirical studies I referenced on the dynamics of global white supremacy.

In one moment, the French scholar would acknowledge systematic racism and forms of white privilege, but in the next breath she withdrew the very same recognition. "*Of course* I recognize that privileges exist!" she said. But when I pointed out that she, as someone who identifies as white and is socially read as white, therefore benefits from white privilege, she demurred. I persisted: "It may not always feel like a privilege but you certainly gain access to resources accorded to people socially read as white as you navigate society—resources that someone like me, a person who is never read as white, does not have access to." The Frenchwoman responded to these social facts with outrage and denial, shaking her head, flustered and angry.

She both recognized her whiteness by claiming it ("I'm white . . .") but also criticized me for recognizing race ("We shouldn't do that!"). In so doing, she weaponized both her white and mixed-race identities to acknowledge the social construction of race while denying the existence of systemic white supremacy and the need to analyze these dynamics empirically. At one point, she made the nonsensical suggestion that scholars should "study racism without studying race"—a common argument against the use of racial classifications made by organizations in France such as SOS Racisme who promote "antiracism without races" (Bleich 2000). You can imagine my astonishment when I found that in the scholar's own article presented at the conference, she made references to racial categories ("white," "people of color") without ever referring to racism or providing theoretical context regarding the social construction of race. Scholars of color, and particularly Black scholars who have worked in the French context, will not be surprised by this hypocrisy—as it presents yet another example of a nonBlack person giving themselves the authority to reference race while simultaneously claiming that Black people who invoke racial categories or name systemic racism are illegitimate. Under the forces of white supremacy and antiblackness, Black people—including Black scholars—are deprived epistemic authority. We are not, as a rule, viewed as legitimate analysts of anything, much less the racial oppression that we both experience and analyze.

At one point, the woman confessed, her face red with frustration: "I have the feeling that you think you are teaching me things about racism in France that I already know." And it wasn't until much later that I realized she was essentially stating that in her view she had nothing to learn from me, despite the fact that she had no expertise in the study of race or racism and was a postdoctoral fellow without a university position. At the time, I was a tenured professor, the author of an award-winning dissertation and a published book, and an advisor of graduate students and doctoral candidates.

The phrase echoed in my mind—"I have the feeling that you *think* you are teaching me things," she said, as if my expertise and her ignorance were mere figments of my imagination. The woman's sense of self, and her identity as a French person who does not need to be educated about race, were intimately tied to her construction of me, a Black American woman, as someone with nothing of value to teach her.

The Temporal Expansiveness
of French Antiblackness

Hegemonic French reactions to racial critique from Black people on any and all sides of the Atlantic takes the predictable form of denial, evasion, and other forms of epistemic violence. In *White Innocence*, a stunning ethnography of white Dutch self-expression, Gloria Wekker writes that "an unacknowledged reservoir of knowledge and affect based on four hundred years of Dutch imperial rule plays a vital but unacknowledged part in dominant meaning-making processes, including the making of the self, taking place in Dutch society" and submits that "with national variations, a similar configuration is operative in national settings that have an imperial history" (2016, 2, 1). In so doing, Wekker brings white Dutch tactics of denial, disavowal, and elusiveness into view as she dissects the mechanisms of white supremacy in the Netherlands.

I wish to make a similar claim about French disavowal and evasiveness regarding its structural racism and systematic evisceration of Black lives. The denial of French racism reinforces antiblackness and expands its temporal scope. In making this argument, I aim to unveil the racial temporality (Fleming 2017) of French antiblack racism—the ways in which the afterlives of slavery (Hartman 2007) and colonialism continue to haunt and hunt the quotidian experiences of Black existence that are made possible in France. As Fanon made clear, French diminishing of Black life is not simply a thing of the past, confined to centuries of brutal enslavement and the atrocities of colonial rule. Instead, French antiblackness is temporally pervasive—stretching from the past into the present even as it bleeds into the future tense. We see the pervasiveness of French antiblackness in the racist treatment of African migrants seeking refuge and shelter as a result of their worlds being menaced and destroyed. We see the pervasiveness of French antiblackness in the social fact that Blacks (and Arabs) are twenty times more likely to be stopped and frisked in France compared to whites (Pascual and Jacquin 2017). We see French antiblackness in the violent rape by French officers of a young Black man named Theo (Chrisafis 2017). We see the pervasiveness of French antiblackness in the efforts of Anne Hildago, the mayor of Paris, to shut down France's very first Afro-feminist festival in 2017—because the organizers dared to specify that certain events and support groups would be exclusively dedicated to uplifting Black women (Hill 2017). We see the pervasiveness of French antiblackness in the death and rape threats and acts of intimidation directed toward antiracist Black French activist Rokhaya Diallo—and her expulsion from the National Digital Council because she dared to speak a simple truth: that institutional (and state-sponsored) racism exists in France (Schofield 2017). And we see the pervasiveness of French antiblackness in the perverse proclivity of some white French for proudly wearing Blackface and anti-African colonial caricatures.[4] We see the pervasiveness of French antiblackness in the fact that members of the Anti-Negrophobia Brigade—an antiracist group— were recently pelted with flour and urine by white French people in Blackface who insisted that their Blackface was not racist (Druelle 2018).

Although there are multiple dimensions of racialization in the construction of white French identity, I focus here on the relationship between French whiteness and the persistence of antiblack racism, which manifests as Afrophobia, negrophobia, and anti-Antillean discrimination. These forms of antiblack oppression, stigmatization, marginalization, and erasure afflict racialized minorities in mainland France as well as those living in former and present-day French colonial possessions. Haiti is, of course, an ongoing site of French antiblackness. I am going to argue that despite the reflexive denial of white politicians, academics, and everyday people, antiblackness not only exists and persists in France, but is also centrally tied to the social construction of a white French sense of being and belonging in the world.

In raising questions about the social legibility of French antiblackness, I want to highlight the ways in which the white French sense of self flees confrontation with the scene of racial oppression. From this perspective,

racial disavowal can be understood as instances of epistemological ignorance and violence that function to maintain the racial status quo. White
epistemic, cultural, and psychological survival involves not only the negation of blackness, but also the denial of antiblack racism. The pose of color
blindness, the refusal to see racism from the perspective of those who are
systemically disadvantaged by it, shores up the legitimacy of French identity and the French state's mythic positioning of itself as nonracist, or, at
the very least, less racist than the United States.

Having traveled back and forth to France over the last seventeen years,
I've become keenly aware of the varied statuses involved in my being embodied, racialized, gendered, and classed as a Black woman academic from
the United States engaged in empirical research on and criticism of French
racism. In so doing, I have directly experienced the mechanisms of denial
and deflection that characterize the response that many French people
have toward critique of racial oppression in their society—particularly
when such critique is articulated by a Black woman. In dialogue with
women of color feminists such as Gloria Wekker (2016) and Sara Ahmed
(2012), who incorporate their own reflexive accounts of European racism
and intersectional oppression, I include here my own experiences and
observations as part of the archive of French antiblackness and white supremacist racism more broadly.

Against scholarly and popular tropes that either erase or minimize
French antiblackness, this essay considers how French repertoires of
denial and disavowal of antiblack racism persist and survive, like immor-
tal cockroaches, despite centuries of French state violence and economic
exploitation directed toward Afro-descended people. My personal observations of French antiblackness include being directly and indirectly in-
sulted by white French scholars and everyday people for critiquing French
racism; being told that the real racial problem in France pertains to the
Maghrebin or the Roma; observing white French people and French multiracial people make denigrating comments about Africans; having my
critique of French racism met with white French people and nonBlack
French people framing interracial relationships as a cure for racism or as
evidence that racism in France does not exist. These scenes of antiblackness reveal some of the rhetorics and practices by which French society
insulates itself from critique.

Elsewhere, I've argued that very few studies of French racism bring together analyses of antiblackness with a critique of French white supremacy

(Fleming 2017). In exploring the contours of French antiblackness, I draw upon Frantz Fanon's critical insights regarding the mutual imbrication of colonialism and racism as well as the salience of antiblackness in the white French cultural imaginary (Go 2016). For Fanon, racism and colonial domination were inextricably linked. Thus, antiblackness cannot be understood solely as the afterlife of slavery, again to borrow Saidiya Hartman's (2007) formulation. Rather, the unmattering of Black life is always already infused with the colonizer/colonized relation.

In a well-known passage in *Black Skin, White Masks* (1967a), Fanon describes his own encounter with imposed objectification, or "thingification," within the context of colonial oppression. When a white boy points at him and shouts, "Look! A negro!," Fanon experiences the psychological trauma of being captured and contained within the denigrating, white supremacist conception of Blackness. From a Fanonian perspective, antiblack racism is fundamentally a question of nonrecognition—the refusal to admit the person socially defined as Black (read: demonic, inferior, exploitable, chattel) into membership in the category "human." This is also what Fanon means by the "zone of non-being"—the ontological obliteration of those trapped within the colonial, white supremacist gaze.

Is it any wonder that Fanon remains almost entirely unknown, intellectually, in his own homeland? French scholars and politicians have largely excluded his work from educational curricula and public debate. The very few French people I know who have read Fanon told me that they discovered his work in the United States. Fanon's trenchant denunciation of French racism—as well as his support for the Algerian resistance and his paean to revolutionary violence—did not endear him to the French white intelligentsia. And then there is, of course, the fact of his Blackness, which is to say, his disposability. To be Black within a white supremacist society is, at the very least, to be dismissed, antagonized, or ignored by those who wish to defend the racial status quo.

Racism generally, and antiblack racism in particular, is a basic, constituent social fact of French society. In his incisive essay "Racism and Culture," Frantz Fanon put it this way: "The racist in a culture with racism is therefore normal. He has achieved a perfect harmony of economic relations and ideology in his environment. . . . In fact, race prejudice obeys a flawless logic. A country that lives, draws its substance from the exploitation of other peoples, makes those people inferior. Race prejudice applied to those people is normal" (Fanon 1967b: 40–41). The normalization of racism in France is the logical consequence of its centuries-long colonial oppression of people defined and subjected as racial others.

While a detailed chronology of the construction of race in France is beyond the scope of this chapter, a brief review of the relevant historical context is useful for understanding the persistence of antiblackness in France today. Historian William Cohen's ([1980] 2003) classic text *The French Encounter with Africans: White Response to Blacks, 1530–1880* chronicles the *longue durée* of French aggression and hostility toward people of African descent. Importantly, Cohen argues that contemporary French racism was rooted in class conflict between Caucasians within French society, including ancient beliefs about the racial superiority of the aristocracy vis-à-vis other social groups.[5] These class frictions would provide the building blocks for racial logics and practices of exclusion that were eventually directed toward African, Indigenous, Arab, and Asian people. Beginning in the seventeenth century, France joined other European powers in expanding their empire overseas through settler colonialism and genocide directed against Indigenous Caribs living in the islands that would later become known as Saint-Domingue, Guadeloupe, and Martinique. After failed experiments with indentured servitude targeting other Europeans, the French transitioned to enslaving Africans and eventually kidnapped and received approximately 1.5 million enslaved individuals during the transatlantic trade—nearly 4.5 times more than the number of slaves sent to the lands that would become the United States (Fleming 2017; Moitt 2001).

France maintained slave plantations throughout the Caribbean as well as in colonies located in the Indian Ocean and in South America. Louis XIV's 1685 Code Noir (Black Code) promulgation institutionalized a brutal racial order built on white supremacy and antiblackness. Over the course of the next century, the French state would establish a series of antiblack laws, including the Edict of 1716, the Declaration of 1738, and the Police des Noirs policies of 1777 that restricted the flow of Afro-descendants into France. As Jennifer Palmer (2006, 27) notes:

> Laws mandated, for example, that owners could only bring slaves into France for two reasons: to be educated in the Catholic religion or to learn a trade. Additionally, slaves had to leave France within a period of three years. Going even further, the 1777 Police des Noirs law, a piece of legisla-

tion based on skin color alone, mandated that all people of color, slave or free, register with the Admiralty office. No people of color were allowed to enter France, and those who were already there were encouraged to leave.

The 1800s ushered in a new era of colonial expansion for France during the so-called scramble for Africa during which European nations competed for the opportunity to seize and oppress African societies and resources. France's subsequent (and violent) imposition into Algeria, West Africa, and Asia (particularly Indochina) as well as Mexico was designed to increase France's economic and political standing (Givens 2014, 120). As colonial rule metastasized throughout Africa, French scientists and philosophers like Buffon and de Gobineau established white supremacist ideologies and antiblack thought which, in turn, justified and glorified colonial plunder as a civilizing mission. In this way, colonial violence, theft, and exploitation were routinely and grotesquely depicted as a generous form of outreach for inferior people.

When France abolished slavery in its colonial possessions (first in 1794 and again in 1848), white slave owners were paid reparations while the formerly enslaved continued to toil under the weight of exploitation and racialized oppressed (Fleming 2017: 182). The historian Frédéric Regent estimates that colonists in Guadeloupe, Martinique, French Guiana, and Réunion were compensated 126 million francs as repayment for the economic costs of abolition (2007, 288). For literary scholar Marlene Daut, France's singularly antiblack oppression of Haiti and its demand that Haitians pay for their own freedom represents "the greatest heist in history."[6] Accordingly, Daut reminds us that "the indemnity Haiti paid to France is the first and only time a formerly enslaved people were forced to compensate those who had once enslaved them."

France's systemic antiblackness was also interwoven into the nation's educational curricula. Thus, Cohen writes:

School textbooks from the 1920s and 1930s, by emphasizing the civilizing mission of French imperial rule in Africa, reinforced the notions of Black barbarism and savagery. Colonial novels in the interwar years were particularly powerful in conveying an image of African savagery and bestiality; their accusations of Black cannibalism were even stronger than those made prior to the colonial era. Films about Africa represented whites heroically; African societies were merely the backdrops providing the French an opportunity to show more love of adventure and resoluteness. . . . French popular opinion during the first three quarters of the twentieth century not only placed Africans low on the evolutionary scale of humanity, but also often embraced the racist view that, condemned by their biology to an inferior existence, Blacks were suited only to serve whites and to live dependent on them. ([1980] 2003, 284)

Given this context of institutionalized antiblackness within the French educational system, it is no mystery why my interviews with Afro-Caribbeans of Martinican and Guadeloupean heritage revealed experiences of alienation and racial marginalization in the classroom (Fleming 2011).

Yet despite centuries of deeply entrenched antiblack racism, France nonetheless gained an unwarranted reputation as a racial haven in comparison to the United States—particularly in the interwar period. What explains this paradox? Cohen underscores the importance of recognizing that French interracial intimacy coexisted with racist beliefs. "In the abstract," he writes, "the French might well have thought that Blacks were inferior, but in actual contacts they could treat Africans with affection and esteem" ([1980] 2003, 286). In the twentieth century, France's apparent embrace of interracial social life (including sex and marriage) situated the country as a refuge for African Americans, notably veterans who served in World Wars I and II.

Until fairly recently, antiblackness and anti-African sentiment were not explicitly highlighted in much international research on racism in France. According to Michaël Privot (2014, 32), the director of the European Network Against Racism (ENAR), Afrophobia and antiblackness were not specifically integrated into the group's mission until 2011—a staggering thirteen years after its founding. Anti-Semitism has long been a recognized category in the fight against racism in Europe, but antiblackness lags behind. Privot suggests that "[in] part, the failure to recognize the struggle against Afrophobia is rooted within the socio-economic status of the community and its restricted means to engage in the development of a meaningful power relationship with relevant authorities." Noting the relatively large population of first-generation migrants among Africans in Europe, Privot (2014, 33–34) argues that the economic precarity and low status of Afro-descended people contribute to the illegibility of antiblackness. Perhaps more usefully, Privot draws attention to white Europeans' uneasiness with directly addressing racism due to their fear of losing power vis-à-vis Blacks. As Black Europeans have begun standing up for their rights and dignity, others (most notably, white leftists and antiracists) have accused them of being divisive or communitarian:

> The increasing visibility of Afrophobia as a concern primarily articulated by Black-led civil society organisations and supported by more mainstream/generalist antiracist organisations such as ENAR and some of its members has been correlated with accusations of "communitarianisation" or "fragmentation" of the anti-racist struggle. These calls have particularly come from majority/White-led anti-racist organisations or individual activists or researchers. Within the anti-racist and equality fields that have often been White-led, "fragmentation" and "communitarianisation" are in some instances code words to express a fear of loss of White entitlement to partake in the struggle against racism. Discourses about Blackness and exclusion imply, as an implacable and logical corollary, discourses about Whiteness and structures of privileges . . . accusations of "fragmentation" may be more of a defence mechanism to preserve the current status quo of majority-led anti-racist efforts. (Privot 2014, 35–37)[7]

The fact that antiblack racism was not even on the radar for ENAR, despite the participation of European countries in the transatlantic slave trade, colonial oppression of Africa, and the elaboration of modern racism as we know it, is remarkable indeed.

In *Resurrecting Slavery*, I argue that far too many scholars of global race and racism have also ignored or minimized the realities of antiblackness in France. There are multiple factors that explain this oppressive obfuscation. Traditionally, many scholars of group relations and inequality in France have preferred to study social class or immigration rather than race and racism. In part, this has to do with the legacy of the Holocaust, mentioned earlier—namely, the desire on the part of some on the left to avoid racial categories altogether due to their disastrous use during the Shoah. A second factor has to do with the way antiblackness is often framed as less salient or less prominent in France compared to anti-Arab or anti-Maghrebin sentiment. But, as I also point out, antiblack racism has been extensively documented in France despite the absence of racial statistics in the census (Beauchemin et al. 2009, Bickerstaff 2012, Bovenkerk et al. 1979). A recent report produced by the French National Consultative Commission on Human Rights affirms that "[in] terms of opinions, Black people constitute, along with Jews, the most accepted minority in France. However, from the perspective of behaviors, they are amongst the most discriminated" (CNCDH 2019, 7).[8] A third factor, explored below, that explains the hegemonic illegibility of French antiblackness is the role of the United States in rendering France a rosy, racial haven by comparison.

On the U.S. Reference and the Whataboutism of French White Supremacy

Europeans' discomfort with confronting their racism and antiblackness in particular is compounded by the bogeyman role of the United States. As a notorious and globally recognized site of racial oppression, discourses that center racism in the U.S. while obscuring global formations of antiblackness and white supremacy play a key role in suppressing widespread recognition and condemnation of French racism. Historically, some African Americans have also contributed to the minimization of antiblack racism in France. Framing French society as particularly welcoming to Black Americans functions to sustain France's image as a nonracist and even Afrophilic society. Indeed, France's exceptional treatment can sometimes provide some Black Americans a first sense of what it feels like to be accepted as American—abroad.

But most expatriates and frequent visitors that I know are well aware of the privileges that go along with being viewed as Black American rather than Black French. In one instance, an African American colleague confessed that they were not outspoken about racism in France because they wanted to continue to be able to travel to the country. This concern is understandable. For all the talk about how the French love Black Americans, the truth is that they very often stop loving us at the precise moment we begin critiquing systemic racism in France. As racialized pawns, Black Americans are only useful to white French to the degree that we shame or silence French people of color and help French whites cover or minimize their racism.

As many others have observed, being African American in France and Europe more broadly is not like being viewed as an African or a colonial migrant. Many Black expatriates and tourists I know who have spent time in France know the importance of keeping their passport with them at all times—as a protective measure against racial profiling. In prior work, I've written about my own experience of being treated exceptionally while living and conducting research in Paris (Fleming 2017). It was not lost on me, at the time, that my preferential treatment was intimately tied to the oppression of Black and brown French people. At a conference I attended on the legacies of French slavery, a Black European scholar expressed to me his view that African Americans' exceptional treatment in France does not reflect the absence of antiblackness or the absence of color prejudice, but rather, a kind of genuflection before the global status and hegemony of the United States. I would hasten to add that this global status was itself established through antiblackness and genocide committed against Indigenous people.

Rokhaya Diallo, mentioned earlier in the chapter, is one of the most visible antiracist activists in France. A forty-two-year-old Black woman and a Muslim who speaks multiple languages and identifies as an intersectional feminist, Diallo frequently denounces systemic racism, Islamophobia, and sexism in the public sphere. She is also just as frequently subjected to harassment, including death threats and rape threats—some, at times, even issued by other women of color.[9] Following her expulsion from the National Digital Council for her antiracist speech, I logged onto social media to express support for Diallo's activism. In the context of the controversy, I wrote the following on Twitter:

La France est un pays raciste.
La France est un pays raciste.
La France est un pays raciste.
La France est un pays raciste.
La France est un pays raciste.
La France est un pays raciste.
La France est un pays raciste.
La France est un pays raciste.[10]

The English translation is straightforward enough—France is a racist country. The responses to this indisputable observation were revelatory. As of this writing, these words have been read by over 300,000 people, retweeted nearly two thousand times, and liked over two thousand times. But the tweet also garnered over seven hundred responses from French or francophone individuals, many of them explicitly racist. This simple truth, repeated eight times, provoked an avalanche of (French) white fragility (DiAngelo 2018), racist hostility, antiblack insults, revisionism, denial, and justification. Several users assumed that I was a French minority and suggested that I "go back to Africa." A sampling of other responses includes these:

Yeah, we don't like dummies—you represent a sub-race.
You don't make any nuance between "France is racist" and "There are some racist people in France?"

Racist and proud of it—go fuck yourself![11]

Aside from these apoplectic responses, one of the most frequent techniques of disavowal was the appropriation of racism in the United States to deflect attention from criticism of French racial oppression. Deploying the logical fallacy that racism in the U.S. somehow excuses or negates racism in France—or implicitly suggesting that it is not possible to condemn racism in both countries—many French and francophone deflectors gleefully instrumentalized the suffering of African Americans in order to exculpate France:

> France offers real social security[.] France didn't elect Trump[,] doesn't let the KKK march in the middle of the street[.] France is an open country[.] You need to see the difference between "There are some racists in France" (like everywhere) and "France is racist."

> Look at your country which kills Blacks because they're Blacks and you dare to say we're racist.[12]

Of course, the racist, dismissive, and hostile responses to my tweet illustrate the racism that was being denounced. As an African American scholar, French deflection and denial cannot pose a serious threat to my career or well-being. This is not the case, however, for many Black French people and people of color, some of whom have confided in me that their academic careers would be derailed if they ever dared to openly denounce French racism and white supremacy. The use of African Americans to minimize French racism is, therefore, especially noxious, given that so many of us are privileged in the French context and, therefore, have a unique opportunity to speak up, standing in solidarity with French minorities to raise consciousness about the transnational realities of antiblack racism.

Beyond the instances detailed in this chapter, I have often observed trolls and everyday racists alike often reverting to informal logical fallacies (e.g., whataboutism or faulty "not as bad" comparisons) in order to deflect legitimate critique of French racism. Given my status as a U.S. citizen, white French racists and minority apologists frequently respond to analyses of French racism by comparing France favorably to the United States. Against the backdrop of the U.S.-as-racist-hellhole, defenders of France portray their society as either much less racist or welcoming and generous to non-Europeans.

I refer to this phenomenon as "white supremacist whataboutisms"— efforts to deflect or silence antiracism critique by pointing to other, supposedly more racist societies (or political parties). Such comparisons are fundamentally racist, as they are attempts to avoid addressing racism and maintain the white supremacist status quo. White supremacist what-aboutism is yet another manifestation of epistemological ignorance involving multiple logical fallacies—the idea that racism in one setting can excuse racism in another; the unsubstantiated notion that racism is actually worse in the United States; the flawed and obscene suggestion that there is an acceptable level of racism; and the illogical contention that our only option is to condemn racism in one context (rather than across contexts).

Taken together, the racist hostility directed toward me as well as attacks from French trolls and far-right racists directed toward Rokhaya Diallo and other prominent Black women like former French minister of justice Christiane Taubira demonstrate the efforts on the part of the white majority (and their apologists) to police and suppress antiracism.

Conclusion

As the afterlife of chattel enslavement and ongoing colonial domination, French antiblackness is structurally embedded within the nation's social, cultural, economic, and political institutions. Utilizing a critical race lens, this chapter forges critical connections between the histories of enslavement and colonialism in France and contemporary instances of antiblack racism and repression. In so doing, I have analyzed French antiblackness reflexively, drawing temporal connections between the history of racial slavery and colonialism and contemporary scenes of French antiblackness. My contention is that French antiblackness resurges with regularity because the conditions that birthed it have not been undone—as evidenced by massive uprisings protesting the killing of Adama Traoré and current mobilizations for Black lives in France.[13]

This chapter has also drawn attention to another, oft-ignored aspect of French antiblackness—its reliance on the trivialization of Black suffering in both France and the United States. French racists and apologists point to the U.S. as a racial bogeyman, while invoking African American suffering in order to silence and invalidate critique of French racism. Simultaneously, popular tropes suggest that Black and brown suffering in France is minimal or meaningless by comparison, thus negating the value of Black life and Black dignity across the Atlantic. Against these anti-Black maneuvers, Black French advocates, including French Black women, draw critical connections linking the fight against the unmattering of Black lives in France to global struggles against systemic antiblackness, as seen in mobilization of activists like Rokhaya Diallo, Assa Traoré, Maboula Soumahoro and MWASI Collectif, among many others.[14]

Too often, the French are falsely described as "color-blind"—but my empirical evidence (Fleming 2011, 2017) and personal experiences demonstrate that race is in fact socially recognized at every level of analysis in French society—from the macro down through the meso and micro levels. Despite the official color-blind stance of the nation, French politicians, policies, intellectuals, and social actors have not only selectively recognized race but have also enacted and maintained a white supremacist racial hierarchy. This is the case, ironically, even though recent commemorations of slavery and antiracist protests have brought greater attention to the legacies of colonism and racial oppression in France.

In closing, it is important to note that the French do not always engage in color-blindness rhetoric or complete racial denial in order to minimize the legacies of slavery and frame their country as nonracist. At times, as seen earlier, the French in fact admit the existence of individual prejudice or even antiblack denigration but generally insist that the presence of racist individuals or racist ideas does not provide evidence of systemic, institutional, or societal racism. This refusal to admit that France is a thoroughly racialized society that systematically benefits whites at the expense of Blacks and other nonwhites is why, undoubtedly, many Black French activists like Rokhaya Diallo are regularly subject to absurd claims of reverse racism or antiwhite racism—discourses that rest upon a violent false equivalence between the positionality of French whites and nonwhites. Indeed, Diallo herself has been on the forefront of arguing that "anti-white racism does not exist."[15]

Reverse racism arguments (which also exist in the United States) find particular sway in France due to the relative absence of recognition accorded to structural racism. Thus, the superficial acknowledgment of racism that emerges within some commemorations of slavery and public discourse about inequality rest upon the continued erasure of the white French majority and the nonrecognition of its social, political, and economic dominance. As such, a full and honest reckoning with French white supremacy and structural antiblackness as the continuing legacies of chattel enslavement remain taboo.

CRYSTAL M. FLEMING

Notes

1   Note that France is the only country in the world to have abolished slavery twice—first in 1794 in the midst of the French Revolution and again in 1848. Between the two dates, Napoleon reinstated slavery in 1802, which ultimately accelerated the Haitian Revolution and the emergence of the world's first Black republic in 1804.

2   See Comité pour la Mémoire de l'Esclavage (2005, 13). Author's translation of the original text: "Les sociétés nées de l'esclavage et du colonialisme contre lesquels elles ont lutté restent marquées par cet héritage, qui se traduit: d'une part, par un héritage d'inégalités, de racisme, de dévalorisation du « Noir » ayant servi à légitimer son statut d'esclave, et par l'héritage d'un sentiment de honte attaché à ce passé d'infamie; d'autre part, par la création de sociétés qui sont dès leur naissance multiculturelles, multiethniques et plurireligieuses. Situées dans des zones de contact culturel et humain diversifiées (la zone Caraïbe et l'océan Indien), elles sont demeurées des terres d'immigration." Note that the Comité pour la Mémoire de l'Esclavage was later renamed the Comité pour la Mémoire et l'Histoire de l'Esclavage (Committee for the Memory and History of Slavery).

3   In my work, I define white supremacy as the "social, political and economic dominance of people socially defined as white" (Fleming 2018: 14).

4   On colonial Blackface in contemporary France, see news coverage of the Nuit des Noirs (Night of the Blacks) carnival in the northern city of Dunquerque.

5   "Racism took on a powerful influence in France because it had become a common method of thought. It had originated not as a means to distinguish between Europeans and non-Europeans, but rather as a concept in the internal dispute over social class in France. Beginning in the 1560s the French nobility faced a double attack from both kings and commoners; in order to uphold its prerogatives, the nobility created the myth of a common racial origin. . . . Polemicists argued that the blood of nobles had certain virtues. . . . By the late sixteenth century the aristocracy claimed that it was superior to the other orders of society because it was descended from the Germanic conquerors of France" (Cohen [1980] 2003, 96). On the historical construction of whiteness and racial distinctions in Europe, see also Painter (2011).

6   Marlene Daut, "When France extorted Haiti—the greatest heist in history," *The Conversation*, June 30, 2020, https://theconversation.com/when-france -extorted-haiti-the-greatest-heist-in-history-137949.

7   In a similar vein, see my analysis of anticommunitarianism as a component of French white supremacy (Fleming 2017).

8   Author's translation. It's worth noting that this report on French antiblack racism cites W. E. B. Du Bois but ignores Frantz Fanon.

9   L'express.fr with AFP, "Condamné pour avoir appelé au viol de Rokhaya
     Diallo sur Twitter," *L'express*, January 24, 2014, https://www.lexpress.fr
     /actualite/societe/condamne-pour-avoir-appele-au-viol-de-rokhaya-diallo
     -sur-twitter_1317162.html. See also Twitter, February 19, 2018, https://
     twitter.com/RokhayaDiallo/status/965502969058865152. Fatiha Boudjahlat,
     a French Arab Muslim schoolteacher who calls herself a "feminist" in her
     Twitter bio, publicly called for the rape of Rokhaya Diallo as a response to
     Diallo's support of women who choose to wear the veil.

10   Twitter, December 18, 2017, https://twitter.com/alwaystheself/status
     /942888838682349569.

11   My translation from the original French. See Twitter, December 26,
     2017, https://twitter.com/ChienneCarla/status/945662845450059781;
     December 27, 2017; December 23, 2017, https://twitter.com/2g077/status
     /944657123606065152; December 23, 2017, https://twitter.com/Le_Slog
     /status/944680687155728384.

12   See Twitter, @Le_Fumier, December 19, 2017, https://twitter.com/le
     _fumier/status/943257897433223168; December 24, 2017, https://twitter
     .com/aymerick_guerot/status/944876668488908800.

13   Rokhaya Diallo, "France is Still in Denial About Racism and Police Brutal-
     ity," Aljazeera, June 11, 2020, https://www.aljazeera.com/indepth/opinion
     /2017/08/police-violence-france-justice-adama-170804091317713.html

14   Nouvel Observateur. 2017. "Qui est Mwasi, l'organisateur du festival
     afroféministe accusé d'être "interdit aux Blancs" ? May 29, https://www
     .nouvelobs.com/societe/20170529.OBS9974/qui-est-mwasi-l-organisateur
     -du-festival-afrofeministe-accuse-d-etre-interdit-aux-blancs.html.

15   France 24, "Pour Rokhaya Diallo, le 'racisme anti-blanc,'" YouTube, Octo-
     ber 10, 2019, https://www.youtube.com/watch?v=-H0sZ1Td6NM.

LATINO ANTIBLACK BIAS AND THE CENSUS CATEGORIZATION OF LATINOS: RACE, ETHNICITY, OR OTHER?

TANYA KATERÍ HERNÁNDEZ

"But I'm Puerto Rican," my father said in a low, slow voice, rubbing his bruises. "They don't care what kinda nigger you is, Guhz-man." Because before people called me a spic, they called me a nigger.
PABLO "YORUBA" GUZMÁN, "Before People Called Me a Spic, They Called Me a Nigger"

For the last few years the U.S. Census Bureau has been considering a proposal to add Latino and Hispanic to the list of government-defined races on its decennial population survey questionnaire, among other changes.[1] This would be a marked shift from treating Latino/Hispanic as an ethnicity to instead treating it as a race. Since the 1980 census, "Hispanic origin" has been part of a separate ethnicity question rather than being listed as an option in the question about race on the census (Cohn 2010). Such a two-part formulation in 2010 enabled Latinos to indicate their ethnic origin as Hispanic and simultaneously indicate their racial identity as white, Black, Asian, American Indian, or Native Hawaiian. Yet, much to the dismay of the Census Bureau, Latinos more than any other group indicate that their race is "Some Other Race" while writing in responses such as Mexican, Hispanic, or Latin American. Thirty-seven percent of Latinos did so on the 2010 census, as did 42 percent on the 2000 census (Parker 2015). In preparation for the 2020 census, the 2018 American Community Survey of 2018 estimates a 25.8 percent Some Other Race reporting rate for Latinos. The Census Bureau prefers to diminish the numbers of Latinos and others who use the Some Other Race option out of concern for how the capaciousness of the Some Other Race option presumably hinders the ability to make empirically precise data comparisons across years. The federal government proposes to solve this "problem" by removing the Hispanic-origin ethnicity question and instead inserting the Hispanic/Latino category into a single listing of possible races a respondent can self-select. Despite the fact that the 2020 Decennial Census Program decided to continue to use the existing format with two separate questions, the Census Bureau remains interested in supporting a change to the single-question format in the future.

Significantly, because so many Latinos have used the Some Other Race category option, the Census Bureau believes that Latinos are confused by the array of North American constructed racial categories (Frank, Akresh, and Lu 2010). The Census Bureau presumes that Latinos do not comprehend the stark racial census categories because of their fluid Latin American approach to racial identity and racial mixture. And there is certainly plenty of Latino rhetoric asserting such a position, despite the fact that many Latinos refuse to avail themselves of the opportunity to fluidly enumerate their multiple racial ancestries by checking multiple census racial categories (Hitlin, Brown, and Elder 2007).

The large majority of Latinos who choose Some Other Race are from Central America (Hogan 2017). It is possible that some of those Central American Latinos select the Some Other Race category as a mechanism for denoting their Indigenous ancestry, inasmuch as the census category American Indian seemingly excludes them with its instruction to print the name of the enrolled tribe or principal tribe with which they are affiliated. As a result, Latino respondents of Indigenous origin may very well view the American Indian race box demand for enrolled tribe status as pertaining solely to persons of North American Indigenous ancestry.

Yet an overall examination of Latino responses to the census and other racial data collections contravenes the notion that Latinos never or cannot view race in stark terms. When provided the ability to check as many racial boxes as apply in ways that could reflect a fluid mixed-race identity, the majority of Latinos instead prefer to solely check white. For example, on the

TANYA KATERÌ HERNÁNDEZ

Census Bureau's 2018 annual American Community Survey, 68.61 percent of Latinos still elected to choose a single racial category apart from the Some Other Race response, and the single race chosen 65 percent of the time was white. Moreover, when Latino census respondents alter their choice of racial categories from one census decade to another, they do so primarily by moving from Some Other Race to white. For instance, 2.5 million respondents who said they were Hispanic and Some Other Race on the 2000 census later told the census in 2010 that they were Hispanic and white (Cohn 2014). In their pursuit of whiteness, Latinos are the largest race or ethnic group to alter their selection of racial categories from one census year to another.

Similarly, when recent Latino immigrants are surveyed and not given the option of choosing Some Other Race, 79 percent choose the single white category regardless of skin color (Frank, Akresh, and Lu 2010). Moreover, those Latinos who are most integrated into U.S. society (based on the duration of residence in the United States and English language proficiency) are more likely than others not to choose an enumerated racial category. In short, a recently arrived cultural confusion with presumably U.S. racial categories is not the driving explanation for the Latino use of Some Other Race responses.

It is the preference for whiteness and its twin flight from Blackness that is a more accurate reflection than any presumed Latino cultural expression on the census form. In contrast to the many reports of a Latino preference for mixed-race census categories, there is a strong Latino preference for the white racial category, and some Latino groups like Cubans disproportionately select the white racial category (Darity, Hamilton, and Dietrich 2010). Moreover, a closer study of Latino racial preferences across generations in the Latino National Political Survey, found that a substantial majority of respondents chose to self-identify as white (Golash-Boza and Darity 2008). The study indicated that the white racial category is particularly preferred by recent immigrants of all skin color shades. And when later generations do move away from the white racial category, they do so in favor of collective national ethnic labels like Latino or Hispanic.

Census data from Latin American countries show the same proclivity for the white racial category regardless of actual skin color in response to the Latin American disdain for African and Indigenous ancestry (Telles 2014). Latin American census experiences suggest that the U.S. Latino selection of Some Other Race may instead be an outgrowth of the cultural preference for whiteness and its companion disdain for Indigeneity and

Blackness. A brief consideration of the Latin American racial context will help illuminate how the proposed census reform to treat Latinos as a racial category rather than an ethnic one may become another mechanism for refusing to officially acknowledge Indigenous and particularly African ancestry within the Latino community.

Latin American Racism Comparison

Racism and in particular antiblack racism is a pervasive and historically entrenched fact of life in Latin America and the Caribbean. Over 90 percent of the approximately 10 million enslaved Africans brought to the Americas were taken to Latin America and the Caribbean, whereas only 4.6 percent were brought to the United States (Slave Voyages: The Trans-Atlantic Slave Trade Database 2020). And so the historical legacy of slavery is pervasive in Latin America and the Caribbean.

In Latin America and the Caribbean, like the United States, having lighter skin and European features increases the chances of socioeconomic opportunity, while darker skin and African/Indigenous features severely limit such opportunity and social mobility (Hernández 2013). Predictably, the poorest socioeconomic class is populated primarily by Afro-Latinos, while the most privileged class is populated primarily by whites, and an elastic intermediary socioeconomic standing exists for some light-skinned mulattoes (mixed-race Blacks) and mestizos (mixed-race Indigenous persons). For instance, until the Cuban Revolution in 1959, certain occupations had explicit color preferences for hiring mulattoes to the complete exclusion of dark-skinned Afro-Cubans, based on the premise that mulattoes were superior to dark-skinned Afro-Cubans but not of the same status as whites (Rout 1976). Such white supremacy is deeply ingrained and continues into the present in Cuba and the rest of the region (Cleland 2017; Sawyer 2006).

For instance, in research conducted in Puerto Rico, the overwhelming majority of college students interviewed described "Puerto Ricans who are 'dumb' as having 'dark skin'" (Hall 2000). Such negative perspectives about African ancestry are not limited to the college study participants. In 1988, when the presiding governor of Puerto Rico publicly stated that "the contribution of the black race to Puerto Rican culture is irrelevant, it is mere rhetoric," it was in keeping with what social scientists describe as the standard paradox in Puerto Rico: Puerto Ricans take great pride in their claim to be the whitest people of the Caribbean islands, while simultaneously asserting themselves as nonracist. The pride of being a presumably white population is a direct reaction to the Puerto Rican understanding that "black people are perceived to be culturally unrefined and lack ambition" (Torres 1998, 297).

Over thirty-one years later, another Puerto Rican governor would again be revealed as a racist in the debacle known as "Telegramgate," "Chatgate," and "RickyLeaks." On July 8, 2019, Puerto Rico's Center of Investigative Journalism released over 800 pages of a group chat between then Governor Ricardo Rosselló and members of his staff on the messaging application Telegram (Valentín and Minet 2019). Included within Governor Rosselló's homophobic and sexist message exchanges, were racist comments about Afro-styled Black hair and the use of Aunt Jemima imagery to belittle the female Mayor of San Juan, Carmen Yulín Cruz, whom he opposed. Protests broke out regarding the sexist messages that predominated. The Puerto Rican public was particularly galvanized to protest the jokes Rosselló made about impoverished islanders who died during Hurricane Maria. Because of the political scandal Rosselló resigned, but the racialized stereotypes he made use of have remained. Research on racial segregation in Puerto Rico only confirms these racialized attitudes (Dinzey-Flores 2013; Godreau 2015). In this respect, the Puerto Rican example is emblematic of the racial attitudes throughout the Caribbean and Latin America (Hernández 2013).

As in the United States, the disparagement of Black identity is not limited to mulattoes and whites, but also extends to darker-skinned Afro-Latinos who can harbor internalized racist norms. The internalization manifests itself in a widespread concern among Afro-Latinos with the degree of darkness in pigmentation, width of nose, thickness of lips, and quality of one's hair—with straight, presumably European hair denominated literally as "good" hair. This concern with European skin and features also influences Afro-Latino assessments of preferred marriage partners. Marrying someone lighter is called *adelantando la raza* (improving the race) under the theory of *blanqueamiento* (whitening), which prizes the mixture of races precisely to help diminish the existence of Afro-Latinos (Martinez-Echazabal 1998). Even familial affection has been observed to be influenced by the extent of one's Black appearance (Bonilla-Silva 2010). It should not be so surprising, then, that migrants from Latin America and the Caribbean travel to the United States with their culture of antiblack racism well intact along with all other manifestations of their culture (Torres-Saillant 2002). And that, in turn, this facet of Latino culture is transmitted to some degree to younger generations along with all other transmissions of Latino culture in the United States.

Afro-Latinos in the United States

For Latinos in the United States, "being, or becoming, anything other than black is preferable" (Cruz-Janzen 2007, 83). Furthermore, the Latino imaginary consistently identifies a white face as the quintessential Latino (DiFulco 2003, 86). Even for those Latinos who do acknowledge their African ancestry, there is cultural pressure to publicly emphasize their Latino ethnicity as a mechanism for distancing themselves from public association with the denigrated societal class of Anglo-Blacks (Pessar 1995, 44). This truism is highlighted by the popular refrain, "The darker the skin, the louder the Spanish" (Howard 2001, 114–15). Thus, compounding the Latin American cultural legacy of antiblackness is the Latino resistance to a U.S. framework in which Latinos of all shades are often viewed as nonwhite depending on the context.

While commentators in the United States are seemingly oblivious to the native antiblack racism of Latinos, the one arena in which Latino antiblack racism has been discussed in the United States is the apparent racial caste system of Spanish-language television that presents Latinos as almost exclusively white (Fletcher 2000). In fact, because of the scarce but derogatory images of Afro-Latinos in the media, activists even considered a lawsuit against the two major Spanish-language networks to challenge their depiction of Afro-Latinos. Some Latino activists see a direct parallel between the whiteness of Spanish-language television and Latino politics. One such activist states, "Latino leaders and organizations do not want to acknowledge that racism exists among our people, so they have ignored the issue by subscribing to a national origin strategy. This strategy identifies Latinos as a group comprising different nationalities, thereby creating the false impression that Latinos live in a color-blind society" (Flores 2001, 30–31).

But many concrete examples demonstrate that Latinos are not color-blind, nor do they emanate from color-blind contexts. To begin with, Afro-Latinos in the United States consistently report racist treatment at the hands of other Latinos in addition to being perceived as outsiders to the construction of Latino identity. For example, Afro-Latinos are frequently mistaken for African Americans in their own communities and, upon identifying themselves as Afro-Latinos, are told, "But you don't look Latino" (Comas-Diaz 1996). Indeed, the Pew Hispanic Center 2002 National Survey of Latinos indicated that Latinos with more pronounced African ancestry, such as many Dominicans, more readily identify color discrimination as an explanation for the bias they experience from other Latinos. Moreover, the 2010 National Survey of Latinos found that after immigrant status, skin color discrimination is the most prevalent perceived form of discrimination for Latinos. The 2019 Pew Research Center survey of Latinos found that Latinos with darker skin are more likely to experience discrimination than those with lighter skin (Gonzalez-Barrera 2019). Indeed, skin-tone bias has been empirically connected to a strong wage penalty for darker-skinned Latin American immigrants that is often nonexistent or much less pronounced among other national-origin populations (Rosenblum et al. 2016). Moreover, discrimination case allegations against Latinos often implicate antiblack bias in Latino discrimination against Afro-Latinos and African Americans (Hernández, forthcoming; Hernández 2007). Even the presumably more enlightened spaces of academia are not immune, as Afro-Latino college students report that "Latino spaces have always been the most violent" on college campuses (Haywood 2017).

Furthermore, Latino life circumstances are influenced not only by the social meaning of having Hispanic origin but also by how facial connections to Africa racialize a Latino as also Black. Studies suggest that the socioeconomic status of Afro-Latinos in the United States is more akin to that of African Americans than to other Latinos or white Americans. Latinos who identify themselves as Black have lower incomes, higher unemployment rates, higher rates of poverty, less education, and fewer opportunities and are more likely to reside in segregated neighborhoods than those who identify themselves as white or "other" (Logan 2003; López and Gonzalez-Barrera 2016; Monforti and Sanchez 2010).

In addition, despite the fact that Afro-Latino health behaviors are similar to those of the Latino ethnic groups they pertain to culturally, Afro-Latino health outcomes of meager access to health insurance and health services are racially distinctive and more in line with the racially disparate health outcomes of African Americans (LaVeist-Ramos et al. 2012). Even high blood pressure rates have been observed to vary with socially perceived racial differences unrelated to actual scientific degrees of pigmentation, such that those perceived as Afro–Puerto Rican have higher blood pressures and rates of hypertension than Puerto Ricans socially perceived as more European descended (Gravlee, Dressler, and Bernard 2005). Furthermore, socially perceived Blackness is more predictive of Latino mental health status than Latino racial self-identification (López et al. 2018). Given the significance of how much African phenotype, hair, and skin shade influence the socioeconomic status of Latinos, some studies indicate that interviewer observations of racial appearance provide the most accurate tool for monitoring discrimination among Latinos of varying shades (Roth 2010).

In fact, sociologist Nancy López (2013) notes that there is mounting evidence of distinct social outcomes in terms of intermarriage, housing segregation, educational attainment, prison sentencing, and the labor market that vary for Latinos according to externally perceived racial status. Thus, the ability to document the racial disparity within Latino ethnic communities is fundamentally advanced by having census data that separately asks Latinos to indicate both their Hispanic-origin ethnicity and their racial ancestry (López 2013). Treating Hispanic-origin ethnicity as a homogenous group signifier obscures the complexity of the socioeconomic racial hierarchy that exists across Latino communities that census racial data was designed to help measure.

Equality Law Census Racial Data Uses

The Office of Management and Budget racial and ethnic classifications that the Census Bureau uses were devised in 1977 for the specific purpose of facilitating the enforcement of civil rights laws. Census racial data is principally used to enforce the civil rights mandates against discrimination in employment, in the selling and renting of homes, and in the allocation of mortgages. The U.S. Department of Housing and Urban Development uses census racial data to determine where to locate low-income and public housing. Census racial data is also used in voting-rights redistricting to improve the political participation of people of color. In short, when the census collects racial data, the primary concern is not with how a person individually identifies, but rather with how society differentiates that person for the purpose of measuring any possible racial disparity.

For this reason, the Census Bureau's consideration of modifying the census demographic questions by removing the Hispanic/Latino option as an ethnic choice and instead presenting it as a racial category distinct from Black and all others has been viewed with alarm by Afro-Latino activists (Reyes 2014). Collapsing Latino and Hispanic ethnic identity into the list of racial categories with Black, in particular, risks obscuring the number of Afro-Latinos and the monitoring of socioeconomic status differences of Latinos across race.

Unfortunately, many Latino leaders assert whiteness as a key component of their identity, which is especially apparent in their lack of concern with the need to monitor racial disparity among Latinos (Haney López 2003). Moreover, national Latino organizations are so focused on promoting Latino unity however well-intentioned, that they too can be shortsighted about the distinctive rights of Afro-Latinos. For instance, the National Association of Latino Elected and Appointed Officials (NALEO) Educational Fund, the Mexican American Legal Defense and Education Fund, and the National Council of La Raza all publicly endorsed the Census Bureau's recommendation to treat Hispanic as a homogenous racial category, with the assertion that there would be very little loss in necessary data since Afro-Latinos could always elect to check both the Hispanic race box and the Black race box to indicate their Afro-Latino identity (NALEO Education Fund 2017).

What such a perspective underappreciates is how over time Latino antiblack bias will inhibit the count of Afro-Latinos in ways that the Census Bureau's experiments with test questions could not readily appreciate. When Hispanic is juxtaposed as a racial category distinct from others, Latinos perceive the other categories as pertaining only to non-Hispanics. This helps to explain why Puerto Ricans in Puerto Rico differ in their use of the Some Other Race box compared to Puerto Ricans living in the mainland United States. Only 11 percent of Puerto Ricans in Puerto Rico selected Some Other Race or Two or More Races on the 2010 census, as compared with 30.8 percent of mainland Puerto Ricans that selected Some Other Race or Two or More Races (Hogan 2017). On the island of Puerto Rico, Puerto Ricans can view the racial categories as pertaining to themselves and not exclusively to North American census takers. As a result, over 75 percent of Puerto Ricans on the island self-identified as white on the 2010 Census, and only 3.3 percent of respondents indicated Two or More Races (Allen 2017).

The island Puerto Rican embrace of whiteness despite contestation over whether white appearance is empirically as dominant as the Puerto Rico census numbers suggest also raises a parallel hindrance to the count of Afro-Latinos—the Latino cultural flight from Blackness. Juxtaposing Hispanic as a race distinct from others also situates Blackness as uniquely African American inasmuch as Latinos historically prefer to view Blackness as always situated outside of their national identities (Hernández 2003).

The distancing of Blackness in Puerto Rico thus enables Puerto Ricans to view Blackness as imbued primarily in their Dominican neighbors, while Dominicans instead view Blackness as imbued primarily in their Haitian neighbors (Duany 2002). A similar racial distancing happens in other Latin American countries where Blackness is presumed to be contained to geographically limited spaces rather than being a fundamental part of the nation-state (Minority Rights Group 1995). Latino Blackness is never within but instead displaced elsewhere. For U.S.-based Latinos, real Blackness is only imbued in African Americans along with English-speaking Afro-Caribbeans and Africans. Again, Blackness is always somewhere else. Even in Miami, Florida's large Caribbean population, Blackness is often exclusively associated with African Americans, such that Afro-Cubans consistently report not feeling welcomed by their fellow white Cuban residents (Gosin 2017).

Collapsing Hispanic ethnicity into the census racial categories rather than keeping it as a separate ethnicity question shields Latinos from confronting their own possible Blackness. In contrast, retaining two separate questions enables all Latinos to demarcate their Hispanic origin as an ethnicity with the first question, and then reflect on their racial origins with the second question specifically on race. Forcing the confrontation with the racial question on the census form can be a very productive navigation of the Latino cognitive dissonance with Blackness. This is borne out by the narratives of Afro-Latinos relating how the census race question brings out from the shadows family discussions of Blackness and race (Hoy 2010).

The concern of Latino leaders that the current two-question ethnicity/race census survey framework may hinder the ability to use census data to accurately portray and challenge the societal exclusion of Latinos qua Latino misapprehends how equality law jurisprudence assesses anti-Latino discrimination. The Supreme Court enforces the constitutional protections against racial discrimination for all Latinos, not because they are viewed as a race but because Latinos are a group distinguished by bias in "the attitude of the community" despite not being uniformly distinguishable based on race or color.[2] Civil rights statutory protections against racial discrimination are also accorded to Latinos because "race includes ethnicity" when Latino ethnicity is subject to adverse differentiation compared to Anglo whiteness or other racial and ethnic groups.[3] When allegations of anti-Latino discrimination are presented in court, claimants are thus authorized to use the census count of Hispanic-origin ethnicity responses with which to compare their disparate exclusion.

For instance, in an allegation of employment discrimination, the comparison between a city's large census numbers of employable Hispanic-origin respondents with the low to nonexistent hiring of Latinos at a particular workplace can be probative of discrimination when the employer has no legitimate nondiscriminatory reason for the exclusion.[4] In this way, the census Hispanic-origin ethnicity data can be effectively used to assess the moments in which Latinos are discriminated against as Latinos. Indeed, the Census Bureau findings show that Latinos overwhelmingly answer the Hispanic-origin question (U.S. Census Bureau 2015). There is no need to conflate the ethnicity question with the race question to gather the data needed to assess the socioeconomic disparities of Latinos qua Latinos. It is possible to recognize that Latinos can be racialized as Latinos distinctive from other races, without sacrificing the additional data about the racial differentiation within Latino groups that would denote the distinct racial positioning of Afro-Latinos.

Moreover, the unilateral treatment of Latino ethnicity as a race itself can be particularly ill advised in contexts where the equality needs of various Latino communities differ sharply. For instance, Latino voters are not monolithic, and the view of Latinos as a single race "polemicizes equitable representation under the umbrella term Latino," which can disserve the needs of Latinos that can vary by racial and ethnic subgroup, geographic location, immigration status, age, and so on (Astrada and Astrada 2017, 253). It is for this very reason that noted race scholar Ian Haney López (1997) suggests that context should be examined when trying to gauge when and how Latinos are being differentiated based upon ethnicity, nationality, or a racialized treatment of their status.

The invisibility of status differences between Afro-Latinos and white-presenting Latinos is especially problematic when trying to prove racial discrimination in a court case. *Arrocha v. CUNY* serves as a paradigmatic example of the analytical problems of conflating Latino ethnic identity with racial identity where the racial diversity of Latino ethnic groups is in conflict.[5] In *Arrocha*, a self-identified Afro-Panamanian tutor of Spanish sued the City University of New York (CUNY) for failure to renew his appointment as an adjunct instructor, claiming a violation of the legal prohibition against race and national-origin discrimination. The claimant alleged that the Latino heads of the Medgar Evers College Spanish department discriminated against "*Black* Hispanics" and that there was "a disturbing culture of favoritism that favor[ed] the appointments of *white* Cubans, Spaniards and *white* Hispanics from South America." Yet the court dismissed his race and national-origin discrimination claims because the judge did not understand how a racial hierarchy informs the ways in which Latinos subject other Latinos to racism and national-origin bias. Indeed, the lawsuit was dismissed because five of the eight adjunct instructors who were reappointed instead of Afro-Panamanian Arrocha were natives of other Latin American countries such as Argentina, Peru, and Mexico, as well as the Dominican Republic.

In dismissing the lawsuit because the Afro-Panamanian claimant's employer reappointed natives from other Latin American countries instead of him, the *Arrocha* court treats all Latinos as racially interchangeable and incapable of discrimination against other Latinos. The *Arrocha* decision thus directly contravenes the Supreme Court case law mandate not to presume that intraethnic and intraracial discrimination cannot exist.[6] The perspective that Latinos are racially interchangeable in *Arrocha* completely fails to appreciate the ways in which internal Latino national-origin ethnic bias is rooted in a racialized hierarchy of Latin American countries, where countries perceived as European are viewed as more advanced than those more significantly populated with people of Indigenous or African descent.

In the list of countries the judge thought equivalent to one another in the published court decision, Latin American racial constructs would rank Argentina as a highly valued white country, followed by Peru and Mexico with their Indigenous populations, closing with the Dominican Republic and the claimant's own country of origin, Panama, because they are populated by more people of African descent. For Latinos influenced by Latin American racial paradigms where each country has a racial identification, a diverse workforce of Latinos is not the immediate equivalent of a bias-free context. Nor is a color preference divorced from a racialized ideology within the Latino context. The *Arrocha* court's mistaken treatment of the panethnic identifier of Latino/Hispanic as precluding discrimination between various Latinos will only proliferate with a Census Bureau conflation of Latino ethnicity with race.

Conclusion

> The demand for full representation of all Latin@s cannot be sacrificed at the altar of "unity."
>
> **EDUARDO BONILLA-SILVA**, "Reflections about Race by a Negrito Acomplejao"

TANYA KATERÎ HERNÂNDEZ

What this chapter has attempted to demonstrate is that the Latino use of the Some Other Race category need not be viewed by the Census Bureau as a problem that needs to be solved. Rather, the Some Other Race usage provides relevant information about the persistence of Latino antiblack bias in the flight from considering race. That insight should be viewed as an invitation to provide a forum for confronting race and its social salience.

Various Latin American countries like Argentina and Brazil have begun a very similar project by mounting public campaigns to make race relevant and not taboo to consider (Nobles 2000). As a result, increasing numbers of Latin Americans are identifying with Blackness on the census. In Brazil alone, the proportion of people declaring themselves of African ancestry on the 2010 census rose from 44.7 to 50.7 percent, making Afro-Brazilians the official majority for the first time (Phillips 2011). Notably, Brazil's census bureau attributed the increase in part to the Afro-Brazilian social justice movement's campaign to increase valorization of identity among Afro-descendants.

In Argentina, after one hundred years of omitting a race question on the census with the national insistence on a white identity, the 2005 census showed 5 percent of the population as Afro-descended (*Clarín* 2006). Similarly, in Uruguay, after 150 years without a racial question on the census, and the same insistence on a white national identity, on the 2011 census 7.8 percent of the population indicated they had some African ancestry (Cabella, Nathan, and Tenenbaum 2013). When the 2010 Ecuadorian census reported that 7.2 percent of the population was of African ancestry, the assertion of African ancestry in such an Indigenous-identified nation was attributed to the public campaign Identify Yourself Family: Proudly Afro-Ecuadorian (*El Telégrafo* 2011). All of this demonstrates that antiblackness can be addressed through public policy that intervenes in the flight from Blackness on a census survey. Indeed, sociologist Nancy López (2013) has proposed that the U.S. Census Bureau mediate the U.S. Latino flight from Blackness with an inquiry into "street race" that invites respondents to reflect on how they are visually perceived by others.

In sum, given the racial diversity of Latinos in the U.S., the preexisting census format of two separate questions about Hispanic ethnicity and racial identity seems quite logical and should be retained. With the current two-part questionnaire structure, the count of Afro-Latinos is not subsumed and made invisible within a simple count of persons of Hispanic origin. In contrast, the proposed Census Bureau reform of collapsing Hispanic ethnicity into a single list of racial categories will hinder an ability to collect the statistical data that concretely demonstrates the subordinated status of Afro-Latinos that is distinctive from broader Hispanic ethnic groups. Because census racial data is principally used to enforce civil rights mandates against discrimination, it would be a disservice to this country's pursuit of racial equality to institute a census change that would mask the civil rights harms perpetrated against Latinos with visible African ancestry. "If you can't measure it, you can't improve it" (Drucker 1955).

Notes

1   This chapter often uses the Spanish-language term "Latino" rather than the explicitly gender-inclusive "Latina/o" and "Latin@" or the gender-neutral "Latinx," for pragmatic ease of presentation to an audience not as familiar with the evolution in the multiplicity of preferred identity terms, in addition to its concordance with Spanish-language usage and the contemporary census forms at issue in this chapter (Salinas and Lozano 2017). The simplicity of "Latino" as a term is also more inclusive of Latinos across generations and geographic spaces that have yet to embrace the explicitly gender-inclusive "Latina/o," and "Latin@" or the gender-neutral "Latinx" that has become to be preferred by college students and inhabitants of some large cities. However, the choice to use the Spanish language "Latino" is in no way a rejection of the desire to be inclusive that the "x" suffix is meant to offer, but rather a recognition of its awkward English language imposition. My hope is that all readers regardless of their own personal preferences regarding terminology will be able to appreciate what the chapter has to offer.

2   *Hernandez v. Texas*, 347 U.S. 475, 479–80 (1954).

3   *Village of Freeport v. Barrella*, 814 F.3d 594, 598 (2nd Cir. 2016).

4   *Teamsters v. United States*, 431 U.S. 324 (1977).

5   *Arrocha v. CUNY*, 2004. wl 594981 (E.D.N.Y. Feb. 9, 2004), litigating Civil Rights Act of 1964 Title VII discrimination claims.

6   *Castaneda v. Partida*, 430 U.S. 482, 499 (1977).

BORN PALESTINIAN, BORN BLACK:

ANTIBLACKNESS AND THE WOMB OF

ZIONIST SETTLER COLONIALISM

SARAH IHMOUD

I was born a Black woman
and now
I am become a Palestinian
JUNE JORDAN, *Moving towards Home*

They killed her on a Wednesday. Maram Saleh Abu Ismael, 23, and her unborn child, as she tried to cross the checkpoint to reach a doctor's appointment in Jerusalem. It didn't matter that she had gone through the extensive process they demanded to obtain a permit to cross the border. It didn't matter that the soldier who shot her was standing behind a concrete blockade (UN 2016).

The soldier guarding the checkpoint was afraid. Afraid of her pregnant belly as she walked in the wrong direction. So afraid, he shot her 15 times; kept shooting to "confirm the kill" even after she lay lifeless on the ground.

Why do they fear us? Why do they fear our unborn children? As Palestinian feminists, we have asked this question and sought the answers countless times. Across space and time, the gendered Palestinian body and the Palestinian womb have been intimate sites of surveillance and state violence (Shalhoub-Kevorkian 2014). Historically, Israel has discouraged growth among Palestinians with policies aimed at "containing Palestinians and their fertility" (Kanaaneh 2002, 253). Limited access to medical care and facilities during pregnancy and childbirth hinder the possibility for Palestinian women to have a healthy and safe pregnancy (Giacaman et al. 2006), as they are shaped by the necessity of navigating militarized geographies (Shalhoub-Kevorkian 2015, 1191). Indeed, "between 2000 and 2002 alone, 52 women gave birth and 19 women and 29 newborns died in military checkpoints in the occupied Palestinian Territories" (Erturk 2005, cited in Shalhoub-Kevorkian 2015, 1191). As twenty-nine-year-old Rula recounted her story of being forced to give birth at the *Beit Furik* checkpoint,

> At the checkpoint there were several soldiers; they were drinking coffee or tea and ignored us . . . I was in pain and felt I was going to give birth there and then; I told Daoud [her husband] who translated what I said to the soldiers but they did not let us pass. I was lying on the ground in the dust and I crawled behind a concrete block by the checkpoint to have some privacy and gave birth there, in the dust, like an animal. I held the baby in my arms and she moved a little but after a few minutes she died in my arms. (Amnesty International 2015)

Crossing checkpoints often exposes pregnant Palestinian women to political violence. As Aseel, a woman interviewed in another study, explained,

> A soldier was going to hit me once while I was pregnant because I [verbally] challenged him at a checkpoint. I had just come back from visiting my mom in Jerusalem and the checkpoint was closed. Everyone was pushing and there was tear gas. I said I was pregnant and my son was waiting for me at home but he wouldn't let me through. The others [Palestinians waiting to cross] warned me to stay away and said that he has hit women before. . . . The moment he turned his head, I passed and he started shouting and pulled my clothes. (Hamayel et al. 2017, S91)

The severe stress of crossing the checkpoint and militarized spaces during the time of pregnancy can result in not only adverse psychological but also bodily effects, as some women have reported having miscarriages immediately after crossing the checkpoint and other aspects of navigating the carceral geography of occupied territory (Hamayel et al. 2017, S91).

SARAH IHMOUD

In this chapter, I place Black and Indigenous feminist scholarship in conversation to consider the racialized politics of the womb, a project grounded in a political moment that has given birth to a resurgence of movement building and intellectual production centered on an analysis that highlights similarities (and dissonances) between structures of racial violence that devalue Black and Palestinian life across white settler states.[1] Ironically, the (much deserved) attention to the hypervisible forms of violence that form the basis for contemporary practices of solidarity—from blatant legal discrimination, police killings in the street, and mass incarceration to the walls (both literal and figurative) that ghettoize communities into territories of dispossession—has left fundamental questions concerning the nature of the relationship between antiblackness and Indigenous erasure in the Israeli settler colony as structures of violence largely unattended. In fact, the tendency of such politics has been an implicit erasure of antiblackness as a foundational logic animating Zionist settler colonialism, a collapsing of racialized positionalities in liberatory projects, and an elision of the gendered character of structures of violence.[2]

This chapter offers a more intimate scale from which to examine the relationality between structures of antiblackness and Palestinian erasure. Drawing on Black and Indigenous feminist scholarship on the spatial politics of the body, and building on Joy James's (2016) theorization of the womb and concept of the "captive maternal," it argues for an acknowledgment of the interplay between logics of antiblackness and Palestinian dispossession in the Israeli settler colony through an examination of the racialized politics of national reproduction, or the politics of the womb. Zionist settler colonial epistemologies and technologies of governance that fuel contemporary exercises of violence against Palestinians in occupied territory, it argues, are energized by an antiblack logic that seeks to purify and secure the Jewish body—and hence, the national body—from the imagined threat of racial contamination.

In order to do so, it examines Zionism's historical project of increasing Jewish demographic presence in Palestine through pronatalist policies that situate women's bodies as symbolic national peripheries. Beyond encouraging birth and expanding Jewish families to fight in what national leaders have referred to as a "demographic war," pronatalist policies continue to labor towards purifying the Jewish nation in the image of European (white) supremacy, and maintaining the racial exclusivity of the "chosen people." It proceeds by examining how these essentially eugenicist politics are instrumental in fomenting growing racial panics concerning a Palestinian demographic "threat" and Israel's internal racial others, fueling violent policies of antiblackness and Indigenous erasure within the colony.

I conclude by sharing some reflections on the question of transnational feminist struggles against racialized gendered violence within the context of white settler nation-states. Drawing on Tiffany King's (2016, 1026) theorization of Black fungibility as a "spatial methodology," I suggest that a centering of the gendered Palestinian body as territory or geography opens space for what Shanya Cordis (2019) calls a praxis of "relational difference" between the entangled logics of "gendered anti-blackness" (Vargas 2012) and "racial Palestinianization" (Goldberg 2008). Examining Israel as a white settler colony invested in the colonial body politics to which antiblackness is foundational forces consideration of critical theories and activist praxes invested in dismantling the settler-spatial order that fall outside of the liberal humanist frame.

Race, Space, and the Body: The Womb of Zionist Settler Colonialism

The production of space and racialized positionalities in the Israeli settler colonial context is often overdetermined by a binary understanding of Palestinian native and Israeli settler bodies and lives. While other scholars have noted the traveling of racial logics between, for example, the United States and Israel through shared imperial relations of power (e.g., Abu-Laban and Bakan 2008), I am less interested in identifying causal relationships than in the ways in which antiblackness and Palestinian erasure map onto each other in the Israeli settler colony. The gendered racial politics of the production of settler space, which I call the womb of Zionist settler colonialism, is a promising lens through which a relationality between antiblackness and Palestinian erasure can be further explored. I deploy the term "womb" here in relation to Joy James's conceptualization of "Womb Theory" or Western theory, "the historical context that married democracy with slavery" (2016, 256).

The embodiment of space has long been a concern of feminist scholars, who have drawn attention to the ways in which women's bodies have been constructed as a symbolic national periphery in a variety of contexts (e.g., Aretxaga 1997; Yuval-Davis 1997), as "biological reproducers of members of ethnic collectivities" and "reproducers of the boundaries of ethnic/national groups" (Yuval-Davis and Anthias 1989). Women are constructed as "symbolic border guards" (Yuval-Davis 1997, 23), embodying the nation's boundaries and becoming contested geographies. In settler colonial contexts, biopolitical surveillance and control over women's bodies and reproductive capacities are closely tied to eliminatory policies that seek to destroy Indigenous peoples in order to replace them with a settler entity (Shalhoub-Kevorkian 2015; Wolfe 2006).

Native feminist scholars have further argued that Indigenous women's bodies within settler regimes are saturated with meaning, signifying Indigenous political orders, land, and perhaps most dangerous of all, the possibility of reproducing native life itself—and with it, "other life forms, other sovereignties, other forms of political will" (Simpson 2016, 28)—a challenge to the very legitimacy of the settler state. As such, women's bodies have been subjected as inherently "rapeable" (Smith 2003), violable and disposable entities in the march toward settler accumulation by dispossession. Thus, while territoriality is widely understood as settler colonialism's "specific, irreducible element" (Wolfe 2006, 388), the native body must be centered as geographic space in theorizing territoriality. In the drive toward native "elimination" (388), the native body is a locus of racialized, gendered processes of colonial dispossession.

Concomitantly, Black feminist scholars have argued that antiblackness is embedded in the spatial projects of colonialism. Sylvia Wynter's (1994) work considers the foundational role of Blackness in shaping the epistemological terms of the Enlightenment, the figure of the human, and hence the very terms of conquest. In doing so, she opens space for thinking beyond the native/settler binary, urging a consideration of antiblackness in projects of Indigenous erasure. In discussing the territoriality of the racial-sexual body, critical geographer Katherine McKittrick (2006, 45) draws attention to the ways in which geographic conquest and expansion are "extended to the reproductive and sexually available body" of Black women. That is, through histories of enslavement, captivity, and racial rape, Black women's bodies—their "reproductive organs, capacities, and sexualities" (47)—became units of spatial production. Tiffany King extends these analyses to understand the Black female body as "a process that is constituted by and constitutes landscapes" (2013, 16). Thus, "anti-black racism's productive and repressive power are also in play when the settler is eliminating the native from the land" (16).

I want to think with both Indigenous and Black feminist analyses that identify the ways in which race and racism are necessary for the production of space (McKittrick 2006, 12), in considering how the Palestinian condition enters into conversation with Blackness. How might the power of antiblackness be at play in Israel's ongoing project of eliminating Palestinian presence from the land? I suggest that the figurative womb of Zionist settler colonialism—its position as a "fulcrum of U.S. imperial exploits in the Middle East" (Erakat and Hill 2019, 8), one shaped by global histories of colonialism and white supremacy (and hence a gendered regime of antiblackness)—is centered in the politics of the womb, or the gendered politics of bodily reproduction. While womb politics, or the ways in which the womb has been a generative space in birthing national projects grounded in biological racism (James 2016), carry the particularities of racial histories and contexts, they can be fertile grounds for considering the intimate entanglements of antiblackness and Indigenous erasure. Antiblackness is embedded in the spatial project of Zionist settler colonialism through its presence/absence in the gendered body politics of white settler nationalism. In turn, Zionist settler colonialism enacts erasure against native Palestinians (seeking to disappear them from the landscape), while, at the same time, energizing antiblack racism in Israel.

In the following section, I investigate how intimate surveillance and the politics of birth, situated within a political context of racial elimination, coupled with Israel's pronatalist fertility regime, work to engineer Zionist settler colonialism as an aggregate of a particular kind of racialized Jewish bodies, creating Israel as a white settler nation in the image of Europe.

Antiblackness and the Politics of the Womb: Producing the White Settler Nation

Black feminist scholars have been at the forefront of drawing attention to the ways in which the womb has been a primary site of racialized control, dispossession, and violence at the heart of national reproduction of white settler states such as the United States (e.g., Bridges 2008; Roberts 1997; Threadcraft 2016), where the terrorizing of Black reproductivity through racial rape, histories of racial slavery, and its afterlife became a primary means of political control (James 2013). In the legitimization of Black captivity during racial slavery, Black women's wombs were a site of commodification of value; in the post-Emancipation era, the Black female body has been used to naturalize Black criminality, leading to a disfiguring of Black maternity, a window on the afterlife of slavery as a gendered regime.

SARAH IHMOUD

While the United States "grew a womb" by consuming the "generative properties of the maternals it held captive" (James 2016, 256), the Zionist project has consumed the wombs of Palestinian women as intimate sites of surveillance, violence, and erasure (e.g., Shalhoub-Kevorkian 2015), while simultaneously consuming the wombs of Jewish women for their capacities to regenerate the Jewish people as a nation.

In historical Palestine, numerous scholars have catalogued the ways in which the Zionist movement devised surveillance and population management strategies as early as the 1920s in order to deal with the inevitable problem arising from the formation of the settler nation: how to rid the territory of its Indigenous Palestinian population (e.g., Sa'di 2014; Sayegh 1965; Zureik et al. 2011). Within this context, Palestinian women's wombs have been constructed by the colonial state as the vessels of an imagined "Arab demographic threat" that should be controlled and eliminated, producing them as sites of surveillance and state violence (Shalhoub-Kevorkian 2015). Histories of gender and sexual violence, including the historical restrictions of Palestinian women's fertility (Kanaaneh 2002), coupled with restrictions on bodily autonomy during the time of birth, legalized mechanisms of family separation (i.e., the Citizenship law), and mobility and access to reproductive health care (Giacaman, Abu-Rmeileh, and Wick 2006), along with other factors (Hamayel, Hammoudeh, and Welchman 2017), as noted earlier, serve the interests of the Zionist project in eliminating Palestinian presence. Violence against the gendered native body and land are intertwined. As Maya Xinca feminist Lorena Cabnal articulates it, being an Indigenous woman in contexts of ongoing colonialism is complex because "your body becomes the first disputed territory for patriarchal power" (2019, 115).

At the same time that Israel has sought to decrease the Palestinian population, it has worked to increase Jewish demographic presence in historical Palestine. As Yuval-Davis and Anthias explain, the issue of national reproduction, "both in terms of its ideological boundaries and in terms of the reproduction of its membership" (1989, 92), has been at the center of Zionist discourse. Israeli demographic policies have historically sought to "increase Jewish domination in Israel" (94). The Zionist project conceptualized the survival of Israel as a "demographic race" (94) early on, as leadership believed that sovereignty could not be fomented without a Jewish demographic majority. While Jewish immigration (*aliyah*) and settlement was considered to be the quickest and most efficient method of increasing Jewish presence, the need for establishing a Jewish demographic advantage remained a preoccupation of Zionist leadership (Yuval-Davis and Anthias 1989, 92). Thus, Jewish family size became a matter of "security and a sacred national mission," and natality "(having large families) was tantamount to patriotism" (Tal 2016, 80, 81).

Beyond encouraging birth and expanding Jewish families to fight in the demographic war, pronatalist policies worked to purify the Jewish race and maintain exclusivity of the chosen people. Indeed, as Ronit Lentin highlights in her discussion of Israel's construction as a racial state, "the prominent Israeli genetics professor Rafael Falk reads the entire history of Zionism as a eugenicist project, aiming to save the Jewish genetic pool from the degeneration forced upon the Jews by diaspora existence (Falk 2006, cited in Lentin 2008); prominent Zionist thinkers perpetuated the idea that Jews were a separate "race," adopting "the terminology of Volk—a racial nation shaped by 'blood and soil'" (Falk 2006, 18–19, cited in Lentin 2008, 8). Hence, within this context, where Jewish women's bodies became the vessel for national reproduction, an emphasis was placed on the importance of Jewish motherhood in producing the new Jew, a process of "rehabilitating" the denigrated Jewish body that lay at the heart of regenerating the Jewish Nation. As Meira Weiss (2002) highlights, Zionism has a "unique bodily aspect" that, stemming from the denigration of the Jewish people throughout Europe for centuries, sought to rehabilitate a Jewish identity and especially Jewish masculinity (e.g., Boyarin 1997; Gilman 1991). Rather than challenging the orientalist image that excluded and subjugated Jews in Europe, Zionism "internalized and reproduced them":

> Zionism modeled the "new Jew" on white European values and culture in purposeful opposition to Eastern cultural markers carried by Middle Eastern Jews and certainly by Muslim and Christian Arabs. As a derivative of Enlightenment Europe, Zionism reproduced the polarized binaries of the superior, enlightened West and the inferior, primitive East. It claimed that Jews as a national entity belonged to the superior, enlightened West despite their geographical origins in the East and sought to enlighten (read: colonize) its primitive peoples. (Erakat 2015, 78–80)

Thus, Israel's founders reified European supremacy in ascribing new value onto Jewish subjectivity and nationality in relation to the racialized Palestinian Other.[3]

Through an assertion of Zionism, "the non-white Jewish victims of anti-Semitism could assert a bridge from non-whiteness to whiteness, identifying with European global hegemony" (Abu-Laban and Bakan 2008, 646). In its alliance with global white supremacy, Zionism absorbed the antiblack logics foundational to Enlightenment Europe. The legal architecture of the colonial project, which sprang from the British mandate for Palestine, further evidences this fact. As Yael Berda (2017, 18) details, the legal framework of the occupation was based on British colonial emergency laws, which sought to manage the civilian population in accordance with the laws of war: "The colonial regulations carried with them the administrative memory of colonial rule, which involved not only laws but organizational practices and political dispositions, primarily the legitimacy to use separate legal systems for different populations based on race" (19). Demographic governance and management of the occupied native population grew out of a larger, global project of Western imperialism.

Over time, Israelis came to "occupy the structural positions of whiteness in the racial hierarchy of the Middle East. Arabs, accordingly—most notably in the person of Palestinians—are the antithesis. . . . Historically, politically, religiously and culturally, Arabs are neither Jew nor (as such) white" (Goldberg 2009, 117). The state's preoccupation with engineering the new Jewish body in the image of European supremacy has thus energized the policing of other nonwhite bodies within the settler nation, particularly Mizrahi (Jews of Middle Eastern descent) and African Jews (see Shohat 2003; Lavie 2014). In what has come to be known as the Yemenite Children Affair, for example, it is estimated that hundreds to thousands of children were kidnapped from their Jewish mothers and fathers who had fled Yemen in the 1950s, before being given or sold to Jewish Ashkenazi families, that is, Jewish families of European descent (Fezehai 2019). In 2013, Israel admitted giving Ethiopian Jewish immigrants forced contraceptives without their knowledge or consent (Dawber 2013). While the Israeli Ministry of Health previously denied the practice, suspicions were raised by an investigative journalist who interviewed more than thirty Ethiopian women in an attempt to understand why birth rates in the community had fallen dramatically. The theft of Yemeni children and the policing of Ethiopian women's reproductive autonomy are cases that point to continued attempts to purify the Jewish race, highlighting Israel's construction as a white settler state animated by logics of antiblackness and invested in the control and management of women's bodies and reproductive capacities. This is to say nothing of the mass detention and deportation of African asylum seekers, and other crude forms of racial violence and antiblackness openly endorsed by Israel's political leadership (see, for example, Pierre 2015).

Pronatal policies continue today through a variety of reproductive technologies and practices such as reproductive genetics (e.g., Hashiloni-Dolev 2006) that enable the production of the Jewish body and homeland in the image of European whiteness and the disappearance of the Palestinian body and body politic. Such practices go beyond pronatalism, bordering on a form of racial eugenics aimed at purifying the Jewish nation (e.g., Nahman 2013), highlighting the interlocking logics of antiblackness and Palestinian erasure that undergird the white nationalist character of the state.

Born Palestinian, Born Black: Palestine's Captive Maternal

The centrality of bodily reproduction and its entanglement with the continuous uprooting and erasure of Indigenous Palestinians situates the womb of Zionist settler colonialism as a space that has absorbed the antiblack logics foundational to the terms of conquest and global white supremacy. These politics form the core of a racist social structure that aims to create Israel in the image of a European nation and, in doing so, eliminate not only the Indigenous Palestinian, but also non-Ashkenazi (European descent) presence within the boundaries of that nation. Attempts to purify the Jewish national body bring to the fore the extent to which Israel's epistemologies and technologies of governance are energized by a fundamentally antiblack animus.

Tiffany King argues that "the symbol of the Black body plays a paradigmatic role in spatial expansion, and geographic humanity" (2016, 1024). Thus, the ways in which Blackness is imagined "in relation to space, residency, Indigenous and conquistador/settler communities is of critical importance" (1024) in undoing the settler order. While situated from within a U.S. settler context, I find resonance between her analysis of the spatial logics of Black fungibility and the spatial logics of Zionist settler colonialism. While the structural positionalities of Black women and Palestinian women in white settler states differ, I want to suggest that the terrain of the gendered body, read through the spatial logics of Black fungibility, and of Palestinian elimination in the settler colony, opens up space for thinking through a politics of what Shanya Cordis calls "relational difference."[4] According to Cordis, "Rather than a discomfiting collapse of racialized difference that perpetuates the so-called ruse of analogy, relational difference centers particularity even as it articulates horizontal connections across ongoing colonial violence" (2019, 30).

The embodied, gendered politics of Zionist settler colonialism provide a ground for thinking through a politics of relationality between eliminatory logics of antiblackness and Indigenous erasure as they traffic in the bodies and lives of women between and across white settler states. The reproductive and productive labor of the Black "captive maternal" (James 2016) may not be visible at first glance; her figure nonetheless energizes the womb of Zionist settler colonialism and the spatial project of Indigenous erasure in historical Palestine.

The title of this piece is a reference to Palestinian poet Suheir Hammad's collection of the same title (2010), which itself is a play on June Jordan's 1985 poem, "Moving towards Home," written in the aftermath of the 1982 Philangist-Israeli massacre of Palestinian refugees in Lebanon's Sabra and Shatila camps.

I was born a Black woman

and now

I am become a Palestinian

The passage, as Jodi Melamed analyzes it, "exemplifies the conjoined epistemological-political project of women of color feminism: it works as politics in the first place by innovating ways of knowing that abrogate normal politics" (2011, 79).

In this chapter, I want to challenge us to think further with this feminist "poetics of relation" (Glissant 1997) as analytics, by exploring the intimate geographies of the body as sites where racial and gendered histories of dispossession push up against each other, and further, ground possibilities for renewed political imaginaries of solidarity based on shared vulnerabilities to violence and a desire for "living room" (Jordan [1985] 2011). Still, to think with the insights of Black feminisms in considering the Palestinian condition in the settler colony is not to elide or erase difference between racialized positionalities, but to consider how antiblackness as a global structure shapes the contours of possibility for Palestinian life and survival. I have ventured to explore here merely one aspect of this womb work, the ways in which the racialized politics of birth at the center of the Zionist project's ongoing colonization of Palestine is imbricated with the foundational gendered logics of antiblackness. In other words, examining Israel as a white settler colony invested in the carceral logics and gendered body politics to which antiblackness is foundational forces consideration of critical theories and activist praxes invested in dismantling the settler spatial order that falls outside of the liberal humanist frame. The current political moment calls for feminist analytics and political projects that attend to the specificities of gendered violence and dispossession, while also contesting the elision of antiblack logics that give rise to the eliminatory politics of Zionist settler colonialism.

Notes

The author would like to thank Shanya Cordis, Noura Erakat, and Melissa F. Weiner, along with the editors, for their thoughtful and incisive comments on earlier drafts of this piece. Any errors are my own.

1   This has included conversations between communities around overlapping systems of oppression and resistance to state violence; delegations of Black activists to occupied territory, and Palestinian activists to Ferguson, Missouri; and internal conversations within Arab diaspora communities around antiblack racism, all of which, it is important to note, build on longstanding histories of Black internationalism, anticolonial solidarity, transnational political analyses, and movement building between communities (e.g., Alhassen 2017; Erakat and Hill 2019; Feldman 2015; Lubin 2014).

2   In this chapter I use the terms *Zionist settler colonialism* and *Israeli settler colonialism* interchangeably to refer to what Fayez A. Sayegh called the "Zionist settler-state of Israel" (1965, 21), a formation characterized by "(1) its *racial complexion* and *racist conduct pattern*; (2) its *addiction to violence*; and (3) its *expansionist stance*." This is grounded in an understanding of Zionism as an ideology and political movement that has subjected Palestinians to structural forms of violence and erasure across space and time in the pursuit of a new Jewish state and society (e.g., Salamanca et al. 2012).

3   The "rehabilitation" of the Oriental Jew by making him European was a decidedly gendered endeavor. As Weiss's (2002) work explains, the construction of this new Jew as a sacralized, chosen body is the attempt of the diaspora Jew as Other to reinvent himself by embodying the hegemonic, European body, resting on the collective construction of a masculine, healthy body in service of the Jewish nation. The Hebrew man, whose reconstructed body symbolizes this national recovery, thus energizes a racialized hierarchy of bodies in Israel.

4   While I refer to them here as structural positionalities, it is important to note that this bifurcation of Palestinian and Black is, in the context of historical Palestine, necessarily a false one, as even in Jerusalem there is a historical community of Afro-Palestinians who identify as both Black and Palestinian.

NOT YET: INDIGENEITY, ANTIBLACKNESS, AND ANTICOLONIAL LIBERATION

JODI A. BYRD

The United States has a fundamental problem that it cannot figure out how to either resolve or move beyond. It cannot even decide how to name the problem. Sourcing through Christianity, people often turn to the concept of original sin to identify something rotten at the core of the empire liberalism built. Part of the difficulty is the fact that multiple candidates are rallied as contenders: conquest, slavery, genocide, racism, misogyny, capitalism, settlement, white supremacy, or colonialism. But even in the listing of them, the gesture of identifying some baseline evil requires a choice, a divining down to a singularity as origin. It is as if there can be only one sin at the bottom of an irreducible trauma that serves as the core wound the nation needs to face in order to resolve and heal. And for all the effort, the assumption is that the U.S. will finally be redeemed in its democratic mission to be a beacon of liberty for the world. Rooting out the source, and fighting causes over symptoms, we are told, is the only way to cure what ails any body or body politic. And so, the nation grapples with pointing and naming, trying to figure out what originates where, with whom, when to start keeping scores, and then how to weight the prior and the ante alongside the now and the anti. Left fumbling with meanings and words in the hopes of finding a way to articulate something solid and fixed at the exact moment meaning and fact have become completely unhinged, we turn to realism and a direct correlation to reality to finally bear witness to the truth of history. And when reality fails truth, we look to fiction and fantasy to alter history in a way that can redeem the present and impel us toward an ever more just future. Hope pushes us past the grimiest of details that realism demands, and it offers us transformative reframings that might this time, finally, make all the difference that will matter.

Lin-Manuel Miranda's Broadway musical *Hamilton* is, to my mind, one of those hopeful, grasping attempts to wrest U.S. history away from its originary violences and oppressions and toward its liberatory horizons without ever having to approach or engage the core wound directly. Wildly popular and enormously successful, with over eleven Tony awards recognizing its creative genius, the show was notoriously difficult to get tickets to see even before it was filmed for online subscription streaming. Miranda's musical revels in its deeply held and fundamental love for the United States as an affective site of initial failure and then belatedly realized liberation, justice, and inclusion. Taking its cues and inspiration from Caribbean literary antecedents including Jean Rhys, Aimé Césaire, and Junot Díaz, *Hamilton* rewrites the founding fathers of America through a postcolonial recasting that centers diasporic Latinx, Black, and Caribbean cultural, intellectual, and political traditions. Along the way, it tries to forecast a sequel to the Declaration of Independence where women are finally included alongside the self-evident truth that "all men are created equal." With the Indian-killing, slave-owning George Washington, Thomas Jefferson, Aaron Burr, Alexander Hamilton, and the Marquis de Lafayette reimagined as Afro-Caribbean and Black revolutionary freedom fighters, *Hamilton* compels its audiences to consider the possibilities of rising up against racist, classist, and xenophobic tyranny in the name of liberation. Its vision, then, takes literally the idea that the United States was founded out of the noblest of ideals as each of these leaders ventriloquizes a future anterior revolution that simultaneously historicizes and anticipates a social transformation to come out of a classed, diasporic, and raced rebellion: "Rise up! / When you're living on your knees, you rise up! / Tell your brother that he's gotta rise up / Tell your sister that she's gotta rise up!" (Miranda 2015a). The lesson of *Hamilton* is first that immigrants and refugees are the driving force of U.S. history, and second that one can never waste a shot to make a difference, achieve freedom, or, if not either of those, then perhaps just a lasting historical relevance.

JODI A. BYRD

That the show is beloved and award winning is no revelation. Transforming the stodgy square dancing of shows like *Oklahoma!* into showstopping numbers built through references to blues, hip-hop, beatbox, and freestyle rap, Miranda's music combines classic Broadway motifs with Americana and then updates them both to the twenty-first century. It is a show that rewards audiences and listeners with a compelling historical character study of the man behind the face on the ten-dollar bill while also showcasing just how successful casting beyond racial expectation can be in realizing the fulfillment of America's multicultural dream. In prioritizing Alexander Hamilton's humble start in the Caribbean as an allegory for scrappy immigrant bootstrap self-starter survival, the musical unabashedly reads the American colonies and their propulsion toward revolution through the claim Helen Tiffin, Bill Ashcroft, and Gareth Griffiths make in *The Empire Writes Back* that "the American experience and its attempts to produce a new kind of literature can be seen to be the model for all later post-colonial writing" (2002, 16). As the Schuyler Sisters sing in R&B girl-group triplicate: "Look around, look around at how lucky we are to be alive right now! / History is happening in Manhattan and we just happen to be in the greatest city in the world" (Miranda 2015b). Sampling past and present, remixing literary allusions with popular culture, and anachronistically reading historical references to hurricanes, orphans, political machinations, and failed fathers and marriages through Anthropocene climate change and globalization, the musical captures the hope the new world colonies supposedly offered the world at the birth of the United States.

But it also repeats some of the idealistic progressivism born out of the post-2008 optimism that a hoped-for social transformation had been realized with the election of the first Black man to the presidency of the United States. *Hamilton*, with an almost pandering desire to prove the United States as always already postracial through historical revision, offers audiences a triumphal narrative of transnational diasporic inclusion as the foundation of the United States as a country built by and for immigrants. It was also a version of progressive U.S. optimism that came to a crashing halt when Donald J. Trump won the 2016 presidential election. Ten days after what the national media decried as a shocking, entirely unpredictable upset that saw Hillary Clinton defeated in her bid to be the first female U.S. president, vice president-elect Mike Pence attended the November 18, 2016, performance of *Hamilton* on Broadway, and the cast confronted him with a letter at the end of the show. For a tense few moments that many on social media described as a confrontation between two radically different

Americas, the multiracial cast joined together at curtain call to express their fears about the future of the country under a return to the regressive white supremacist nationalism, xenophobia, homophobia, antiblack racism, and misogyny that Trump's political campaign augured. Brandon Dixon, who performed that night as Aaron Burr, addressed Pence on behalf of the cast: "We, sir, are the diverse America who are alarmed and anxious that your new administration will not protect us: our planet, our children, our parents, or defend us and uphold our inalienable rights, sir. But we truly hope this show has inspired you to uphold our American values and to work on behalf of all of us. All of us" (Loughrey 2016).

As accounts of that night's performance with Pence in attendance circulated, reports came through of audiences giving standing ovations for a number of the performances, with others joking about how past presidential excursions to the theater had been met and handled. President-elect Trump tweeted late in the evening that the cast had harassed Pence, and, after declaring the theater should always be a safe space, he then demanded the *Hamilton* cast apologize. But it was reportedly the brief but standout exchange between Hamilton and Lafayette from the scene "Yorktown (The World Turned Upside Down)" that drew the longest standing ovation from an audience anxious to demonstrate their resistance to Trump/Pence: "Immigrants," the two historical figures say to each other on the battlefield before high-fiving, "we get the job done" (Mele and Healy 2016). With the threats to immigration reform hanging in the balance in the aftermath of Trump's Republican win, along with his constant campaign trail calls for Muslim immigration bans and a Mexican-funded border wall to keep the global south from migrating north, this on-stage moment was especially poignant for theatergoers that night as they weighed out the actual historical intent of U.S. history alongside their own deeply felt and passionate desires for a narrative arc of ever-increasing tolerance, prosperity, peace, and inclusion.

That moment and the arc it envisioned was so poignant that Lin-Manuel Miranda released a mixtape for the show a few months later. Featuring a range of hip-hop artists and pop stars including Busta Rhymes, The Roots, Kelly Clarkson, Usher, Sia, Ben Folds, and Alicia Keys, who helped reimagine many of the well-beloved songs from the musical, the centerpiece for the compilation was a new song titled, "Immigrants (We Get the Job Done)." Built around that moment of standing ovation and then released as a music video to help amplify #SanctuaryForAll and #HereToStay during the first summer of Trump's presidency, the song used fictional news commentary to reflect on the pitched political battles of the day, with an unnamed radio commentator disdainfully noting the ironies that a country built by immigrants has suddenly made "immigrant" a bad word. The lyrics that then follow punctuate just how far immigrants and refugees have had to come—across transatlantic passages and war-torn borders littered with dead, working four jobs, hoping for "a lap dance from Lady Liberty"—to make their way into America as the abjected, underpaid, and unwanted workforce doing the hard-time labor to just barely make ends meet in the hopes that to do so will finally secure a place for themselves. As "America's ghost writers, where the credit is only borrowed," immigrants represent the precarity of arrival, the stamina to overcome, and the sheer will to build a country from the land up (Miranda 2016a). Pitching its vision to that diverse America that the *Hamilton* cast claimed to represent, and hoping to remind white folks that the United States was, from the beginning, a nation of immigrants, Lin-Manuel Miranda's *Hamilton* and its *Mixtape* companion caution a "not yet" temporality of freedom that requires hard work and vigilance to ensure that the United States will someday fulfill the promise of its founding.

The problem, of course, is that this desired narrative arc of U.S. exceptionalism has never been the actual story of the United States. Two days after Pence saw *Hamilton* on Broadway, North Dakota mobilized over seventy-six militarized police forces from at least ten surrounding states to confront water protectors at Standing Rock Indian Reservation and spray them with water, concussion grenades, and explosive tear gas canisters in subzero temperatures throughout the night of November 20, 2016 (Dresslar 2016). Culminating after months of protests against the Dakota Access Pipeline that cut through North Dakota, Iowa, and Illinois, which were, in fact, as Nick Estes (2016) has pointed out, tied to "the longer histories of Oceti Sakowin (The Great Sioux Nation) resistance against the trespass of settlers, dams, and pipelines across the Mni Sose, the Missouri River," the events of that night were a spectacle in conquistador logics that testify to the degree to which American Indians and our lands remain under constant siege even as the occupying U.S. national community itself prepared for the difficult and personal battles of Thanksgivings at home with relatives of contesting political (and racist) views. Buried within the hashtags proclaiming this country a sanctuary where all have the right to come and then stay as long as they are willing to do the work is a fundamental disavowal of the plundering, slavery, and genocide that made this country possible at all.

The United States has, in other words, never been just a nation built by hardworking immigrants, and its precious devotion to individual freedoms has only ever been formed in relation to those who never counted as human to be free in the first place. This country is, instead, a nation built through those foreclosed from the teleology of immigration as the path to humanity—descendants of Africans brought to the new world via the slave trade as well as the descendants of those Indigenous peoples who were already here and who survived genocide and the dispossession of their lands. Neither can ever cohere presence under the conditions of belonging, rights, and subjectivity that the U.S. demands. Though the historical violences of slavery and colonization still compete with each other to claim primacy as the original sin of this nation's founding—and in that competition contribute to the discursive means through which Indigenous and Black oppression continue—the lasting repercussions of slavery, Jim Crow racism, and the hypervisible subjections of quotidian antiblackness, police brutality, poverty-to-prison pipelines on the one hand and the ongoing colonization of Indigenous peoples and lands that render American Indians statistical nonentities erased within the archive as well as the contemporary moment on the other, work in tandem. In reading the cognitive dissonances that emerged after a statue of Columbus in Boston was defaced with red paint and the words Black Lives Matter painted at its feet, Tiffany Lethabo King suggests that the new-world grammars of conquest that Hortence Spillers and Sylvia Wynter theorize contain within them the approaches necessary for understanding the conditions of possibility that have created the present state of racialized politics in the Americas. "The making of the Conquistador—as the human," Lethabo King (2016) writes, "can be tracked methodologically as bloody, bodily, discursive, sensual (and affective) enactments of perverse and gratuitous violence as well as theoretically approached and narrated as a way of deftly and surgically reading the minutia of its quotidian discursive moves and affectations." Conquest, as Lethabo King argues, inaugurated both slavery and genocide in the new world; as such, it is already a capacious enough frame through which to theorize both as the historical intent of the United States as empire.

So, even with declarations that the election of Barack Obama signified that the inherent racism of the nation's founding had finally been overcome, as Keeanga-Yamahtta Taylor observes, "the United States does not passively contend that it is a colorblind society; it actively promotes its supposed colorblindness as an example of its democratic traditions and its authority to police the globe" (2016, 5). And though Taylor does not address it outright in her analysis of Black liberation, the implications of U.S. territoriality mean that were the United States able to somehow actualize its postracial ideal and end white supremacy, antiblackness, and xenophobia without also upending the political economies and structures of the nation-state and capitalism (which Taylor is clear is not possible), the ongoing colonization of Indigenous peoples would continue unabated. The spectacular state-sanctioned violence targeting Black Americans, the rise of #BlackLivesMatter to confront, protest, and stop it, and the #NoDAPL protests at Standing Rock all emerged first under Obama's presidency, and that timing was in many ways a direct result of the fact that the imperial presidency's authority to police the globe did not substantively transform under the policies of the first Black president. The idea that the United States is fundamentally a meritocracy accompanies the insistence that the United States is a postracial, color-blind, and immigrant society, and as Taylor states further, "where there is bad treatment on the basis of race, it is viewed as the product of lapsed personal behavior and morality" (2016, 4). The election of Donald J. Trump that followed the optics of the first Black family in the White House in many ways only serves to drive home the fundamental ideal of white conquistador supremacy, that not only was the United States exceedingly and already color-blind, it was to a fault, that it had forgotten to prioritize whiteness and the sanctity of borders as that which made America great from the start.

Wait for It

As border walls, transmisogyny, sexual abuse and harassment, gun violence, homophobia, environmental collapse, and antiblack racism have come to define the hours, days, weeks, months, and now years that have followed Donald J. Trump's presidential apotheosis, the durative question of original sin and subsequent calls for reconciliation, redress, reparation, or atonement have fostered a number of ongoing public performances and responses that swing from Canada's constant apologies that elicit the prodigious tears of Prime Minister Justin Trudeau to Trump's daily harangues and belligerent bullying of almost everyone, from the removal of Confederate statues to militarized police forces mobilized to brutally suppress and murder Black and Indigenous lives, from the daily drumbeat of men accused and fired for sexual harassment to ever growing and expansive anti-Muslim immigration bans and the rise of migrant detention centers.

Or the U.S. recognition of Jerusalem as the capital of Israel. Every day is another crisis that only reaffirms the hegemony of white masculinity, racial capitalism, and the dispossessive logics that have made plunder the most profitable means to an ends. The sources and culpabilities of evil, dispossession, and oppression are almost too prolific to process at this point, let alone apprehend. And the lateral violences and horizontal competitions for attention as the most pressing issue among pressing issues only ensure that settlement never relinquishes white supremacy within the cacophony that is its raison d'être.

Within this cultural moment, academia has seen the rise of two strands of intellectual thought grappling with the legacies of slavery and colonialism that served as the founding violences of the settler states in the Americas. Indigenous critical theory and Afropessimism both seek to confront the structural and interlocking histories and oppressions of colonial, racial, and gendered capitalism that have maintained the dispossessive economies at the heart of U.S. empire. Providing some genealogy into how critiques of settler colonialism and antiblackness have arisen almost coterminously, Justin Leroy (2016) suggests that "recent work in black studies, on the one hand, and indigenous and settler colonialism studies, on the other, has made claims to exceptionalism that leave the two fields at an impasse." Given the irreducibility of the historical violences encapsulated by slavery and antiblackness and the colonization of American Indian peoples and lands, that impasse is as much about temporality as it is about subjectivity and territoriality. "Either colonialism or slavery," Leroy (2016) observes, "must be subordinated to the other, forcing them into aporetic tension. Each field reduces the other to a variation on the theme of liberal multiculturalism to maintain the integrity of its own exceptionalist claims." Neither alone, he concludes, can account for the messiness of history.

Indeed, in "The *Vel* of Slavery," Jared Sexton suggests that Indigenous scholars, as their work intervenes within and against the theories and practices of antiracism, "draw from and contribute to the discourse of post-racialism by diminishing or denying the significance of race in thinking about the relative structural positions of black and non-black populations, not in order to assert the colorblind justice of American or Canadian society or to extol the respective virtues and vices of 'model' and 'problem' minorities, but rather to establish the contrasting injustice of their settler colonial relations with indigenous peoples" (2016b, 584). In diagnosing the aporias at the heart of the field, Sexton concludes that "Native Studies scholars misrecognize 'the true horror of slavery' as de-culturalization or the loss of sovereignty because they do not ask what slavery is in the most basic sense—its local and global histories, its legal and political structures, its social and economic functions, its psychosexual dynamic, and its philosophical consequences" (591). Raising the caution that Indigenous studies' insistence on sovereignty might itself reflect antiblackness, Sexton finally advocates for the relinquishment of land and the abolishment of sovereignty altogether as providing any recourse to humanity and as the radical gesture of affirmation of the condition of what Sexton identifies as the nonsovereign and the slave. It is "the landless inhabitation of selfless existence" that will finally liberate all from the ravages of antiblack white supremacy (593).

Responding back to Sexton's concerns that Indigenous studies scholars have failed to apprehend race and racism in prioritizing Indigenous struggles for land and sovereignty, Iyko Day points out that at the core of his argument lie the key precepts of Afropessimism, that "no other oppression is reducible to antiblackness," and that "the relative totality of antiblackness is the privileged perspective from which to understand racial formation more broadly" (2015, 112). In advocating for no ground on which to stand, Day suggests, Sexton makes Blackness the only ground, where "the slave's nonrelation to her body precedes and exceeds any other body's relation to land" (Day 2015, 112). Further, Sexton's landless inhabitation of no ground on which to stand is, for American Indians, the *terra nullius* and empty lands that Europeans proclaimed to have discovered all along. Problematizing what Day sees as the impetus to dismantle "the validity of settler colonial critique by recourse to the issue of Native sovereignty," she further cautions against assumptions that "settler colonial racial capitalism is a zero sum game" (117). Instead, she provides a rigorous and detailed discussion of the limitations of Marxist critique to resolve the dialectical traps of primitive accumulation, and advocates for further engagement with Indigenous studies given its precarious and belated presence within discussions of race in American studies, postcolonial studies, and ethnic studies.

In many ways, Day's essay can and should serve as the final word on the matter, especially as she charts the distinctions between settler colonial studies and Indigenous studies and outlines productively some ways to consider how racial capitalism has always also been colonial capitalism, where the labor of U.S. empire has served the dispossession of Indigenous peoples and the theft of lands even as Indigenous people have themselves been precluded and foreclosed from any mode or means of production. However, I find that I remain troubled by the continued back-and-forth rejoinders that one field must in the end give way for the other without sitting longer with the fact that all of our scholarship is produced in the context of ongoing colonialism that uses the logics of dispossession, racial capitalism, and antiblackness to further entrench what Aileen Moreton-Robinson terms "the white possessive," a mode of colonial relationality that disavows Indigenous sovereignty and uses racialization as "the process by which whiteness operates possessively to define and construct itself as the pinnacle of its own racial hierarchy" (2015, xx). Rather than defend or indict either field, or continue to gesture to a both/and as a way forward, I want to instead pause to consider further how Indigeneity situates itself in and benefits from antiblackness even within the ongoing and daily violences enacted by U.S. colonialism and imperialism that render American Indians past-tense presences whose terra nullius absence is the necessary given so that Indigenous lands might come to hold all other formations of relationality.

One of the biggest challenges facing U.S.-based Indigenous activists, scholars, theorists, and nations themselves, then, is the fact that the conditions of our existence—and the stakes of our political survival—are tied to and produce white supremacy, antiblack racism, and the legitimacy of nation-state formations. I want to state this outright and in response to Sexton's charge so that I can elaborate further the implications of what such an admission might mean to how we understand both Indigeneity and Blackness. Moreton-Robinson has further suggested that "blackness functions as a white epistemological tool servicing the social construction of whiteness in its multiple and possessive forms, displacing Indigenous sovereignties and rendering them invisible through a civil rights discourse," and in so doing, she performs the very move of making Blackness somehow the subsidiary function of white settler colonization of Indigenous peoples, as Sexton suggests (Moreton-Robinson 2015, xxi). The same could be said for my own book, The Transit of Empire: Indigenous Critiques of Colonialism (Byrd 2011). Meanwhile, to be native to the lands stolen to provide the space, territoriality, and resources for people who arrived from elsewhere to build the country, state, culture, population, and laws to which you are rendered not only foreign but deferred as unwanted excess is to be both absolutely necessary to the founding narrative and simultaneously and entirely denied as having ever existed at all. Required but unwanted, Indigenous peoples serve as the structuring rationale through which sovereignty, subjectivity, and humanity come to be defined for settlers who have proclaimed themselves to be both the real and only natives and masters. In the context of a performance such as Lin-Manuel Miranda's (2016b) *Hamilton*, this structuring rationale means that the only time that American Indians or Indigeneity is ever mentioned in the context of the soundtrack for the Broadway show as well as its spinoffs is in an insult Hamilton makes to Congress on a demo of "Valley Forge" included on the *Hamilton Mixtape*: "Congress, I beg of you, justify your existence / Are you men or just a bunch of indigenous infants?"

In his work on the structural formations of settler colonialism, Patrick Wolfe asserts that the goal of settlement is only ever the elimination of the native, that settlers not only "come to stay," they "destroy to replace" (2006, 388). In distinguishing settler colonialism from other forms of administrative or bureaucratic colonialism, Lorenzo Veracini similarly suggests that settlers, unlike migrants, "are *founders* of political orders and carry their sovereignty with them," that while "migrants, by definition, move to *another* country and lead diasporic lives, settlers, on the contrary, move . . . to *their* country" (2010, 3). While such distinctions of elimination and founding might on the surface seem entirely commonsensical even as they appear to parse out the power differentials for those who merely migrate to arrive from those who move with the inherent sovereignty to settle wherever they go, they also naturalize the entirely taken for granted material, discursive, political, cultural, legal, and imperial machinations necessary to accomplish this sleight of hand that transforms Indigenous lands into the settler's—but not the migrant's—own home and native country from the start. It is a process of oscillation between presence and absence, significance and deferral, that resides in the very nature of sovereignty and the formation of the human. According to Lisa Lowe, "Liberal forms of political economy, culture, government, and history propose a narrative of freedom overcoming enslavement that at once denies colonial slavery, erases the seizure of lands from native peoples, displaces migrations and connections across continents, and internalizes these processes in a national struggle of history and consciousness" (2015, 3). Nowhere is this more evident than in white claims to Indigenous identity that manifest in vague gestures to Indian blood, high cheekbones, and Cherokee princess great-great-great-grandmothers on the one hand and the emotional attachment to native mascotry and dancing headdresses on the other. As Jamaica Kincaid's titular character asks with trenchant clarity in her novel *Lucy*, "How do you get to be the sort of victor who can claim to be the vanquished also?" (2002, 41).

Within such Derridian deconstructive registers of signification and différance at work in the delineation of Indigeneity and whiteness that serve as the thresholds of sovereignty in the new world, the dispossession of Indigenous lands becomes the structure, or perhaps the better word is container, that holds both antiblackness and settler colonialism. Heidi Kiiwetinepinesiik Stark's analysis of the significance of U.S. and Canadian colonial law in producing the lawless savage is useful here in demonstrating how the political and legal economies of the United States and Canada do not deny the seizure of Indigenous lands, nor do they eliminate Indigenous peoples outright. Instead, they "require Indigenous sovereignty as their own legitimacy as nation-states is constituted through the treaties that are intended to at least provide the perception of legality" (Stark 2016). Further, Stark observes, "these two nation-states could not, or would not, unequivocally dismiss or deny the existence of Indigenous sovereign authority. Instead, both nations developed and drew on legal narratives that discursively transformed and anchored the political attributes of Indigenous nations by framing treaties away from ongoing relationships to contractual events that were temporally and geographically fixed." In attaching their own settler sovereignty to the simultaneous requirement and refusal of Indigenous sovereignty, the settler states of the United States and Canada stacked the deck to ensure a continually generative and recursive inversion: that iterations of Indigenous sovereignty—and in fact, Indigenous identity itself—will likewise interpellate the settler in a dialectical feedback loop that continually reifies antiblack white supremacy even within articulations of what can only ever be perceived as Indigenous illiberal, xenophobic, and criminal resistance and resurgence.

Unfortunately, the system is rigged from the inside, and the ways to theorize ourselves outside of the impasse themselves turn on the degree to which antiblackness is always already imbricated within settler colonialism; in the process of resistance either we run the risk of obscuring lived consequences in trying to make flattened equivalencies or we risk reinscribing the ongoing discourses of both Indigenous dispossession and antiblackness. For instance, the Hegelian master-slave dialectic is often evoked within Indigenous studies as an allegory where Hegel's slave, or bondsman, stands in for the "other" that contains Indigeneity in its subordinated position within settler colonialism. But, and in spite of good-faith efforts to theorize the complexities of the colonial encounter dictated on the terms given to us all by Western philosophies, reading Hegel as just allegory to understand Indigeneity produces antiblackness as its trace when the field does not also address the simultaneous literal meanings attached to Hegel's use of the word "slave." So, when Glen Coulthard deploys Fanon's reading of Hegel to argue that, in the context of "nation-states and the sub-state national groups that they 'incorporate' into their territorial and jurisdictional boundaries," he argues that the master "does not require recognition from the previously self-determining communities upon which its territorial, economic, and social infrastructure is constituted" (Coulthard 2014, 40). And when Audra Simpson builds on Coulthard's reading to argue that "Indigeneity and its imbrication with settler colonialism question the conditions of seeing (perhaps of writing) that are laid out in the master-bondsman allegory," she asserts that "settler colonialism structures justice and injustice, in particular ways, not through the conferral of recognition of the enslaved but by the conferral of the disappearance in subject. This is *not seeing* that is so profound that mutuality cannot be achieved" (2014, 23). The *not seeing* that is the disappearance in subject is the reason why there can be nothing exceptional to point to in Indigenous colonization that does not already bring along all other global histories of oppressions and why anti-Indianness as a callout cannot mobilize any urgency connected to the present as a discourse to confront structural racism, violence, and exclusion.

But, and to follow after an angle Manu Vimalassery, Juliana Hu Pegues, and Alyosha Goldstein have already asked us to consider, the question before us still remains: "What, for example, might Indigenous politics of refusal, so far as they are critically articulated through the Hegelian lord/bondsman dialectic, look like when re-read through the lens of Blackness?" (2017, 1045). For both Coulthard and Simpson, the Hegelian dialectics of recognition and an Indigenous refusal to be eliminated require a willingness to, in Simpson's words,

> turn away from the oppressor, to avert one's gaze and refuse the recognition itself. This moment of turning away can turn us toward Haudenosaunee assertions, which in different ways tell a story about a territory of willingness, a willingness to "stay enslaved." We could see this as a political strategy that is cognizant of an unequal relationship, understands the terms of bondage, and chooses to stay within them in order to assert a greater principle: nationhood, sovereignty, jurisdiction by those who are deemed to *lack* that power, a power that is rooted in historical precedent but is conveniently forgotten or legislated away. (2014, 24)

In the context of antiblackness, that story of willingness to "stay enslaved" is for some not a matter about being willing, it is a matter of no choice at all, and here we are again at the impasse, where Indigeneity cannot be thought of outside antiblackness.

Who Tells Your Story

I first listened to the soundtrack to Lin-Manuel Miranda's *Hamilton: An American Musical* on the eight-hour drive from Champaign, Illinois, to Oxford, Mississippi, in July 2016 for a conference on Faulkner and the Native South. As an obsessed fan of Broadway musicals in high school, the buzz surrounding *Hamilton* had been constantly on my periphery for over a year as I saw it get referenced more and more often by friends on my social media feeds, and somehow I still had not managed to find the few quick minutes to track it down to give it a listen. In my anxiety about driving to Mississippi by myself as Chickasaw and gender-nonconforming queer, I figured that soundtrack would be as good a way as any to distract myself from the stretches of road and time it would take me to pass through southern Illinois, Missouri, and Tennessee to finally reach the heart of the Mississippi Delta. It was a trip that carried a fraught historical significance for me on what would be my first visit to the state—though my great-great-grand-uncle and Chickasaw Nation governor William L. Byrd had been born in what was left of Chickasaw homelands in Holly Spring, Mississippi, no one in my direct family line had lived there since he was forced to remove to Indian Territory with his parents and the ten slaves they forced with them when he was three months old. The route through Illinois to Mississippi has always been one weighted by the histories of slavery and removal, conquest and war, and Jim Crow racisms and "Mississippi Goddamn" circuits of antiblack violence that include the murders of Emmett Till, Medgar Evers, Andrew Goodman, Michael Schwerner, and James Chaney, to name just a few. As Clyde Woods observes, "Although often described as anathema to enlightened American forms of democracy and capitalism, the Mississippi Delta plantation regime is actually emblematic of a deeply rooted American form of social organization and philosophy that have provided neo-liberalism with its core organizing principles" (2007, 56). To drive to and through Chickasaw homelands where generations of my ancestors had lived, walked, and died as a now only temporary and itinerant visitor felt surreal and, frankly, sad. To do so thinking about Faulkner,

Chickasaw slave owning, and our own complicit histories in the oppressions that have defined this beloved geography felt crushing.

It turns out that *Hamilton* was the perfect soundtrack to that trip; its gleeful musical and historical riffs, its knowing callouts and ins, and its joy in form and play have made it successful for a reason. Among my favorites were the songs "Burn" and "It's Quiet Uptown," but it was Jonathan Groff's vamp as a queer King George promising to "kill your friends and family to remind you of my love" that had me replaying and relistening to the lyrics (Miranda 2015c). And yet, in the midst of that glee, and inflected by my own relation to the geography and its history outside my car windows, I found myself unable to stop the critical background voice in my head from analyzing and questioning Miranda's choices, especially with the masculinist fantasies that make women handmaids to "great men," not to mention the portrayal of Thomas Jefferson and Sally Hemings. Driving into the county in Mississippi that is named for the Marquis de Lafayette and is also Faulkner's Yaknapatawpha County (itself a Chickasaw word meaning "furrowed land"), where Faulkner's home still stands outside Oxford and his grave still receives libational offerings from fans and foes of his work, the surrealistic dissonances between the musical and Mississippi became more and more glaring, and I felt moments of deep frustration that Lin-Manuel Miranda had also reimagined Lafayette as a Haitian revolutionary leader fighting the American Revolution, as if the birth of the United States had been some fight for an anticolonial third-world liberation in a musical that does not ever even once mention American Indians. How do we chart and talk across such complex, interwoven, and violent histories in ways that help us transform them toward some kind of justice that does not require the field clearing of conquest to make Indigeneity and Blackness legible?

"In what I am calling the weather," Christina Sharpe writes, "antiblackness is pervasive *as* climate. The weather necessitates changeability and improvisation; it is the atmospheric condition of time and place; it produces new ecologies" (2016, 106). Built out of what Sharpe calls the singularity of slavery, "emancipation did not make black life free," it only proliferated the conditions of antiblackness that have now created the toxic atmospherics that steal breath, life, and air from everyone in the wake of transatlantic slavery. In a supplemental essay for *Cultural Anthropology*, Paiute scholar Kristen Simmons (2017) draws on Sharpe to further observe that "the conditions we breathe in are collective and unequally distributed, with particular qualities and intensities that are felt differently through and across time. For indigenous nations, the imbrications of U.S. militarism, industrialism, and capitalism have always been palpably felt on indigenous lands and through indigenous bodies, from extraction to experimentation. The regimes of these foundational violences are the surrounds of settler atmospherics." We live in a moment when the additive both/and feels like diffusion and distraction, where the pointing to something specific to a group or experience is deemed exceptional and exclusionary, and where the relational #metoo is both demanded and dismissed for the #onlyme. Every aspect of our political mobilization requires a purity of abjection, where any hint of power or privilege invalidates an entire argument, history, or experience.

Given that U.S. formations of freedom and liberty are built through slavery and Indigenous dispossession, looking to those formations as they are cannot and will never provide any real transformation of sociality toward anticolonial liberation. But neither will looking for a new world or a new system to build; that impulse to discover something new is what got us into this morass in the first place. In what is now Mississippi, where my own people, the Chickasaw, first encountered DeSoto and the Spanish Conquistadors, and then the French and British, where our participation in chattel slavery and plantation economies were a substantive component to how we articulated our rights to nationhood, sovereignty, and jurisdiction, we can see the organizing principles of neoliberalism at work on us. To pivot slightly off Audra Simpson and Jared Sexton, perhaps it is not a matter of choosing to stay enslaved that will lead us to a greater principle, but rather choosing a return to what remains that will allow us to turn away from state, sovereignty, and jurisdiction and toward governance, relationality, kinship, and land.

JODI A. BYRD

Abu El-Haj, Nadia. 2010. "Racial Palestinianization and the Janus-Faced Nature of the Israeli State." *Patterns of Prejudice* 44 (1).

Abu-Jamal, Mumia. 1995. *Live from Death Row*. Reading, MA: Addison-Wesley.

Abu-Laban, Yasmeen, and Abigail Bakan. 2008. "The Racial Contract: Israel/Palestine and Canada." *Social Identities* 14 (5): 637–60.

Adas, Michael. 1974. *The Burma Delta: Economic Development and Social Change on an Asian Rice Frontier*. Madison: University of Wisconsin Press.

Advancement Project. 2011. "No Child Left Behind Catalyzes 'School-to-Prison Pipeline.'" Washington, DC: Advancement Project.

African American Policy Forum. 2014. "Black Girls Matter: Pushed Out, Overpoliced and Underprotected." New York: Center for Intersectionality and Social Policy Studies.

Ahmed, A. F. Salahuddin. 2003. *Social Ideas and Social Change in Bengal*. Calcutta: Papyrus.

Ahmed, Sara. 2012. *On Being Included: Racism and Diversity in Institutional Life*. Durham, NC: Duke University Press.

Ahn, Ji-Hyun. 2013. "Visualizing Race: Neoliberal Multiculturalism and the Struggle for Koreanness in Contemporary South Korean Television." PhD diss., University of Texas, Austin.

AHSI. 1842. *Report of the Agricultural and Horticultural Society of India*. Calcutta: Bishop's College Press.

Alba, Richard. 2018. "What Majority-Minority Society? A Critical Analysis of the Census Bureau's Projections of America's Demographic Future." *Socius: Sociological Research for a Dynamic World* 4: 1–10. doi:10.1177/2378023118796932.

Alcoff, Linda Martín. 2015. *The Future of Whiteness*. Malden: Polity.

Alexander, Claire. 2017. "Breaking Black: The Death of Ethnic and Racial Studies in Britain." *Ethnic and Racial Studies* 41 (6): 1034–54. doi:10.1080/01419870.2018. 1409902.

Alexander, Michelle. 2010. *The New Jim Crow: Mass Incarceration in the Age of Colorblindness*. New York: New Press.

Alhassen, Maytha. 2017. "To Tell What the Eye Beholds: A Post 1945 Transnational History of Afro-Arab Solidarity Politics." PhD diss., Department of American Studies and Ethnicity, University of Southern California.

Ali, Tariq Omar. 2018. *A Local History of Global Capital*. Princeton, NJ: Princeton University Press.

al-Khalili, Jim. 2012. *The House of Wisdom: How Arabic Science Saved Ancient Knowledge and Gave Us the Renaissance*. New York: Penguin.

Allen, Reuben. 2017. "Investigating the Cultural Conception of Race in Puerto Rico: Residents' Thoughts on the U.S. Census, Discrimination, and Interventionist Policies." *Latin American and Caribbean Ethnic Studies* 12: 201–26.

Amin, Shahid. 1984. *Sugarcane and Sugar in Gorakhpur: An Inquiry into Peasant Production for Capitalist Enterprise in Colonial India*. Delhi: Oxford University Press.

Amnesty International. 1995. "Death in Police Custody of Joy Gardner." Amnesty International, August. https://www.amnesty.org/download/Documents/172000/eur450051995en.pdf.

Amnesty International. 2005. "Israel and the Occupied Territories: Conflict, Occupation and Patriarchy; Women Carry the Burden." Amnesty International, March. https://unispal.un.org/DPA/DPR/unispal.nsf/0/ABE29CA944AF099385256FD50055F789.

Amnesty International. 2009. *Disposable Labour: Rights of Migrant Workers in South Korea*. London: Amnesty International.

Andrews, George Reid. 2004. *Afro-Latin America, 1800–2000*. New York: Oxford University Press.

Aretxaga, Begoña. 1997. *Shattering Silence: Women, Nationalism, and Political Subjectivity in Northern Ireland*. Princeton, NJ: Princeton University Press.

Aristotle. 2013. *Aristotle's Politics*. 2nd ed. Edited and translated by Carnes Lord. Chicago: University of Chicago Press.

Arnold, David. 2005. "Agriculture and 'Improvement' in Early Colonial India: A Prehistory of Development." *Journal of Agrarian Change* 5 (4): 505–25.

Arvind, T. T. 2012. "'Though It Shocks One Very Much': Formalism and Pragmatism in the Zong and Bancoult." *Oxford Journal of Legal Studies* 32 (1): 113–51.

Asaka, Ikuko. 2017. *Tropical Freedom: Climate, Settler Colonialism, and Black Exclusion in the Age of Emancipation*. Durham, NC: Duke University Press.

Astrada, Scott B., and Marvin L. Astrada. 2017. "Being Latino in the 21st Century: Reexamining Politicized Identity and the Problem of Representation." *University of Pennsylvania Journal of Law and Social Change* 20: 245–72.

Ayers, William, Bernadine Dohrn, and Rick Ayers. 2001. *Zero Tolerance: Resisting the Drive for Punishment in Our Schools. A Handbook for Parents, Students, Educators, and Citizens*. New York: New Press.

Back, Les. 1996. *New Ethnicities and Urban Culture*. London: University College Press.

Bahk, Eun-ji. 2015. "Rep. Kim Moo-sung Sorry for Skin-Color Joke." *Korea Times*, December 18. http://www.koreatimes.co.kr/www/news/nation/2015/12/116_193519.html.

Bailey, Anne C. 2017. *The Weeping Time: Memory and the Largest Slave Auction in American History*. Cambridge: Cambridge University Press.

Bailey, Benjamin. 2001. "Dominican-American Ethnic Racial Identities and U.S. Social Categories." *International Migration Review* 35: 677–708.

Baldwin, James. 1962. *The Fire Next Time*. New York: Dell.

Baldwin, James. 1993. *Nobody Knows My Name*. New York: Vintage.

Ballagh, James Curtis. 1909. *The South in the Building of the Nation*, vol. 5. Richmond: Southern Historical Publication Society.

Baptist, Edward. 2010. "Toxic Debt, Liar Loans, and Securitized Human Beings: The Panic of 1837 and the Fate of Slavery." *Common-Place* 10 (3).

Beauchemin, Cris, Christelle Hamel, and Patrick Simon. 2009. "Trajectoires et origines: Enquête sur la diversité des populations de France (Documents de Travail #168)." Paris: Institut national d'études demographiques.

Beckert, Sven. 2014. *Empire of Cotton: A Global History*. New York: Knopf.

Behal, Rana P., and Prabhu P. Mohapatra. 1992. "'Tea and Money versus Human Life': The Rise and Fall of the Indenture System in the Assam Tea Plantations, 1840–1908." *Journal of Peasant Studies* 19 (3–4): 142–72.

Bell, Derrick. 1995. "Racial Realism." In *Critical Race Theory: The Key Writings That Formed the Movement*, edited by K. Crenshaw et al., 302–14. New York: New Press.

Bennett, Lerone, Jr. 1984. *Before the Mayflower: A History of Black America*. 5th ed. New York: Penguin.

Berger, Dan. 2014. *Captive Nation: Black Prison Organizing in the Civil Rights Era*. Chapel Hill: University of North Carolina Press.

Bernhard, Eisenach. 1828. *Travels through North America during the Years 1825 and 1826*, vol. 1. Philadelphia: Carey, Lea and Carey.

Berry, Daina Ramey. 2007. *"Swing the Sickle for the Harvest Is Ripe": Gender and Slavery in Antebellum Georgia*. Urbana: University of Illinois Press.

Berry, Daina Ramey. 2017. *The Price for Their Pound of Flesh: The Value of the Enslaved, from Womb to Grave, in the Building of a Nation*. Boston: Beacon.

Bhattacharya, Subhas. 1975. "Indigo Planters, Ram Mohan Roy and the 1833 Charter Act." *Social Scientist* 4 (3): 56–65.

Bhattacharyya, Gargi. 1998. *Tales of Dark-Skinned Women: Race, Gender and Global Culture*. Race and Representation. London: University College of London Press.

Bickerstaff, Jovonne J. 2012. "All Responses Are Not Created Equal: Variations in the Antiracist Responses of First-Generation French Blacks." *Du Bois Review: Social Science Research on Race*. 9 (1): 107–31.

Birla, Ritu. 2016. "Failure via Schumpeter: Market Globality, Empire, and the End(s) of Capitalism." *Social Research* 83 (3): 645–71.

Black, Maggie. 1936. *Federal Writers' Project: Slave Narrative Project*, vol. 14: *South Carolina, Part 1, Abrams-Durant*. Washington, DC: Library of Congress. http://hdl.loc.gov/loc.mss/mesn.141.

Blackmon, Douglas A. 2008. *Slavery by Another Name: The Re-enslavement of Black Americans from the Civil War to World War II*. New York: Doubleday.

Blake, Jamila, Betty Ray Butler, Chance W. Lewis, and Alicia Darensbourg. 2011. "Unmasking the Inequitable Discipline Experiences of Urban Black Girls: Implications for Urban Educational Stakeholders." *Urban Review* 43 (1): 90–106.

Bleich, Erik. 2000. "Antiracism without Races." *French Politics, Culture & Society* 18 (3): 48–74.

Blumrosen, Alfred W., and Ruth G. Blumrosen. 2005. *Slave Nation: How Slavery United the Colonies and Sparked the American Revolution*. Naperville, IL: Sourcebooks.

Bonilla-Silva, Eduardo. 2010. "Reflections about Race by a Negrito Acomplejao." In *The Afro-Latin@ Reader: History and Culture in the United States*, edited by Miriam Jiménez Román and Juan Flores, 445–52. Durham, NC: Duke University Press.

Bonilla-Silva, Eduardo, and David R. Dietrich. 2008. "The Latin Americanization of Racial Stratification in the U.S." In *Racism in the 21st Century: An Empirical Analysis of Skin Color*, edited by Ronald E. Hall, 151–70. New York: Springer.

Bonynge, Francis. 1851. "Cultivation of Tea, Indigo, & C." *De Bow's Review*, 45–46.

Bose, Sugata. 1991. *South Asia and World Capitalism*. Oxford: Oxford University Press.

Bosma, Ulbe. 2013. *The Sugar Plantation in India and Indonesia: Industrial Production, 1770–2010*. New York: Cambridge University Press.

Botts, Tina Fernandes, Liam Kofi Bright, Myisha Cherry, Guntur Mallarangeng, and Quayshawn Spencer. 2014. "What Is the State of Blacks in Philosophy?" *Critical Philosophy of Race* 2 (2): 224–42.

Bovenkerk, Frank, Benjamin Kilborne, François Raveau, and David Smith. 1979. "Comparative Aspects of Research on Discrimination against Non-white Citizens in Great Britain, France and the Netherlands." In *Problems in International Comparative Research in the Social Sciences*, edited by Jan Berting, Felix Geyer, and Ray Jurkovich, 105–22. Oxford: Pergamon.

Boyarin, Daniel. 1997. *Unheroic Conduct: The Rise of Heterosexuality and the Invention of the Jewish Man*. Berkeley: University of California Press.

Brennan Center for Justice. 2014. "Shifting Law Enforcement Goals to Reduce Mass Incarceration." New York: Brennan Center for Justice, September 23. https://www.brennancenter.org/sites/default/files/events/Shifting%20Law%20Enforcement%20Goals.Program%20Book.pdf.

Brennan Center for Justice. 2018. "Our Mission." New York: Brennan Center for Justice. https://www.brennancenter.org/about.

Brewster, Lawrence Fay. 1947. *Summer Migrations and Resorts of South Carolina Low-Country Planters*. New York: AMS Press,

Bridges, Khiara. 2008. *Reproducing Race: An Ethnography of Pregnancy as a Site of Racialization*. Berkeley: University of California Press.

Brown, John T. 1875. *Annual Report of the Principal Keeper*. State Prison Commission, Record Group 21-1-1, Georgia Archives, Morrow, Georgia.

Brown, Kimberly Juanita. 2015. *The Repeating Body: Slavery's Visual Resonance in the Contemporary*. Durham, NC: Duke University Press.

Brown, William Wells. 1855. *Sketches of Places and People Abroad*. Boston: John P. Jewett.

Bryan, J. 1832. "On the Culture of Rice." *Southern Agriculturist* 5 (October): 528–32.

Buck-Morss, Susan. 2000. "Hegel and Haiti." *Critical Inquiry* 26 (4): 821–65.

Bukhari, Safiya. 2010. *The War Before: The True Life Story of Becoming a Black Panther, Keeping the Faith in Prison and Fighting for Those Left Behind.* New York: Feminist Press.

Burbank, Jane, and Frederick Cooper. 2010. *Empires in World History: Power and the Politics of Difference.* Princeton, NJ: Princeton University Press.

Burton, Orisanmi. 2016. "Attica Is: Revolutionary Consciousness, Counterinsurgency and the Deferred Abolition of New York State Prisons." PhD diss., Department of Anthropology, University of North Carolina.

Byrd, Alexander X. 2008. *Captives and Voyagers: Black Migrants across the Eighteenth-Century British Atlantic World.* Baton Rouge: Louisiana State University Press.

Byrd, Jodi A. 2011. *The Transit of Empire: Indigenous Critiques of Colonialism.* Minneapolis: University of Minnesota Press.

Cabella, Wanda, Mathías Nathan, and Mariana Tenenbaum. 2013. *Atlas Sociodemográfico y de la Desigualdad del Uruguay.* Montevideo: Ediciones Trilce.

Cabnal, Lorena. 2019. "El relato de las violencias desde mi territorio cuerpo-tierra." In *En Tiempos de Muerte: Cuerpos, Rebeldias, Resistencias,* edited by Xochitl Leyva Solano and Rosalba Icaza, 113–23. Buenos Aires y San Cristobal de Las Casas, Chiapas: CLACSCO, Cooperativo Editorial Retos, ISS/EUR (Tomo IV).

California State Legislature. 2015. California Education Code, Title Elementary and Secondary Education, Chapter 6, Pupil Rights and Responsibilities, Article 1, Suspension or Expulsion. http://leginfo.legislature.ca.gov/faces/codes _displayText.xhtml?lawCode=EDC&division=4.&title=2.&part=27.&chapter=6 .&article=1.

Campbell, Gwyn. 2005. "African Diaspora in Asia." In *Encyclopedia of Diasporas: Immigrant and Refugee Cultures around the World,* edited by Melvin Ember, Carol R. Ember, and Ian Skoggard, 3–15. New York: Springer.

Campion, Karis. 2019. "Diane Abbott and 'Misogynoir': Colourism, Anti-blackness and Sexism in the UK." *The Conversation,* February 1. https://theconversation .com/diane-abbott-and-misogynoir-colourism-anti-blackness-and-sexism-in-the -uk-110413.

Carney, Judith A. 2004. "'With Grains in Her Hair': Rice in Colonial Brazil." *Slavery and Abolition* 25 (1): 1–27.

Carney, Judith. 2009. *Black Rice: The African Origins of Rice Cultivation in the Americas.* Cambridge, MA: Harvard University Press.

Carter, Lashonda, and Tiffany Willoughby-Herard. 2018. "What Kind of Mother Is She? From Margaret Garner to Rosa Lee Ingram to Mamie Till to the Murder of Korryn Gaines." *Theory and Event* 21 (1): 88–105.

Cartwright, Samuel. 1851. "Report on the Diseases and Physical Peculiarities of the Negro Race." *New Orleans Medical and Surgical Journal* (May): 691–715.

Chambers-Letson, Joshua. 2016. "Performance's Mode of Reproduction I: Searching for Dan Võ's Mother." *Women and Performance: A Journal of Feminist Theory* 26 (2–3): 122–45.

Chang, Gordon H. 2003. "Whose 'Barbarism'? Whose 'Treachery'? Race and Civilization in the Unknown United States–Korea War of 1871." *Journal of American History* 89 (4): 1331–65.

Chang, Hao. 1971. *Liang Ch'i-ch'ao and Intellectual Transition in China, 1890–1907.* Cambridge, MA: Harvard University Press.

Chapin, Ralph. (1923) 2003. "Solidarity Forever!" In *I.W.W. Songs to Fan the Flames of Discontent.* 19th ed. Reprint, Chicago: Charles H. Kerr.

Chaplin, Joyce. 1993. *An Anxious Pursuit: Agricultural Innovation and Modernity in the Lower South, 1730–1815.* Chapel Hill: University of North Carolina Press, 1993.

Chen, Chris. 2013. "The Limit Point of Capitalist Equality: Notes toward an Abolitionist Antiracism." *Endnotes* 3. https://endnotes.org.uk/issues/3/en/chris-chen -the-limit-point-of-capitalist-equality.

Chesney-Lind, Meda, and Katherine Irwin. 2008. *Beyond Bad Girls: Gender, Violence and Hype.* New York: Routledge.

Chigwada-Bailey, Ruth. 1991. "The Policing of Black Women." In *Out of Order: Policing Black People,* edited by Ernest Cashmore and Eugene McLaughlin, 134–50. New York: Routledge.

Chigwada-Bailey, Ruth. 2003. *Black Women's Experiences of Criminal Justice: A Discourse on Disadvantage.* Winchester, UK: Waterside.

Childs, Dennis. 2015. *Slaves of the State: Black Incarceration from the Chain Gang to the Penitentiary.* Minneapolis: University of Minnesota Press.

Choe, Sang-Hun. 2016. "Korean Official, Calling for Class System, Hears Woofs, Oinks and Outrage." *New York Times,* July 12. https://www.nytimes.com/2016/07 /13/world/asia/south-korea-education-ministry.html.

Choi, Hyaeweol. 2000. "Women's Literacy and New Womanhood in Late Choson Korea." *Asian Journal of Women's Studies* 6 (1): 88–115.

Chow, Cai-wing. 1997. "Imagining Boundaries of Blood: Zhang Binglin and the Invention of the Han 'Race' in Modern China." In *The Construction of Racial Identities in China and Japan,* edited by Frank Dikötter, 34–52. Honolulu: University of Hawai'i Press.

Chrisafis, Angelique. 2017. "French Police Brutality in Spotlight Again After Officer Charged with Rape." *The Guardian,* February 6. https://www.theguardian.com /world/2017/feb/06/french-police-brutality-in-spotlight-again-after-officer -charged-with.

Christian, Barbara. 1988. "The Race for Theory." *Feminist Studies* 14 (1): 67–79.

Christie, Nils. 2000. *Crime Control as Industry: Towards Gulags, Western Style.* London: Routledge.

Chung, Yuehtsen Juliette. 2002. *Struggle for National Survival: Eugenics in Sino-Japanese Contexts, 1896–1945.* New York: Routledge.

City Rustic. 1828. "On the Pounding of Rice." *Southern Agriculturist* 1 (August): 351–52.

Claiborne, James H. 1828. "Answers: Queries on the Culture of Rice." *Southern Agriculturist* 1 (July): 309–11.

Clarín. 2006. "Casi dos millones de argentinos tienen sus raíces en el Africa negra." *Clarín,* September 6.

Clarke Kaplan, Sara. 2007. "Love and Violence/Maternity and Death: Black Feminism and the Politics of Reading (Un)representability." *Black Women, Gender + Families* 1 (1): 94–124.

Cleland, Danielle Pilar. 2017. *The Power of Race in Cuba: Racial Ideology and Black Consciousness during the Revolution.* New York: Oxford University Press.

Clifton, James M. 1978a. "Charles Manigault's Essay on the Economics of Milling Rice [1852]." *Agricultural History* 52: 104–10.

Clifton, James M. 1978b. *Life and Labor on Argyle Island: Letters and Documents of a Savannah Rice Plantation, 1833–1867.* Savannah: The Beehive Press.

Clifton, James M. 1981. "The Rice Driver: His Role in Slave Management." *South Carolina Historical Magazine* 82: 331–53.

Clifton, James M. 1985. "Jehossee Island: The Antebellum South's Largest Rice Plantation." *Agricultural History* 59 (1): 56–65.

Clinton, Hillary. 1996. "Hillary Clinton Campaign Speech." CSPAN, January 25. https://www.c-span.org/video/?69606-1/hillary-clinton-campaign-speech.

Clinton, Hillary. 2015. Verified Twitter account. https://twitter.com/HillaryClinton /status/593449489207304192.

Coates, Ta-Nehisi. 2017. "The First White President." *The Atlantic*, October. https:// www.theatlantic.com/magazine/archive/2017/10/the-first-white-president-ta -nehisi-coates/537909.

Coclanis, Peter. 1993. "Distant Thunders: The Creation of a World Rice Market and the Transformations It Wrought." *American Historical Review* 98 (4): 1050–78.

Cohen, William B. (1980) 2003. *The French Encounter with Africans: White Response to Blacks, 1530–1880.* Bloomington: Indiana University Press.

Cohn, D'Vera. 2010. "Census History: Counting Hispanics." Pew Research Center Social and Demographic Trends, March 3. https://www.pewsocialtrends.org /2010/03/03/census-history-counting-hispanics-2/.

Cohn, D'Vera. 2014. "Millions of Americans Changed Their Racial or Ethnic Identity from One Census to the Next." Pew Research Center: Fact Tank News in the Numbers, May 4. https://www.pewresearch.org/fact-tank/2014/05/05/millions -of-americans-changed-their-racial-or-ethnic-identity-from-one-census-to-the -next/.

Collins, Patricia Hill. 2019. *Intersectionality as Critical Social Theory.* Durham, NC: Duke University Press.

Comas-Diaz, Lillian. 1996. "LatiNegra: Mental Health Issues of African Latinas." In *The Multiracial Racial Borders as New Frontier*, edited by Maria P. P. Root, 167–90. New York: Sage.

Combahee River Collective. 1983. "The Combahee River Collective Statement." In *Home Girls: A Black Feminist Anthology*, edited by Barbara Smith. New York: Kitchen Table: Women of Color Press. http://circuitous.org/scraps/combahee .html.

Commission Nationale Consultative des Droits de l'Homme. 2019. "Rapport sur la lutte contre le racisme, l'antisémitisme et la xénophobie. Focus: Lutter contre

le racisme anti-noirs." https://www.cncdh.fr/sites/default/files/rapport_racisme
_2019_focus_racisme_anti-noirs_vdef.pdf.

Comité Pour La Mémoire de L'esclavage. 2005. "Mémoires de la traite négrière, de
l'esclavage et de leurs abolitions." April 12. https://www.vie-publique.fr/sites
/default/files/rapport/pdf/054000247.pdf.

Conway, Marshall, and Dominque Stevenson. 2011. *Marshall Law: The Life and Times
of a Baltimore Black Panther*. Oakland, CA: AK Press.

Conyers, Susan. 1894. Clemency Petition. Applications for Clemency 1858–1942. Convict and Fugitive Papers, Record Group 1-4-42, Georgia Archives, Morrow, Georgia.

Cooper, Frederick. 2005. *Colonialism in Question: Theory, Knowledge, History*. Berkeley: University of California Press.

Cordis, Shanya. 2019. "Forging Relational Difference: Racial Gendered Violence and
Dispossession in Guyana." *small axe* 23 (3): 18–33.

Coulthard, Glen. 2014. *Red Skin, White Masks: Rejecting the Colonial Politics of Recognition*. Minneapolis: University of Minnesota Press.

Cox, Jane, and Katherine Sacks-Jones. 2017. *"Double Disadvantage": The Experiences of
Black, Asian and Minority Ethnic Women in the Criminal Justice System*. London:
Agenda: Alliance for Women and Girls at Risk. https://www.womeninprison.org
.uk/perch/resources/double-disadvantage-1.pdf.

Crenshaw, Kimberlé. 1995. *Critical Race Theory: The Key Writings That Formed the
Movement*. New York: New Press.

Crenshaw, Kimberlé. 2012. "From Private Violence to Mass Incarceration: Thinking
Intersectionally about Women, Race, and Social Control." *UCLA Law Review* 59
(6): 1418–72.

Crenshaw, Kimberlé. 2020. *On Intersectionality: Essential Writings*. New York: New Press.

Crenshaw, Kimberlé, and Andrea J. Ritchie with Rachel Anspach, Rachel Gilmer,
and Luke Harris. 2015. "Say Her Name: Resisting Police Brutality against Black
Women." African American Policy Forum. New York: Center for Intersectionality and Social Policy Studies.

Cruz-Janzen, Marta I. 2007. "Madre Patria (Mother Country): Latino Identity and
Rejection of Blackness." *Trotter Review* 17: 79–92.

Curry, Tommy J., and Gwenetta Curry. 2018. "On the Perils of Race Neutrality and
Anti-blackness: Philosophy as an Irreconcilable Obstacle to (Black) Thought."
American Journal of Economics and Sociology 77: 657–87.

Dadouch, Sarah. 2020. "Black Lives Matter Protests Spark Debate over Racism in the
Arab World." *Washington Post*. July 8. https://www.washingtonpost.com/world
/middle_east/black-lives-matter-protests-spark-debate-over-racism-in-the-arab
-world/2020/07/07/83234c5e-b7ab-11ea-9a1d-d3db1cbe07ce_story.html.

Dalla Costa, Mariarosa. 1972. *The Power of Women and the Subversion of the Community*. Bristol, U.K.: Falling Wall.

Danner, Deborah. 2012. "Living with Schizophrenia." January 28. https://assets
.documentcloud.org/documents/3146953/Living-With-Schizophrenia-by
-Deborah-Danner.pdf.

Darity, William, Jr., Darrick Hamilton, and Jason Dietrich. 2010. "Passing on Blackness: Latinos, Race and Earnings in the USA." *Applied Economics Letters* 9: 847–53.

Davis, Adrienne. 2002. "'Don't Let Nobody Bother Yo' Principle': The Sexual Economy of American Slavery." In *Sister Circle: Black Women and Work*, edited by S. Hartley. New Brunswick, NJ: Rutgers University Press.

Davis, Angela Y. 1971. "Reflections on the Black Woman's Role in the Community of Slaves." *Black Scholar* 3 (4): 2–15.

Davis, Angela. 1981. "The Approaching Obsolescence of Housework." In *Women, Race, and Class*, 222–24. New York: Random House.

Davis, Angela Y. 1983. *Women, Race and Class*. New York: Vintage.

Davis, Angela Y. 1998. "From the Prison of Slavery to the Slavery of Prison: Frederick Douglass and the Convict Lease System." In *The Angela Y. Davis Reader*, edited by Joy James, 74–95. Malden, MA: Blackwell.

Davis, David Brion. 2006. *Inhuman Bondage: The Rise and Fall of Slavery in the New World*. New York: Oxford University Press.

Davis, J. E., and W. J. Jordan. 1994. "The Effects of School Context, Structure, and Experiences on African American Males in Middle and High School." *Journal of Negro Education* 63 (4): 570–87.

Dawber, Alistair. 2013. "Israel Gave Birth Control to Ethiopian Jews without Their Consent." *Independent*, January 27. http://www.independent.co.uk/news/world /middle-east/israel-gave-birth-control-to-ethiopian-jews-without-their-consent -8468800.html.

Day, Iyko. 2015. "Being and Nothingness: Indigeneity, Antiblackness, and Settler Colonial Critique." *Critical Ethnic Studies* 1 (2): 102–21.

Dayan, Colin. 2007. *The Story of Cruel and Unusual*. Cambridge, MA: MIT Press.

D'Cruz, J. V., and William Steele. 2000. *Australia's Ambivalence towards Asia: Politics, Neo/Post-colonialism, and Fact/Fiction*. Melbourne: Monash Asia Institute, Monash University Press.

Deb, Radhakanta. 1836a. "On the Cultivation of Cotton and Tobacco in Central India." *Transactions of the Agricultural and Horticultural Society of India* 2: 70–73.

Deb, Radhakanta. 1836b. "On the Culture of Paddy in Twenty Different Districts." *Transactions of the Agricultural and Horticultural Society of India* 2: 193–95.

de Bellaigue, Christopher. 2017. *The Islamic Enlightenment: The Struggle between Faith and Reason, 1798 to Modern Times*. New York: Liveright/W. W. Norton.

De Genova, Nicholas, and Ana Y. Ramos-Zayas. 2003. *Latino Crossings: Mexicans, Puerto Ricans, and the Politics of Race and Citizenship*. New York: Routledge.

Dewan, Angela. 2020. "Indians Are Being Held Up as a Model Minority. That's Not Helping the Black Lives Matter Movement." CNN, June 29. Accessed July 8, 2020. https://www.cnn.com/2020/06/29/world/indians-migrant-minority-black -lives-matter-intl/index.html.

DiAngelo, Robin. 2018. *White Fragility: Why It's So Hard for White People to Talk About Racism*. Boston: Beacon Press.

Dickens, Charles. 1856. "Rice." *Household Words* 33: 6–14.

DiFulco, Denise. 2003. "Can You Tell a Mexican from a Puerto Rican?" *Latina* 8 (1): 86–88.

Dikötter, Frank. 1992. *The Discourse of Race in Modern China*. Stanford, CA: Stanford University Press.

Dikötter, Frank, ed. 1997a. *The Construction of Racial Identities in China and Japan*. Honolulu: University of Hawai'i Press.

Dikötter, Frank. 1997b. "Introduction." In *The Construction of Racial Identities in China and Japan*, edited by Frank Dikötter, 1–11. Honolulu: University of Hawai'i Press.

Dillon, Stephen. 2012. "Possessed by Death: The Neoliberal Carceral State, Black Feminism, and the Afterlife of Slavery." *Radical History Review*, no. 112: 113–25.

Dinzey-Flores, Zaire Zenit. 2013. *Locked In, Locked Out: Gated Communities in a Puerto Rican City*. Philadelphia: University of Pennsylvania Press.

Dongnipsinmungangdokoe. 2004. *Dongnipsinmun Dasi Ikgi*. Seoul: Pureunyeoksa.

Donne, John. (1633) 2004. "At the Round Earth's Imagined Corners (Holy Sonnet 7)." In *John Donne: The Complete English Poems*. New York: Penguin Classics.

Donziger, Steven R., ed. 1996. *The Real War on Crime: The Report of the National Criminal Justice Commission*. New York: HarperCollins.

Douglass, Patrice D. 2018. "Black Feminist Theory for the Dead and the Dying." *Theory and Event* 21 (1): 106–23.

Draper, Nicholas. 2013. *The Price of Emancipation: Slave-Ownership, Compensation and British Society at the End of Slavery*. Cambridge: Cambridge University Press.

Dresslar, Thomas. 2016. "How Many Law Enforcement Agencies Does It Take to Subdue a Peaceful Protest?" ACLU, November 30. https://www.aclu.org/blog /free-speech/rights-protesters/how-many-law-enforcement-agencies-does-it -take-subdue-peaceful.

Drucker, Peter F. 1955. *The Practice of Management*. Oxford: Elsevier.

Druelle, Aline. 2018. "Dunkerque: Une 'Nuit des Noirs' controversée jusqu'au bout." RCI FM, March 10. https://www.rci.fm/infos/societe/dunkerque-une-nuit-des -noirs-controversee-jusquau-bout.

Duany, Jorge. 2002. *The Puerto Rican Nation on the Move: Identities on the Island and the United States*. Chapel Hill: University of North Carolina Press.

Du Bois, W. E. B. (1899) 1996. *The Philadelphia Negro*. Philadelphia: University of Pennsylvania Press.

Du Bois, W. E. B. (1900) 1996. "The Present Outlook of the Darker Races of Mankind." In *The Oxford W.E.B. Du Bois Reader*, edited by E. J. Sundquist, 47–54. New York: Oxford University Press.

Du Bois, W. E. B. (1903) 1965. *The Souls of Black Folk*. In *Three Negro Classics*, 207–389. New York: Avon.

Du Bois, W. E. B. (1903) 1997. *The Souls of Black Folk*, edited by David W. Blight and Robert Gooding-Williams. Boston: Bedford.

Du Bois, W. E. B. (1906) 2005. "The Color Line Belts the World." In *W.E.B. Du Bois on Asia: Crossing the World Color Line*, edited by Bill V. Mullen and Cathryn Watson, 33–34. Jackson: University Press of Mississippi.

Du Bois, W. E. B. 1935. *Black Reconstruction*. New York: Russell and Russell.

Dusinberre, William. 1996. *Them Dark Days: Slavery in the American Rice Swamps*. New York: Oxford University Press.

Dzidzienyo, Anani, and Suzanne Oboler, eds. 2005. *Neither Enemies nor Friends: Latinos, Blacks, Afro-Latinos*. New York: Palgrave Macmillan.

Eberhardt, Jennifer, Phillip Atiba Goff, Valerie J. Purdie, and Paul G. Davies. 2004. "Seeing Black: Race, Crime, and Visual Processing." *Journal of Personality and Social Psychology* 87 (6): 876–93.

Ebrahimji, Alisha, and Alicia Lee. 2020. "Meet the Asian Americans Helping to Uproot Racism in Their Communities." CNN, June 13. Accessed July 8, 2020. https://www.cnn.com/2020/06/13/us/asian-americans-blm-conversations-trnd /index.html.

Eckert, Carter J., Ki-baik Lee, Young Ick Lew, Michael Robinson, and Edward W. Wagner. 1990. *Korea Old and New: A History*. Seoul: Ilchokak.

Egerton, Douglass R. 1999. *He Shall Go Out Free: The Lives of Denmark Vesey*. Lanham, MD: Rowman and Littlefield.

Eisen, Lauren-Brooke, Nicole Fortier, and Inimai Chettiar. 2014. *Federal Prosecution for the 21st Century*. New York: Brennan Center for Justice. http://www .brennancenter.org/sites/default/files/analysis/Federal_Prosecution_For_21st _Century.pdf.

Elgot, Jennifer. 2018. "Theresa May's 'Hostile Environment' at Heart of Windrush Scandal." *The Guardian*, April 17. https://www.theguardian.com/uk-news/2018 /apr/17/theresa-mays-hostile-environment-policy-at-heart-of-windrush-scandal.

Eliav-Feldon, Miriam, Benjamin Isaac, and Joseph Ziegler, eds. 2013. *The Origins of Racism in the West*. New York: Cambridge University Press.

Elliot, E. 1851. "History and Cultivation of Rice." *De Bow's Review* 11: 305–7.

Ellison, Ralph. (1952) 1995. *Invisible Man*. New York: Vintage.

El Telégrafo. 2011. "Los afroecuatorianos en el censo de población 2010." *El Telégrafo*, September 11. http://www.eltelegrafo.com.ec/noticias/columnistas/1/los -afroecuatorianos-en-el-censo-de-poblacion-2010.

Eltis, David. 1993. "Europeans and the Rise and Fall of African Slavery in the Americas: An Interpretation." *American Historical Review* 98 (5): 1399–1423.

Eltis, David, Philip Morgan, and David Richardson. 2007. "Agency and Diaspora in Atlantic History: Reassessing the African Contribution to Rice Cultivation in the Americas." *American Historical Review* 12 (5): 1329–58.

Eltis, David, Philip Morgan, and David Richardson. 2010. "Black, Brown, or White? Color-Coding American Commercial Rice Cultivation with Slave Labor." *American Historical Review* 115 (1): 164–71.

Em, Henry H. 1999. "*Minjok* as a Modern and Democratic Construct: Sin Ch'aeho's Historiography." In *Colonial Modernity in Korea*, edited by Gi-Wook Shin and Michael Robinson, 336–62. Cambridge, MA: Harvard University Press.

Em, Henry H. 2013. *The Great Enterprise: Sovereignty and Historiography in Modern Korea*. Durham, NC: Duke University Press.

Ennis, Sharon R., Merarys-Rios Vargas, and Nora G. Albert. 2011. *The Hispanic Population: 2010*. Washington, DC: U.S. Census Bureau. http://www.census.gov/prod/cen2010/briefs/c2010br-04.pdf.

Erakat, Noura. 2015. "Whiteness as Property in Israel: Revival, Rehabilitation, and Removal." *Harvard Journal on Racial and Ethnic Justice* 31: 69–103.

Erakat, Noura, and Lamont Hill, Marc. 2019. "Black-Palestinian Transnational Solidarity: Renewals, Returns, and Practice." *Journal of Palestine Studies* 48 (4): 7–16.

Estes, Nick. 2016. "Fighting for Our Lives: #NoDAPL in Historical Context." *Red Nation*, September 18. https://therednation.org/2016/09/18/fighting-for-our-lives-nodapl-in-context/.

Falk, Rafael. 2006. *Zionism and the Biology of the Jews*. Tel Aviv, Israel: Resling.

Fanon, Frantz. 1963. *The Wretched of the Earth*. New York: Grove.

Fanon, Frantz. 1967a. *Black Skin, White Masks*. Translated by Charles Lam Markmann. New York: Grove.

Fanon, Frantz. 1967b. *Toward the African Revolution*. New York: Grove.

Fanon, Frantz. 1991. *Black Skin, White Masks*. New York: Grove.

Farley, Anthony. 2005. "Perfecting Slavery." *Loyola University Chicago Law Journal* 36 (1): 221–51.

Feagin, Joe R. 2013. *The White Racial Frame: Centuries of Racial Framing and Counter-framing*. 2nd ed. New York: Routledge.

Federici, Silvia. 2004. *Caliban and the Witch: Women, the Body and Primitive Accumulation*. New York: Autonomedia.

Feldman, Keith P. 2015. *A Shadow over Palestine: The Imperial Life of Race in America*. Minneapolis: University of Minnesota Press.

Ferguson, Ann A. 2001. *Bad Boys: Public Schools in the Making of Black Masculinity*. Ann Arbor: University of Michigan Press.

Ferguson, Roderick A. 2004. *Aberrations in Black: Toward a Queer of Color Critique*. Minneapolis: University of Minnesota Press.

Ferguson, Susan. 2016. "Intersectionality and Social-Reproduction Feminisms." *Historical Materialism* 24 (2): 38–60.

Fezehai, Malin. 2019. "The Disappeared Children of Israel." *New York Times*, February 20. https://www.nytimes.com/2019/02/20/world/middleeast/israel-yemenite-children-affair.html.

Fields-Black, Edda L. 2008. *Deep Roots: Rice Farmers in West Africa and the African Diaspora*. Bloomington: Indiana University Press.

Fish, Isaac Stone. 2014. "Obama, Don't Take It Personally, North Korea Just Hates Black People." *Foreign Policy*, May 8. http://foreignpolicy.com/2014/05/08/obama-dont-take-it-personally-north-korea-just-hates-black-people.

Fisher, Clara Lee. 2009. "Letter to Thomas Jefferson about Barack Obama." *Newsweek*, January 19. http://www.newsweek.com/letter-thomas-jefferson-about-barack-obama-78347.

Fitzpatrick, Ellen. 1990. *Endless Crusade: Women Social Scientists and Progressive Reform*. New York: Oxford University Press.

Fitzpatrick, Pamela. 2006. "Right to Reside: New Rules." Child Poverty Action Group, June 1. http://www.cpag.org.uk/content/right-reside-%E2%80%93-new-rules.

Flannery, Mary Ellen. 2015. "The School-to-Prison Pipeline: Time to Shut it Down." NEA Today, January 5. http://neatoday.org/2015/01/05/school-prison-pipeline -time-shut/.

Fleming, Crystal M. 2011. "The Educational Experiences of Caribbeans in France." In Education in the Black Diaspora, edited by Kassie Freeman, Ethan Johnson, and Kelvin Shawn Sealey, 79–98. London: Routledge.

Fleming, Crystal M. 2017. Resurrecting Slavery: Racial Legacies and White Supremacy in France. Philadelphia: Temple University Press.

Fleming, Crystal M. 2018. How to Be Less Stupid about Race: On Racism, White Supremacy, and the Racial Divide. Boston: Beacon.

Fletcher, Michael A. 2000. "The Blond, Blue-Eyed Face of Spanish TV." Washington Post, August 3, A01.

Flores, Carlos. 2001. "Race Discrimination within the Latino Community." Diálogo 5 (winter/spring): 30–31.

Florio, Christopher. 2016. "From Poverty to Slavery: Abolitionists, Overseers, and the Global Struggle for Labor in India." Journal of American History 102 (4): 1005–24.

Foucault, Michel. 1977. Discipline and Punish: The Birth of the Prison. New York: Vintage.

Frank, Reanne, Ilana Redstone Akresh, and Bo Lu. 2010. "Latino Immigrants and the U.S. Racial Order: How and Where Do They Fit In?" American Sociological Review 75 (3): 378–401.

Franklin, John Hope, and Loren Schweninger. 1999. Runaway Slaves: Rebels on the Plantation. Oxford: Oxford University Press.

Fredrickson, George M. 2015. Racism: A Short History. Princeton, NJ: Princeton University Press.

Freud, Sigmund. (1900) 2010. The Interpretation of Dreams. New York: Basic Books.

Frizell, Sam. 2015. "Hillary Clinton Calls for an End to 'Mass Incarceration.'" Time, April 29. http://time.com/3839892/hillary-clinton-calls-for-an-end-to-mass -incarceration/.

Fuentes, Annette. 2012. "Arresting Development: Zero Tolerance and the Criminalization of Children." Rethinking Schools 26 (2): 18–23.

Fullilove, Courtney. 2017. The Profit of the Earth: The Global Seeds of American Agriculture. Chicago: University of Chicago Press.

Furman, Jason, and Douglas Holtz-Eakin. 2016. "Why Mass Incarceration Doesn't Pay." New York Times, April 21. https://www.nytimes.com/2016/04/21/opinion /why-mass-incarceration-doesnt-pay.html.

Gelb, Joyce. 1989. Feminism and Politics: A Comparative Perspective. Berkeley: University of California Press.

Giacaman, Rita, N. M. E. Abu-Rmeileh, and L. Wick. 2006. "The Limitations on Choice: Palestinian Women's Childbirth Location, Dissatisfaction with the Place of Birth and Determinants." European Journal of Public Health 17: 86–91.

Gillies, Donna, Fiona Taylor, Carl Gray, Louise O'Brien, and Natalie D'Abrew. 2013. "Psychological Therapies for the Treatment of Post-Traumatic Stress Disorder in Children and Adolescents." *Evidence-Based Child Health: A Cochrane Review Journal* 8 (3): 1004–16.

Gilman, Sander. 1991. *The Jew's Body*. New York: Routledge.

Gilmore, Craig. 2019. "On the Business of Incarceration." *Commune*, July 12. https://communemag.com/on-the-business-of-incarceration/.

Gilmore, Ruth Wilson. 2002. "Race and Globalization." In *Geographies of Global Change: Remapping the World*, edited by R. J. Johnston et al. New York: Wiley-Blackwell.

Gilmore, Ruth Wilson. 2007. *Golden Gulag: Prisons, Surplus, Crisis, and Opposition in Globalizing California*. Berkeley: University of California Press.

Gilmore, Ruth Wilson. 2015. "The Worrying State of the Anti-prison Movement." *Social Justice*, February 23. http://www.socialjusticejournal.org/the-worrying-state-of-the-anti-prison-movement/.

Gilmore, Ruth Wilson. 2019. "Prisons and Class Warfare: An Interview with Ruth Wilson Gilmore." *Verso Blog*, August 2. https://www.versobooks.com/blogs/3954-prisons-and-class-warfare-an-interview-with-ruth-wilson-gilmore.

Gilroy, Paul. 1993. *The Black Atlantic: Modernity and Double Consciousness*. Cambridge, MA: Harvard University Press.

Givens, T. E. 2014. "The Impact of the European Union's Racial Equality Directive on Antidiscrimination Policy and Black People in France." In *Visible Invisible Minority: Confronting Afrophobia and Advancing Equality for People of African Descent and Black Europeans in Europe*. Brussels: ENAR. https://www.enar-eu.org/IMG/pdf/book_-_people_of_african_descent_-_final-2.pdf.

Glenn, Evelyn Nakano. 2015. "Settler Colonialism as Structure: A Framework for Comparative Studies of U.S. Race and Gender Formation." *Sociology of Race and Ethnicity* 1 (1): 52–72.

Glissant, Edouard. 1997. *Poetics of Relation*. Ann Arbor: University of Michigan Press.

Glymph, Thavolia. 2008. *Out of the House of Bondage: The Transformation of the Plantation Household*. Cambridge, MA: Harvard University Press.

Go, Julian. 2016. *Postcolonial Thought and Social Theory*. New York: Oxford University Press.

Gobineau, Arthur de. 1999. *The Inequality of Human Races*. New York: Howard Fertig.

Godreau, Isar P. 2015. *Scripts of Blackness: Race, Cultural Nationalism, and U.S. Colonialism in Puerto Rico*. Champaign: University of Illinois Press.

Goeman, Mishuana. 2017. "Ongoing Storms and Struggles: Gendered Violence and Resource Exploitation." In *Critically Sovereign: Indigenous Gender, Sexuality, and Feminist Studies*, edited by Joanne Barker. Durham, NC: Duke University Press.

Goethe, Johann Wolfgang von. (1808) 1985. *Faust*. New York: Bantam.

Goff, Phillip A., Jennifer L. Eberhardt, Melissa J. Williams, and Matthew Christian Jackson. 2008. "Not Yet Human: Implicit Knowledge, Historical Dehumanization, and Contemporary Consequences." *Journal of Personality and Social Psychology* 94 (7): 292–306.

Goh, Daniel P. S. 2007. "Imperialism and 'Medieval' Natives." *International Journal of Cultural Studies* 10 (3): 323–41.

Golash-Boza, Tanya, and William Darity Jr. 2008. "Latino Racial Choices: The Effects of Skin Colour and Discrimination on Latinos' and Latinas' Racial Self-Identifications." *Ethnic and Racial Studies* 31: 899–934.

Goldberg, David Theo. 2002. *The Racial State.* Malden, MA: Blackwell.

Goldberg, David Theo. 2008. "Racial Palestinianization." In *Thinking Palestine*, edited by Ronit Lentin. London: Zed.

Goldberg, David Theo. 2009. *The Threat of Race.* New York: Wiley-Blackwell.

Goldenberg, David M. 2003. *The Curse of Ham: Race and Slavery in Early Judaism, Christianity, and Islam.* Princeton, NJ: Princeton University Press.

Goldenberg, David M. 2013. "Racism, Color Symbolism, and Color Prejudice." In *The Origins of Racism in the West*, edited by M. Elian-Feldon, B. Isaac, and J. Ziegler, 88–108. New York: Cambridge University Press.

Gomez, Michael. 1998. *Exchanging Our Country Marks: The Transformation of African Identities in the Colonial and Antebellum South.* Chapel Hill: University of North Carolina Press.

Gonzalez-Barrera, Ana. 2019. "Hispanics with Darker Skin Are More Likely to Experience Discrimination Than Those with Lighter Skin." Pew Research Center Fact Tank: News in the Numbers, July 2. https://www.pewresearch.org/fact -tank/2019/07/02/hispanics-with-darker-skin-are-more-likely-to-experience -discrimination-than-those-with-lighter-skin/.

Gooding-Williams, Robert. 2009. *In the Shadow of Du Bois: Afro-Modern Political Thought in America.* Cambridge, MA: Harvard University Press.

Gopnik, Adam. 2012. "The Caging of America." *New Yorker*, January 30. https://www .newyorker.com/magazine/2012/01/30/the-caging-of-america.

Gordon, Avery. 1997. *Ghostly Matters: Haunting and the Sociological Imagination.* Minneapolis: University of Minnesota Press.

Gordon, Lewis R. 1995. *Bad Faith and Antiblack Racism.* Atlantic Highlands, NJ: Humanities.

Gordon, Lewis R. 2005. "Through the Zone of Nonbeing: A Reading of *Black Skin, White Masks* in Celebration of Fanon's Eightieth Birthday." *CLR James Journal* 11 (1): 1–43.

Gordon, Lewis R. 2015. *What Fanon Said: A Philosophical Introduction to His Life and Thought.* New York: Fordham University Press.

Gordon-Reed, Annette, and Titus Kaphar. 2017. "Are We Actually Citizens Here?" *On Being*, June 29. https://onbeing.org/programs/annette-gordon-reed-and-titus -kaphar-are-we-actually-citizens-here-jun2017/.

Gosin, Monika. 2017. "'A Bitter Diversion': Afro-Cuban Immigrants, Race, and Everyday-Life Resistance." *Latino Studies* 15: 4–28.

Gracia, Jorge J. E., ed. 2007. *Race or Ethnicity: On Black and Latino Identity.* Ithaca, NY: Cornell University Press.

Gravlee, Clarence C., William W. Dressler, and H. Russell Bernard. 2005. "Skin Color, Social Classification, and Blood Pressure in Southeastern Puerto Rico." *American Journal of Public Health* 95: 2191–97.

Gray, Lewis Cecil. 1933. *History of Agriculture*, vol. 2. Washington, DC: Carnegie Institution of Washington.

Greene, Judith A. 1999. "Zero Tolerance: A Case Study of Police Policies and Practices in New York City." *Crime and Delinquency* 45 (2): 171–87.

Grieco, Elizabeth M. 2010. *Race and Hispanic Origin of the Foreign-Born Population in the United States: 2007*. Washington, DC: U.S. Census Bureau.

Guy-Sheftall, Beverly, ed. 1995. *Words of Fire: An Anthology of African-American Feminist Thought*. New York: New Press.

Guzmán, Pablo "Yoruba." 2010. "Before People Called Me a Spic, They Called Me a Nigger." In *The Afro-Latin@ Reader: History and Culture in the United States*, edited by Miriam Jiménez Román and Juan Flores, 235–43. Durham, NC: Duke University Press.

Hadden, Sally E. 2001. *Slave Patrols: Law and Violence in Virginia and the Carolinas*. Cambridge, MA: Harvard University Press.

Hairong, Yan. 2007. "Position without Identity: An Interview with Gayatri Chakravorty Spivak." *Positions* 15 (2): 429–48.

Haley, Sarah. 2016. *No Mercy Here: Gender, Punishment, and the Making of Jim Crow Modernity*. Chapel Hill: University of North Carolina Press.

Hall, Basil. 1830. *Travels in North America, in the Years 1827 and 1828*. Edinburgh: Robert Cadell.

Hall, Ronald E. 2000. "A Descriptive Analysis of Skin Color Bias in Puerto Rico: Ecological Applications to Practice." *Journal of Sociology and Social Welfare* 27: 171–84.

Hall, Ruth E. 1985. *Ask Any Woman: A London Inquiry into Rape and Sexual Assault: Report of the Women's Safety Survey Conducted by Women against Rape*. Bristol, UK: Falling Wall.

Hall, Stuart. 1980. "Race, Articulation and Societies Structured in Dominance." In *Sociological Theories: Race and Colonialism*, 305–45. Paris: UNESCO.

Hall, Stuart. 2017. *Familiar Stranger: A Life between Two Islands*. Durham, NC: Duke University Press.

Hall, Stuart, Chas Critcher, Tony Jefferson, John Clarke, and Brian Roberts, eds. 2013. *Policing the Crisis: Mugging, the State and Law and Order*. 2nd ed. New York: Palgrave Macmillan.

Hamayel, Layaly, Doaa Hammoudeh, and Lynn Welchman. 2017. "Reproductive Health and Rights in East Jerusalem: The Effects of Militarisation and Biopolitics on the Experiences of Pregnancy and Birth of Palestinians Living in the Kufr 'Aqab Neighbourhood." *Reproductive Health Matters* 25 (suppl. 1): 87–95.

Hamilton, Dell. 2017. *Blues\Blank\Black*. Performed at Mount Holyoke College, May 5.

Hammad, Suheir. 2010. *Born Palestinian, Born Black and The Gaza Suite*. Brooklyn, NY: UpSet Press.

Han, Gil-Soo. 2015. "K-Pop Nationalism: Celebrities and Acting Blackface in the Korean Media." *Continuum* 29(1): 2–16.

Hanchard, Michael. 1999. "Afro-Modernity: Temporality, Politics, and the African Diaspora." *Public Culture* 11 (1): 245–68.

Haney López, Ian F. 1997. "Race, Ethnicity, Erasure: The Salience of Race to LatCrit Theory." *California Law Review* 85: 1143–1211.

Haney López, Ian F. 2003. "White Latinos." *Harvard Latino Law Review* 6: 1–7.

Hannaford, Ivan. 1995. *Race: The History of an Idea in the West.* Baltimore, MD: Johns Hopkins University Press.

Hardy, Paul-A. 2002. "Medieval Muslim Philosophers on Race." In *Philosophers on Race: Critical Essays,* edited by J. K. Ward and T. L. Lott, 38–62. Malden, MA: Blackwell.

Harlan, Chico, and Zachary A. Goldfarb. 2014. "U.S. Criticizes Racist North Korean Screed against Obama." *Washington Post,* May 8. https://www.washingtonpost .com/world/asia_pacific/north-korean-scre . . . 8/9bc7a68f-7b71-4110-b4f1 -85ae05c92777_story.html.

Harney, Stefano, and Fred Moten. 2013. *The Undercommons: Fugitive Planning and Black Study.* New York: Minor Compositions.

Harpham, Geoffrey Galt. 2001. "Elaine Scarry and the Dream of Pain." *Salmagundi* 130/131: 202–34.

Hartman, Saidiya V. 1997. *Scenes of Subjection: Terror, Slavery, and Self-Making in Nineteenth-Century America.* New York: Oxford University Press.

Hartman, Saidiya V. 2002. "The Time of Slavery." *South Atlantic Quarterly* 101 (4): 757–77.

Hartman, Saidiya V. 2007. *Lose Your Mother: A Journey along the Atlantic Slave Route.* New York: Farrar, Straus and Giroux.

Hartman, Saidiya. 2016. "The Belly of the World: A Note on Black Women's Labors." *Souls* 18 (1): 166–73.

Hartman, Saidiya, and Frank Wilderson. 2003. "The Position of the Unthought." *Qui Parle* 13 (2): 183–201.

Hartmann, Heidi, Chandra Childers, and Elyse Shaw. 2015. *Toward Our Children's Keeper: A Data-Driven Analysis of the Interim Report of the My Brother's Keeper Initiative Shows the Shared Fate of Boys and Girls of Color.* Washington, DC: Institute for Women's Policy Research and the African American Policy Forum.

Hartney, Christopher, and Linh Vuong. 2009. *Created Equal: Racial and Ethnic Disparities in the US Criminal Justice System.* Oakland, CA: National Council on Crime and Delinquency.

Harvey, David. 2010. *A Companion to Marx's Capital.* London: Verso.

Hashiloni-Dolev, Yael. 2006. "Between Mothers, Fetuses and Society: Reproductive Genetics in the Israeli-Jewish Context." *Nashim: A Journal of Jewish Women's Studies and Gender Issues,* no. 12 (fall 5767): 129–50.

Hawthorne, Walter. 2015. "The Cultural Meaning of Work: The 'Black Rice Debate' Reconsidered." In *Rice: Global Networks and New Histories.* Cambridge: Cambridge University Press.

Haywood, Jasmine M. 2017. "'Latino Spaces Have Always Been the Most Violent': Afro-Latino Collegians' Perceptions of Colorism and Latino Intragroup Marginalization." *International Journal of Qualitative Studies in Education* 30 (8): 759–82.

Hazareesingh, Sandip. 2013. "Cotton, Climate, and Colonialism in Dharwar, Western India, 1840–1880." *Journal of Historical Geography* 42: 1–17.

Heng, Geraldine. 2018. *The Invention of Race in the European Middle Ages*. New York: Cambridge University Press.

Heng, Geraldine. 2019. *England and the Jews: How Religion and Violence Created the First Racial State in the West*. New York: Cambridge University Press.

Hernández, Tanya Katerí. 2003. "'Too Black to Be Latino': Blackness and Blacks as Foreigners in Latino Studies." *Latino Studies* 1: 152–59.

Hernández, Tanya Katerí. 2007. "Latino Inter-ethnic Employment Discrimination and the 'Diversity' Defense." *Harvard Civil Rights Civil Liberties Law Review* 42: 259–316.

Hernández, Tanya Katerí. 2013. *Racial Subordination in Latin America: The Role of the State, Customary Law, and the New Civil Rights Response*. New York: Cambridge University Press.

Hernández, Tanya Katerí. 2021. *On Latino Anti-Black Bias: "Racial Innocence" and the Struggle for Equality*. New York: Beacon Press.

Hiatt, Jeffrey M. 2012. *Employee's Survival Guide to Change*. 3rd ed. Loveland, CO: Prosci.

Hill, Zahara. 2017. "Black Voices: Afro-Feminist Festival Organizers Call Out Paris Mayor for Accusing Them of Racism." *Huffington Post*, May 30. https://www.huffingtonpost.com/entry/afro-feminist-festival-organizers-call-out-paris-mayor-for-accusing-them-of-racism_us_592d8a3ee4b0df57cbfd7f0b.

Hill-Collins, Patricia. 2000. *Black Feminist Thought: Knowledge, Consciousness, and the Politics of Empowerment*. New York: Routledge.

Hilliard, S. B. 1978. "Antebellum Tidewater Rice Culture in South Carolina and Georgia." In *European Settlement and Development in North America*, edited by J. R. Gibson. Toronto: University of Toronto Press.

Hing, Julianne. 2010. "Georgia Prisoners End Protest but Continue Demands." *Colorlines*, December 15. https://www.colorlines.com/articles/georgia-prisoners-end-protest-continue-demands.

Hitchens, Christopher. 2010. "A Nation of Racist Dwarfs." *Slate*, February 1. http://www.slate.com/articles/news_and_politics/fighting_words/2010/02/a_nation_of_racist_dwarfs.html.

Hitlin Steven, J. Scott Brown, and Glen H. Elder Jr. 2007. "Measuring Latinos: Racial vs. Ethnic Classification and Self-Understandings." *Social Forces* 86: 587–611.

Hobsbawm, Eric. 1989. *The Age of Empire, 1875–1914*. New York: Vintage.

Hogan, Howard. 2017. "Reporting of Race among Hispanics: Analysis of ACS Data." In *The Frontiers of Applied Demography*, 169–91. Cham, Switzerland: Springer International.

Holder, Eric H. 2015. "The Benefits of Shifting Law Enforcement Priorities and Incentives." Keynote address, Shifting Law Enforcement Goals to Reduce Mass

Incarceration, Brennan Center for Justice, New York, September 23. https://
www.youtube.com/watch?v=2xSVJ_VfX-M.

Hong, Grace Kyungwon. 2015. *Death beyond Disavowal: The Impossible Politics of Difference*. Minneapolis: University of Minnesota Press.

Hong, Grace Kyungwon, and Roderick A. Ferguson, eds. 2011. *Strange Affinities: The
Gender and Sexual Politics of Comparative Racialization*. Durham, NC: Duke
University Press.

Hope, R. L. 1895. "A Glimpse into the Life of Fulton County's Poor." *Atlanta Constitution*, January 6, 11.

Hord, Fred Lee (Mzee Lasana Okpara), and Jonathan Scott Lee, eds. 1995. *I Am
Because We Are: Readings in Black Philosophy*. Amherst: University of Massachusetts Press.

Horne, Gerald. 2014. *The Counter-revolution of 1776: Slave Resistance and the Origins of
the United States of America*. New York: New York University Press.

Horry, Ben. 1938. *Federal Writers' Project: Slave Narrative Project*, vol. 14. *South Carolina, Part 2, Eddington-Hunter*. Washington, DC: Library of Congress. http://hdl
.loc.gov/loc.mss/mesn.142.

House, Albert V., ed. 1954. *Planter Management and Capitalism in Ante-bellum Georgia:
The Journal of Hugh Fraser Grant, Ricegrower*. New York: Columbia University
Press.

Howard, David. 2001. *Coloring the Nation: Race and Ethnicity in the Dominican Republic*. Boulder, CO: Lynne Rienner.

Hoy, Vielka Cecilia. 2010. "Negotiating among Invisibilities: Tales of Afro-Latinidades
in the United States." In *The Afro-Latin@ Reader: History and Culture in the
United States*, edited by Miriam Jiménez Román and Juan Flores, 426–30. Durham, NC: Duke University Press.

Hulbert, Homer B. 1896. "Korean Poetry." *Korean Repository* 3: 203–7.

Hunter, Tera. 1997. *To 'Joy My Freedom: Southern Black Women's Lives and Labors after
the Civil War*. Cambridge, MA: Harvard University Press.

Huzzey, Richard. 2010. "Free Trade, Free Labour, and Slave Sugar in Victorian Britain." *Historical Journal* 53 (2): 359–79.

"Industry of the Southern and Western States." 1848. *De Bow's Review* 6 (4–5):
285–304.

Inikori, Joseph. 2002. *Africans in the Industrial Revolution*. Cambridge: Cambridge
University Press.

Isaac, Benjamin. 2004. *The Invention of Racism in Classical Antiquity*. Princeton, NJ:
Princeton University Press.

Israel, Jonathan I. 2001. *Radical Enlightenment: Philosophy and the Making of Modernity, 1650–1750*. New York: Oxford University Press.

Jackson, George L. (1972) 1990. "Letter to a Comrade." In *Blood in My Eye*. Baltimore,
MD: Black Classic Press.

James, C. L. R. 1970. "The Atlantic Slave Trade and Slavery: Some Interpretations of
Their Significance in the Development of the United States and the Western

World." In *Amistad I*, edited by John A. Williams and Charles F. Harris, 119–64. New York: Vintage Books.

James, C. L. R. 1989. *The Black Jacobins: Toussaint L'Ouverture and the San Domingo Revolution*. Rev. 2nd ed. New York: Vintage.

James, James Calhart. 1936. *Federal Writers' Project: Slave Narrative Project*, vol. 8. *Maryland, Brooks-Williams*. Manuscript/mixed material. https://www.loc.gov /item/mesn080/.

James, Joy. 1999. *Shadowboxing: Representations of Black Feminist Politics*. New York: St. Martin's.

James, Joy. 2013. "Afrarealism and the Black Matrix: Maroon Philosophy at Democracy's Border." *The Black Scholar* 43 (4): 124–31.

James, Joy, ed. 2007. *Warfare in the American Homeland: Policing and Prison in a Penal Democracy*. Durham, NC: Duke University Press. https://abolitionjournal.org /warfare-in-the-american-homeland/

James, Joy. 2015. "'Sorrow, Tears, and Bloods': Black Activism, Fractionation, and the Talented Tenth." VIEWPOINT, January 26. https://www.viewpointmag.com/2015 /01/26/sorrow-tears-and-blood-black-activism-fractionation-and-the-talented -tenth/.

James, Joy. 2016. "The Womb of Western Theory: Trauma, Time Theft and the Captive Maternal." *Carceral Notebooks* 12: 253–96.

James, Joy. 2018. "Killmonger's Captive Maternal Is M.I.A.: *Black Panther's* Family Drama, Imperial Masters and Portraits of Freedom." In *Reading Wakanda: Reconciling Black Radical Imaginations with Hollywood Fantasies*. Los Angeles: Southern California Library. http://www.socallib.org/reading-wakanda/captive -maternal.

James, Joy. 2020. "Presidential Powers and Captive Maternals: Sally, Michelle, and Deborah." *Blog of the APA*, May 6. https://blog.apaonline.org/2020/05/06 /presidential-powers-and-captive-maternals-sally-michelle-and-deborah/.

James, Joy, and Tracy Denean Sharpley-Whiting, eds. 2000. *The Black Feminist Reader*. New York: Wiley-Blackwell.

James, Selma. 2012. *Sex, Race, and Class—the Perspective of Winning: A Selection of Writings, 1952–2011*. Oakland, CA: PM Press.

Jiménez Román, Miriam, and Juan Flores, eds. 2010. *The Afro-Latin@ Reader: History and Culture in the United States*. Durham, NC: Duke University Press.

Johnson, Walter. 1999. *Soul by Soul: Life Inside the Antebellum Slave Market*. Cambridge, MA: Harvard University Press.

Johnson, Walter. 2013. *River of Dark Dreams: Slavery and Empire in the Cotton Kingdom*. Cambridge, MA: Harvard University Press.

Johnson, Walter. 2017. "To Remake the World: Slavery, Racial Capitalism, and Justice." *Boston Review Forum* 1: 11–31.

Jones, Janine. 2016. "The Pitfalls of Being the Best Black Surrogate a White Woman Could Hope For." *Abolition*, November 2. https://abolitionjournal.org/pitfalls -best-black-surrogate-white-woman-hope/.

Jones, Nikki. 2009. *Between Good and Ghetto: African American Girls and Inner-City Violence*. New Brunswick, NJ: Rutgers University Press.

Jones, Wilbur Devereux. 1958. *Lord Aberdeen and the Americas*. Athens: University of Georgia Press.

Jordan, June. (1985) 2011. "Moving towards Home." In *The Collected Poems of June Jordan: Directed by Desire*, edited by Jan Heller Levi and Sara Miles, 398. Port Townsend, WA: Copper Canyon Press.

Jordan, Winthrop D. 2012. *White over Black: American Attitudes toward the Negro, 1550–1812*. 2nd ed. Chapel Hill: Omohundro Institute of Early American History and Culture/University of North Carolina Press.

Jorge, Angela. 1979. "The Black Puerto Rican Woman in Contemporary American Society." In *The Puerto Rican Woman*, edited by Edna Acosta-Belén, 134–41. New York: Praeger.

Jung, Moon-Kie. 2015. *Beneath the Surface of White Supremacy: Denaturalizing U.S. Racisms Past and Present*. Stanford, CA: Stanford University Press.

Jung, Moon-Kie. 2019. "The Enslaved, the Worker, and Du Bois's *Black Reconstruction*: Toward an Underdiscipline of Antisociology." *Sociology of Race and Ethnicity* 5 (2): 157–68.

Jung, Moon-Kie, and Yaejoon Kwon. 2013. "Theorizing the U.S. Racial State: Sociology since *Racial Formation*." *Sociology Compass* 7 (11): 927–40.

Kafka, Judith. 2011. *The History of "Zero Tolerance" in American Public Schooling*. New York: Palgrave Macmillan.

Kajstura, Aleks. 2017. "Women's Mass Incarceration: The Whole Pie, 2017." Prison Policy Initiative, October 19. https://www.prisonpolicy.org/reports/pie2017women.html

Kanaaneh, Rhoda. 2002. *Birthing the Nation: Strategies of Palestinian Women in Israel*. Berkeley: University of California Press.

Kang, Hyeok. 2014. "Sesange Hanabakke Eomneun Bullyanga Obamaege Cheonbeoreul! Jaennaebigateun Inganchumul." *Rodongsinmun*, May 3. http://web-uridongpo.com/wp/wp-content/uploads/2014/05/rodong_us140503.html.

Kang, Shin-who. 2009. "Bias against South Asians, Blacks Still Lingers Here." *Korea Times*, January 7. http://www.koreatimes.co.kr/www/news/nation/2009/01/117_37466.html.

Kant, Immanuel. (1784) 1981a. "Idea for a Universal History from a Cosmopolitan Point of View." In *On History*. London: Pearson.

Kant, Immanuel. (1784) 1981b. "What Is Enlightenment?" In *On History*. London: Pearson.

Karl, Rebecca E. 2002. *Staging the World: Chinese Nationalism at the Turn of the Twentieth Century*. Durham, NC: Duke University Press.

Kassem, Fatima. 2011. *Palestinian Women: Narrative Histories and Gendered Memory*. London: Zed.

Kataoka, Sheryl, Audra Langley, Marleen Wong, Shilpa Baweja, and Bradley Stein. 2012. "Responding to Students with Posttraumatic Stress Disorder in Schools." *Child and Adolescent Psychiatric Clinics of North America* 21 (1): 119–33.

Kellor, Frances. 1901. *Experimental Sociology*. New York: Macmillan.

Kemble, Frances Anne. 1863. *Journal of a Residence on a Georgian Plantation in 1838–1839*. New York: Harper and Brothers.

Kennedy, Duncan. 1997. *A Critique of Adjudication*. Cambridge, MA: Harvard University Press.

Kerkoff, Kathinka Sinha. 2014. *Colonising Plants in Bihar: Tobacco Betwixt Indigo and Sugarcane*. Delhi: Partridge.

Kiernan, Victor. 1996. *The Lords of Human Kind: European Attitudes to Other Cultures in the Imperial Age*. 4th ed. London: Serif.

Kilgore, James. 2015. *Understanding Mass Incarceration: A People's Guide to the Key Civil Rights Struggle of Our Time*. New York: New Press.

Kim, Andrew Eungi. 2009. "Global Migration and South Korea: Foreign Workers, Foreign Brides and the Making of a Multicultural Society." *Ethnic and Racial Studies* 32 (1): 70–92.

Kim, Bok Rae. 2003. "Nobi: A Korean System of Slavery." *Slavery and Abolition* 24 (2): 155–68.

Kim, Catherine Y., Daniel J. Losen, and Damon T. Hewitt. 2010. *The School-to-Prison Pipeline Structuring Legal Reform*. New York: New York University Press.

Kim, Claire Jean. 1999. "The Racial Triangulation of Asian Americans." *Politics and Society* 27 (1): 105–38.

Kim, Claire Jean. 2000. *Bitter Fruit: The Politics of Black-Korean Conflict in New York City*. New Haven, CT: Yale University Press.

Kim, Han-Kyo. 1989. "The Declaration of Independence, March 1, 1919: A New Translation." *Korean Studies* 13: 1–4.

Kim, Jae Kyun. 2015. "Yellow over Black: History of Race in Korea and the New Study of Race and Empire." *Critical Sociology* 41 (2): 205–17.

Kim, Kichung. 2003. "Unheard Voices: The Life of the Nobi in O Hwi-mun's 'Swae-mirok.'" *Korean Studies* 27: 108–37.

Kim, Michael. 2004. "Literary Production, Circulating Libraries, and Private Publishing: The Popular Reception of Vernacular Fiction Texts in the Late Choson Dynasty." *Journal of Korean Studies* 9 (1): 1–31.

Kim, Nadia Y. 2008. *Imperial Citizens: Koreans and Race from Seoul to L.A.* Stanford, CA: Stanford University Press.

Kim, Nadia Y. 2015. "The United States Arrives: Racialization and Racism in Post-1945 South Korea." In *Race and Racism in Modern East Asia: Interactions, Nationalism, Gender and Lineage*, edited by Rotem Kowner and Walter Demel, 274–95. Boston: Brill.

Kim, Sookyung. 2012. "Racism in the Global Era: Analysis of Korean Media Discourse around Migrants, 1990–2009." *Discourse and Society* 23 (6): 657–78.

Kim, Tae Koon. 2006. *Korean Travel Literature*. Translated by Lee Kyong-hee. Seoul: Ewha Womans University Press.

Kimura, Mitsuhiko. 1993. "Standards of Living in Colonial Korea: Did the Masses Become Worse Off or Better Off under Japanese Rule?" *Journal of Economic History* 53 (3): 629–52.

Kincaid, Jamaica. 2002. *Lucy*. New York: Farrar, Straus and Giroux.

King, Richard H. 2004. *Race, Culture, and the Intellectuals, 1940–1970*. Baltimore, MD: Johns Hopkins University Press.

King, Tiffany Lethabo. 2013. "In the Clearing: Black Female Bodies, Space and Settler Colonial Landscapes." PhD diss., University of Maryland.

King, Tiffany Lethabo. 2016. "The Labor of (Re)reading Plantation Landscapes Fungible(ly)." *Antipode* 48, no. 4: 1022–39.

Kline, David. 2017. "The Pragmatics of Resistance: Framing Anti-blackness and the Limits of Political Ontology." *Critical Philosophy of Race* 5 (1): 51–69.

Knight, Frederick C. 2010. *Working the Diaspora: The Impact of African Labor on the Anglo-American World, 1650–1850*. New York: New York University Press.

Koshiro, Yukiko. 2003. "Beyond an Alliance of Color: The African American Impact on Modern Japan." *Positions* 11 (1): 183–215.

Kowner, Rotem, and Walter Demel, eds. 2013. *Race and Racism in Modern East Asia: Western and Eastern Constructions*. Boston: Brill.

Kowner, Rotem, and Walter Demel, eds. 2015. *Race and Racism in Modern East Asia: Interactions, Nationalism, Gender and Lineage*. Boston: Brill.

Kumar, Prakash. 2013. *Indigo Plantations and Science in Colonial India*. Cambridge: Cambridge University Press.

Kvach, John F. 2013. De Bow's Review: *The Antebellum Vision of a New South*. Lexington: University of Kentucky Press.

Lady, A. [Maria Eliza Ketelby Rundell and Esther Copley]. ca. 1840. *The New London Cookery*, 9th ed. London: Joseph Smith.

Lai, Sufen Sophia. 2012. "Racial Discourse and Utopian Visions in Nineteenth-Century China." In *Race and Racism in Modern East Asia: Western and Eastern Constructions*, edited by R. Kowner and W. Demel, 327–49. Boston: Brill.

Lake, Marilyn, and Henry Reynolds. 2008. *Drawing the Global Colour Line: White Men's Countries and the International Challenge of Racial Equality*. New York: Cambridge University Press.

Lakoff, George, and Mark Johnson. 2003. *Metaphors We Live By*. 2nd ed. Chicago: University of Chicago Press.

Lambda Legal. 2012. "Transgender Incarcerated People in Crisis." https://www .lambdalegal.org/know-your-rights/article/trans-incarcerated-people.

Lammy, David. 2018. "Windrush Children (Immigration Status)." United Kingdom, House of Commons, *Debates*, 239, April 16. https://hansard.parliament.uk /commons/2018-04-16/debates/7234878F-ACEE-48DD-A94C-9013B38FA465/W indrushChildren(ImmigrationStatus).

Lander, Ernest M. 1954. "Manufacturing in South Carolina, 1815–60." *Business History Review* 28 (1): 59–66.

Lang, Cady. 2020. "The Asian American Response to Black Lives Matter Is Part of a Long, Complicated History." *Time*, June 26. https://time.com/5851792/asian -americans-black-solidarity-history/.

LaVeist-Ramos, Thomas Alexis, Jessica Galarraga, Roland J. Thorpe Jr., Caryn N. Bell, and Chermeia J. Austin. 2012. "Are Black Hispanics Black or Hispanic? Exploring Disparities at the Intersections of Race and Ethnicity." *Journal of Epidemiological Community Health* 66: 1–5.

Lavie, Smadar. 2014. *Wrapped in the Flag of Israel: Mizrahi Single Mothers and Bureaucratic Torture*. Lincoln: University of Nebraska Press.

Lee, Inchoo. 2009. "Situated Globalization and Racism: An Analysis of Korean High School EFL Textbooks." *Language and Literacy* 11 (1): 1–14.

Lee, Kwang-rin, and Yong-ho Ch'oe. 1988. "Newspaper Publication in the Late Yi Dynasty." *Korean Studies* 12: 62–72.

Lee, Yoonkyung. 2009. "Migration, Migrants, and Contested Ethno-Nationalism in Korea." *Critical Asian Studies* 41 (3): 363–80.

Leflouria, Talitha. 2015. *Chained in Silence: Black Women and Convict Labor in the New South*. Chapel Hill: University of North Carolina Press.

Lengermann, Patricia Madoo, and Gillian Niebrugge. 1998. *The Women Founders: Sociology and Social Theory, 1830–1930: A Text/Reader*. Long Grove, IL: Waveland.

Lenin, V. I. (1917) 1976. *State and Revolution*. Beijing: Foreign Languages Press.

Lentin, Ronit, ed. 2008. *Thinking Palestine*. London: Zed Books.

Lepler, Jessica. 2013. *The Many Panics of 1837: People, Politics, and the Creation of a Transatlantic Financial Crisis*. Cambridge: Cambridge University Press.

Leroy, Justin. 2016. "Black History in Occupied Territory: On the Entanglement of Slavery and Settler Colonialism." *Theory and Event* 19 (4). https://muse.jhu.edu/article/633276.

Lethabo King, Tiffany. 2016. "New World Grammars: The 'Unthought' Black Discourse of Conquest." *Theory and Event* 19 (4). https://muse.jhu.edu/article/633275.

Lewis, Bernard. 1992. *Race and Slavery in the Middle East: An Historical Enquiry*. New York: Oxford University Press.

Lewis, Chance W., Bettie Ray Butler, Fred A. Bonner III, and Marcus Joubert. 2010. "African American Male Discipline Patterns and School District Responses Resulting Impact on Academic Achievement: Implications for Urban Educators and Policy Makers." *Journal of African American Males in Education* 1 (1): 7–25.

Li, Victor. 2009. "Necroidealism, or the Subaltern's Sacrificial Death." *Interventions* 11 (3): 275–92.

Lichtenstein, Alex. 1995. *Twice the Work of Free Labor: The Political Economy of Convict Labor in the New South*. New York: Verso.

Littlefield, Daniel. 1981. *Rice and Slaves: Ethnicity and the Slave Trade in Colonial South Carolina*. Baton Rouge: Louisiana State University Press.

Logan, Frenise A. 1974. "A British East India Company Agent in the United States, 1839–1840." *Agricultural History* 48: 267–76.

Logan, John R. 2003. "How Race Counts for Hispanic Americans." Lewis Mumford Center, State University of New York at Albany. http://mumford.albany.edu/census/BlackLatinoReport/BlackLatino01.htm.

López, Gustavo, and Ana Gonzalez-Barrera. 2016. "Afro-Latino: A Deeply Rooted Identity among U.S. Hispanics." Pew Research Center Fact Tank: News in the Numbers, March 1. https://www.pewresearch.org/fact-tank/2016/03/01/afro -latino-a-deeply-rooted-identity-among-u-s-hispanics/.

López, Nancy. 2013. "Killing Two Birds with One Stone? Why We Need Two Separate Questions on Race and Ethnicity in the 2020 Census and Beyond." *Latino Studies* 11: 428–38.

López, Nancy, Edward Vargas, Melina Juarez, Lisa Cacari-Stone, and Sonia Bettez. 2018. "What's Your 'Street Race'? Leveraging Multidimensional Measures of Race and Intersectionality for Examining Physical and Mental Health Status among Latinx." *Sociology of Race and Ethnicity* 4 (1): 49–66.

Lorde, Audre. 1984. *Sister Outsider*. Berkeley, CA: Crossing Press.

Losen, Daniel J., and Russell J. Skiba. 2010. *Suspended Education: Urban Middle Schools in Crisis*. Montgomery, AL: Southern Poverty Law Center.

Loughrey, Clarisse. 2016. "Read Hamilton Cast's Surprise Statement to Vice President-Elect Mike Pence in Full." *Independent*, November 21. http://www.independent .co.uk/arts-entertainment/theatre-dance/news/hamilton-mike-pence-booed -statement-in-full-watch-new-york-vice-president-elect-a7429251.html.

Lowe, Lisa. 1986. "The Orient as Woman in Flaubert's *Salammbo* and *Voyage en Orient*." *Comparative Literature Studies* 23 (1): 44–58.

Lowe, Lisa. 2015. *The Intimacies of Four Continents*. Durham, NC: Duke University Press.

Lowe, Lisa, and Kris Manjapra. 2019. "Comparative Global Humanities after Man: Alternatives to the Coloniality of Knowledge." *Theory, Culture and Society* 36 (5): 23–48.

Loyd, Jenna M., Matt Mitchelson, and Andrew Burridge, eds. 2012. *Beyond Walls and Cages: Prisons, Borders, and Global Crisis*. Athens: University of Georgia Press.

Lubin, Alex. 2014. *Geographies of Liberation: The Making of an Afro-Arab Political Imaginary*. Chapel Hill: University of North Carolina Press.

Ludden, David. 1985. *Peasant History in South India*. Princeton, NJ: Princeton University Press.

Lyons, William, and Julie Drew. 2006. *Punishing Schools: Fear and Citizenship in American Public Education*. Ann Arbor: University of Michigan Press.

Malaklou, M. Shadee, and Tiffany Willoughby-Herard. 2018. "Notes from the Kitchen, the Crossroads, and Everywhere Else, Too: Ruptures of Thought, Word, and Deed from the 'Arbiters of Blackness Itself.'" *Theory and Event* 21 (1): 2–67.

Mancini, Matthew J. 1996. *One Dies, Get Another: Convict Leasing in the American South, 1866–1928*. Columbia: University of South Carolina Press.

Marable, Manning. 2007. *Race, Reform, and Rebellion: The Second Reconstruction and Beyond in Black America, 1945–2006*. Jackson: University Press of Mississippi.

Marriott, David. 2000. *On Black Men*. New York: Columbia University Press.

Marriott, David. 2007. *Haunted Life: Visual Culture and Black Modernity*. New Brunswick, NJ: Rutgers University Press.

Marriott, David. 2011. "Inventions of Existence: Sylvia Wynter, Frantz Fanon, Sociogeny, and 'the Damned.'"*New Centennial Review* 11 (3): 45–89.

Martinez-Echazabal, Lourdes. 1998. "Race and National Identity in the Americas." *Latin American Perspectives* 25: 21–42.

Marx, Karl. (1863) 1975. *Theories of Surplus-Value*. Moscow: Progress.

Marx, Karl. (1867) 1990. *Capital*, vol. 1. London: Penguin.

Marx, Karl. (1891) 1978. *Wage-Labour and Capital*. New York: International.

Marx, Karl. 1976. *Capital*, vol. 1. London: Penguin.

Massey, Douglas, and Nancy Denton. 1993. *American Apartheid: Segregation and the Making of the Underclass*. Cambridge, MA: Harvard University Press.

Mauer, Marc, and Meda Chesney-Lind, eds. 2002. *Invisible Punishment: The Collateral Consequences of Mass Imprisonment*. New York: New Press.

May, Vivian M. 2007. *Anna Julia Cooper, Visionary Black Feminist: A Critical Introduction*. New York: Routledge.

Mbembe, Achille. 2001. *On the Postcolony*. Berkeley: University of California Press.

McBride, B. 1830. "Directions for Cultivating the Various Crops Grown at Hickory Hill." *Southern Agriculturist* 3 (May): 288.

McKay, Claude. (1919) 2004. "If We Must Die." In *The Norton Anthology of African American Literature*, edited by H. L. Gates Jr. and N. Y. McKay, 1007. 2nd ed. New York: Norton.

McKittrick, Katherine. 2006. *Demonic Grounds: Black Women and the Cartographies of Struggle*. Minneapolis: University of Minnesota Press.

McKittrick, Katherine. 2014. "Mathematics Black Life." *Black Scholar* 44 (2): 16–28.

McKittrick, Katherine, ed. 2015. *Sylvia Wynter: On Being Human as Praxis*. Durham, NC: Duke University Press.

Melamed, Jodi. 2011. "Reading Tehran in *Lolita*: Making Racialized and Gendered Difference Work for Neoliberal Multiculturalism." In *Strange Affinities: The Gender and Sexual Politics of Comparative Racialization*, edited by Grace Kyungwon Hong and Roderick A. Ferguson, 76–112. Durham, NC: Duke University Press.

Mele, Christopher, and Patrick Healy. 2016. "'Hamilton' Had Some Unscripted Lines for Pence. Trump Wasn't Happy." *New York Times*, November 19. https://www.nytimes.com/2016/11/19/us/mike-pence-hamilton.html.

Mies, Maria. 1986. *Patriarchy and Accumulation on a World Scale: Women in the International Division of Labour*. London: Zed.

Mills, Charles W. 1997. *The Racial Contract*. Ithaca, NY: Cornell University Press.

Mills, Charles W. 2007. "White Ignorance." In *Race and Epistemologies of Ignorance*, edited by S. Sullivan and N. Tuana, 13–38. Albany: State University of New York Press.

Mills, Charles W. 2008. "Racial Liberalism." PMLA 123 (5): 1380–97.

Mills, Charles W. 2013. "An Illuminating Blackness." *Black Scholar* 43 (4): 32–37.

Mills, Charles W. 2015. "Global White Ignorance." In *Routledge International Handbook of Ignorance Studies*, edited by M. Gross and L. McGoey, 217–27. New York: Routledge.

Mills, Charles W. 2020. "The Racial State." In *Routledge International Handbook of Contemporary Racisms*, edited by J. Solomos, 99–109. New York: Routledge.

Mills, Heather. 1999. "A Life without Joy." *The Guardian*, March 7. https://www.theguardian.com/celldeaths/article/0,2763,195387,00.html.

Millward, Jessica. 2016. "Black Women's History and the Labor of Mourning." *Souls* 18 (1): 161–65.

Minority Rights Group, ed. 1995. *No Longer Invisible: Afro-Latin Americans Today.* London: Minority Rights.

Miranda, Lin-Manuel. 2015a. "My Shot." *Hamilton: An American Musical.* Original Cast Recording. Atlantic Records.

Miranda, Lin-Manuel. 2015b. "The Schuyler Sisters." *Hamilton: An American Musical.* Original Cast Recording. Atlantic Records.

Miranda, Lin-Manuel. 2015c. "You'll Be Back." *Hamilton: An American Musical.* Atlantic Records.

Miranda, Lin-Manuel. 2016a. "Immigrants (We Get the Job Done)." *The Hamilton Mixtape.* Atlantic Records.

Miranda, Lin-Manuel. 2016b. "Valley Forge (Demo)." *The Hamilton Mixtape.* Atlantic Records.

Mirza, Heidi Safia. 1992. *Young, Female, and Black.* New York: Routledge.

Mirza, Heidi Safia. 1997. *Black British Feminism: A Reader.* New York: Routledge.

Mirza, Heidi Safia. 2009. *Race, Gender and Educational Desire: Why Black Women Succeed and Fail.* New York: Routledge.

Mirza, Heidi Safia, and Yasmin Gunaratnam. 2014. "'The Branch on Which I Sit': Reflections on Black British Feminism." *Feminist Review* 108 (1): 125–33.

Moitt, Bernard. 2001. *Women and Slavery in the French Antilles, 1635–1848.* Bloomington: Indiana University Press.

Monforti, Jessica Lavariega, and Gabriel Sanchez. 2010. "The Politics of Perception: An Investigation of the Presence and Sources of Perception of Internal Discrimination among Latinos." *Social Science Quarterly* 91 (1): 245–65.

Monroe, Carla R. 2006. "African American Boys and the Discipline Gap: Balancing Educators' Uneven Hand." *Educational Horizons* 84 (2): 102–11.

Montag, Warren. 2008. "Spirits Armed and Unarmed: Derrida's Specters of Marx." In *Ghostly Demarcations: A Symposium on Jacques Derrida's Specters of Marx*, edited by Michael Sprinker. New York: Verso.

Moon, Katharine H. S. 1997. *Sex among Allies: Military Prostitution in U.S.-Korea Relations.* New York: Columbia University Press.

Moon, Katharine H. S. 2015. *South Korea's Demographic Changes and Their Political Impact.* Washington, DC: Center for East Asia Policy Studies, Brookings Institution.

Moreton-Robinson, Aileen. 2015. *The White Possessive: Property, Power, and Indigenous Sovereignty.* Minneapolis: University of Minnesota Press.

Morgan, Jennifer L. 2004. *Laboring Women: Reproduction and Gender in New World Slavery.* Philadelphia: University of Pennsylvania Press.

Morgan, Jennifer, Christina Sharpe, and Stephanie Smallwood. 2017. "Slavery and Its Afterlives." Presentation at Scenes @ 20: A Symposium Celebrating the 20th Anniversary of Saidiya Hartman's *Scenes of Subjection: Terror, Slavery, and Self-Making in Nineteenth-Century America* and Its Impact on Studies of Black Lives in the Past, Present and Future. Rutgers University, New Brunswick, NJ, October 6–7.

Morgan, Philip D. 1982. "Work and Culture: The Task System and the World of Lowcountry Blacks, 1700 to 1880." *William and Mary Quarterly* 39 (4): 563–99.

Morris, Edward W. 2007. "Ladies or Loudies? Perceptions and Experiences of Black Girls in Classrooms." *Youth and Society* 38 (4): 490–515.

Morris, Monique. 2012. *Race, Gender and the School-to-Prison Pipeline*. Washington, DC: African American Forum.

Morris, Monique. 2015. *Pushout: The Criminalization of Black Girls in Schools*. New York: New Press.

Morrison, Toni. (1970) 2007. *The Bluest Eye*. New York: Vintage International.

Mosse, George L. 1997. *Toward the Final Solution: A History of European Racism*. New York: Howard Fertig.

Moten, Fred. 2003. *In the Break: The Aesthetics of the Black Radical Tradition*. Minneapolis: University of Minnesota Press.

Movement Advancement Project, Center for American Progress, and Youth First. 2017. *Unjust: LGBTQ Youth Incarcerated in the Juvenile Justice System*. http://www.lgbtmap.org/criminal-justice-youth-detention.

Muhammad, Khalil Gibran. 2011. *The Condemnation of Blackness: Race, Crime, and the Making of Modern Urban America*. Cambridge, MA: Harvard University Press.

Mukherjee, Mukul. 1983. "Impact of Modernisation on Women's Occupations: A Case Study of the Rice-Husking Industry of Bengal." *Indian Economic and Social History Review* 20 (1): 29.

Munnerlyn, Charles. 1828. "Answers: Queries on the Culture of Rice." *Southern Agriculturist* 1 (May): 220–21.

Murdach, Allison D. 2008. "Frances Kellor and the Americanization Movement." *Social Work* 53 (1): 93–95.

Myers, B. R. 2010. *The Cleanest Race: How North Koreans See Themselves—and Why It Matters*. New York: Melville House.

NAACP and National Women's Law Center. 2014. "Unlocking Opportunity for African American Girls." http://www.nwlc.org/resource/unlocking-opportunity-african-american-girls-call-action-educational-equity.

Nahman, M. 2013. *Extractions: An Ethnography of Reproductive Tourism*. Hampshire, UK: Palgrave Macmillan.

NALEO Education Fund. 2017. "The Census Bureau's Proposed 'Combined Question' Approach Offers Promise for Collecting More Accurate Data on Hispanic Origin and Race, but Some Questions Remain." National Association of Latino Elected and Appointed Officials. https://d3n8a8pro7vhmx.cloudfront.net/naleo/pages/190/attachments/original/1497288838/Hispanic_Origin_and_Race_Brief_fin_05-17.pdf.

National Center for Transgender Equality. 2018. "LGBT People Behind Bars: A Guide to Understanding the Issues Facing Transgender Prisoners and Their Legal Rights." https://transequality.org/sites/default/files/docs/resources /TransgenderPeopleBehindBars.pdf.

Nesbitt, Nick. 2008. *Universal Emancipation: The Haitian Revolution and the Radical Enlightenment*. Charlottesville: University of Virginia Press.

Newham Monitoring Project. 1992. *Annual Report 1991/2*. London: Newham Monitoring Project.

Newham Monitoring Project. 1993. *Annual Report 1992–93*. London: Newham Monitoring Project.

Newham Regeneration Planning and Property Directorate. 2010. *Newham, London: Local Economic Assessment, 2010–2027*. London: London Borough of Newham.

"The New Trade in Rough Rice." 1828. *Southern Agriculturist* 1 (October): 460.

Nichols, Robert. 2015. "Disaggregating Primitive Accumulation." *Radical Philosophy* 194: 18–28.

Ninde, William X. 1895. "An Interesting Communication: To the Editor of the Korean Repository." *Korean Repository* 2: 119.

Nobles, Melissa. 2000. *Shades of Citizenship: Race and the Census in Modern Politics*. Stanford, CA: Stanford University Press.

Nocella, Anthony, II, Priya Parmer, and David Stovall. 2014. *From Education to Incarceration: Dismantling the School to Prison Pipeline*. New York: Peter Lang.

Noguera, Pedro. 2008. *The Trouble with Black Boys: And Other Reflections on Race, Equity, and the Future of Public Education*. San Francisco: Jossey-Bass.

Nolan, Kathleen. 2011. *Police in the Hallways: Discipline in an Urban High School*. Minnesota: University of Minnesota Press.

"North Korea Media Calls President Barack Obama a 'Wicked Black Monkey.'" 2014. *Huffington Post UK*, May 9. http://www.huffingtonpost.co.uk/2014/05/09/north -korea-media-president-barack-obama-_n_5293445.html.

Nusairat, Tuqa. 2020. "Black Lives Also Matter in the Arab World." *New Atlanticist Blog*, June 12. https://www.atlanticcouncil.org/blogs/new-atlanticist/black-lives -also-matter-in-the-arab-world/.

Obama, Barack. 2015. "Remarks by the President at the NAACP Conference." July 14. Washington, DC: White House. https://www.whitehouse.gov/the-press-office /2015/07/14/remarks-president-naacp-conference.

Obama, Michelle. 2015. "Remarks by the First Lady at Tuskegee University Commencement Address." Tuskegee University, Tuskegee, Alabama, May 9. https:// obamawhitehouse.archives.gov/the-press-office/2015/05/09/remarks-first-lady -tuskegee-university-commencement-address.

Obama, Michelle. 2016. "Remarks by the First Lady at the Jackson State University Commencement." Jackson State University, Jackson, Mississippi, April 23. https://obamawhitehouse.archives.gov/the-press-office/2016/04/23/remarks -first-lady-jackson-state-university-commencement.

"Objects of This Journal." 1841. *British Indian Advocate* 1 (January 1): 2.

O'Carroll, Chad. 2014. "President Obama a 'Wicked Black Monkey'—North Korean State Media." NK News, May 8. https://www.nknews.org/2014/05/president-obama-a-wicked-black-monkey-north-korean-state-media.

Oguma, Eiji. 2002. *A Genealogy of "Japanese" Self-Images*. Melbourne: Trans Pacific Press.

Ohlinger, Franklin S., and Bertha Ohlinger. 1898. "Editorial Department—Oppression." *Korean Repository* 5: 193–94.

Oliver, Melvin, and Thomas Shapiro. 1995. *Black Wealth, White Wealth: A New Perspective on Racial Inequality*. New York: Routledge.

Olmstead, Alan. 2017. "Antebellum U.S. Cotton Production and Slavery in the Indian Mirror." *Agricultural History* 91 (1): 5–33.

Olmsted, Frederick Law. 1856. *A Journey in the Seaboard Slave States*, vol. 1. New York: Dix and Edwards.

O'Neil, Ruari Cahir. 2011. "Residence as Condition for Social Security in the United Kingdom: A Critique of the UK Right to Reside Test for Accessing Benefits and How It Is Applied in the Courts." *European Journal of Social Security* 13 (2): 226–47.

O'Neill, Onora. 1993. "Justice, Gender, and International Boundaries." In *The Quality of Life*, edited by M. Nussbaum and A. Sen, 303–23. New York: Clarendon.

Oparah/Sudbury, Julia Chinyere. 1998. *"Other Kinds of Dreams": Black Women's Organization and the Politics of Transformation*. New York: Routledge.

Oparah/Sudbury, Julia Chinyere. 2001. "(Re)constructing Multiracial Blackness: Women's Activism, Difference and Collective Identity in Britain." *Ethnic and Racial Studies* 24 (1): 29–49.

Oparah/Sudbury, Julia Chinyere. 2016. "Rethinking Anti-violence Strategy: Lessons from Black Women's Movement in Britain." In *Color of Violence: The INCITE! Anthology*, edited by INCITE! Women of Color against Violence, 13–24. Durham, NC: Duke University Press.

Oshinsky, David. 1996. *"Worse Than Slavery": Parchman Farm and the Ordeal of Jim Crow Justice*. New York: Free Press.

Outram, Dorinda. 2005. *The Enlightenment*. 2nd ed. New York: Cambridge University Press.

Pai, Hyungil. 2000. *Constructing "Korean" Origins*. Cambridge, MA: Harvard University Press.

Painter, Nell I. 2011. *The History of White People*. New York: Norton.

Pak, No-ja. 2001. *Dangsindeurui Daehanminguk*. Seoul: Hangyurye Sinmunsa.

Pak, Seong-jin. 2003. *Sahoejinhwarongwa Singminjisahoesasan*. Seoul: Seonin.

Palmer, Jennifer. 2006. *Creating and Belonging to Community: Race and Gender in Eighteenth-Century La Rochelle*. Ann Arbor: Scholarly Publishing Office, University of Michigan Library.

Park, Bongsoo. 2010. "Intimate Encounters, Racial Frontiers: Stateless GI Babies in South Korea and the United States, 1953–1965." PhD diss., University of Minnesota.

Park, Chung-Shin. 2003. *Protestantism and Politics in Korea*. Seattle: University of Washington Press.

Parker, Kim. 2015. *Multiracial in America: Proud, Diverse and Growing in Numbers*. Washington, DC: Pew Research Center. http://assets.pewresearch.org/wp-content/uploads/sites/3/2015/06/2015-06-11_multiracial-in-america_final-updated.pdf.

Pascual, Julia, and Jean-Baptiste Jacquin. 2017. "Le Défenseur des droits dénonce les contrôles « au faciès.»" *Le Monde*, January 20. https://www.lemonde.fr/police-justice/article/2017/01/20/le-defenseur-des-droits-denonce-les-controles-au-facies_5066029_1653578.html.

Patterson, Orlando. 1982. *Slavery and Social Death: A Comparative Study*. Cambridge, MA: Harvard University Press.

Patterson, Orlando. 2018. "Preface, 2018." In *Slavery and Social Death*, vii–xxvi. Cambridge, MA: Harvard University Press.

Patterson, Orlando, and Xiaolin Zhuo. 2018. "Modern Trafficking, Slavery, and Other Forms of Servitude." *Annual Review of Sociology* 44: 407–39.

Patton, Michael Q. (1990). *Qualitative Evaluation and Research Methods*. New York: Sage.

Peltier, Leonard. 1999. *Prison Writings: My Life Is My Sun Dance*. New York: St. Martin's.

Pessar, Patricia R. 1995. *A Visa for a Dream: Dominicans in the United States*. Needham Heights, MA: Allyn and Bacon.

Peterson, Mark. 1985. "Slaves and Owners; or Servants and Masters? A Preliminary Examination of Slavery in Traditional Korea." *Transactions of the Royal Asiatic Society, Korea Branch* 60: 31–41.

Pew Hispanic Center. 2010. "National Survey of Latinos." https://www.pewresearch.org/hispanic/dataset/2010-national-survey-of-latinos/.

Pew Hispanic Center and Kaiser Family Foundation. 2002. "National Survey of Latinos." https://www.pewresearch.org/hispanic/2002/12/17/2002-national-survey-of-latinos/.

Phillips, Tom. 2011. "Brazil Census Shows African-Brazilians in the Majority for the First Time." *The Guardian*, November 17. https://www.theguardian.com/world/2011/nov/17/brazil-census-african-brazilians-majority.

Phillips, Ulrich Bonnell. 1929. *Life and Labor in the Old South*. Boston: Little, Brown.

Picot, Pauline. 2016. "Quelques usages militants du concept de *racisme institutionnel* : Le discours antiraciste postcolonial (France, 2005–2015)." *Migrations Société* 1(163): 47–60.

Pierre, Jemima. 2015. "Zionism, Anti-Blackness, and the Struggle for Palestine." *Savage MindsBlog*, November 10. https://savageminds.org/2015/11/10/zionism-anti-blackness-and-the-struggle-for-palestine/.

Pieterse, Jan Nederveen. 1995. *White on Black: Images of Africa and Blacks in Western Popular Culture*. New Haven, CT: Yale University Press.

Pilkington, Edward. 1990. *Beyond the Mother Country: West Indians and the Notting Hill White Riots*. London: I. B. Tauris.

Plato. 2012. *The Republic*. Edited by G. R. F. Ferrari and translated by Tom Griffith. New York: Cambridge University Press.

Polk, James. 1888. "Polk's Special Message, 23 March 1846." In *Tariff from the White House, Extracts from the Messages*. Washington, DC: Gray and Clarkson.

Pool, Hannah. 2007. "The Police Are Meant to Be on My Side, but I Am More Than a Little Frightened of Them." *The Guardian*, March 9. http://www.guardian.co.uk /uk/2007/mar/09/ukcrime.gender1.

Poon, Linda. 2016. "Why South Korean Businesses Can Legally Refuse to Serve Foreigners." *Citylab*, March 11. http://www.citylab.com/politics/2016/03/why-south -korean-businesses-can-legally-refuse-to-serve-foreigners/473220.

Porter, George Richardson. 1851. *The Progress of the Nation in Its Various Social and Economic Relations from the Beginning of the Nineteenth Century*. London: John Murray.

Postone, Moishe. 1993. *Time, Labor, and Social Domination: A Reinterpretation of Marx's Critical Theory*. Cambridge: Cambridge University Press.

Postone, Moishe. 2004. "Critique and Historical Transformation." *Historical Materialism* 12 (3): 53–72.

Potok, Mark. 2017. "The Year in Hate and Extremism." *Intelligence Report*, spring. Montgomery, AL: Southern Poverty Law Center. https://www.splcenter.org /fighting-hate/intelligence-report/2017/year-hate-and-extremism.

Prison Reform Trust. 2016. "Prison: The Facts, Bromley Briefing Summary 2016." http://www.thebromleytrust.org.uk/files/2016factfile.pdf.

Privot, Michaël. 2014. "Afrophobia and the 'Fragmentation of Anti-racism.'" In *Visible Invisible Minority: Confronting Afrophobia and Advancing Equality for People of African Descent and Black Europeans in Europe*, 31–38. Brussels: ENAR. https://www .enar-eu.org/IMG/pdf/book_-_people_of_african_descent_-_final-2.pdf.

Pruneah, Leigh Ann. 1997. "All the Time Is Work Time: Gender and the Task System on Antebellum Low Country Rice Plantations." PhD diss., University of Arizona.

"Public Health." 1863. *Sixth Report of the Medical Officer of the Privy Council*. With appendix. London.

Punishment Reports of Individual Camps. 1885–1908. Corporal Punishment Monthly Reports, Record Group 21-1-11, Georgia Archives, Morrow, Georgia.

Q.E.D. 1832. "Answer to Queries of an Observer on the Culture of Rice." *Southern Agriculturist* 5 (December): 630–31.

Quijano, Anibal. 2000. "Coloniality of Power, Eurocentrism and Latin America." *Nepanthla: Views from the South* 1 (3): 533–80.

Randhawa, M. S. 1983. *A History of Agriculture in India*, vol. 3. New Delhi: Indian Council of Agricultural Research.

Ransby, Barbara. 2018. *Making All Black Lives Matter: Reimagining Freedom in the Twenty-First Century*. Oakland: University of California Press.

Rawls, John. 1999. *A Theory of Justice*. Rev. ed. Cambridge, MA: Harvard University Press.

Reanne Frank, Ilana Redstone Akresh, and Bo Lu. 2010. "Latino Immigrants and the U.S. Racial Order: How and Where Do They Fit In?" *American Sociological Review* 75: 378.

Rediker, Marcus. 2007. *The Slave Ship: A Human History*. New York: Penguin.

Régent, Frédéric. 2007. *La France et ses escalaves: De la colonization aux abolitions, 1620–1848*. Paris: Grasset.

"Report from the Society of Arts on Nipal Rice, Thibet Wool, Safflower, &C." 1839. *Transaction of the Agricultural and Horticultural Society of India* 3: 120.

Reyes, Raul A. 2014. "Afro-Latinos Seek Recognition and Accurate Census Count." *NBC News*, September 21. http://www.nbcnews.com/storyline/hispanic-heritage -month/afro-latinos-seek-recognition-accurate-census-count-n207426.

Reynolds, Tracey. 2002. "Re-thinking a Black Feminist Standpoint." *Ethnic and Racial Studies* 25 (4): 591–606.

Richie, Beth. 1996. *Compelled to Crime: The Gender Entrapment of Battered Black Women*. New York: Routledge.

Richie, Beth. 2012. *Arrested Justice: Black Women, Violence, and America's Prison Nation*. New York: New York University Press.

Robb, Peter. 1990. "Ideas in Agrarian History: Some Observations on the British and Nineteenth-Century Bihar." *Journal of the Royal Asiatic Society* 1: 17–43.

Robb, Peter. 1992. "Peasants' Choices? Indian Agriculture and the Limits of Commercialization in Nineteenth Century Bihar." *Economic History Review* 45 (1): 97–119.

Robb, Peter. 1994. "Labour in India 1860–1920: Typologies, Change and Regulation." *Journal of the Royal Asiatic Society* 4 (1): 37–66.

Robb, Peter. 2007. *Peasants, Political Economy, and Law*. Oxford: Oxford University Press.

Roberts, Dorothy. 1997. *Killing the Black Body: Race, Reproduction, and the Meaning of Liberty*. New York: Pantheon.

Roberts, Dorothy. 2011. "Prison, Foster Care, and the Systemic Punishment of Black Mothers." *UCLA Law Review* 59: 1474.

Robinson, Cedric J. 1983. *Black Marxism: The Making of the Black Radical Tradition*. Chapel Hill: University of North Carolina Press.

Robinson, Cedric. 2000. *Black Marxism: The Making of the Black Radical Tradition*. Chapel Hill: University of North Carolina Press.

Robinson, Michael. 2007. *Korea's Twentieth-Century Odyssey: A Short History*. Honolulu: University of Hawai'i Press.

Rodríguez, Dylan. 2006. *Forced Passages: Imprisoned Radical Intellectuals and the US Prison Regime*. Minneapolis: University of Minnesota Press.

Rodríguez, Dylan. 2014. "'Allow One Photo Per Year': Prison Strikes (Georgia 2010, California 2011–2012) as Racial Archive, from 'Post-Civil Rights' to the Analytics of Genocide." In *The Nation and Its Peoples: Citizens, Denizens, Migrants*, edited by John S. W. Park and Shannon Gleeson, 70–91. New York: Routledge.

Rodríguez, Dylan. 2018. "To Define 'Incarceration' as Against 'Mass Incarceration.'" *Scholars for Social Justice Blog*. http://scholarsforsocialjustice.com/ssj-blog-to -define-incarceration-against-mass-incarceration-by-dylan-rodriguez/.

Rodríguez, Dylan, and Casey Goonan. 2016. "Policing and the Violence of White Being: An Interview with Dylan Rodríguez." *Propter Nos* 1 (1): 8–18.

Roscoe, H., W. Frere, and S. D. Glenbervie. 1831. *Reports of Cases Argued and Determined in the Court of King's Bench: In the Nineteenth, Twentieth, and Twenty-First [Twenty-Second, Twenty-Third, Twenty-Fourth, and Twenty-Fifth] Years of the Reign of George III [1778–1785]*, vol. 4, 299–302. London: Reed and Hunter.

Rosenblum, Alexis, William Darity Jr., Angel L. Harris, and Tod Hamilton. 2016. "Looking through the Shades: The Effect of Skin Color on Earnings by Region of Birth and Race for Immigrants to the United States." *Sociology of Race and Ethnicity* 2 (1): 87–105.

Rosenblum, Nina, dir. 1991. *Through the Wire* (film). New York: New Video Group.

Rosenthal, Caitlin. 2016a. "Seeking a Quantitative Middle Ground: Reflections on Methods and Opportunities in Economic History." *Journal of the Early Republic* 36: 659–80.

Rosenthal, Caitlin. 2016b. "Slavery's Scientific Management: Masters and Managers." In *Slavery's Capitalism: A New History of American Economic Development*, edited by Sven Beckert and Seth Rockman. Philadelphia: University of Pennsylvania Press.

Roth, Wendy D. 2010. "Racial Mismatch: The Divergence between Form and Function in Data for Monitoring Racial Discrimination of Hispanics." *Social Science Quarterly* 91: 1288–1311.

Rout, Leslie B., Jr. 1976. *The African Experience in Spanish America*. Princeton, NJ: Markus Wiener.

Roy, Natasha, and Agnes Constante. 2020. "75 Ways Asian Americans and Pacific Islanders Are Speaking Out for Black Lives." NBC News, June 12. https://www.nbcnews.com/news/asian-america/75-ways-asian-americans-pacific-islanders-are-speaking-out-black-n1230551.

Rushdy, Ashraf H. A. 2012. *American Lynching*. New Haven, CT: Yale University Press.

R.W.R. 1846. "Utility of Machinery." *Southern Agriculturist* 2 (9, September): 466.

Ryu, Dae Young. 2008. "The Origin and Characteristics of Evangelical Protestantism in Korea at the Turn of the Twentieth Century." *Church History* 77 (2): 371–98.

Sa'di, Ahmed. 2014. *Thorough Surveillance: The Genesis of Israeli Policies of Population Management, Surveillance and Political Control towards the Palestinian Minority*. Manchester, UK: Manchester University Press.

Sahlins, Marhsall D. 1987. *Islands of History*. Chicago: University of Chicago Press.

Said, Edward. 1978. *Orientalism*. New York: Vintage.

Salamanca, Omar Jabary, Mezna Qato, Kareem Rabie, and Sobhi Samour. 2012. "Past Is Present: Settler Colonialism in Palestine." *Settler Colonial Studies* 2, no. 1: 1–8.

Saldaña, Johnny. 2012. *The Coding Manual for Qualitative Researchers*. New York: Sage.

Salinas, Cristobal, Jr., and Adele Lozano. 2017. "Mapping and Recontexualizing the Evolution of the Term *Latinx*: An Environmental Scanning in Higher Education." *Journal of Latinos and Education* 18 (4): 302–15. https://www.tandfonline.com/doi/abs/10.1080/15348431.2017.1390464.

Saltman, Kenneth J. 2007. *Capitalizing on Disaster: Taking and Breaking Public Schools*. New York: Routledge.

Saltman, Kenneth J., and David Gabbard. 2011. *Education as Enforcement: The Militarization and Corporatization of Schools*. New York: Routledge.

Samantrai, Ranu. 2002. *AlterNatives: Black Feminism in the Postimperial Nation*. Stanford, CA: Stanford University Press.

Sartre, Jean-Paul. 1976. *Anti-Semite and Jew*. Translated by George J. Becker. New York: Schocken.

Saul, Heath. 2014. "North Korea Labels President Obama a 'Cross-Breed Black Monkey' in Racist Attack." *Independent*, May 8. http://www.independent.co.uk/news/world/asia/north-korea-labels-president-obama-a-cross-breed-in-racist-attack-9339926.html.

Sautman, Barry. 1997. "Racial Nationalism and China's External Behavior." *World Affairs* 160 (2): 78–95.

Sawyer, Mark. 2006. *Racial Politics in Post-revolutionary Cuba*. New York: Cambridge University Press.

Sawyer, Wendy, and Peter Wagner. 2019. "Mass Incarceration: The Whole Pie." *Prison Policy Initiative*, March 19. https://www.prisonpolicy.org/reports/pie2019.html.

Sayegh, Fayez A. 1965. *Zionist Colonialism in Palestine*. Beirut: Research Center, Palestine Liberation Organization.

Scarborough, William Kauffman. 2011. *The Allstons of Chicora Wood: Wealth, Honor, and Gentility in the South Carolina Lowcountry*. Baton Rouge: Louisiana State University Press.

Schmid, Andre. 2002. *Korea between Empires, 1895–1919*. New York: Columbia University Press.

Schrottky, Eugene C. 1876. *The Principles of Rational Agriculture Applied to India and Its Staple Products*. Bombay: Times of India Office.

Schwalm, Leslie. 1997. *A Hard Fight for We: Women's Transition from Slavery to Freedom in South Carolina*. Urbana: University of Illinois Press.

Schofield, Hugh. 2017. "Row over French Anti-racist Lands Minister in Mess." BBC *News*, December 20. https://www.bbc.com/news/world-europe-42426276.

Segal, Ronald. 2002. *Islam's Black Slaves: The Other Black Diaspora*. New York: Farrar, Straus and Giroux.

Seijas, Tatiana. 2014. *Asian Slaves in Colonial Mexico: From Chinos to Indians*. New York: Cambridge University Press.

Sell, Zach. 2016. "White Overseers of the World." *Salvage* 3 (August 22). http://salvage.zone/in-print/white-overseers-of-the-world/.

Sengupta, Syamalendu. 1990. *A Conservative Hindu of Colonial India: Raja Radhakanta Deb and His Milieu*. New Delhi: Navrang.

Sentencing Project. 2015. "Criminal Justice Facts." Washington, DC: Sentencing Project. http://www.sentencingproject.org/criminal-justice-facts/.

Sewell, William H., Jr. 2005. *Logics of History: Social Theory and Social Transformations*. Chicago: University of Chicago Press.

Sexton, Jared. 2007a. "The Obscurity of Black Suffering." In *What Lies Beneath: Katrina, Race, and the State of the Nation*, edited by the South End Press Collective, 120–31. Boston: South End.

Sexton, Jared. 2007b. "Racial Profiling and the Societies of Control." In *Warfare in the American Homeland: Policing and Prison in a Penal Democracy*, edited by J. James, 197–218. Durham, NC: Duke University Press.

Sexton, Jared. 2008. *Amalgamation Schemes: Antiblackness and the Critique of Multiracialism*. Minneapolis: University of Minnesota Press.

Sexton, Jared. 2010. "People-of-Color-Blindness Notes on the Afterlife of Slavery." *Social Text* 28 (2): 31–56.

Sexton, Jared. 2011. "The Social Life of Social Death: On Afro-Pessimism and Black Optimism." *InTensions Journal* 5.

Sexton, Jared. 2015. "Don't Call It a Comeback: Racial Slavery Is Not Yet Abolished." Open Democracy, June 17. https://www.opendemocracy.net/beyondslavery /jared-sexton/don't-call-it-comeback-racial-slavery-is-not-yet-abolished.

Sexton, Jared. 2016a. "Afro-Pessimism: The Unclear Word." *Rhizomes: Cultural Studies in Emerging Knowledge*, no. 29. http://www.rhizomes.net/issue29/sexton .html.

Sexton, Jared. 2016b. "The *Vel* of Slavery: Tracking the Figure of the Unsovereign." *Critical Sociology* 42 (4–5): 583–97.

Sexton, Jared. 2017. *Black Masculinity and the Cinema of Policing*. New York: Palgrave Macmillan.

Shalhoub-Kevorkian, Nadera. 2009. *Militarization and Violence against Women in Conflict Zones: A Palestinian Case-Study*. Cambridge: Cambridge University Press.

Shalhoub-Kevorkian, Nadera. 2014. "Terrorism and the Birthing Body in Jerusalem." In *At the Limits of Justice: Women of Colour on Terror*, edited by Suvendrini Perera and Sherene Razack. Toronto: University of Toronto Press.

Shalhoub-Kevorkian, Nadera. 2015. "The Politics of Birth and the Intimacies of Violence against Palestinian Women in Occupied East Jerusalem." *British Journal of Criminology* 55 (6): 1187–1206.

Shapiro, Thomas. 2004. *The Hidden Cost of Being African American: How Wealth Perpetuates Inequality*. New York: Oxford University Press.

Sharma, Jayeeta. 2006. "British Science, Chinese Skill and Assam Tea: Making Empire's Garden." *Indian Economic and Social History Review* 43 (4): 429–55.

Sharma, Suniti. 2013. *Girls Behind Bars: Reclaiming Education in Transformative Spaces*. New York: Bloomsbury Academic.

Sharpe, Christina. 2010. *Monstrous Intimacies: Making Post-Slavery Subjects*. Durham, NC: Duke University Press.

Sharpe, Christina. 2016. *In the Wake: On Blackness and Being*. Durham, NC: Duke University Press.

Shaylor, Cassandra. 1998. "'It's Like Living in a Black Hole': Women of Color and Solitary Confinement in the Prison Industrial Complex." *New England Journal on Criminal and Civil Confinement* 24: 385–416.

Shih, Shu-Mei. 2013. "Race and Revolution: Blackness in China's Long Twentieth Century." *PMLA* 128 (1): 156–62.

Shin, Gi-Wook. 2005. "Asianism in Korea's Politics of Identity." *Inter-Asia Cultural Studies* 6 (4): 616–30.

Shin, Gi-Wook. 2006. *Ethnic Nationalism in Korea: Genealogy, Politics, and Legacy.* Stanford, CA: Stanford University Press.

Shin, Gi-Wook. 2013. "Racist South Korea? Diverse but Not Tolerant of Diversity." In *Race and Racism in Modern East Asia: Western and Eastern Constructions*, edited by Rotem Kowner and Walter Demel, 369–90. Boston: Brill.

Shin, Julia Jiwon. 2009. "The Gendered and Racialised Division in the Korean Labour Market: The Case of Migrant Workers in the Catering Sector." *East Asia* 26: 93–111.

Shin, Michael D. 2003. "Major Trends in Korean Historiography in the U.S." *Sungkyun Journal of East Asian Studies* 3 (1): 151–75.

Shohat, Ella. 2003. "Rupture and Return: Zionist Discourse and the Study of Arab Jews." *Social Text* 21 (2): 49–74.

Simmons, Kristen. 2017. "Settler Atmospherics." *Cultural Anthropology* 12: 21. https://culanth.org/fieldsights/1221-settler-atmospherics.

Simpson, Audra. 2014. *Mohawk Interruptus: Political Life across the Borders of Settler States.* Durham, NC: Duke University Press.

Simpson, Audra. 2016. "The State Is a Man: Theresa Spence, Loretta Saunders and the Gender of Settler Sovereignty." *Theory and Event* 19 (4).

Siok-Hwa, Cheng. 1968. *The Rice Industry of Burma, 1852–1940.* Singapore: University of Malaysia Press.

Skiba, Russell J., and Kimberly Knesting. 2001. "Zero Tolerance, Zero Evidence: An Analysis of School Disciplinary Practice." *New Directions for Youth Development* 92: 17–43.

Skiba, Russell J., Robert S. Michael, Abra Carroll Nardo, and Reece L. Peterson. 2002. "The Color of Discipline: Sources of Racial and Gender Disproportionality in School Punishment." *Urban Review* 34 (4): 317–42.

Skiba, Russell J., and Reece L. Peterson. 2000. "School Discipline at a Crossroads: From Zero Tolerance to Early Response." *Exceptional Children* 66 (3): 335–96.

"S. Korean Presidential Frontrunner Sorry for Racist Joke." 2015. *Al Jazeera*, December 19. http://www.aljazeera.com/news/2015/12/korean-presidential-frontrunner-racist-joke-151219051135138.html.

Slave Voyages: The Trans-Atlantic Slave Trade Database. "Trans-Atlantic Slave Trade—Estimates." Accessed July 7, 2020. https://slavevoyages.org/assessment/estimates.

Sloan, Alaistar, and Eric Allison. 2015. "Sharp Rise in Proportion of Young Black and Minority Ethnic Prisoners." *The Guardian*, June 24. https://www.theguardian.com/society/2015/jun/24/rise-proportion-black-ethnic-minority-young-prisoners-stop-and-search.

Smallwood, Stephanie. 2017. "What Slavery Tells Us about Marx." *Boston Review*, winter: 78–82.

Smith, Andrea. 2003. "Not an Indian Tradition: The Sexual Colonization of Native Peoples." *Hypatia* 18 (2): 70–85.

Smith, Andrea. 2005. *Conquest: Sexual Violence and American Indian Genocide*. Boston: South End.

Smith, Christen. 2016. "Facing the Dragon: Black Mothering, Sequelae and Gendered Necropolitics in the Americas." *Transforming Anthropology* 24 (1): 31–48.

Smith, Sara. 2012. "Intimate Geopolitics: Religion, Marriage, and Reproductive Bodies in Leh, Ladakh." *Annals of the American Association of Geographers* 102: 1511–28.

Society for Promoting Christian Knowledge. 1854. *Substances Used as Food, as Exemplified in the Great Exhibition*. London: Society for Promoting Christian Knowledge.

Spargo, Clifton R. 2004. *The Ethics of Mourning: Grief and Responsibility in Elegiac Literature*. Baltimore, MD: Johns Hopkins University Press.

Spillers, Hortense J. 1984. "Interstices: A Small Drama of Words." In *Pleasure and Danger: Exploring Female Sexuality*, edited by Carol Vance, 73–100. Boston: Routledge and Kegan Paul.

Spillers, Hortense. 1987. "Mama's Baby, Papa's Maybe: An American Grammar Book." *Diacritics* 17 (2): 64–81.

Spillers, Hortense. 2003. *Black, White, and in Color: Essays on American Literature and Culture*. Chicago: University of Chicago Press.

Spillers, Hortense, Saidiya Hartman, Farah Jasmine Griffin, Shelly Eversley, and Jennifer L. Morgan. 2007. "'Whatcha Gonna Do?' Revisiting 'Mama's Baby, Papa's Maybe: An American Grammar Book': A Conversation with Hortense Spillers, Saidiya Hartman, Farah Jasmine Griffin, Shelley Eversley, & Jennifer L. Morgan." *Women's Studies Quarterly* 35 (1–2): 299–309.

Springs, John, III. 1996. "Gentlemen Dealing in Slaves." *South Carolina Historical Magazine* 97 (1): 6–29.

Stannard, David. 1992. *American Holocaust: The Conquest of the New World*. New York: Oxford University Press.

Stark, Heidi Kiiwetinepinesiik. 2016. "Criminal Empire: The Making of the Savage in a Lawless Land." *Theory and Event* 19 (4). https://muse.jhu.edu/article/633282.

Starobin, Robert. 1970. *Industrial Slavery in the Old South*. Oxford: Oxford University Press.

"Steam Rice Mills." 1824. *Washington Quarterly Magazine of Arts, Science and Literature* 1 (2): 133.

Stein, Sandra J. 2004. *The Culture of Education Policy*. New York: Teachers College Press.

Steinmetz, George. 2003. "'The Devil's Handwriting': Precolonial Discourse, Ethnographic Acuity, and Cross-Identification in German Colonialism." *Comparative Studies in Society and History* 45: 41–95.

Steinmetz, George. 2007. *The Devil's Handwriting: Precoloniality and the German Colonial State in Qingdao, Samoa, and Southwest Africa*. Chicago: University of Chicago Press.

Steinmetz, George. 2008. "The Colonial State as Social Field: Ethnographic Capital and Native Policy in the German Overseas Empire before 1914." *American Sociological Review* 73: 589–612.

Steinmetz, George. 2016. "Social Fields, Subfields and Social Spaces at the Scale of Empires: Explaining the Colonial State and Colonial Sociology." *Sociological Review Monographs* 64 (2): 98–123.

Stone, Chris. 2014. "Ending Mass Incarceration." Open Society Foundations, November 7. https://www.opensocietyfoundations.org/voices/ending-mass-incarceration.

Strickland, Debra Higgs. 2003. *Saracens, Demons, and Jews: Making Monsters in Medieval Art*. Princeton, NJ: Princeton University Press.

Stuckey, Sterling. 2013. *Slave Culture: Nationalist Theory and the Foundations of Black America*. New York: Oxford University Press.

Suh, Michael. 2013. *2010 National Survey of Latinos*. Washington, DC: Pew Research Center Hispanic Trends Project. http://www.pewhispanic.org/2013/07/19/2010-national-survey-of-latinos/.

Sullivan, Michael T. 1994. "The 1988–89 Nanjing Anti-African Protests: Racial Nationalism or National Racism?" *China Quarterly* 138: 438–57.

Sullum, Jacob. 2013. "Eric Holder Condemns Mass Incarceration (Again)." *Forbes*, November 22. http://www.forbes.com/sites/jacobsullum/2013/11/22/eric-holder-condemns-mass-incarceration-again/.

Sun, Jiang. 2012. "Blumenbach in East Asia: The Dissemination of the 'Five-Race Theory' in East Asia and a Textual Comparison." *Orients Extremus* 51: 107–53.

Swan, Dale E. 1972. "The Structure and Profitability of the Antebellum Rice Industry, 1859." PhD diss., University of North Carolina.

Tadman, Michael. 1989. *Speculators and Slaves: Masters, Traders, and Slaves in the Old South*. Madison: University of Wisconsin.

Tadman, Michael. 1996. "The Hidden History of Slave Trading in Antebellum South Carolina: John Springs III and Other 'Gentlemen Dealing in Slaves.'" *South Carolina Historical Magazine* 97 (1): 6–29.

Tajima, Atsushi, and Michael Thornton. 2012. "Strategic Solidarity: Japanese Imaginings of Blacks and Race in Popular Media." *Inter-Asia Cultural Studies* 13 (3): 345–64.

Takezawa, Yasuko. 2005. "Transcending the Western Paradigm of the Idea of Race." *Japanese Journal of American Studies* 16: 5–30.

Tal, A. 2016. *The Land Is Full: Addressing Overpopulation in Israel*. New Haven, CT: Yale University Press.

Tayler, Samuel. 1945. Letter to Elizabeth Frances Blyth (September 2, 1838). In *The South Carolina Rice Plantation as Revealed in the Papers of Robert F. W. Allston*, edited by J. H. Easterby, 339. Chicago: University of Chicago Press.

Taylor, Keeanga-Yamahtta. 2016. *From #BlackLivesMatter to Black Liberation*. Chicago: Haymarket.

Taylor, Keeanga-Yamahtta, ed. 2017. *How We Get Free: Black Feminism and the Combahee River Collective*. Chicago: Haymarket.

Telles, Edward. 2014. *Pigmentocracies: Ethnicity, Race, and Color in Latin America*. Chapel Hill: University of North Carolina Press.

Thomas, Piri. 1967. *Down These Mean Streets*. New York: Knopf.

Thompson, George. 1839. "Speech of George Thompson." *British India Addresses*, June 1, 5.

Thornton, Michael C. 1986. "Collective Representations and Japanese Views of African-Descent Populations." *International Journal of Sociology and Social Policy* 6 (1): 90–101.

Threadcraft, Shatema. 2016. *Intimate Justice: The Black Female Body and the Body Politic*. Oxford: Oxford University Press.

Tiffin, Helen, Bill Ashcroft, and Gareth Griffiths. 2002. *The Empire Writes Back: Theory and Practice*. New York: Routledge.

Tikhonov, Vladimir. 2010. *Social Darwinism and Nationalism in Korea*. Boston: Brill Academy.

Tikhonov, Vladimir. 2013. "The Race and Racism Discourses in Modern Korea, 1890s–1910s." *Korean Studies* 36: 31–57.

Torres, Arlene. 1998. "La Gran Familia Puertorriqueña 'Ej Prieta de Belda' (The Great Puerto Rican Family Is Really Really Black)." In *Blackness in Latin America and the Caribbean*, vol. 2, edited by Arlene Torres and Norman E. Whitten Jr., 285–306. Bloomington: Indiana University Press.

Torres-Saillant, Silvio. 2002. "Problematic Paradigms: Racial Diversity and Corporate Identity in the Latino Community." In *Latinos: Remaking America*, edited by Marcelo M. Suarez-Orozco and Mariela M. Paez, 435–55. Berkeley: University of California Press.

Trouillot, Michel-Rolph. 2015. *Silencing the Past: Power and the Production of History*. 20th anniversary ed. 2nd revised ed. Boston: Beacon.

Uniform Crime Reporting Statistics. 2014. "Estimated Crime in the United States: Total (1970–2014)." Washington, DC: US Bureau of Justice Statistics. https://www.bjs.gov/ucrdata/Search/Crime/State/RunCrimeStatebyState.cfm.

United Nations. 2016. "Grave Breaches of International Humanitarian and Human Rights Law by Israel—Letter from Palestine." April 29. https://www.un.org/unispal/document/auto-insert-181742/.

U.S. Census Bureau. 2015. "2020 Census Operational Plan." https://www2.census.gov/programs-surveys/decennial/2020/program-management/planning-docs/2020-oper-plan-exe-sum.pdf.

U.S. Census Bureau. 2018. "American Community Survey Table of Hispanic or Latino Origin Population by Race." https://data.census.gov.

U.S. Census Bureau. 2019. Quick Facts: United States. https://www.census.gov/quickfacts/fact/table/US/RHI225218#RHI225218.

U.S. Department of Education. 2014. *Office of Civil Rights: Civil Rights Data Collection*. Washington, DC: Department of Education.

U.S. Department of Education. 2015. "Subpart 3: Gun Possession." In *Elementary and Secondary Education Act Title IV, 21st Century Schools, Part A, Safe and Drug-Free Schools and Communities*. http://www2.ed.gov/policy/elsec/leg/esea02/pg54.html.

Valentín, Luis J., and Carla Minet. 2019. "Las 889 páginas de Telegram entre Rosselló Nevares y sus allegados." *Centro de Periodismo Investigativo*, July 13. http://periodismoinvestigativo.com/2019/07/las-889-paginas-de-telegram-entre-rossello-nevares-y-sus-allegados/.

Vallières, Pierre. 1972. *White Niggers of America: The Precocious Autobiography of a Quebec Terrorist*. Translated by Joan Pinkham. Toronto: McClelland and Stewart.

van Deusen, Nancy E. 2015. *Global Indios: The Indigenous Struggle for Justice in Sixteenth-Century Spain*. Durham, NC: Duke University Press.

Vargas, João H. Costa. 2004. "Hyperconsciousness of Race and Its Negation: The Dialectic of White Supremacy in Brazil." *Identities* 11 (4): 443–70.

Vargas, João H. Costa. 2008. *Never Meant to Survive: Genocide and Utopias in Black Diaspora Communities*. Lanham, MD: Rowman and Littlefield.

Vargas, João H. Costa. 2012. "Gendered Antiblackness and the Impossible Brazilian Project: Emerging Critical Black Brazilian Studies." *Cultural Dynamics* 24 (1): 3–11.

Vargas, João H. Costa. 2018. *The Denial of Antiblackness: Multiracial Redemption and Black Suffering*. Minneapolis: University of Minnesota Press.

Vasquez, Jesse. 2018. "Female Inmates Help Battle Fires." *San Quentin News*, January 18. https://sanquentinnews.com/female-inmates-help-battle-fires/.

Veracini, Lorenzo. 2010. *Settler Colonialism: A Theoretical Overview*. New York: Palgrave Macmillan.

Vimalassery, Manu, Juliana Pegues, and Alyosha Goldstein. 2017. "Colonial Unknowing and Relations of Study." *Theory and Event* 20 (4): 1042–54.

Viswanath, Rupa. 2014. *The Pariah Problem: Caste, Religion, and the Social in Modern India*. New York: Columbia University Press.

Wacquant, Loïc. 1999. *Prisons of Poverty*. Minneapolis: University of Minnesota Press.

Wagner, Peter, and Alison Walsh. 2016. "States of Incarceration: The Global Context 2016." Northampton, MA: Prison Policy Initiative, June 16. https://www.prisonpolicy.org/global/2016.html.

Walcott, Rinaldo. 2014. "The Problem of the Human: Black Ontologies and 'the Coloniality of Our Being.'" In *Postcoloniality—Decoloniality—Black Critique: Joints and Fissures*, edited by Sabine Broeck and Carsten Junker, 93–105. New York: Campus Verlag.

Wald, Johanna, and Daniel J. Losen. 2003. "Defining and Redirecting a School-to-Prison Pipeline." *New Directions for Youth Development* 99: 9–15.

Wallace, John M., Jr., Sara Goodkind, Cynthia M. Wallace, and Jerald G. Bachman. 2008. "Racial, Ethnic, and Gender Differences in School Discipline among US High School Students: 1991–2005." *Negro Educational Review* 59 (1–2): 47–62.

Warren, Calvin. 2017. "Onticide: Afro-pessimism, Gay Nigger #1, and Surplus Violence." *GLQ* 23 (3): 391–418.

Washbrook, David. 1990. "South Asia, the World System and World Capitalism." In *South Asia and World Capitalism*, edited by Sugata Bose, 40–84. Oxford: Oxford University Press.

Watson, Iain. 2012. "Paradoxical Multiculturalism in South Korea." *Asian Politics and Policy* 4 (2): 233–58.

Watson, Jini Kim. 2007. "Imperial Mimicry, Modernisation Theory and the Contradictions of Postcolonial South Korea." *Postcolonial Studies* 10 (2): 171–90.

We Charge Genocide. 2015. "An Open Letter to the ACLU of Illinois Regarding Stop and Frisk." August 12. http://wechargegenocide.org/an-open-letter-to-the-aclu-of-illinois-regarding-stop-frisk/.

Weeks, Kathi. 2011. *The Problem with Work: Feminism, Marxism, Antiwork Politics, and Postwork Imaginaries.* Durham, NC: Duke University Press.

Weheliye, Alexander. 2014. *Habeas Viscus: Racializing Assemblages, Biopolitics, and Black Feminist Theories of the Human.* Durham, NC: Duke University Press.

Weiner, Melissa F. 2012. "Toward a Critical Global Race Theory." *Sociology Compass,* 6 (4): 332–50.

Weiner, Michael. 1995. "Discourses of Race, Nation and Empire in Pre-1945 Japan." *Ethnic and Racial Studies* 18 (3): 433–56.

Weiner, Michael, ed. 1997. *Japan's Minorities: The Illusion of Homogeneity.* New York: Routledge.

Wekker, Gloria. 2016. *White Innocence: Paradoxes of Colonialism and Race.* Durham, NC: Duke University Press.

Wells, Kenneth M. 1990. *New God, New Nation: Protestants and Self-Reconstruction Nationalism in Korea, 1896–1937.* Honolulu: University of Hawai'i Press.

Wells-Barnett, Ida B. 1895. "A Red Record." In *On Lynchings.* Amherst, NY: Humanity.

Widra, Emily. 2017. "Incarceration Shortens Life Expectancy." *Prison Policy Initiative,* June 26. https://www.prisonpolicy.org/blog/2017/06/26/life_expectancy/.

Wilderson, Frank, III. 2003. "Gramsci's Black Marx: Whither the Slave in Civil Society?" *Social Identities* 9 (2): 225–40.

Wilderson, Frank, III. 2008. *Incognegro: A Memoir of Exile and Apartheid.* Boston: South End.

Wilderson, Frank, III. 2010. *Red, White, and Black: Cinema and the Structure of U.S. Antagonisms.* Durham, NC: Duke University Press.

Williams, Eric. (1944) 1994. *Capitalism and Slavery.* Chapel Hill: University of North Carolina Press.

Williams, Patricia. 1992. *Alchemy of Race and Rights.* Cambridge, MA: Harvard University Press.

Williamson, Terrion L. 2017. *Scandalize My Name: Black Feminist Practice and the Making of Black Social Life.* New York: Fordham University Press.

Wimmer, Andreas, and Nina Glick Schiller. 2003. "Methodological Nationalism, the Social Sciences, and the Study of Migration: An Essay on Historical Epistemology." *International Migration Review* 37 (3): 576–310.

Winant, Howard. 2001. *The World Is a Ghetto: Race and Democracy since World War II.* Boston: Basic Books.

Wittgenstein, Ludwig. 2009. *Philosophical Investigations.* 4th ed. New York: Wiley Blackwell.

Wolf, Eric R. 1982. *Europe and the People without History*. Berkeley: University of California Press.

Wolfe, Patrick. 2006. "Settler Colonialism and the Elimination of the Native." *Journal of Genocide Research* 8 (4): 387–409.

Women in Prison. 2017. "Key Facts: A Roundup and Latest Key Statistics Regarding Women Affected by the Criminal Justice System." http://www.womeninprison.org.uk/research/key-facts.php.

Wood, Betty. 1995. *Women's Work, Men's Work: The Informal Economies of Lowcountry Georgia*. Georgia: University of Georgia Press.

Wood, Peter. 1974. *Black Majority: Negroes in Colonial South Carolina from 1670 through the Stono Rebellion*. New York: Alfred A. Knopf.

Woodman, Harold. 1968. *King Cotton and His Retainers: Financing and Marketing the Cotton Crop of the South, 1800–1925*. Lexington: University of Kentucky Press.

Woods, Clyde Adrian. 1998. *Development Arrested: The Blues and Plantation Power in the Mississippi Delta*. New York: Verso.

Woods, Clyde. 2007. "'Sittin' on Top of the World': The Challenges of Blues and Hip Hop Geography." In *Black Geographies and the Politics of Place*, edited by Katherine McKittrick and Clyde Woods. Toronto: Between the Lines.

Wun, Connie. 2014. "Unaccounted Foundations: Black Girls, Anti-black Racism, and Punishment in Schools." *Critical Sociology* 42 (4–5): 737–50.

Wun, Connie. 2016. "Against Captivity: Black Girls and School Discipline Policies in the Afterlife of Slavery." *Educational Policy* 30 (1): 171–96.

Wynter, Sylvia. 1971. "Novel and History, Plot and Plantation." *Savacou* 5: 95–102.

Wynter, Sylvia. 1994. "1492: A New World View." In *Race, Discourse and the Origin of the Americas*, edited by Vera Lawrence and Rex Nettleford, 5–57. Washington, DC: Smithsonian.

Wynter, Sylvia. 2003. "Unsettling the Coloniality of Being/Power/Truth/Freedom: Towards the Human, After Man, Its Overrepresentation—an Argument." CR: *The New Centennial Review* 3 (3): 257–337.

Wynter, Sylvia, and David Scott. 2000. "The Re-enchantment of Humanism: An Interview with Sylvia Wynter." *Small Axe* 8 (1): 119–207.

Yancey, George. 2004. *Who Is White? Latinos, Asians, and the New Black/Nonblack Divide*. Boulder, CO: Lynne Rienner.

Yang, Anand. 1989. *The Limited Raj: Agrarian Relations in Colonial India, Saran District, 1793–1920*. Berkeley: University of California Press.

Yi, Gwang-rin. 1969. *Hangukgaehwasayeongu*. Seoul: Iljogak.

Yi, Taek-hwi, Un-tae Kim, Yang Jae-in, Sin Bok-ryong, Sang-cheol Yi, and Yi U-jin. 1993. *Seo Jae-pil*. Seoul: Mineumsa.

Yoon, Christine. 2020. "Why Asian Americans Should Care about Black Lives Matter." *The Chronicle*, June 11. https://www.dukechronicle.com/article/2020/06/why-asian-americans-should-care-about-black-lives-matter.

Yoon, Min-sik. 2015. "Saenuri Chief Apologizes for Racist Remark." *Korea Herald*, December 18. http://www.koreaherald.com/view.php?ud=20151218000803.

Young, Benjamin R. 2013. "North Korea's Uncomfortable Race Relations." *NK News*, October 11. https://www.nknews.org/2013/10/north-koreas-uncomfortable-race -relations.

Young, Benjamin R. 2015. "The Struggle for Legitimacy: North Korean-African Relations, 1965–1992." *BAKS Papers* 16: 97–116.

Yu, Gil-jun. (1895) 2004. *Seoyugyeonmun*. Seoul: Seohaemunjip.

Yuval-Davis, N. 1997. *Gender and Nation*. Thousand Oaks, CA: Sage.

Yuval-Davis, N., and F. Anthias. 1989. *Women-Nation-State*. Houndmills, UK: Macmillan.

Zureik, Elia, David Lyon, and Yasmeen Abu-Laban, eds. 2011. *Surveillance and Control in Israel/Palestine: Population, Territory and Power*. New York: Routledge.

CONTRIBUTORS

MOHAN AMBIKAIPAKER is Associate Professor in critical race theory and postcolonial studies in the Department of Communication at Tulane University, USA. He works on the interlocking forms of globalized racisms across different national contexts (United States, United Kingdom, and Malaysia). He is the author of *Political Blackness in Multiracial Britain* (2018), an ethnographic study of the experiences of racial and state violence as well as resistance among African Caribbean and South Asian communities in London.

JODI A. BYRD is a citizen of the Chickasaw Nation of Oklahoma and Associate Professor of English and gender and women's studies at the University of Illinois at Urbana-Champaign, where she is also a faculty affiliate at the National Center for Supercomputing Applications. She is the author of *Transit of Empire: Indigenous Critiques of Colonialism* (2011), and her work on critical Indigenous studies, queer Indigenous studies, and critical technology studies has appeared most recently in *Critical Ethnic Studies*, *Settler Colonial Studies*, *Social Text*, and *South Atlantic Quarterly* and in Joanne Barker's edited collection *Critically Sovereign: Indigenous Gender, Sexuality, and Feminist Studies* (2017).

IYKO DAY is Associate Professor of English and Critical Social Thought at Mount Holyoke College and a faculty member in the Five College Asian/Pacific/American Studies Program. She is the author of *Alien Capital: Asian Racialization and the Logic of Settler Colonial Capitalism* (Duke University Press, 2016), and she coedits the book series *Critical Race, Indigeneity, and Relationality*.

ANTHONY PAUL FARLEY is the Peter Rodino Distinguished Visiting Professor at Rutgers Law School (Spring 2020) and the Matthews Distinguished Professor of Jurisprudence at Albany Law School.

Farley, a member of the American Law Institute and the Board of Governors of the Society of American Law Teachers, is a graduate of Harvard Law School and the University of Virginia. His work on racism addresses questions of law, philosophy, psychoanalysis, and political economy. Farley is currently working on a book, a general theory of antiblackness.

CRYSTAL MARIE FLEMING is Professor of Sociology, Africana studies and women's, gender and sexuality studies at Stony Brook University. Her work contributes to interdisciplinary scholarship at the nexus of sociology, critical race theory, and Black studies. She is the author of *How to Be Less Stupid About Race: On Racism, White Supremacy and the Racial Divide* and *Resurrecting Slavery: Racial Legacies and White Supremacy in France*. Her current line of research and theory explores the implications of spirituality, meditation, and mindfulness for Black practitioners of meditation.

SARAH HALEY is Associate Professor of gender studies and African American studies at the University of California, Los Angeles. She has research and teaching investments in Black feminism, abolition, women's and gender history, carceral state history, and working class history. She is the author of *No Mercy Here: Gender, Punishment, and the Making of Jim Crow Modernity* and has published articles and essays in interdisciplinary venues including *Women and Performance, Souls, Signs,* and *GLQ*. Her in-progress book examines the relationship between Black domestic space and the intensification of carceral power from the 1970s through the present.

TANYA KATERÍ HERNÁNDEZ is the Archibald R. Murray Professor of Law at Fordham University School of Law. She is the author of *Racial Subordination in Latin America: The Role of the State, Customary Law and the New Civil Rights Response* (including Spanish and Portuguese translation editions), *Research Perspectives in Comparative Law: Racial Discrimination,* and *Multiracials and Civil Rights: Mixed-Race Stories of Discrimination*. Her forthcoming book is *On Latino Anti-Black Bias: "Racial Innocence" and the Struggle for Equality*.

SARAH IHMOUD is Assistant Professor of anthropology at the College of the Holy Cross. She is a member of *Insaniyyat*, the Society of Palestinian Anthropologists.

JOY JAMES is Ebenezer Fitch Professor of the Humanities at Williams College. She is the author of *Resisting State Violence, Transcending the Talented Tenth, Shadowboxing: Representations of Black Feminist Politics*, and *Seeking the Beloved Community*. Editor of *States of Confinement, The Angela Y. Davis Reader, The Black Feminist Reader* (with T. D. Sharpley-Whiting), *Imprisoned Intellectuals, The New Abolitionists*, and *Warfare in the American Homeland*, James writes on the "captive maternal"; advocates for political prisoners; and works with the Abolition Collective Black Internationalist Unions.

MOON-KIE JUNG teaches sociology and antisociology at the University of Massachusetts, Amherst.

JAE KYUN KIM is a Visiting Assistant Professor in the Department of Sociology at Davidson College. His research interests center around the singular significance of antiblack racism and its relation to the construction of modernity and global racial order. He is currently working on his book manuscript, *Yellow over Black: The Precolonial and Colonial History of Race in Korea, 1883–1945*.

CHARLES W. MILLS is a Distinguished Professor of Philosophy at the Graduate Center, City University of New York. He works in the general area of oppositional political theory, with a special focus on race. He is the author of six books: *The Racial Contract* (1997); *Blackness Visible: Essays on Philosophy and Race* (1998); *From Class to Race: Essays in White Marxism and Black Radicalism* (2003); *Contract and Domination* (with Carole Pateman, 2007); *Radical Theory, Caribbean Reality* (2010); and *Black Rights/White Wrongs: The Critique of Racial Liberalism* (2017).

DYLAN RODRÍGUEZ is President of the American Studies Association (2020–21), Chair of the University of California Riverside Academic Senate (2016–20), and Professor in the Department of Media and Cultural Studies at the University of California, Riverside. He is the author of *White Reconstruction: Domestic Warfare and the Logics of Genocide* (2021).

ZACH SELL is Visiting Assistant Professor of history at Drexel University. He is the author of *Trouble of the World: Slavery and Empire in the Age of Capital* (2021).

JOÃO H. COSTA VARGAS works at the University of California, Riverside, plantation.

FRANK B. WILDERSON III is chair of African American studies, a core faculty member in the Culture & Theory PhD Program at the University of California, Irvine, and an award-winning writer whose books include *Afropessimism* (2020), *Incognegro: A Memoir of Exile and Apartheid* (Duke University Press, 2015), and *Red, White, & Black: Cinema and the Structure of U.S. Antagonisms* (Duke University Press 2010). He spent five and a half years in South Africa, where he was one of two Americans to hold elected office in the African National Congress during the apartheid era. He also was a cadre in the underground. His literary awards include the American Book Award, the Zora Neale Hurston/Richard Wright Legacy Award for Creative Nonfiction, the Maya Angelou Award for Best Fiction Portraying the Black Experience in America, and a National Endowment for the Arts Literature Fellowship. Wilderson was educated at Dartmouth College (AB/Government and Philosophy), Columbia University (MFA/Fiction Writing), and the University of California, Berkeley (PhD/Rhetoric).

CONNIE WUN, PhD, is the cofounder of AAPI Women Lead. She is also the founder of Transformative Research, a research consultancy that trains community-based organizations on participatory action and community-driven research. She has been a recipient of the National Science Foundation Fellowship, Ed-Trust West Senior Fellowship, American Association for University Women Postdoctoral Fellowship, the University of California, Berkeley, Chancellor's Fellowship, Mills College Research at the Intersections Fellowship, and UC Berkeley Center for Race and Gender Fellowship. Her work has been published in *Critical Sociology*, *Educational Policy*, *Educational Theory and Practice*, and *Race, Ethnicity, and Education*. She has also written for the *Feminist Wire* and *Truthout* and is currently working on her book manuscript on schools as sites of antiblack violence.

Page numbers in italics refer to figures.

Census, U.S., 13; Afro-Latinos and, 290–91; "Some Other Race," 284–86, 295

Césaire, Aimé, 310

Chambers-Letson, Joshua, 79

Chaney, James, 322

Chase-Riboud, Barbara, 247

Chen, Chris, 68

Chesney-Lind, Meda, 187

Chigwada-Bailey, Ruth, 206

Childers, Chandra, 233

Christie, Chris, 179

Christie, Nils, 186

citizenship: British, 204, 207, 215–16; race and, 151, 156

Clark, Darcel D., 259

class: antiblackness and, 83; empire and, 28; modernity and, 27; race and, 92; racial formation and, 92–93

Clinton, Bill, 226, 253

Clinton, Hillary, 190, 191, 256; "super-predators" rhetoric of, 176, 191, 253

Coates, Ta-Nehisi, 254

Code Noir (Black Code), 266

Cohen, William, 272, 273–74, 282n5

colonialism: antiblackness and, 272–73; commodities trade, 121–22; Enlightenment and, 28; Japanese, 159–61; race and, 146–47, 271; rice cultivation and, 120–21; white supremacy and, 27. *See also* settler colonialism

color blindness, 245, 254, 314–15; French, 270; Latinos and, 288

Combahee River Collective, 36

Committee for the Memory of Slavery, 264

commodification: of enslaved people, 108–9; of labor, 85–86, 104n4

communism, 42, 69–70

Cooper, Anna Julia, 266

Cordis, Shanya, 300, 306–7

Corner, Toni, 205

cotton cultivation, 108

Coulthard, Glen, 321

criminalization: of African Caribbean women, 210, 206; antiblack, 173–74, 191–92; of Black girls, 233–34, 238–39; of Black men, 206–7; of Black women, 132, 134–36, 175–76, 206, 225, 231–32, 238; mass incarceration and, 187; race

and, 193; reproduction and, 131, 175–76; of student behavior, 227, 229–32, 240–41

critical race theory, 84, 101, 265

Critical Resistance, 139–40, 187

Croce, Cherry, 207

Cruz, Carmen Yulín, 287

Curse of Ham, 22, 32

Danner, Deborah, 13, 244, 256–59; as anti-FLOTUS, 245–46, 259

Daut, Marlene, 273

Davis, Adrienne, 74

Davis, Angela Y., 131–32, 175

Day, Iyko, 317

Deb, Radhakanta, 123

Defend the Deane Family Campaign, 212, 223n7

de Gobineau, Arthur, 273

dehumanization, 196, 200; antihumanization, 9; of Black people, 8–9, 206, 222

Deleuze, Gille, 51

Dessalines, Jean-Jacques, 102

Diallo, Rokhaya, 269, 277, 278, 279

Díaz, Junot, 310

Dickens, Charles, 110–11

Diderot, Denis, 26

Dikötter, Frank, 147

Dillon, Stephen, 239

dispossession, 90–92, 308; equality and, 88–89; freedom and, 88–89, 99–100; Indigenous, 314, 316, 319–22, 324; labor and, 100; politics of, 318; primal accumulation and, 96–97, 101; surplus value and, 100

Dixon, Brandon, 312

Dongnipyeopoe (Independence Club), 156–57

Donne, John, 82

Douglass, Patrice, 11

Du Bois, W. E. B., 5, 8, 34, 144; on Black labor, 7, 14n10; on the color line, 102, 147; on the human, 148; labor in, 66; Marxism and, 7; patriarchy in, 66; on second sight, 26; on slavery, 2, 108

Ellis, Eddie, 186

Ellison, Ralph: *Invisible Man*, 18

Em, Henry, 160

discourse, 64, 66; on emancipation, 72; on Indigenous studies, 316–18; on libidinal economy, 78

sex trafficking, 236–37

sexuality, racialized, 6

Sharma, Jayeeta, 122

Sharpe, Christina, 131–32, 134, 323

Shaw, Elyse, 233

Shin, Gi-Wook, 150

Simmons, Kristen, 323–24

Simpson, Audra, 321–22, 324

slave labor, 72–75; as human capital, 81n4

slave rebellions, 249; Haitian revolution, 26, 102, 281n1

slavery, 324; afterlife of, 4, 10, 131, 134, 198, 225, 238–43, 268, 271, 302; antiblackness and, 4, 9, 13, 83, 109, 128–29; antiblack racism and, 263–65; as antisocial, 3; Blackness and, 32–34, 264; British abolition of, 202, 249; capitalism and, 3, 34, 70–72; commemorations of, 263, 264; commodification of, 108–9; as death, 82; empire and, 3; in France, 272; gendered afterlife of, 134; gendered inheritance, 67; Greek, 72; the human and, 251; international trade and, 108–12, 120–23; kinship under, 107–8; in Korea, 161; Marxism and, 69–73; modernity and, 3–4, 23, 194–95; as prehistory of capitalism, 69; premature death and, 119; prisons and, 194–95; property and, 97–98; race and, 23; reproductive labor and, 78; resistance to, 237–39; segregation and, 82, 87; value and, 70, 81n4; violence of, 108, 113, 184; white supremacy and, 27

slave trade, 108, 121, 129n2; in France, 263

Smallwood, Stephanie, 134

Smith, Christen, 223n10

Smith, Gillian, 198–99, 208–22, 223n2, 223n10

Smith, Gold, 151

Smith, Mark, 217–21

Social, the, 2–4; antiblackness and, 6–9

social Darwinism, 148, 150, 161–62

social death, 4, 43, 57; of Black women, 202–3; Marxism and, 69

social sciences: racial slavery and, 2–4

solidarity: Black-Palestinian, 299

Somerset, James, 249

Somerset v Stewart, 202, 249

Soumahoro, Maboula, 280

sovereignty, 13, 317–20, 324; antiblackness and, 317; Indigenous, 320

Spillers, Hortense J., 6, 40, 131, 175, 316; on Black flesh, 43, 221; on Black women's invisibility, 78–79; on gender, 63–64, 79; on kinship, 3–4; "Mama's Baby, Papa's Maybe," 62; on marked Black women, 60; on Moynihan Report, 64

Spinoza, Baruch, 26

Standing Rock protests, 313, 315

standpoint theory, 25, 35–36

Stark, Heidi Kiiwetinepinesiik, 320

Steinmetz, George, 146

Strickland, Debra Higgs, 20–21

subjectivity: antiblackness and, 10; Black, 8; Blackness and, 46–47

suffering, Black, 6, 41–42, 45–46, 50, 57

Sullivan, Stephen, 257

surveillance, 183; antiblackness and, 12; biopolitical, 301; of Black girls, 225, 228–30, 232, 237–39; of Black people, 266; of Palestinian women's bodies, 298, 302–3; of students, 225, 227

Taubira, Christiane, 279

Tayler, Samuel, 107, 110, 116, 129n1

Taylor, Breonna, 1, 64

Taylor, Keeanga-Yamahtta, 314–15

technology: rice cultivation and, 118–19; surplus value and, 74–75

Thompson, George, 112

Tiffin, Helen, 311

Till, Emmett, 79, 322

Till Mobley, Mamie, 79

Tometti, Opal, 36

torture, 50–52

Traoré, Adama, 279

Traoré, Assa, 280

trauma, 309; of accumulation, 84–85

Trudeau, Justin, 315

Trump, Donald, 245, 254, 278, 311, 312–16; sexual assault allegations, 249–50

Trump, Melania, 254